THE PRESIDENCY REAPPRAISED

Reappraised

SECOND EDITION

edited by
Thomas E. Cronin and Rexford G. Tugwell

This new and extensively revised edition of *The Presidency Reappraised* shares with concerned Americans a variety of post-Watergate reappraisals of the American Presidency—its powers, paradoxes, and limitations. Essays by seventeen leading scholars and journalists examine the highly personalized institution that is now a central focal point for the nation, a symbol of the nation's hopes and aspirations, and the most visible target for criticism and blame when things go wrong.

Although the contributors to this book differ among themselves about solutions, they share the view that we need to refashion the capacity of the Presidency to furnish needed political leadership while the office remains at the same time accountable and responsive to the American public.

The questions posed here and the answers suggested provide varied, provocative views of America's most powerful institution and the responsibilities and challenges it presents to any man who occupies it.

The Presidency Reappraised

Second Edition

edited by

Thomas E. Cronin

Brandeis University

and

Rexford G. Tugwell

Center for the Study of Democratic Institutions

 Praeger Publishers • New York

Copyright Acknowledgments

"The Carter Presidency: Plans and Priorities," prepresidency interviews with Jimmy Carter conducted by Neal R. Peirce, is reprinted by permission of *National Journal*, 1730 M Street, N.W., Washington, D.C. 20036.

"Lyndon Johnson's Political Personality" by Doris Kearns, is reprinted with permission from *Political Science Quarterly* 91 (Fall 1976) 385-408.

"The President and the Press," by Daniel P. Moynihan, is reprinted by permission of the author from *Commentary*, March, 1971. Copyright 1971 by Daniel P. Moynihan.

"Congress and the Making of American Foreign Policy," by Arthur Schlesinger, Jr., is reprinted by permission from *Foreign Affairs*, October, 1972. Copyright 1972 by Council on Foreign Relations, Inc.

"Making War: The President and Congress," by Graham T. Allison, with the assistance of Richard Huff, is reprinted, with permission, from a symposium on Presidential Power: Sources of Growth and Means of Constraint appearing in *Law and Contemporary Problems* (Vol. 40, No. 2, Spring 1976), published by Duke University School of Law, Durham, North Carolina. Copyright © 1976 by Duke University.

Published in the United States of America in 1977
by Praeger Publishers
200 Park Avenue, New York, N.Y. 10017

© 1977 by Praeger Publishers
A Division of Holt, Rinehart and Winston, Publishers

Library of Congress Cataloging in Publication Data

Main entry under title:

The Presidency reappraised.

In the 1st ed. R. G. Tugwell's name appeared first on t.p.
        Bibliography: p. 345.
        Includes index.
        1. Presidents—United States—Addresses, essays, lectures.   2. Presidents—United States—History—Addresses, essays, lectures.   3. Executive power—United States—Addresses, essays, lectures.
I. Cronin, Thomas E.   II. Tugwell, Rexford Guy, 1891–   III. Tugwell, Rexford Guy, 1891–
JK516.T82 1977   353.03'13   76-41955
ISBN 0-275-24140-8
ISBN 0-275-64810-9 pbk.

789 074 987654321

Printed in the United States of America

Preface

The American Presidency is approximately 188 years old as Jimmy Carter assumes office as the nation's thirty-ninth President. When George Washington took office on April 30, 1789, he was painfully aware that the job of President would be a difficult one—fraught with conflicts, high expectations, and inevitably judged sternly by the citizenry when it grew uneasy with its leadership. When Washington accepted the high office, he did so with solemn anxiety and a full realization that while he would give his best, he would doubtless have to give up nearly all expectations of personal privacy and perhaps of private happiness as well. For him the job was a very public as well as taxing duty, as he noted in these grave words written a few months after his inauguration:

The establishment of our new government seemed to be the last great experiment for promoting human happiness by a reasonable compact in civil society. It was to be, in the first instance, in a considerable degree, a government of accommodation as well as a government of laws. Much was to be done by prudence, much by conciliation, much by firmness. Few who are not philosophical spectators can realize the difficult and delicate part which a man in my situation had to act. All see, and most admire, the glare which hovers round the external happiness of elevated office. To me there is nothing in it beyond the lustre which may be reflected from its connection with power of promoting human felicity. In our progress towards political happiness my station is new, and, if I may use the expression, I walk on untrodden ground. There is scarcely an action the motive of which may not be subject to a double interpretation. There is scarcely any part of my conduct which may not hereafter be drawn into precedent.[1]

When Washington began his duties, there was no White House staff, no Cabinet, no Executive Office of the President; nothing save a President and a Congress. Indeed, there was no White House, the government being located in New York City. When President Carter begins his duties, he will preside over a national government comprising nearly 5 million civilian and military public servants. He will enter a White House that, during the last months under President Ford, had nearly five hundred employees and a cabinet of eleven departments, with about another ten individuals also accorded Cabinet status, such as the Vice President, the ambassador to the United Nations, and the director of the Office of Management and Budget.

Carter will have assumed the Presidency at a time when there is much division about the precise character of presidential powers and what, if anything, should be done about them. During Watergate, many people called for the weakening of the Presidency. Some Americans plainly sought retribution against the institution itself for the abuses made by incumbent presidents and their advisers during Vietnam and Watergate. Others claimed that Watergate and Vietnam came about not only because there had been a definite excess of presidential authority and power. Thus, they called for strengthening the Congress, as well as reining in the Presidency.

But even at the peak of this period of reappraisal, a much larger group of Americans called for the continuation of a strong Presidency. Of course, they differed over their definitions of presidential strength, but it became clear, as Watergate receded, that few of them wanted to recast the Presidency in any fundamental way. It became the majority view that the President's primacy had been founded in the necessities of the American order. Most agreed that grave social and economic problems—widespread unemployment and inflation, the fiscal crises in many of our older cities, racial divisiveness, and the persistence of high crime rates—require the attention of a rigorous and persistent President who can provide the necessary political leadership.

Most people agreed, too, that the larger the country's population becomes, the more its people need a common reference point for social and economic regeneration. The Presidency, they felt, serves, or can serve, as a source of unity in diversity, of continuity in change, of relative order during periods of upheaval; thus, the view that the United States needs a strong government and a strong leadership institution to attain that government. Writing in 1975, Vice-President Walter Mondale, then a senator, summed up the problem well when he stressed that what was needed was strength and accountability: We must, he wrote, "arrive at a working concept of the Presidency which is strong, yet legal; capable of leading, but without dictating. We have reaped the bitter harvest of fundamental failure in the accountability of our Presidency; now we must rebuild that accountability to ensure the success of our government."[2] Some observers even went so far as to suggest that the reaction to Vietnam and Watergate might result in another period of congressional government, not unlike the period that followed the Civil War. Samuel Huntington declares that exaggerated criticism and the resulting loss of public confidence had badly damaged the legitimacy of the Presidency. Others, of course, believe that Lyndon B. Johnson and especially Richard M. Nixon had done the damage—not the critics or reformers. Nonetheless, the Huntington thesis is as follows:

> Probably no development of the 1960s and 1970s had greater import for the future of American politics than the decline in the authority, status, influence, and effectiveness of the Presidency. The effects of the weakening of the Presidency will be felt throughout the body politic for years to come.[3]

As a result, Huntington adds, even our political leaders had questions about the "legitimacy of hierarchy, coercion, discipline, secrecy, and deception—all of which are, in some measure, inescapable attributes of the process of government."[4]

Rexford Tugwell reminds us, however, that there is an old aphorism that truth is elusive and appears different to different people. Different observers have drawn decidedly different lessons from the Vietnam and Watergate periods, or the 1960s and 1970s. Political scientist Bruce Miroff, for example, concludes his study of the Kennedy presidency and the 1960s by saying that the Presidency in fact is the chief stabilizer of the existing order and that the presidential claim to be moral leader or the spokesman of reform for the American public can no longer be taken seriously. On the contrary, Miroff declares:

> The record of the Kennedy presidency should serve as a warning to those who still believe that major changes in American society can be instituted if only the right liberal makes it to the White House. Liberals will no doubt regain the Presidency in the future. But they will hardly refashion it into an instrument for the progressive transformation of American politics. That transformation can be accomplished only by those who have a stake in change. It is likely to be impeded by Presidents—who are, after all, the most successful products of the existing order.[5]

Still others who have examined recent presidential performance have come away with the view that the only productive study of the Presidency is achieved by examining the biographies and the character of presidents. This view holds that the Presidency is in fact a one-man show, and nearly everything—tone, initiatives, and outcomes—revolves around and depends on a single person. Study the man, not the office, a thesis James David Barber cogently argues.[6] Doris Kearns' essay in this volume is illustrative.

The purpose of *The Presidency Reappraised* is to share with concerned Americans a variety of fresh reappraisals of the American Presidency—its powers, paradoxes, limitations, and responsibilities. The Presidency is indeed a highly personalized institution, but it is also much more than that; it is now an important national focal point, a symbol of the nation's hopes and aspirations, and the inevitable target of criticism and blame when things go wrong. It is also a large bureaucracy. The contributors to this volume share the view that we need to refashion the capacity of the Presidency to furnish needed political leadership while remaining, at the same time, accountable and responsive to the American public. Another recurring theme throughout the book is the need to appreciate the variety and critical importance of central constraints and incentives that shape presidential performance.

Rexford G. Tugwell initiated the idea for the first edition of this book, and he encouraged some twenty or more papers to be written and presented at various meetings sponsored by the Center for the Study of Democratic Institutions during the early 1970s. Most of those papers formed the basis of the first edition. That edition having been well received, we were encouraged to produce a greatly revised and extended new edition—in part because so much has happened both to the Presidency and to our thinking about the institution during the last few years. Only six of the essays in the first edition are included again, and some of these are considerably revised and updated. Seven of the new essays were commissioned and written in 1976 expressly for publication in the new edition, while a few of the others are reprinted from journals or, having been commissioned for conferences, are published here for the first time.

We are delighted that this second edition has been able to follow up on the themes outlined in the first edition, and to update, amend, and enlarge upon the debates that arose among the distinguished authors who contributed to the earlier edition. In addition, this new edition is able to appraise the Nixon-Ford era and the varying reforms and recommendations about the Presidency that poured forth during these often troubled years.

Since the appearance of the first edition, there has been a welcome and noticeable increase of scholarly attention devoted to the Presidency and presidential performance. In gathering together a variety of assessments of the office, we have necessarily had to neglect important new research contributions. No single book aimed at the general reader can any longer comprehensively survey the American Presidency, its problems, and the insightful commentary they stimulate. However, we feel we have reached out to some of the best-informed students of the subject, including two distinguished White House correspondents who have joined us in this edition—Philip Shabecoff of *The New York Times* and Dom Bonafede of *The National Journal*. We asked authors to present their findings succinctly, and some of the often cumbersome trappings of scholarship—extensive footnotes, tables, graphs, and jargon—have been kept to a minimum or eliminated altogether. Scholars and advanced students who want further evidence or data may contact individual authors directly. Readers are also encouraged to go beyond this book and seek out the numerous new and often excellent studies listed in the bibliography at the end of the book.

Each essay gives its own interpretations and evaluates, in historical and political contexts, how the job and the office of the Presidency evolved from original conceptions of it. Each author writes about a different aspect of the office, and each writes from a different vantage point. Not surprisingly, these differing perspectives lead to different kinds of conclusions, a fact that may trouble a few readers. But paradoxes, ambiguities, and unsettled questions are so characteristic of the institution that the reader should not expect consensus.

As we conclude the 1970s and approach 1984, we need to reconsider not only the evolution of the Presidency but also the social, psychological, economic and political realities that have so fundamentally molded its character and responsibilities. We hope this volume will stimulate thousands more to join us in this quest to understand the requirements and demands of contemporary democratic leadership.

By all means, however, argue with these authors, take issue with their conclusions, and develop different ideas and interpretations in the much needed venture of reevaluating the strengths and flaws of the Presidency—an essential institution that seems increasingly inconsistent with many of the cherished ideals of a democratic society.

I want to thank Rexford Tugwell who began this enterprise several years ago and vigorously encouraged me to undertake and organize this second edition. He has been a splendid teacher and a generous colleague. Together, we both express special thanks to Denise Rathbun, senior editor at Praeger Publishers, and a political scientist in her own right, who has given again of her uncommon talents to make this an especially attractive book.

Thomas E. Cronin

Milton, Mass.
November 26, 1976

Notes

1. George Washington's diary, quoted in Henry Cabot Lodge, *George Washington,* Vol. 2 (Boston: Houghton Mifflin, 1889), p. 50.

2. Walter F. Mondale, *The Accountability of Power: Toward a Responsible Presidency* (New York: McKay, 1975), p. 278.

3. Samuel Huntington, "The Democratic Distemper," in Nathan Glazer and Irving Kirstol, eds., *The American Commonwealth, 1976* (New York: Basic Books, 1976), pp. 24-25.

4. *Ibid,* p. 24.

5. Bruce Miroff, *Pragmatic Illusions: The Presidential Politics of John F. Kennedy* (New York: McKay, 1976) p. 295.

6. James David Barber, *The Presidential Character*, rev. ed. (Englewood Cliffs, N.J.: Prentice Hall, 1977). President Carter's prepresidency views about his own character and roots can be found in *Why Not The Best?* (New York: Bantam, 1976).

Contents

PART ONE

Presidential Powers

The Editors

Thomas E. Cronin, a former White House Fellow and White House staff assistant in the mid-1960s, has taught political science at the University of North Carolina and at Brandeis University. He has served on the staffs of The Brookings Institution and the Center for the Study of the Presidency, is the author of *The State of the Presidency,* and co-author of several other works including *Government by the People* and *Policy and Politics in America.*

Rexford G. Tugwell, a former Professor of Political Economy and Planning at Columbia University and the University of Chicago, was a member of President Franklin D. Roosevelt's "brains trust." He also served as Under-Secretary of Agriculture and as the wartime Governor of Puerto Rico. A long time senior fellow at the Center for the Study of Democratic Institutions, he is the author of numerous books, among them *The Democratic Roosevelt, The Enlargement of the Presidency, The Emerging Constitution,* and, most recently, *The Compromised Constitution.*

1. The President's Constitutional Position

C. Herman Pritchett

The Presidency looms so large in our national history, and we are so accustomed to the President as a necessary and familiar fact of life, that it is difficult to conceive of any other way we could institutionalize the executive power. For that reason, it may be helpful to the reader to begin this survey of current constitutional problems with respect to *presidential powers* by returning to 1787 and reviewing the alternatives as the Founders saw them and the proposals from among which they made the choices that created the Presidency.

What were the attitudes toward executive power in the Founding period? The fear of monarchy was basic to all considerations of the executive office. The shadow of George III was heavy on the land. Executive authority was symbolized by the royal governors. As Corwin says, "The colonial period ended with the belief prevalent that 'the executive magistracy' was the natural enemy, the legislative assembly the natural friend of liberty."[1] The Virginia constitution of 1776 stipulated that the executive powers of government were to be exercised according to the laws of the commonwealth, and that no power or prerogative was ever to be claimed "by virtue of any law, statute, or custom of England." The intention was to cut the executive power off entirely from the resources of the common law and of English constitutional usage.

But, between 1776 and 1787, there was enough experience with state legislatures to destroy naive assumptions about their inherent goodness. Madison was critical of the state constitutions, which, in their concern with the "over-grown and all-grasping prerogative of an hereditary magistrate," did not realize the "danger from legislative usurpation, which, by assembling all power in the same hands, must lead to the same tyranny as is threatened by executive usurpations."[2] Gouverneur Morris, reversing the earlier pattern, saw the executive as the protector and the legislature as the threat, saying the "Executive Magistrate should be the guardian of the people, even of the lower classes, agst. Legislative tyranny, against the Great & the wealthy who in the course of things will necessarily compose—the Legislative body."[3]

The principal theoretical writers with whom the Founders were familiar likewise supplied support for a strong executive. Particularly impressive is Locke's description of "prerogative" in Chapter 14 of his *Second Treatise of Government,* which argues that

> . . . the good of the society requires that several things should be left to the discretion of him that has the executive power. . . . For the legislators not being able to foresee and provide by laws for all that may be useful to the community, the executor of the laws, having the power in his hands, has by the common law of Nature a right to make use of it for the good of the society.

Montesquieu's doctrine of the separation of powers, holding that the three departments of government must be kept separate and that each must be able to defend its characteristic functions from intrusion by either of the other departments, provided another source of defense for the executive against legislative supremacy.

The problem, then, as the Founders saw it, was how to secure an executive power capable of penetrating to the remotest parts of the Union for the purpose of enforcing national laws and bringing assistance to the states in emergencies of domestic disorder, yet avoiding, at the same time, stirring up the widespread popular fear of monarchy.

The Decisions that Established the Constitutional Dimensions of the Presidency

Rejection of a collegial executive or a council. The one decision about the executive that was basic to all others was that it should be an individual and not a board or committee. Some thought a one-person executive would be too much like a monarch. In the discussions at the Convention, Sherman said that the number of the executive should "not be fixed, but . . . the legislature should be at liberty to appoint one or more as experience might dictate." Randolph then proposed an executive council of three men, contending that "unity in the Executive magistracy" would be the "foetus of monarchy." But Gerry thought that, in military matters, a plural executive would be a "general with three heads."[4]

James Wilson was the leader of the strong executive faction. He wanted a "single magistrate, as giving most energy, dispatch, and responsibility to the office."[5] Unity in the executive would be the "best safeguard against tyranny." As chairman of the Committee of Detail, Wilson had the opportunity to incorporate his conception of the office into the draft. In Articles VI and X of the Committee's report of August 6, 1787, the issue was settled in favor of a single executive.

There was still the issue of restraining the executive by a Council. On September 7, while discussing the provision for the President to require the opinion in writing of the heads of departments, Mason said that, in rejecting a Council to the President, "we were about to try an experiment on which the most despotic Governments had never ventured—the Grand Signor himself had his Divan." He proposed a Council of State for the President, made up of six members—two from the Eastern, two from the Middle, and two from the Southern states—with a rotation and duration of office similar to those of the Senate, and appointed by Congress or the Senate. Franklin approved; he thought a Council "would not only be a check on a bad President but be a relief to a good one." Morris replied that the Committee had considered a Council and rejected the idea; "it was judged that the President by persuading his Council—to concur in his wrong measures, would acquire their protection for them." The proposal was defeated, eight to three.[6]

Rejection of election by the legislature. Election of the President by the legislature, which was very nearly adopted, would inevitably have made the Presidency a much different institution. There was a close relationship between the method of election and the term of office. If the executive were to be chosen by Congress, then a fairly long term, with no re-eligibility, was favored, to reduce the possibility of intrigue with Congress for a second term. If the President could be chosen in some other fashion, then re-eligibility was not objectionable, and a shorter term was possible.

The Virginia Plan called for a national executive to be named by electors chosen by Congress. Sherman wanted the executive to be only an "institution for carrying the will of the legislature into effect," and consequently executive officials should be "persons . . . appointed by and accountable to the legislature only."[7] Early discussion by the Committee of the Whole left the Virginia Plan unchanged.

Choice of the President by electors chosen by the people was proposed by Wilson on June 2 and defeated, eight to two. Morris again proposed popular election on July 17, at which time Mason made his famous comment that "it would be as unnatural to refer the choice of a proper character for chief Magistrate to the people, as it would, to refer a trial of colours to a blind man."[8] The popular-election plan failed, and the Convention then reaffirmed legislative election unanimously. But Morris and Madison contended that the executive should be independent of the legislature. The convention then switched to electors, but provided for their choice by the state legislatures.

On July 24, the Convention flopped back to the original scheme for legislative election, with a seven-year term and no re-eligibility. In this posture, the matter went to the Committee of Detail, which had to decide how Congress would vote for President. Would the houses vote separately (they might not agree) or jointly (the larger states would dominate)? Joint election was adopted on August 24, but an effort to have the votes cast by states, each with one vote, failed by a six-to-five margin. Here, Morris again urged popular election and lost only by six to five. The matter was so completely in dispute that it was turned over to the Committee of Eleven, including Morris. This committee proposed the plan that was finally adopted—electors equaling in number senators and representatives from the states and appointed by the states.

A broad appointing power for the President. The appointing power went to the President only after prolonged opposition. The Virginia Plan called for the election of judges as well as the President by the Congress, but the judicial provision was soon eliminated. On June 5, Wilson argued for appointment of judges by the President. "A principal reason for unity in the Executive was that officers might be appointed by a single, responsible person."[9] Madison inclined toward appointment of judges by the Senate, as the more stable and independent branch of the legislature.

On July 18, Gorham's proposal for executive appointment, with Senate advice and consent, was rejected by a tie vote. Senate appointment was reaffirmed on July 21, and the decision then went to the Committee of Detail. Its report gave the general appointing power to the President, but left judges and ambassadors with the Senate. The Committee of Eleven, reporting on September 4, gave the appointment of Supreme Court justices and ambassadors, and all other officers of the United States whose appointment was not otherwise provided for, to the President, with Senate advice and consent. This formula was accepted by the Convention on September 7.

The grant of power as Commander in Chief to the President and the power to declare war to Congress. In giving Congress the power to declare war, the Convention clearly intended to vest the power to embark on a war in the body most representative of the people, in contrast to the power of the British sovereign to initiate war on his own prerogative. In the draft that came from the Committee of Detail, the language was that Congress should have the power to "make" war.

This clause remained in its original form in the committee drafts for several weeks after other foreign relations powers had been transferred from the whole Congress to the Senate and then to the President.

On August 17, Pinckney opposed the vesting of this power in Congress—"its proceedings were too slow." He thought the "Senate would be the best depositary, being more acquainted with foreign affairs." Butler was "for resting the power in the President, who will have all the requisite qualities, and will not make war but when the Nation will support it." But Gerry said he "never expected to hear in a republic a motion to empower the Executive alone to declare war."[10]

It was Gerry and Madison who moved to substitute "declare" for "make," "leaving to the Executive the power to repel sudden attacks." Mason supported the change; he was against "giving the power of war to the Executive, because [he could] not (safely) . . . be trusted with it." King pointed out that the phrase "make war" might be understood to mean "conduct war," which was clearly an executive function—an argument Ellsworth found convincing. The change was made by a vote of seven to two.[11] Thus, the purpose of the change from "make" to "declare" was by no means to limit the role of Congress to a declaratory formality; the intention was to vest in Congress the full power and responsibility of initiating war.[12]

The power of the President to act as Commander in Chief was not much discussed, according to Madison's notes. There is no evidence that it was thought of as a source of power for the President. Since the clause contains nothing to indicate the purposes for which the President may exercise the power thus granted to command the troops, these purposes must ultimately be found in other provisions of Article II. According to Hamilton, in No. 69 of the *Federalist*, the power "would amount to nothing more than the supreme command and direction of the military and naval forces, as first General and admiral of the Confederacy."

The power to make treaties. The draft of the Constitution, as reported by the Committee of Detail on August 6, gave the Senate the power to make treaties as well as to appoint ambassadors and judges of the Supreme Court. On August 15, Mercer objected. The power of treaties, he contended, "belonged to the Executive department," adding that "Treaties would not be final so as to alter the laws of the land, till ratified by legislative authority." Madison, on August 23, agreed, saying "that the Senate represented the States alone, and that for this as well as other obvious reasons it was proper that the President should be an agent in Treaties."[13]

On September 4, the Committee of Eleven reported the new language giving the President the power to make treaties by and with the advice and consent of the Senate, with a two-thirds vote required. It

was adopted on September 7, unanimously, after the Convention
voted down, ten to one, Wilson's proposal that treaties be approved by
the House of Representatives also.

*The President's power to take care that the laws be faithfully exe-
cuted.* The most general statement of presidential power to come from
the Founders was the provision that the President should take care
that the laws be faithfully executed. Obviously, the executive had to
have some general authorization to enforce the laws. The only question was how this grant of power was to be phrased. The original
Virginia Plan gave the national executive a "general authority to execute the National laws," as well as the "Executive rights vested in
Congress by the Confederation."[14] On June 1, this language was
amended in the Committee of the Whole to read "with power to carry
into execution the national laws." The additional provision, "to execute such powers, not legislative or judiciary in their nature, as may
from time to time be delegated by the national legislature," was voted
down.[15] The subsequent change to the present language was a change
in style, not in content or intention.

The Grant of Executive Powers in Practice

How did these key textual decisions of the Convention pertaining to
executive powers work out in practice?

1. The establishment of a single President is, of course, the foundation on which the entire subsequent development of the Executive
Office rests. A collegial executive surely would have collapsed almost
immediately. Under President Washington's wise and responsible
exploration of presidential powers, fears of an executive monarchy
gradually faded away. While the institution of the Cabinet developed,
it hardly filled the role of a Council to the President that some had
urged in the Convention. Executive responsibility rested solely on
the President, and each incumbent has had ample opportunity to re-
create the office in his own image.

2. Equally portentous was the Convention's rejection of congressional election of the President. Such an arrangement would certainly
have diminished the potential of the office, making the President subservient to Congress, and perhaps opening the way to some version of
the parliamentary system.[16]

The choice the Convention made, as close to popular election as
seemed feasible at the time, proved to be rather readily adaptable to a
system of full popular election (with the necessary qualifications that
the Electoral College system requires). The direct link between the
President and the national electorate must be regarded as the primary

condition of presidential power, providing him with a legitimacy possessed by no other official of the government. This legitimacy is slightly diminished when the President is elected with less than 50 percent of the popular vote, or when the margin between the two leading candidates is very narrow. It would be seriously eroded if, in a future election, the workings of the Electoral College awarded the Presidency to a candidate who actually secured fewer popular votes than his opponent.

3. The appointment power is the President's most important instrument for effectuating his control of the executive branch and ensuring that the laws are faithfully executed. The principal limitations on this power derive from the necessity of securing Senate confirmation for his appointments to a very large number of offices, a number extending far beyond positions with substantial policy-forming powers. Normally, however, the great bulk of these appointments are confirmed routinely.

The occasional Senate rejection of a presidential appointee takes place under two circumstances. First, nominees who are to fill positions in a state may be rejected because a senator from that state announces to the Senate that the nominee is personally obnoxious to him, in which event the rule of senatorial courtesy almost invariably results in rejection of the nomination. Second, a majority of the Senate may reject a nominee because he is deemed unqualified for the post or, for some other reason, personally unfit or politically undesirable. Examples are the rejections of Nixon nominees Clement F. Haynsworth and G. Harrold Carswell for the Supreme Court, Kennedy nominee Francis X. Morrissey for the federal district bench, and Eisenhower nominee Lewis B. Strauss as Secretary of Commerce. Such rejections are embarrassing defeats for the President, but they occur very rarely.

Another technique Congress might employ to limit presidential discretion in appointments has been used very seldom, and that is to specify qualifications that nominees for a position must have. Thus, members of federal regulatory commissions must come from both parties, and members of the boards of the Federal Reserve banks must come from certain occupational areas. The various proposals that have been made to require the President to appoint only men with prior judicial experience to the Supreme Court have all failed.

The President's appointing power was interpreted and safeguarded by the Supreme Court in *Buckley* v. *Valeo* (1976). When setting up the Federal Election Commission in 1974 to supervise the new plan for public financing of presidential elections, Congress provided that four of its six voting members should be appointed by the President pro tempore of the Senate and the Speaker of the House, with only two being presidential appointees. The Court ruled that the Commission was an administrative agency with wide rule-making and enforcement powers, and that under Article II, section 2, clause 2, its members must be appointed by the President. Congress then amended the act accordingly.

Attempts to limit the President's power of removal have led to some classic and well-known constitutional arguments, but any restraints imposed as a result are of greater theoretical than practical significance. The requirement that the Senate be consulted on removals as on appointments was declared unconstitutional by Chief Justice Taft in *Myers* v. *United States* (1926). An exception for officials in quasi-judicial positions, where Congress had manifested an intention that they be removable only for cause, was created by the Court in *Humphrey's Executor* v. *United States* (1935), an exception extended in *Wiener* v. *United States* (1958) to all positions created by Congress with quasi-judicial duties, whether or not the legislature specified removal only for cause. While these rulings suggest to the President a certain caution in removing members of the regulatory commissions, their practical effect on the President's control over personnel is otherwise negligible.

4. The power that the President has asserted as Commander in Chief would have been most surprising to the Founders. The Hamiltonian view, that this provision merely placed the President at the top of the military hierarchy, was endorsed half a century later by Story, who interpreted this power in his *Commentaries* as "to give orders and have a general superintendency" over the armed forces. In a Supreme Court opinion by Chief Justice Taney (*Fleming* v. *Page* [1850]), the Court spoke of the President's duty and power as "purely military."

Corwin describes the transformation that occurred in 1861, as Lincoln met the secession crisis:

> The sudden emergence of the "Commander-in-Chief" clause as one of the most highly charged provisions of the Constitution occurred almost overnight in consequence of Lincoln's wedding it to the clause that makes it the duty of the President "to take care that the laws be faithfully executed." From these two clauses thus united, Lincoln proceeded to derive what he termed the "war power," to justify the series of extraordinary measures that he took in the interval between the fall of Fort Sumter and the convening of Congress in special session on July 4, 1861.[17]

In World War I, no such reliance had to be placed on the Commander-in-Chief power, since the war was initiated by a congressional declaration, and Congress provided authority to the President to conduct the war either by substantive legislation or by broad delegation of legislative power. Even so, Wilson called on his power as Commander in Chief to create such war agencies as the Committee on

Public Information, the War Industries Board, and the War Labor Board. He invoked the same authority at the outbreak of the war in closing German wireless stations and subjecting communications companies to regulation with respect to messages received from or going abroad.

The World War II situation was similar, but the emergency started before the declaration of war and extended further beyond it. The destroyer deal with Britain on September 3, 1940, was directly in violation of at least two statutes and represented an exercise by the President of a power specifically assigned to Congress, but it was defended by Attorney General Jackson as based on the President's powers as Commander in Chief. During the war, President Roosevelt created no fewer than thirty-five executive agencies, generally invoking as authority his powers as "Commander-in-Chief in time of war." In only one case, involving the War Labor Board, was the constitutional legitimacy of these agencies questioned, and then unsuccessfully.[18]

When the President uses American armed forces abroad in the *absence* of a congressionally declared war, his reliance on the Commander-in-Chief power is even more crucial. It seems likely that the framers never intended troops to be used outside the country without congressional consent. Since neither a standing army nor a navy was contemplated, naturally any military operations abroad would necessarily require congressional participation in securing the troops and providing the funds. However, the availability of a navy made possible three undeclared naval wars—the war with France (1798–1800) and the first (1801–5) and second (1815) Barbary wars. But Jefferson forbade the navy to attack Tripoli in 1801 on the ground that Congress had not declared war, and Madison, in 1812, refused to retaliate against British provocations until Congress declared war.

By the latter half of the nineteenth century, it had become a well-established presidential practice to use troops abroad for the purpose of protecting American lives and property. In the present century, both Roosevelts, Wilson, Truman, Eisenhower, Kennedy, Johnson, and Nixon have all moved American troops into action or across national frontiers with little or no effort to secure advance congressional assent. Since 1950, there have been presidential moves into Korea, Lebanon, Cuba, the Dominican Republic, Vietnam, Cambodia, and Laos, as well as distant naval operations, undercover plots, military advisory programs, and aerial overflights of foreign countries that risked conflict—all with no opportunity for congressional review.

The two major examples of undeclared wars are of course the Korean War (1950–53) and the Vietnam War (1964–75). In the Korean War, justification for the executive action was provided by the U.N. resolution condemning aggression by North Korea. In 1955, President

Eisenhower secured from Congress a joint resolution authorizing his employment of the armed forces, if required, to protect Taiwan from Chinese attack. Again, in 1957, he requested from Congress authorization to use force against Communist aggression in the Middle East when asked to do so by a victim of such aggression. Under Democratic leadership, the Senate concluded that it would be constitutionally improper to "authorize" the President to take action he already had power to take as Commander in Chief, and so changed the language to read that, "if the President determines the necessity thereof, the United States is prepared to use armed forces" on behalf of nations requesting assistance against armed aggression.

These precedents were used by President Johnson in 1964. At a time when there were only twenty thousand American troops in Vietnam, and after alleged North Vietnamese torpedo-boat attacks on two U.S. destroyers in the Gulf of Tonkin, the President asked Congress for a joint resolution of support to strengthen his hand in dealing with the Vietnam situation. Almost unanimously, Congress adopted the Tonkin Gulf Resolution, approving and supporting the "determination of the President, as Commander-in-Chief, to take all necessary measures to repel any armed attack against the forces of the United States and to prevent further aggression."

President Johnson subsequently relied on this resolution as authorizing and justifying the tremendous escalation of military operations in Vietnam and the bombing of North Vietnam. Assistant Secretary of State Nicholas Katzenbach argued before the Senate Foreign Relations Committee that the resolution gave the President as much authority as a declaration of war. In fact, he alarmed the senators by referring to declarations of war as "outmoded," and contended that a declaration of war would not "correctly reflect the very limited objectives of the United States with respect to Vietnam."[19]

Efforts by members and committees of Congress to recapture some control of the war-making power were tremendously accelerated in 1970 by President Nixon's precipitate expansion of military activities into Cambodia with no prior consultation with Congress, but they had only limited success. Congress did repeal the Tonkin Gulf Resolution in 1970, but this action had no effect, because by then the official justification for continued military operations was the necessity to protect American troops until they could be withdrawn. Various "end the war" and withdrawal resolutions failed, but Congress did eventually order the bombing of Cambodia stopped by August 15, 1973. Efforts to involve the Supreme Court failed, as it rejected all attempts to have it consider whether the Vietnam War was unconstitutional because there had been no declaration of war by Congress.[20]

5. Naturally, it has made a great difference that the President, and not the Senate, negotiates treaties. However, the requirement that

treaties secure ratification by a two-thirds vote of the Senate has been a substantial limitation on the President's power. To a considerable degree, Presidents have met this challenge by the extensive use of executive agreements, which have the same legal effect as treaties. The principal limitations on their use are political in nature—the degree to which it is wise to exclude the Senate from this constitutional foreign-policy role. The serious but unsuccessful drive for the Bricker Amendment in the early 1950s sought to prevent the use of executive agreements as alternatives to treaties. In 1972 discovery by the Senate of a number of secret foreign commitments, particularly an agreement permitting American use of Spanish bases in return for substantial grants, led Congress to adopt the Case Act, which requires the Secretary of State to submit to Congress within sixty days the text of any international agreement.

6. The power to take care that the laws be faithfully executed was, as already noted, joined by Lincoln to the Commander-in-Chief power at the outbreak of the Civil War to justify his emergency acts. Standing alone, this power also has been the subject of significant reliance in supporting presidential action, and it is a principal reliance for the theory of implied presidential powers.

That the President possesses not only the specific powers mentioned in the Constitution but also the powers necessary and proper for the performance of the executive function finds the broadest support in the first sentence of Article II: "The executive power shall be vested in a President of the United States." It has always been a nice constitutional question whether these words constitute a grant of power or are a mere designation of an office. The former interpretation is consistent with the Lockean notion of executive power as "residual," and it is also supported by the so-called decision of 1789, in which the First Congress relied on the "executive power" provision in deciding that the President already had the power of removal under the Constitution without any authorization by Congress.

The "faithful execution of the laws" clause was authoritatively interpreted by the Supreme Court in the well-known case of *In re Neagle* (1890), where it held that the "laws" that the President was to execute included not only statutes enacted by Congress but also "any obligation fairly and properly inferrible from [the Constitution], or any duty . . . to be derived from the general scope of . . . duties under the laws of the United States." The President's duty to see that the laws are faithfully executed, the Court went on, is not "limited to the enforcement of acts of Congress . . . according to their express terms," but includes also "the rights, duties and obligations growing out of the Constitution itself, our international relations, and all the protection implied by the nature of the government under the Constitution."

The same position was taken by the Court in *In re Debs* (1895), where it upheld the power of the President to order his Attorney General to secure a court injunction against the Pullman railroad strike despite the fact that there was no explicit statutory basis for the injunction.

The principal Supreme Court ruling limiting the implied powers of the Presidency is the famous steel-seizure case of 1952, in which President Truman's seizure of the steel mills to prevent a strike that would impair the flow of munitions to the troops in Korea was invalidated. That decision, however, turned on the special circumstances of the case and should not be read as imposing any serious limitations on the President's emergency powers. It was the fact that Congress, in passing the Taft-Hartley Act, had specifically considered giving seizure powers to the President and decided against it (though adopting no language at all on the subject) that convinced the swing justices, Jackson and Frankfurter, that this nonaction had stripped the President of powers he might otherwise have had.

In *New York Times Co.* v. *United States* (1971), involving the Nixon Administration's attempt to enjoin the press from publishing the so-called Pentagon Papers,[21] the Court likewise rejected, by a vote of six to three, a presidential claim to inherent power that was unsupported by statutory authorization. But two of the majority justices, Stewart and White, were willing to grant the existence of a "sovereign prerogative power" to protect the confidentiality of materials related to the national defense, and only voted against the President because they could not say that disclosure of the Pentagon Papers would "surely result in direct, immediate, and irreparable damage to our Nation or its people." Speaking for the three dissenters, Harlan would have granted the President's inherent power to act, subject only to a judicial determination that the issue lay within the "proper compass of the President's foreign relations power," and a determination by the Secretary of State or Secretary of Defense that "disclosure of the subject matter would irreparably impair the national security."

The Impact of Watergate on the Presidency

The Watergate scandals destroyed Nixon's "imperial Presidency" and provoked an unprecedented reconsideration of presidential powers. One major issue was the validity of the claim of "executive privilege," which Nixon had initially put forth to justify refusal to respond to congressional requests for information, and later in denying White House tapes and other records demanded by congressional investigating committees, the Watergate special prosecutor, and judges in the several Watergate cases. In *United States* v. *Nixon*

(1974), the Supreme Court unanimously denied the President's right to make a final, nonreviewable claim of executive privilege, saying:

> Neither the doctrine of separation of powers, nor the need for confidentiality of high-level communications, without more, can sustain an absolute, unqualified, presidential privilege of immunity from judicial process under all circumstances.

The Court did grant that there was a limited executive privilege with a constitutional base, mentioning particularly the need to protect military, diplomatic, or sensitive national-security secrets, and assured that the Court would recognize claims of confidentiality related to the President's ability to discharge his constitutional powers effectively. But no national-security claims were involved in this case, which concerned White House tapes subpoenaed in connection with the trial of former Attorney General John Mitchell and White House aides H. R. Haldeman and John Ehrlichman.[22]

United States v. *Nixon*, as well as a ruling by the Court of Appeals for the District of Columbia in *Nixon* v. *Sirica* (1973), established that the President is subject to subpoena. There had been some doubt on this subject because of the obvious enforcement problem if he chose to resist. The principal precedent was Chief Justice Marshall's subpoena to President Jefferson in the 1807 treason trial of Aaron Burr. Although Marshall's opinion clearly asserted that the President was not immune from subpoena, later developments in the case were confused, and the subpoena was not actually enforced.[23]

Later, in *Mississippi* v. *Johnson* (1867), the Supreme Court declined to issue an injunction against the President, pointing out that if he refused obedience, the Court would be "without power to enforce its process." When Judge John J. Sirica subpoenaed Nixon's tapes in 1973 for use by the Watergate grand jury, he considered it immaterial "that the court has not physical power to enforce its order to the President." He simply relied on the "good faith of the executive branch." In fact Nixon did yield to both subpoenas.

Another constitutional issue raised by Watergate was whether a President is subject to criminal indictment while in office. The Watergate grand jury was convinced by the evidence it received that Nixon had participated in the cover-up and proposed to indict him along with the other principals. It was dissuaded, however, by Special Prosecutor Leon Jaworski, who told the grand jury that the President was constitutionally protected against indictment.

Watergate led to the inauguration of impeachment proceedings against a President for only the second time in American history. The unsavory character of the impeachment effort against President Andrew Johnson a century earlier was generally thought to have so discredited the impeachment device as to preclude its future use against a President. But as evidence of Nixon's participation in the Watergate cover-up accumulated, impeachment proceedings were begun before the House Judiciary Committee, and three articles of impeachment were ultimately voted. Although impeachment action was dropped after Nixon's resignation, the Judiciary Committee did clarify a long-disputed issue as to the meaning of "high crimes and misdemeanors," the terms used by the Constitution to define impeachable offenses.

One possible view is that an impeachable offense is whatever a majority of the House of Representatives considers it to be. The opposite position is that impeachment can be voted only on proof of serious, indictable crimes. The Judiciary Committee majority adopted a middle position—that violation of a criminal statute is not a prerequisite for impeachment, as long as the offense is a serious one.[24]

One month after assuming office, President Ford granted a full pardon to Nixon for any crimes he "has committed or may have committed" during his Presidency, though Nixon had not been indicted for crime or admitted any criminal acts. While the pardon was strongly criticized, there was no way of challenging its validity, and as a precedent it seemed to establish that pardons can be granted for criminal offenses in advance of any legal proceedings.

Watergate exposed some problems with the Twenty-fifth Amendment. It was invoked for the first time in October 1973, as Nixon named Gerald Ford to fill the vacancy in the Vice-Presidency caused by the resignation of Spiro Agnew. Then, in August 1974, Ford succeeded to the Presidency on Nixon's resignation and named as Vice-President, Nelson Rockefeller, who was confirmed by Congress after a four-month delay. Thus the Twenty-fifth Amendment did not succeed in its intention never to permit a vacancy in the Vice-Presidency, and resulted for almost two and one-half years in a President and a Vice-President, neither of whom had been elected by the people.

Balance Sheet on Presidential Power

The conventional wisdom on the American Presidency, confirmed by our review of the decisions made by the framers in 1787, is that the Presidency was intended to be an office of great power, and that the successful operation of the American constitutional system requires that this power be used. Presidents who do not use their power vigorously are condemned as weak and as failures in office. The unity, dispatch, and national outlook of the President are contrasted with the divisiveness, the delay, and the parochialism of the legislature. Let us attempt to appraise the character and extent of presidential power in the principal executive roles and determine whether the effective performance of these roles requires any changes in presidential powers.

As Head of State

The President gains support for his other roles from his status as symbolic and ceremonial head of the nation. On the other hand, his performance as head of state is handicapped because he is a partisan for whom almost half the electorate, and often more than half, did not vote. No practical plan has ever been suggested for providing the Republic with a nonpartisan chief of state, leaving the President with his other executive duties. Thus, the ultimate symbols of unity have to be inanimate objects—the flag and the Constitution.

As Opinion-Molder

The President occupies incomparably the "best bully pulpit" in the land, particularly as supplemented by ready access to television. Certainly, nothing could or should be done about this. If he appears on the tube too often, overexposure will bring its own redress. The principal problem is to provide some balance in presentation of opposing views. One issue is: Who speaks for the opposition when it has no recognized national leader?

Legislative Function

Clearly Congress has failed to live up to the original constitutional expectations in the field of legislative performance, encouraging the President to assume a greater role than was anticipated in formulating legislative programs. Presidential success in the legislative arena, however, has been limited by factors such as the following:

1. Separation of powers makes it possible for the opposition party to be in control of one or both of the houses.
2. There may be substantial opposition to the President within his own congressional party, and he may not even be on particularly good terms with his party's leadership in Congress.
3. The seniority system gives committee chairmen the powers of small-time monarchs.
4. The unwieldy size of the House and the principle of unlimited debate in the Senate do not facilitate expeditious action.
5. The effectiveness of both majority- and minority-party leadership in both houses is often quite limited.

Efforts to reform legislative procedures or to achieve party responsibility in Congress have repeatedly failed. Similar failure has marked proposals for institutional changes that would strengthen the President vis-à-vis Congress—for example, giving the President the item veto on appropriation bills or providing four-year terms for members of the House with the purpose of making it more likely that a majority of representatives would be from the President's party. Separation of powers has thus left the responsibility for adopting coherent legislative programs thoroughly confused.

As Chief Administrator

The President's position as administrative chief is guaranteed by his control over personnel, organization, and funds. As we have seen, the Senate's role in confirmation of appointees is troublesome to him only on rare occasions, while the power to remove presidential appointees is practically unlimited.

As for organization of the federal establishment, Congress has largely abdicated to the President by a series of reorganization acts giving the President power to set up new organizational structures or arrangements. Such authority was used, for example, by President Nixon to create the Office of Management and Budget. Congress retains only the power to refuse to approve reorganization plans.

In the area of fiscal policy, Congress by the Budget and Accounting Act of 1921 gave the President responsibility for preparation of the budget, and congressional efforts to control or even effectively to review the budget have been progressively less successful. Even such fiscal autonomy as Congress had preserved was challenged by President Nixon in a full-scale assault on the integrity of legislative spending decisions when between 1971 and 1973 he sought to impound some $25 billion in appropriations for projects he disapproved or in amounts he deemed unwise. This assertion of executive power was too blatant, however, and was partially countered by judicial decisions and legislative reaction.[25] Congress recognized that its own slipshod fiscal practices, which never required appropriations to be considered in relation to anticipated revenues, had furnished the President with some justification for his actions. Consequently a serious effort was made to reform congressional budget procedures by adoption of the Congressional Budget and Impoundment Control Act of 1974. Briefly, the act created budget committees in each house to oversee expenditures and revenues, and established a congressional budget office to give Congress the type of expertise available to the President through his Office of Management and Budget. The act also specified procedures by which Congress can force the President to spend funds he has impounded.

In spite of the constitutional powers and position of the executive, all recent presidents have found it difficult to exercise policy control over the federal establishment because of its size, bureaucratic rigidity, and ties to protectors and sponsors in Congress. Beginning with the development of the Executive Office of the President under Franklin Roosevelt, efforts have been made to achieve a greater measure of executive control, without marked success. Again it remained for President Nixon to make a frontal assault on the problem by greatly increasing the Executive Office staff and by an unprecedented concentration of administrative control in the White House by the appointment as Cabinet members of men who had no independent political base, by placing in key positions in the departments and independent agencies men who had proved their loyalty to the President in service on the White House staff, and by setting up four super-department heads directly under the President. These arrangements collapsed in the Watergate holocaust.

As Party Leader

This is an extraconstitutional role. The President is, by virtue of his election, the leader of his party, but this does not guarantee that he will perform the function effectively. Moreover, he will make trouble for himself if he seems to be giving priority too consistently to partisan motives.

The Presidency at Home versus the Presidency Abroad

This summary view of the powers of the President in and through his different roles affords some measure of understanding of his resources for performing his domestic functions. His great powers of leadership, initiative, and action are balanced by countervailing forces inherent in the separation-of-powers system. No President is ever able to develop a domestic program without working within this system. Roosevelt was able to get what he wanted from Congress, without fighting for it, only during the first hundred days of his New Deal administration. Nixon's artfully planned and vigorously implemented effort to maximize executive power and subordinate or ignore Congress would no doubt have encountered increased resistance even if Watergate had not occurred.

When we consider the President's foreign-policy functions and his access to the war power, however, the situation becomes quite different. Here, there is a real basis for concern whether the system is in balance, for events have repeatedly demonstrated that presidential powers of initiative are greater and the possibilities of restraint fewer. Some of the reasons for this contrast are suggested in the following summary:

1. The President monopolizes the sources of information about foreign affairs to a much greater degree than he does the sources of domestic information, and much of it is not made public, so that the President can always contend that his actions are based on data not available to Congress or the public.
2. The President directs diplomatic negotiations, which must proceed largely in secret.
3. The necessity for emergency action, not permitting consultation, is much greater, the ultimate example being the need to counter a threatened nuclear attack.
4. As Commander in Chief, the President is in control of a vast engine of force that can move into immediate operation on his command, as compared with the civil establishment, which the President can put in motion or redirect much more slowly, and sometimes not at all.
5. Recommendations for military action come up to the President through a military hierarchy that typically presents specific and coordinated policy proposals, compared with the conflicting and uncoordinated advice he usually receives on domestic matters.
6. The doctrine of political questions generally prevents the Supreme Court from reviewing any challenges to the constitutionality of executive action in the field of foreign affairs, in contrast to the full power of judicial review over domestic controversies.[26]

In certain foreign-policy matters, Congress does participate fully, and admittedly its record is not always one to inspire great confidence in congressional capacity. The Senate's action, or inaction, in the ratification of treaties has been a long-standing cause for complaint. The annual foreign-aid appropriation is another field where Congress has not been reluctant to substitute its judgment for that of the President. There are matters with domestic ramifications, such as the closing of military posts, where Congress has often reversed presidential judgment. On the other hand, appropriations for the CIA are hidden completely from the public and from most members of Congress, and the general appropriations for military supply and procurement are seldom seriously questioned.[27]

Congress's frustration over its impotence in attempting to end the Vietnam War ultimately resulted in adoption of the War Powers Act, passed in 1973 over President Nixon's veto. The law sets a sixty-day limit on any presidential commitment of U.S. troops abroad without specific congressional authorization. The commitment can be extended for another thirty days if necessary for the safe withdrawal of troops. Unauthorized commitments can be terminated before the sixty-day deadline by congressional adoption of a concurrent resolution, a measure that does not require presidential signature. Moreover, the act requires the President to consult with Congress in every possible situation before introducing armed forces into hostilities or areas where imminent involvement in hostilities is clearly indicated. Whereas President Nixon condemned the statute as an unconstitutional and dangerous restriction on the power of the Commander in Chief to meet emergencies, some liberal members of Congress voted against it on the opposite ground that the statute, in fact, recognized the President's right to start a war.

The collapse of the South Vietnamese regime in April 1975 was so sudden that Congress was precluded from acting on President Ford's request for authorization to use U.S. troops to evacuate American citizens from Vietnam. But within two weeks another situation arose calling for application of the War Powers Act—the seizure of the American merchant vessel *Mayaguez* by Cambodian naval forces. Not until the sea and air rescue operation ordered by President Ford, including bombing of the Cambodian mainland, was under way did Ford call congressional leaders to the White House to "advise" them of the military moves. The widespread support for the President's prompt action suggested that the War Powers Act was unlikely to prove a very effective limitation on presidential military initiatives.

Congress did, however, find other methods of participating more actively in the field of foreign affairs, highlighted by a congressionally imposed arms embargo against Turkey in 1974, in response to the Turkish invasion of Cyprus, and a ban on funds and military aid to factions in the Angolan civil war in 1975. Both actions were strongly condemned by the executive as congressional meddling in foreign affairs. Disclosure of CIA covert activities and assassination plots led both the House and Senate to create special intelligence committees in 1975 to investigate these reports. As a result the Senate in 1976 created a new fifteen-member select committee charged with oversight of all the nation's secret intelligence services, with absolute authority to approve the CIA budget. The intelligence agencies were required to keep the committee fully and currently informed as to their operations, including any significant anticipated activities.[28]

A review of these recent experiences with executive-legislative relationships in the field of foreign affairs suggests the following conclusions:

1. Because of the inherent differences between domestic and foreign problems, the President may legitimately claim greater freedom of action in the foreign field, particularly the power to take emergency measures in the use of military forces.
2. The broad claims for executive autonomy in the use of military

forces, based on the Commander-in-Chief power, in other than emergency situations, find support in the practices of the past hundred years, but are not justified by the intentions of the framers and are not consistent with the American system of representative government and checks and balances.

3. Congress has the right and the obligation to use its appropriating and legislating power to fix outer limits for American foreign and military policy and to review and revise ongoing foreign and military commitments.

4. Under present conditions, the congressional declaration of war, which was relied upon so strongly by the framers as a limitation on the executive, is probably obsolete, for it encourages what is no longer acceptable—the use of unlimited force. Limited war is all that can now be contemplated, and the determination of those limits is a matter for joint action by the President and Congress. Development of such machinery may require adaptation in present procedures, particularly for emergency actions. When longer-range policies are involved, it would seem feasible for Congress to set limits on presidential autonomy by the normal processes of legislation and appropriation.

Notes

1. Edward S. Corwin, *The President: Office and Powers, 1787–1957* (New York, 1957), pp. 5–6.
2. *The Federalist*, No. 48.
3. Max Farrand, *The Framing of the Constitution of the United States* (New Haven, 1913), vol. II, p. 52.
4. *Ibid.*, vol. I, pp. 65, 66, 97.
5. *Ibid.*, p. 65.
6. *Ibid.*, vol. II, pp. 541–42.
7. *Ibid.*, vol. I, p. 65.
8. *Ibid.*, vol. II, p. 31.
9. *Ibid.*, vol. I, p. 119.
10. *Ibid.*, vol. II, p. 318.
11. *Ibid.*, p. 319.
12. See Charles A. Lofgren, "War-Making Under the Constitution: The Original Understanding," 81 *Yale Law Journal* 672 (1972).
13. Farrand, *op. cit.*, vol. II, pp. 297, 392.
14. *Ibid.*, vol. I, p. 21.
15. *Ibid.*, pp. 63–64.
16. There have been periodic proposals for grafting features of the parliamentary system onto the American system of separate powers. The most common suggestion has been for congressional question periods during which Cabinet members would appear before the House or Senate to defend administration policies. Representative Henry Reuss's proposal

for a congressional vote of no confidence in the President is the subject of a symposium in 43 *George Washington Law Review* 327 (1975).

17. Corwin, *op. cit.*, p. 229.
18. *Ibid.*, p. 243.
19. *New York Times*, August 18, 1967.
20. Anthony A. D'Amato and Robert M. O'Neil, *The Judiciary and Vietnam* (New York: St. Martin's Press, 1972). The Supreme Court denied certiorari in a number of cases, including *Mora* v. *McNamara* (1967), *Mitchell* v. *United States* (1967), and *Sarnoff* v. *Shultz* (1972). See also *Massachusetts* v. *Laird* (1970) and *Holtzman* v. *Schlesinger* (1973).
21. Martin Shapiro, *The Pentagon Papers and the Courts* (San Francisco: Chandler, 1972); Louis Henkin, "The Right to Know and the Duty to Withhold: The Case of the Pentagon Papers," 120 *University of Pennsylvania Law Review* 271 (1971); Peter D. Junger, "Down Memory Lane: The Case of the Pentagon Papers," 23 *Case Western Reserve Law Review* 3 (1971).
22. See "Symposium: *United States* v. *Nixon*," 22 *UCLA Law Review* 1 (1974); Paul A. Freund, "On Presidential Privilege," 88 *Harvard Law Review* 13 (1974); Raoul Berger, *Executive Privilege: A Constitutional Myth* (Cambridge, Mass.: Harvard University Press, 1974). All the documents in the case are collected in Leon Friedman (ed.), *United States v. Nixon: The President Before the Supreme Court* (New York: Chelsea House, 1974).
23. Raoul Berger, "The President, Congress, and the Courts—Subpoenaing the President: Jefferson v. Marshall in the Burr Case," 83 *Yale Law Journal* 1111 (1974).
24. Raoul Berger, *Impeachment: The Constitutional Problems* (Cambridge, Mass.: Harvard University Press, 1973); Charles L. Black, Jr., *Impeachment: A Handbook* (New Haven: Yale University Press, 1974); House Committee on the Judiciary, 93d Cong., 1st sess., *Impeachment: Selected Materials* (Washington, D.C.: Government Printing Office, 1973).
25. *Train* v. *City of New York* (1975); Louis Fisher, *Presidential Spending Power* (Princeton, N.J.: Princeton University Press, 1975), chaps. 7–8.
26. See Louis Henkin, "Is There a 'Political Question' Doctrine?" 85 *Yale Law Journal* 597 (1976); Michael Tigar, "Judicial Power, the 'Political Question' Doctrine, and Foreign Relations," 17 *UCLA Law Review* 1135 (1970).
27. In *United States* v. *Richardson* (1974), the Supreme Court rebuffed an effort to make the CIA budget public. See also "The CIA's Secret Funding and the Constitution," 84 *Yale Law Journal* 608 (1975).
28. "National security" has been invoked to justify invasions of privacy, including wiretapping and opening of mail, by executive intelligence agencies such as the FBI and the CIA. Attorney General John Mitchell contended that the Crime Control Act of 1968 permitted the executive to conduct electronic surveillance without prior judicial warrant even in domestic security investigations. The Supreme Court rejected this claim in *United States* v. *United States District Court* (1972), but left the constitutionality of wiretapping without warrant in foreign intelligence actions uncertain by failing to review *Ivanov* v. *United States* (1974).

2. Appraising Presidential Power: The Ford Presidency

Philip Shabecoff

I

Reflections on the American Presidency by scholars and other commentators in recent years have tended to employ a vocabulary peppered with royal and absolutist terms. To Arthur M. Schlesinger, Jr., for example, the Presidency is "imperial." George E. Reedy calls the office the "American Monarchy," while Richard E. Neustadt views it as an elective "kingship." And in another chapter in this volume, F. G. Hutchins finds that the Presidency has become the "tyranny" foreseen by Thomas Jefferson.

But this kind of regal language was manifestly inappropriate to describe the Presidency of Gerald R. Ford in 1976, two years after he moved into the White House to complete the unexpired term of Richard M. Nixon. While imperial trappings remained, Ford emerged in media portrayals more as the court jester than as the king. A prevailing image of Ford was an amiable, bumbling pratfall artist, prone to tumbling down airplane steps and banging his head against the sides of swimming pools. It was hardly the image of an all-powerful tyrant.

President Ford's weakness was reflected by more than mere imagery, however. Despite his incumbency, which he put to full use, he was embarrassingly unable to shake off a challenge by Ronald Reagan, an ex-actor turned governor of California, for the presidential nomination of his own party.

Even while he was struggling through the primary process, public-opinion polls indicated he would be a decided underdog in the general election despite the fact that recent history shows that incumbent presidents seeking election do not lose. Observers who traveled with past presidents noted that public appearances by Ford did not produce the kind of reverence, awe, and even hysteria that almost invariably had been generated among crowds by past chief executives.

In Washington, President Ford lost to Congress a number of policy battles—chiefly in foreign policy but also in such areas as taxes and energy—that presidents normally win, even if they are minority presidents.

Ford came to power at a time of deep national crisis as an unelected President from a minority party. Considering the handicaps he faced, he appears to have performed with reasonable competence in office. Compared to conditions that prevailed when he took office, including turmoil in the executive branch, the aftermath of the Vietnam War still producing social unrest, and a dangerous recession building up a head of steam, the country appeared to be in relatively decent shape in mid-1976. What, then, accounted for the seeming weakness of Gerald Ford and his Presidency?

One reason certainly involved the personality and style of the man himself. It is undoubtedly true, as the White House staff insisted, that descriptions of President Ford as a dumb, maladroit fumbler were grossly unfair. The staff pointed out that he was a well-coordinated athlete and, at age sixty-three, was in far better physical—and probably mental—health than most of his recent predecessors. He also proved himself bright enough to come to grips with and grasp quickly the many complex issues a President must master, from fiscal and monetary policy to strategic arms-limitations negotiations and the politics of the Atlantic Alliance.

But Ford also presented a bland and uninspiring public façade. His oratorical style was yawn-inducing and his leadership continued to reflect the techniques of accommodation, compromise, and dealmaking that characterized his tenure as House Minority Leader. When he raised a banner—whether his "WIN" campaign to "Whip Inflation Now" or, indeed, his own candidacy for a full term in office—he found it difficult to inspire people to follow. He simply did not act like a powerful President.

President Ford's own view that Government has grown too big and must play a more passive role in the affairs of the nation also contributed to the general impression that presidential power ebbed during his administration. In part responding to what he perceived as the political mood of the country and in part because of his own conservative convictions, Mr. Ford deliberately sought to reduce the role of the federal government and, therefore, the powers of his own office as well.

Another part of the apparent weakness of the Ford Presidency stemmed from the fact that Ford was a nonelected President, the first to take office under the Twenty-fifth Amendment. As Joseph A. Califano, a former White House domestic adviser to President Johnson pointed out during one of Mr. Ford's confrontations with Capitol Hill, "the only elected people in town" were in Congress. Without an electoral mandate, the President could not, as many of his predecessors liked to do, invoke the authority of the plebiscite to overcome his opposition.

Still another source of apparent weakness in the Ford Administration was the overwhelming domination of Congress by the opposition Democratic Party by a majority of better than two to one. Mr. Ford handled his congressional relations skillfully and exercised his veto frequently, but the majority on Capitol Hill was an important constraint on presidential power during his administration.

All of these drains on the powers of the Presidency were related to the officeholder himself or to current and perhaps temporary circumstances. But there were other limitations placed on the White House and executive branch that sprang from external sources and that might or might not prove to be of a lasting nature. They sprang from a variety of causes, many of them reflecting reaction to the unpopular lost war in Vietnam and the Watergate scandal, which had destroyed the previous administration and driven its leader from office in disgrace.

II

Potentially the most significant check on presidential power was the seeming determination by Congress in the wake of Watergate and Vietnam to try to reassert its authority as a coequal branch of the federal government, a role it had been slowly abdicating in previous decades. In his thoughtful book *The Accountability of Power*, Senator Walter F. Mondale, writing in 1975 prior to his Vice-Presidency, sums up the long-term trend:

> The cause for concern was—and still is—a real one. Over a period of decades, the power of the Congress—intended to be both a force for positive government and the principal check against executive branch tyranny—had been systematically eroded and weakened. A potent combination of Presidential action and Congressional inaction had shifted the balance of power, particularly in foreign affairs, undercutting much of Congress's role as a restraint against the arbitrary exercise of Presidential power.

As Senator Mondale notes, it was by no means certain that this trend had been more than temporarily arrested. But when Mr. Ford moved into the White House, and, indeed, even in the last year or so of the aborted Nixon presidency, Congress took action after action in resistance to presidential pressures that previously had seemed irresistible.

"For the time being at least, Congress is resurgent," said Mike Mansfield, the Senate Democratic leader, during an interview early in 1976. He added that "Congress is now trying to bring about an equality of power between the executive and legislative branches."

Much of this new assertiveness by Congress appeared in the field of foreign policy, where the growth of presidential power had been most abundantly nourished. "The Imperial Presidency," Arthur M. Schlesinger, Jr., writes in his book of that title, "was essentially the creation of foreign policy." Certainly the reach of presidential power was most dramatically demonstrated during the tragic war in Vietnam.

It was in response to the unilateral exercise of war powers by Presidents Johnson and Nixon—and to the debilitating domestic and international results of those acts—that Congress passed the War Powers Act. Basically, the act requires the President to consult with Congress when committing American forces abroad and gives Congress the right to recall those forces after sixty days. Just how much of a limit the resolution places on the President's ability to take the nation to war on his own initiative—if any at all—is a matter of considerable dispute. There is a strain of thought that considers the legislation a bad mistake on the ground that it gives legitimacy to presidential war-making power where there was previously no written assertion of such power but only ambiguous precedent.

Schlesinger, in an interview, called the War Powers Act a "lot of nonsense." In fact, he said, it will have a negative effect because "it makes legal the President's ability to take the nation into war. I think, on the whole, it increases Presidential power." He cited the *Mayaguez* incident, in which the President committed air, sea, and land forces to rescue an American merchant ship and its crew that had been captured by Cambodian gunboats, as an example of how the President's war-making powers had been untouched.

Some members of Congress also share the belief that the War Powers Act may have been a mistake. Senator James Abourezk, Democrat of South Dakota, called the resolution "misguided." "It gives him [the President] more power. Jesus! The power of 60 days to make war!"

But other observers, while conceding that the resolution allows the President wide discretion to commit American forces to foreign adventures, insist that it puts limits on that discretion that did not exist before. While the President can still do what he wants in a *Mayaguez* situation—admittedly a great deal and with the potential for dragging the country into a major war—he cannot keep the nation in a protracted Vietnam type of situation without the approval and consent of Congress.

Raoul Berger, the constitutional scholar, writes that the passage of the War Powers Act marked the "end of an era." "Henceforth, unilateral warmaking by the President would not go unchallenged," he notes. "The resolution premised that there are constitutional metes and bounds to warmaking by the President; and it signalled that Congress meant to resume its place in the sun. Watergate served to hammer home the lesson of Vietnam—presidential disregard of Constitutional limits threatens our democratic system."

This view was shared by a number of members of Congress and, even more to the point, by foreign-policy and national-security officials within the Ford Administration. One high-ranking national-security aide in the White House commented that "power, to a certain extent, is what is perceived," and then went on to say that whatever the War Powers Act does or does not do, outside forces—friends and foes alike—are bound to conclude that it restricts the ability of the President of the United States to act.

Change in the relationship between Congress and the President in the area of foreign policy was signaled by more than the War Powers Act. Congress, by a wide variety of actions, some of them major and some relatively insignificant, consciously sought to drop its rubber-stamp role in foreign policy.

As Columbia University professor Louis Henkin pointed out, the Presidency early acquired "dominant influence" in foreign policy by the simple process of making foreign policy on a day-to-day basis as the sole communicator with other governments. The President, in effect, pre-empted foreign policy in increasingly absolute fashion, with Congress only coming into the picture when a policy already instituted required congressional legitimization in the form of a treaty, a statute, a declaration of war, or an appropriation of funds.

Although there may have been no fundamental change in this relationship, Congress has displayed in the past couple of years an increasing readiness to take an active role in the formulation and, to an extent, the conduct of foreign policy. The congressional role was largely negative in that it blocked presidential initiatives, but it was, nonetheless, a check on the accustomed freedom of the White House to determine what the nation's foreign policy shall be.

Congress specifically resisted, for example, President Ford's efforts to provide economic and military aid to the anti-Communist governments of South Vietnam and Cambodia in the weeks preceding the collapse of these governments. It declined to give the President the means to conduct open or covert operations in Angola, it resisted military aid to Turkey after the Turks had invaded Cyprus, and it passed a bill with restrictions on trade with the Soviet Union despite urgent opposition from the White House. It also passed a military-appropriation bill with requirements that certain actions authorized by the law be reviewed by Congress after they were already taken by the executive branch—a bill that President Ford vetoed.

While it is too early at this writing to determine the eventual results of the congressional-oversight hearings on covert foreign operations by the Central Intelligence Agency and other intelligence arms of the executive branch, it seems safe to assume that the freewheeling activities by those groups will be curbed by the revelations alone, at least for the time being. Finally, Congress has seemed inclined to resist the making of foreign policy through executive agreements and to insist on its treaty-ratifying rights.

Time will tell whether this post-Vietnam, post-Watergate congressional assertiveness in foreign policy will have any lasting significance, but in 1976 it could be stated that certain assumptions about the relative roles of the legislative and executive branches had been reopened to questioning.

Within the White House itself, constraints on the President's ability to make foreign policy were certainly a matter of real concern. A high-ranking national-security policy official insisted to an interviewer:

> The President's powers to safeguard national security and conduct foreign policy have been seriously weakened by the combined effects of Vietnam and Watergate. There is a general sense in Congress that there has been an accretion of presidential power and that now is the time to move in and redress the imbalance. . . . Nothing is permanent but there has been a relative shift of power to Congress which probably will remain for a long time.

One of the problems with congressional activism in foreign policy, the official said, is that

> there is no coherent Congressional alternative to presidential policy in foreign affairs and national security. Congressional impact is almost entirely negative and nihilistic. . . . The most serious implication is that our opponents will perceive a paralysis to action [*sic*] in what are more or less marginal areas that could produce serious confrontation. Less perceptible and perhaps less dangerous but harder to reverse is the perception by friends and allies that they really have to make other arrangements, that people we've told we're behind explicitly or implicitly will lose faith and confidence.

If, as Senator Mondale claims in his book, "a renaissance of power has begun on Capitol Hill," it is most dramatically apparent in the field of foreign policy because that is where the President has been paramount. But it also may be taking place in domestic areas, particularly in the all-important field of budget-making.

Senator Mondale expresses the belief that "Congressional power over spending is the cornerstone of the constitutional balance between Congress and the President." In "Federalist Paper Number 59," James Madison declares that "this power over the purse may, in fact, be regarded as the most complete and effectual weapon with which any constitution can arm the immediate representatives of the people, for obtaining a redress of every grievance and for carrying into effect every just and salutary measure."

Over the years, however, the President assumed more and more of this power for some of the same reasons he was able to dominate foreign policy—his executive branch had the staff and information with which to make decisions, and, most important, he could make those decisions unilaterally, while Congress was being divided and rendered indecisive by the pressures of competing interest groups. The result was that the national budget increasingly became the President's budget and not the budget of the "immediate representatives of the people." Congress's function became more and more a matter of rearranging or supplementing the basic budget program that emerged from the White House. President Nixon carried presidential control over the budget to new heights by refusing to use or deferring the expenditure of funds appropriated for the budget.

To Senator Mondale, the "wave of $18 billion in [budget] impoundments announced by the Nixon Administration in the spring of 1973 clearly brought home the fact that the practice of impoundment had gradually grown into a major vehicle for Presidential disregard of Congressional policies in legislation which the President himself had signed."

The new budget-control procedure adopted by Congress to restore order to budget-making on Capitol Hill and to regain some mastery over the process puts stringent limits on the President's power to impound or defer expenditure of funds appropriated by the legislative branch. President Ford frequently attempted to impose his conservative economic positions on the Democratic Congress through "recisions" and "deferrals" of appropriated funds for a wide variety of programs. His efforts were defeated time after time with only a few billion dollars in spending actually affected.

A probably even more significant feature of the Budget Control Act is the requirement that Congress set an overall budget ceiling and then remain within that limitation when voting appropriations. The significance of this provision is that it gives Congress overall responsibility for the budget process and the end result of the process—a function that had gone to the President almost by default.

Of course, the new budget process is still largely untested, and it will take at least until well into the Ninety-fifth Congress (1977–79) to tell whether it will prove to be of significance over the long run. The early performance of the congressional budget committees was encouraging, however. Even skeptics who believed a shift in the balance of power between the White House and Capitol Hill was highly unlikely conceded that the new budget process could have substantial impact.

Writing in *The Public Interest*, Aaron Wildavsky of the University of California enumerates reasons he believes presidents will gain rather than lose power despite Watergate and Vietnam. But he also writes that "the exception is budget reform. If successful, it would, by relating revenue to expenditure, enable Congress to maintain its power of the purse." He adds, however, that "the prognosis is problematic."

Congress successfully fought President Ford on a number of other major domestic legislative fronts. It declined to tie a tax-cut extension to a specific spending ceiling. It provided more funds for employment, housing, education, and other social programs than Mr. Ford had asked for or deemed necessary. Congress also defeated the President on energy policy, to which Mr. Ford had assigned one of his highest domestic priorities, by refusing to curtail demand through the mechanism of higher prices.

It was not only in battles over specific legislation or issues that Congress sought to limit and turn back the growth of presidential power over the past few years. It employed an array of constitutional and institutional tools in an effort to reassert its authority.

One such tool was the *legislative veto*, which, to the dismay of the White House and the executive branch, was embedded in legislation with increasing frequency. This device enables Congress to review the President's execution of a law or otherwise modify executive actions.

For example, the Senate approved a $3 billion foreign-military-aid bill that reserved to Congress the right to veto arms sales abroad after they had been made. The energy bill adopted by Congress authorized the administration to take action to increase, develop, and conserve fuel but required the Federal Energy Administration (FEA) to report back to Congress and allowed Congress to reverse actions already taken by the FEA.

Congress has been much more zealous in exercising its oversight function since Vietnam and Watergate. The most dramatic examples during the Ford Administration were the investigations of the government's intelligence-gathering organizations, but there were many other examples—less publicized but probably more effective—in a broad range of areas.

Still another demonstration of stiffened will by Congress was its resistance to claims of executive privilege, a resistance helped by the bad repute into which such claims had fallen because of their misuse by President Nixon. Congress and the White House went nose to nose on a claim of executive privilege by President Ford to prevent Secretary of State Henry A. Kissinger from having to turn over documents describing covert foreign operations that had been demanded by the House Select Committee on Intelligence. The committee threatened a congressional contempt citation against Kissinger, and the White House backed down, giving the committee the information it sought.

The defeat was cloaked as a compromise in which the documents themselves were not physically turned over to Congress.

Finally, the Senate indicated a new congressional combativeness by refusing to confirm a significantly high number of presidential appointments to federal agencies. Until recently, the Senate turned down such appointments only in rare circumstances, generally treating them as a matter of courtesy. But it rejected Ford appointments to the Home Loan Bank Board, the Corporation for Public Broadcasting, the Tennessee Valley Authority, and other agencies.

III

Congress was not the only force to vie with, limit, or otherwise act as a constraint on presidential power in the post-Watergate period. Changing attitudes in the bureaucracy and among the press and public that were a result of Watergate and the unpopular lost war in Vietnam, and also of shifting social, economic, political, and geopolitical forces, seemed to make an impact on the strength of the Presidency under Gerald R. Ford.

Ford's control over the federal bureaucracy clearly was not as great as that of his immediate predecessors. Certainly he was not able to plant White House operatives in the departments and agencies to make sure that the will of the President was being carried out—a practice followed by Nixon. There is some evidence that the bureaucracy, emboldened by the downfall of a President who tried to exercise autocratic control over the agencies, is willing to exercise somewhat more independent judgment. And President Ford apparently has found it expedient to give freer rein to the bureaucracy.

This has meant, among other things, that a degree of power has been restored to Cabinet officers and that Ford has shared more power with members of his Cabinet than recent presidents. The Cabinet as an institution remained pretty much in the low estate to which it had steadily sunk. President Ford called meetings of the Cabinet somewhat more frequently than his immediate predecessors, but it did not reassume any significant policy-making function.

Philip W. Buchen, chief legal counsel in the Ford White House, said:

> One effect of Watergate was to make it incumbent on Presidents to impose less interference and less direct control over the operation of departments and agencies. Departments ought to be operating agencies but every President since Roosevelt violated that principle. This President is letting cabinet officers function and respects their prerogatives. He is not letting the White House staff interfere with them. Cabinet officers, when appointed, should expect they will be treated as cabinet members and not as

a tool for manipulation by the White House. The effect is not so much a weakening of the power of the President as a dispersal of that power.

The backlash from Watergate, along with economic factors, also put pressure on the President to hold down the size of the White House staff. Not that the staff size has shrunk by any significant amount—it numbered nearly five hundred full-time employees just before the 1976 election. In fact, the size of the federal bureaucracy as a whole was not perceptibly reduced during the Ford presidency. But, at least, the steady spiraling growth of the White House staff and Executive Office of the President was slowed and, for a time, even stopped.

Presidential power, of course, derives from many sources. Over the years, particularly in this century, presidents have used the prestige of their office to increase their power through direct appeals to public opinion.

There seems to be little doubt at this juncture that the Vietnam War and the departure of President Nixon in disgrace as a result of the Watergate scandal drained large reserves of prestige from the Presidency and reduced the legitimacy of paramount presidential power.

Historian Henry Graff of Columbia University believes that Vietnam and Watergate have "de-mythologized" the President and that because the office has become "tarnished" it has also become more prone to defeat. The public, Professor Graff suggests, no longer attributes to a President a mysterious "he knows" quality.

Ron Nessen, the Ford White House press secretary, said that the treatment of President Ford by the news media, as well as the prevailing climate of public opinion, indicates that "the majesty and awe have gone out of the Presidency." President Ford, he told an interviewer in 1976,

has been able to regain some moral authority because he is truthful and honest. But there is a public mood that anything is possible from the President. There is an inclination to disbelieve anything the President says or does. That is the damage Nixon did. He made everybody cynics. There is a legacy of a breakdown in public confidence in the President. Actually it applies to all public officials, but the President is so much more in the spotlight that he is affected most of all.

The traumatic Vietnam experience also seems to have discredited the presidential war to some degree. Even observers who see little lasting change in presidential power concede that a President cannot at this point in history simply sound a trumpet and expect the nation to follow him to war. Without that ability, a President is shorn of one of his bases of power. As Arthur M. Schlesinger, Jr., puts it, there has been "some withdrawal of consent from the President's war making powers."

A highly revealing indication of the low esteem and loss of legitimacy suffered by the Presidency was the fact that in 1976 many of the candidates for the presidential nomination from both parties, including Jimmy Carter, George Wallace, Ronald Reagan, and President Ford himself, ran "anti-Washington" campaigns in response to what they perceived to be the mood of the country. This anti-Washington mood applied to all branches, of course, but, springing as it did from the Watergate scandal and Vietnam, it would seem to have applied most of all to presidential government.

There were many other factors, unrelated or not directly related to Watergate and Vietnam, or even to domestic politics, that affected the powers of the Presidency. For example, in an era of detente, the President's ability to initiate and carry out foreign policy has been restrained in several ways. Joseph A. Califano, Jr., a former key aide to President Johnson and author of *A Presidential Nation*, commented that the mere invocation of "national security" by a President is losing its potency, and a President can no longer cow his adversaries by appealing to it.

In part, the national-security appeal is debased coin because it was so badly abused by President Nixon and others. But it is also dying a natural death. President Ford's Attorney General, Edward H. Levi, commented that the nation is finally emerging from the "overhanging shadow" of the national emergency of World War II and that, therefore, the national-security rationale for the exercise of presidential power has lost much of its persuasiveness.

New institutions are arising, meanwhile, that are less susceptible to presidential authority. As Professor Graff points out, multinational companies, based in the United States but having global interests, "have become like the multinational church—they are largely free of presidential control." Many of the multinationals, in fact, may have a greater stake in the power of a foreign sovereign than in that of the President of the United States. An oil company, for example, may find it expedient and profitable to demonstrate its chief loyalty to the potentate of an Arab oil-producing country.

Finally, amorphous, hard-to-define social forces have probably been nibbling away at the prestige and authority of the President. For example, there is generally conceded to have been in recent years an erosion of respect for authority figures of all kinds—parents, churches, teachers. Obviously a President is not immune to this trend. A father figure is not what it used to be.

IV

The extent of the constraints on presidential power that have developed in recent years is probably somewhat underestimated. But it also is undoubtedly true that what has been taken away is a shallow scratch on the surface of what remains. A U.S. President—even a seemingly weak President such as Gerald Ford—retains enormous inherent and acquired constitutional powers and the ability to build upon those powers in the future.

Obviously, Congress continues to delegate power with every piece of legislation it passes and, in so doing, increases presidential power virtually daily. In a complex world of domestic and international problems, the President, in the view of many observers, remains the one center of power that can function efficiently on a day-to-day basis. "Look at the institutional, economic and social problems and where the solutions are going to come from," commented Joseph A. Califano. "It has to be the White House. Congress has shown it cannot act. Cities and states don't have the power to deal with narrow interests."

Although Congress did seek to restore a balance of authority with the President after Watergate, it remained, in the absence of strong leadership, relatively ineffectual as an alternative to presidential power. Some observers felt that the weakness of Congress actually served to weaken the President as well because the White House could never be certain that Capitol Hill would follow up on ideas and programs initiated in the executive branch.

But despite his lack of an electoral mandate, despite the inherited burden of Vietnam and Watergate, despite the fact that Congress was controlled by the opposition party, and despite his own personal weaknesses, President Ford was able to impose much of his conservative social and economic philosophy on federal policy in the two years of President Nixon's unexpired term. He also was able to obtain some specific legislation from Congress, as well as to block some programs favored by congressional liberals.

One surprising victory by the President was the acceptance, virtually intact, of his $112 million defense budget for fiscal year 1977 by a Congress that for years had been slicing away military spending. Ford was also successful in beating back repeated congressional efforts to reduce unemployment at a more rapid rate through federal job-creating programs, though some of his defenses on this line began to crumble as the election neared.

Among other things, Ford's successes underscored the significance of the veto as a prime instrument of presidential power. He used his veto well over fifty times in his first two years in office, and the vetoes were overridden just ten times. So frequently—his critics said, "promiscuously"—did the President employ his veto that one member of Congress was moved to comment that "Jerry Ford uses the veto as if he were still the minority leader voting 'Nay.' "

But Ford used his veto because it was effective—perhaps the most effective tool he possessed in a weak administration. His use of this tool supported the observation by James Bryce in *The American Commonwealth* that "the strength of Congress consists in the right to pass statutes; the strength of the President in his right to veto them."

President Ford's handling of the *Mayaguez* incident was another vivid example of the continuing strength of the Presidency. He committed land, sea, and air forces to recover an American merchant ship and its crew that had been captured by Cambodian gunboats and then informed leaders of Congress of what he had done, asserting that he had thereby satisfied the requirement of the War Powers Act that Congress be "consulted" by a President committing forces overseas.

Although American casualties in the *Mayaguez* operation were far higher than the number of seamen rescued and although there were indications that the ship and crew might have been recoverable without any fighting at all, Ford's handling of the incident was uncritically praised by the public and most of Congress, and his popularity rating in the polls temporarily rose.

The *Mayaguez* incident demonstrated anew the ability of a President to act unilaterally and quickly. It also demonstrated that the President alone is suited to respond to demands by the public for decisive, effective, and immediate action to solve problems. It also showed that the office of the President is the ideal stage from which to command national and world attention.

Despite Ford's liabilities, both personal and circumstantial, he retained the same trappings of power as the strongest presidents. He could command fleets of jet aircraft and limousines; he had access to worldwide communications networks; he was chief executive of a vast bureaucracy and Commander in Chief of awesomely powerful armed forces. When he gave press conferences, they were carried on national television (with a few controversial exceptions), and his every move was dutifully observed by the press and duly recorded for posterity.

Finally, as many commentators have pointed out, presidential power is enhanced by the weakness of competing power centers, particularly the political parties. This remained true in the Ford Administration, though Ford himself bent like a reed before the pressures of his party's right wing in his effort to secure the Republican presidential nomination in 1976.

V

It would seem, then, that the powers of the Presidency remained reasonably intact in the wake of Watergate and Vietnam. Gerald Ford, who came to office by virtue of the Twenty-fifth Amendment, an appointee of his disgraced predecessor (whom he subsequently pardoned) and was, therefore, an "accidental" President, was able to carry out the duties of his office just as if he were a "real" President. If he was less effective than most presidents, it was only a matter of degree.

But it is also clear that there have been some changes. In the two years during which President Ford filled the unexpired term of

Richard Nixon, he did not use or abuse the powers of his office as his predecessor had. Nor, for that matter, did he exercise his authority the way Presidents Johnson, Kennedy, and even Eisenhower had. President Ford quite obviously functioned under a variety of constraints, described above, imposed by outside forces, such as Congress, or self-imposed for political reasons. Unlike other presidents of the recent past, Ford conducted a circumspect and cautious administration.

In mid-1976 there was considerable disagreement over the significance and durability of these changes among scholars, members of Congress, and professional politicians, and within the White House itself. Some observers, particularly those in academia or otherwise outside the government, were certain that the constraints on the President are a temporary phenomenon and that the powers of the Presidency will be fully restored, perhaps as soon as an elected President is installed in the White House in January 1977. Others, including members of Congress and some officials within the White House, think that there has been a shift of power away from the President that will last for some time.

President Ford himself, in a written response to a query I submitted to him, expressed the opinion that the President had not lost "his basic powers." But he did feel that there had been a shift of the historical "pendulum" within the federal government in which Congress has sought to acquire more power at the expense of the executive. He wrote:

> Frankly, I believe that Congress recently has gone too far in trying to take over powers that belong to the President and the executive branch.
>
> This probably is a natural reaction to the steady growth of executive branch power over the past forty years. I'm sure it is a reaction to Watergate and Vietnam. And the fact that I came to this office through a Constitutional process and not by election also may have something to do with current efforts by the Democratic Congress to take away some of the powers of the President.
>
> As a member of Congress for twenty-five years, I clearly understand the powers and obligations of the Senate and House under our Constitution. But as President for eighteen months, I also understand that Congress is trying to go too far in some areas.

Ford's Attorney General, Edward H. Levi, commented that the nation may have entered a period of "reaction" to what was perceived, because of Watergate and Vietnam, as the accumulation of excessive presidential power. Levi contended that the perception was wrong and that the problem was not that the Presidency had grown too strong but that Congress had failed to carry out adequately its legislative and oversight functions. Levi expressed the fear that the reaction that seemed to have set in could lead to a "cycle" of congressional ascendancy and presidential weakness similar to what followed the Civil

War. The remedy for abuses of presidential power is to have a strong Congress *and* a strong executive, not to weaken the Presidency, which, he said, would greatly weaken the authority of the U.S. Government as a whole.

Several members of Congress expressed the conviction that the reaction to Watergate and Vietnam presented the legislative branch with an opportunity to begin recovering some of its long-term loss of authority to the executive branch. Senator Mondale declared, "The tide has been turned. The punishment of Nixon should make the change last for my lifetime in politics." Senator Mike Mansfield, the Senate Democratic leader, said that Congress had taken the initiative, and added, "I believe that Congress will retain momentum. There will be a slow and deliberate effort by Congress to reassert its own power. Of course we have to be sure the pendulum doesn't swing too far in the other direction. But the President will not continue to accumulate power at the expense of Congress. There will be no more Vietnams."

Professor Graff believes that the President is losing power for a number of reasons, one of which is that people seem to have been "exhausted" by presidential activism. "It may be like the Harding era—people only wanted to play." The desire for a weaker President shows that "we live in fear of history," he said. "We are shaped by the Vietnam war and to a lesser extent by Watergate. My fear is that we have learned the wrong lessons. All wars and all presidents are not bad because of Vietnam."

But other observers believe that Watergate, Vietnam, and all the other developments of recent years have made scarcely a dent in the enormous accumulation of presidential power—and that only temporarily.

In a new introduction to his *Presidential Power*, Richard E. Neustadt finds that despite all the changes that have affected the Presidency in the past quarter century,

> . . . plainly there has been no revolution. Overall, the landmarks stand. He [the President] still shares most of his authority with others and is no more free than formerly to rule by sheer command. . . . But some at least of those with whom he deals appear less formidable than before. Despite the legislative aftermath of Watergate, his own advantages, while dented here and there, may still have suffered relatively less than theirs over the years. And this shows up in his autonomy from them, his freedom, relatively speaking, to deal with them on his terms, not theirs.

Neustadt asserts that the duties of a President—"from bombs to jobs, to racial strife, to prices and resources"—can be handled by no other center of authority. He also finds, however, that "Congressional and public moods since Watergate, piled on electoral politics since 1968, drain all stability and certainty out of the terms on which a

President once sought support from others with authority or influence to lend. The gap between responsibility and capability grows wider."

Wildavsky writes that "in the backlash of Watergate it has become all too easy to imagine a weakening of the Presidency. Not so. Does anyone imagine that fewer groups will be interested in influencing a President's position in their own behalf or that his actions will matter less to people in the future? The question answers itself. The weakening of the Presidency is about as likely as the withering away of the state."

In fact, Wildavsky believes that presidents will accumulate so much power that they will find it expedient to give some of that power away to others to relieve political pressures. "Future presidents," he writes, "will be preoccupied with operating strategic levers, not with making tactical moves. They will see their power stakes in giving away their power; like everyone else they will have to choose between what they can keep and what they must give up. Not so much running the country but seeing that it is running will be their forte."

Joseph Califano's comment that "the perception of shrunken presidential power is really the perception of Ford as a weak political leader and also of his lack of popularity" is a view shared by a number of commentators. Like Califano, they believe that "all of that goes when a new President is elected, be it a Democrat or a Republican— but especially if it is a Democrat. Then, almost instantly, the President will be very powerful again."

To Arthur M. Schlesinger, Jr.,

> the Ford experience shows us the relative indestructibility of presidential power. The only people who ever voted for him are in the Fifth District of Michigan. He bears the stigma of illegitimacy. He does not even have the loyalty of his own party. He seems to be in a very weak position. Yet he has vetoed more bills in a few months than Nixon did in six years of office. He did his best to get us into a secret war in Angola. . . . Why has Watergate had so little effect? Because of the continued passivity of Congress. We still don't have a general statute on privilege, a classification system, a statute on C.I.A.

VI

The Ford presidency, then, has provided no definitive answers about permanent changes, if any, in presidential power in the wake of Vietnam and Watergate—at least, not from the perspective of late 1976. But the experience of the past two years does allow a few generalities to be set forth with a fair degree of assurance:

1. The Presidency, despite the deep scars left by Vietnam, Watergate, and other exposed abuses, remains a powerful and vital institution, even under a weak President.

2. The accretion of power by the White House has been slowed and in certain areas rolled back. The President and his staff cannot as easily as before lead the nation into foreign adventures, dominate the budget process, cow the bureaucracy, or impose their own priorities on public policy.

3. The abuse of presidential power has been curbed, at least for the moment. In the aftermath of Watergate and Vietnam, the checks and balances of the Congress, the courts, and public opinion have been reinvigorated. The President and his administration know that they cannot with impunity break the law, spy on citizens, order arbitrary arrests, subvert the political process, enter into secret agreements with foreign powers, or treat the federal budget as a private purse.

4. The President, to exercise his powers effectively, must to a greater degree seek some form of consensus with Congress, with the federal bureaucracy, with state and local governments, and with the public. President Nixon treated these other power centers with contempt; President Ford assiduously courted them.

Ford worked very hard on his congressional relations, and the fact that his programs succeeded at all reflects his skill and perseverance in winning congressional support or, at least, in neutralizing congressional opposition. To restore "trust" and "openness" to the White House, an achievement about which he frequently boasted during his campaign for the Republican presidential nomination, he made himself more accessible to the press and to the public than any other President of recent years. He traveled widely about the country, even well before the 1976 campaign. Under arrangements made by his public-liaison office, headed by William Baroody, he met delegations representing major interest groups—business, labor, religious, ethnic, and others—sometimes on almost a daily basis.

In short, Ford, unlike his recent predecessors, acted as if a President requires contact and support from a number of diverse social, political, and economic elements in order to be able to run the country.

Also unlike his recent predecessors, he acted as if the President of the United States is, like other citizens, subject to the law of the land.

VII

How long these generalities will apply remains to be seen. Some answers about the future of the Presidency began emerging when President Carter took office on January 20, 1977, with a slim electoral mandate—and with an implicit understanding that he is not held accountable for the sins of Vietnam and Watergate.

Because the United States is a democracy, and because the Constitution is flexible, the Presidency has been and should in the future be more or less what we want it to be. At this point, however, there does not seem to be any strong kind of consensus about what kind of President we want.

For most of the past forty-five years or so, the American people have opted for a strong President capable of dealing quickly and decisively with economic, social, and international crises. Many still feel that in an increasingly complex and dangerous world, a powerful, relatively uninhibited President is still desirable.

But in the wake of Watergate, there is wide concern that presidents have been too strong, arrogant, and unrestrained and that the constitutional balance created by the Founders has gotten out of alignment. In this view, new restraints—legal and binding—must be placed on the Presidency to prevent a new Watergate and to ensure that there is no erosion of democracy and liberty.

There are even some indications that Americans want not just a weaker Presidency but a weaker government generally, one that will play a diminishing role in the everyday life of the nation. That, at least, is how some political candidates in 1976 interpreted the supposed "anti-Washington" mood around the country.

Many of those in Washington who have thought seriously about the Presidency in light of recent history—people like Senators Mondale and Mansfield—have concluded that what is needed is not a weaker Presidency, because the needs of governance dictate a strong executive in this age. What *is* needed, they believe, is a strengthened Presidency, along with a strengthened Congress, judicial system, Cabinet, and bureaucracy, and the strengthening of other institutions that make up and buttress American democracy.

If that is brought about, the President may continue to provide leadership and unity to the nation while the checks and balances of the other institutions more effectively prevent abuse of existing power and arrogation of new power by the White House.

VIII

Whatever the future may hold, it can be said with certainty that at present the debate about what the federal government is and should be is as lively and intense—both in and out of government—as it has been in many, many years. Congressman Peter Rodino, who presided over the historic impeachment proceedings conducted by the House Judiciary Committee, noted that "the Constitution is now being debated and discussed more than at any other time in my lifetime."

It is, somehow, quite appropriate that in its bicentennial year, the Republic engaged in a meaningful debate over the kind of government bequeathed to it by the Founding Fathers.

3. The Carter Presidency: Plans and Priorities

Prepresidency Interviews with Jimmy Carter by Neal R. Peirce

In two lengthy interviews with Neal R. Peirce of the *National Journal*, Jimmy Carter gave several indications as to the shape of his presidency. Veteran reporter and columnist Peirce interviewed Carter during June 1976, once at Sea Island, Georgia, and again in New York City. This informative exchange was an advance indication of how Carter planned to deal with Congress, his staff, the Cabinet, and the bureaucracy and what kinds of policy shifts he was likely to initiate during his first term in the White House. This is doubtless one of the best previews of what we can expect from President Carter. Whether he can keep all these pledges remains to be seen. (Eds.)

Presidential Leadership

Q. *Would you describe in your own words the style and character of leadership you would bring to the presidency?*
A. The President ought to be a strong leader. . . . The nation is best served by a strong, independent and aggressive President, working with a strong and independent Congress, in harmony for a change, with mutual respect, in the open.

I have a great respect for the Congress, but I don't consider the Congress to be inherently capable of leadership. I think the Founding Fathers expected the President to be the leader of our country. The President is the only person who can speak with a clear voice to the American people and set a standard of ethics and morality, excellence, greatness. He can call on the American people to make a sacrifice and explain the purpose of the sacrifice, propose and carry out bold programs to protect, to expose and root out injustice and discrimination and divisions among our population. He can provide and describe a defense posture that will make our people feel secure, a foreign policy to make us proud once again.

The degree of strength of the White House is probably proportionate to the confidence and trust of the people in the office of President. There is not a time for timidity, but there is a time for careful, cautious consideration of complicated issues, searching for harmony among the disparate groups that comprise American society. I think the Democrats, and indeed the nation, are looking for an end to distrust. I think we've already seen strong evidence of this desire in the evolution of the Democratic platform, where very controversial issues were handled with sensitivity, and with an adequate degree of aggression, but still an inclination to arrive at a harmonious answer to complicated questions.

The consummation of the platform promises ought to begin in the fall elections when candidates seeking offices of Congress, Senate, possibly governorships, will comment in their own campaigns . . . on the Democratic Party commitments. This would be a good way to bridge the gap among the President and the other office seekers so that during and after that period detailed legislation might be evolved jointly by the President and congressional leaders to carry out the approaches of our party. I think that would be good politics and would also add some substance to the platform promises, which quite often in the past have not been adequately used.

Here is where the President should provide the leadership, and I intend to do that in my major statements during the fall campaign, to cover the items in the platform plus others I might add, to provide a general debate and a framework on which we Democrats can make commitments. So in relationship with Congress and the population of the country and other officials, the leadership, the role of the President is perhaps most important of all. I intend to provide that leadership as a candidate and hopefully as a President.

Q. *Would you say that the general tone and mode of leadership that you would exercise as President would be close to or substantially different from the tone and mode of leadership you exercised as governor of Georgia?*
A. It would be similar. I can't change my basic character or basic approach. I learned a lot as governor that would stand me in good stead as President. I think I can do a better job now of being aggressive and innovative and dynamic as a leader and also have a closer relationship with the Congress.

Everything I did as governor was done jointly with the legislature.

It had to be. But there was room for improvement in personal relationships between myself as governor and the leadership of the legislature that I would hope to realize as President with the leaders of Congress.

Q. *Some people have likened your approach to Theodore Roosevelt's—aggressiveness, activism, personal discipline, the theme of moral revitalization in American life. Do you see any parallel there in your own reading of American history?*
A. That's a great compliment to me. It's too early to say that I would like to be able to measure up to that kind of standard. But I think it's too early just looking at the campaign to say what kind of President I would be. I've always admired Theodore Roosevelt. Truman had the same approach to the presidency in a much more quiet and less dramatic way. And I think to some degree, Franklin Roosevelt did too. I've spent a lot of time in the last three to four years reading about various Presidents and their attitude toward the position. I think I would be strong and aggressive—maybe a good deal quieter about it than Theodore Roosevelt.

Q. *Is the description by James David Barber of an active-positive President along the lines you'd like to bring to the office?*
A. Yes, I think so. Again, it's a very subjective expectation and analysis, I would guess. I would be active and, I think, positive in approach. I don't feel ill at ease. I don't feel afraid of the job. I think I would be able to admit a mistake publicly when one was made.

I would not be reticent to use the office of the White House. I think I would be sure enough about my performance to strip away a maximum amount of secrecy that surrounds the President's function.

Decision Making

Q. *How do you arrive at a decision on a major policy issue?*
A. Exact procedure is derived to some degree from my scientific or engineering background— I like to study first all the efforts that have been made historically toward the same goal, to bring together advice or ideas from as wide or divergent points of view as possible, to assimilate them personally or with a small staff, to assess the quality of the points of view and identify the source of those proposals and, if I think the source is worthy, then to include that person or entity into a group I then call in to help me personally to discuss the matter in some depth. Then I make a general decision about what should be done involving time schedules, necessity for legislation, executive acts, publicity to be focused on the issue. Then I like to assign task forces to work on different aspects of the problem, and I like to be personally involved so that I can know the thought processes that go

into the final decisions and also so that I can be a spokesman, without prompting, when I take my case to the people, the legislature or Congress.

I have always promised the people willing to help me that we would not yield to political expediency—only when absolutely necessary to save the whole project. I think this gives volunteer contributors a sense of purpose and feeling the governor or President will indeed pursue the ideas proposed aggressively and without reticence. Most of the studies that have been made in the past . . . (on welfare, tax reform, etc.) have wound up in a beautiful bound volume and the President has never put the force of his office behind it. But I don't intend to do that.

Q. *Many people suggest that after the many inputs have been made, you make the decision essentially alone. Is that a correct perception?*
A. Yes, it is to some degree. In reorganization, the members of the legislature, the civil service workers, the business, professional and educational communities were intimately involved in the process from the beginning. They also thought they had a role to play in it. Somebody has to make the final decision in areas of controversy. To some degree that circumstance can be minimized by the degree of harmony that you are able to weld among those who do the basic work, and to the extent that the executive leader is part of the whole process. Then the isolated decision-making role can be minimized.

Q. *Some persons say that though they admire your decision-making process, that either on policy or strategy, it takes heaven and earth to move you thereafter. Is that allegation of stubbornness on your part fair criticism?*
A. I think so. But you have to be certain the position you propose is best, and it can't be a unilateral decision. You have to have a mutual agreement this is the best road to pursue.

Quite often there are alternative decisions that can be made on the same subject with very little to choose one above the other. In gray areas, the necessity to compromise is obvious.

I've always been inclined on a matter of principle or importance not to compromise until it's absolutely necessary. I don't see any reason to compromise away a position early in the stage of negotiation or early in the stage of passage through the Congress or the legislature.

There is a final forum that even transcends the inclination of the legislative body. That's the people themselves. When you do have a difference of opinion with the legislative body, then the people themselves ought to be acquainted with the discussion. I've never had the inclination nor the knowledge about the process to twist arms or force people to vote different from what they thought. But I've always seen the effectiveness of convincing the constituents back home about the question and then giving the legislative members maximum credit for the success achieved. If the legislative leaders can be involved in the initial stages of the project, if they can take credit for what is done, and not be placed in a combative attitude, then most of those disharmonies can be avoided.

Q. *Do you see any validity in people's suggestions that when you're convinced the principle is right, the brittleness could be so great you'd get into a Woodrow Wilson–League of Nations type of situation?*
A. I can't recall an incident when that's happened yet in my public life.

I've been through profound changes in the Georgia government that involved prison reform, education reform, government reorganization, judicial reform, mental health programs. I can't remember any instance, minor or major, when an adamant position on my part doomed a desirable goal.

Q. *There were some comments that Jimmy Carter approached being governor like being skipper of a submarine. As President, would you like to avoid that type of feeling and have a more harmonious working relationship?*
A. I don't accept that categorization as accurate. It was made by the present speaker of the Georgia House, Tom Murphy, who's always been a political critic of mine. I never tried to be autocratic as governor or to run other people's feelings.

If I had, I would have had an adamant resistance from the legislature instead of the cooperation we experienced. But I would be much more able now, with the experience of four years as governor, to assure harmony.

Open Administration

Q. *A constant theme of some observers of the presidency is the dangerous sense of invincibility and infallibility that pervades the White House, especially after there's been a successful campaign and the winning team and its leader are in office. Some talk of "groupthink"—a mutually reinforcing idea that we've conquered the opposition and therefore whatever problem lies ahead of us, even like a Bay of Pigs in the early '60s under Kennedy, we can conquer also. Have you thought about that type of occurrence in your presidency and do you see a way to prevent it happening?*
A. Yes, I've thought about it. Obviously I've seen it in other administrations. It's a serious enough matter to make every effort to remember the possibility and also to prevent the eventuality. One obvious measure that can help to prevent that kind of circumstance is a maximum

degree of openness in government—a constant relationship between
the President and the people of this country and the President and
Congress. I favor strong sunshine legislation, and I will pursue that
aggressively through executive order. I'll open up as much as I can of
the deliberations of the executive branch of government to public
scrutiny.

Another measure that could prevent a recurrence of those tragedies
is to have foreign and domestic policy shaped with a maximum inter-
relationship with the congressional leaders. I need their help.

I recognize my inexperience in Washington. Many congressional
leaders have already pledged their support to me, if I should become
President, in the most complete way. Another prevention that can be
instituted is to maintain a staff with free access to me and encourage-
ment of an almost unrestricted debate within the White House circles.
I think we had this while I was governor. I guess there were 200
people in the Georgia government who had unimpeded access to me,
through memoranda or personally. This was a problem that sometimes
I had with department heads because the key members within their
departments knew they could come to me directly whenever they
chose. I won't go into detail about the sensitive relationship between
them and their superiors, but it worked well.

I think this kind of mistake can be prevented.

Q. *Do you have persons on your staff who feel free to say "that's
wrong—everybody else in this room is wrong—including you"?*
A. Yes.

Q. *Do you encourage that?*
A. Yes, I do.

Q. *George Reedy says that's impossible to maintain in the White
House.*
A. I've read his book. I recognize that the stature of the presidency
itself is much more awe-inspiring than the stature of a governor or
candidate for President. I hope, I believe, I can maintain my commitment to those preventive steps that I've described to you.

Q. *Are there several members of your staff who feel they have that
freedom?*
A. Yes. . . . We had quite an argument yesterday afternoon, as a matter
of fact, about whether I should release the names of 12 or 15 potential
vice presidential nominees. And there was quite a free-wheeling discussion about that. I don't believe there was any reticence about it at
all.

Q. *Some say your wife also performs this function at times.*
A. She does. You can leave off "at times."

Also, I intend to restore frequent press conferences. I would say every two weeks, at least 20 times a year. And also restore the format of the fireside chat.

I believe an open presentation by the President to the American people of his ideas on matters of controversy or potential seriousness is a very self-disciplinary measure that would require the President to re-examine his position before those positions are made public. Once they are made public, then you have a massive amount of editorial comment. This would apply to our relationships with the Soviet Union or the 200-mile fishing limit or environmental quality or International Monetary Fund or aid to developing countries, for example. Many matters of foreign policy, plus a much larger number of domestic matters. I'm committed to doing that on my word of honor to the American people, and I don't believe I would ever be tempted not to carry out that commitment.

Q. *Do you mean in relationship to these subjects?*
A. Yes, the frequency of the press conferences and also the fireside chat format.

Q. *You've made a suggestion on accountability, of Cabinet members going before a joint session of Congress. Do you see any merit to another proposal that the President might appear two or three times a year with the congressional leadership in a televised discussion of national issues? Does that type of idea have any potential?*
A. Possibly. I don't know how much validity it would have if it was preplanned or staged. I'm not sure.

Q. *Other ideas are people's press conferences or even letting people telephone in occasionally questions to a President in some type of a public format.*
A. I would certainly have no objection to that. While I was governor, we had a similar format, in that I would travel around the state for anywhere from four to eight days at a time. Let the radio stations know in advance when I would be there. They would call in questions ahead of time. The radio station manager would read the questions to me. This would be done live, and I would respond to the questions.

That was always a great pleasure to me. In addition, we had visitors' day once a month when anyone in Georgia who wanted to see me personally could come and do so. That would be a difficult thing to handle as President, but anything I can devise that would maintain a feeling of open access to me by the American people—I would try it.

Q. *You seem to be seeking some historic breakthrough in terms of communications.*
A. Yes, it could prevent recurrence of Watergate. I think we'd also contribute to prevention of another Vietnam or Cambodia, when the President hid behind a veil of secrecy and the people of this country were misled about what was going on.

There would be no sure prevention for mistakes, obviously. But if you can tap on a truly continuing basis the experience and common sense and sound judgment and high moral character of the American people and let that be exemplified within the government of our country through the President and Congress, it's a great insurance against a serious national mistake, such as we've witnessed in recent years.

Q. *The type of open presidency you're describing—does that include "pressing the flesh"—or don't you think that's as essential as the kind of communication you're describing?*
A. I really don't think that's as essential. It's enjoyable and it's great for the ego of the President. It's fairly nonsubstantial as far as communication is concerned. In transient moments of contact with individual persons, there's very little opportunity for exchange of ideas. I think that would probably be of less significance than earlier, but I would certainly do it on occasion.

Q. *People like George Reedy have talked about a republican officer as President—lower case "r"—less emphasis on "Hail to the Chief," great booming guns and so on. Have you given some thought to that?*
A. Yes, I'd like to minimize the pomp and circumstance of the office. And I think the American people would appreciate that. I would not form a secret White House "palace guard." I would expect Cabinet members to play a much larger and more autonomous role, much like the role that was played by the cabinet heads when I was governor of Georgia.

I would try to appoint members of the Cabinet in whom I had complete confidence, who could speak clearly to the American people and had judgment enough to act on their own. I would monitor their performance and try to bring cohesion within the executive branch of government as different departments shared a common purpose. But I would not have anyone within the White House try to administer the affairs of the executive branch of government.

Q. *You have talked about your contact with everyday citizens, the help you felt that gave you to keep in touch with people when you were governor, and the help it could give in avoiding misadventures as President. Could you give me one or two examples of such contacts, when you were governor, that led you to new policy positions or new insights?*
A. Every month I was governor, as I told you before, I had a visitors' day, when anyone who wanted to could come in and see me. On one of the first visitors' days, although my wife and I had already participated publicly in a program for hiring the handicapped, I had a young man with a withered hand who came in to talk to me. He said that it was impossible to take the merit system examination for employment in the state government because he was handicapped. "Well," I said,

"I'm sure that your own relatively minor handicap of having one withered hand would not be an obstacle to employment." He said, "They won't even let me take the examination for employment." And I said, "That cannot possibly be the case." And he said, "Governor, I can tell you for a fact that it is." And so I went over and picked up the phone and called the head of our merit system, which is civil service in Georgia, and reported to the administrator of the system what the young man had reported to me. The head of the merit system said, "Yes, sir, that's right. Four or five governors ago a decision was made that we would not employ handicapped people in the state government." So the policy was changed. We later had an aggressive program for hiring the handicapped. But I could very well have gone through a large portion of my administration pushing hiring of the handicapped in private industry and other ways and then discovered that state government had a policy of not hiring handicapped people.

Another example was during my campaign for governor, when it became obvious toward the end of my campaign that I might very well be governor. People would quite quickly come up to me and say "Governor," or "Jimmy," or "Senator, I've got a handicapped child at home, and I hope you'll do something about it." And I would glibly say, "Yes, this is going to be one of the major thrusts of my administration if I'm elected"—just to get votes. I didn't really think seriously about what I was going to do. And after I got the nomination, one day in a grocery store a fellow came up and touched me on the shoulder, and I turned around and he said, "I'm going to vote for you for governor." I said, "Well, I really appreciate that." And he said, "Do you know why?" And I said, "No, why?" "It's because I've got a retarded child at home." And he turned around and walked away. And I stood there shocked in a way to realize that the kind of political statements that I'd been making in the campaign about retarded children were actually such a deep, personal thing for a lot of Georgians. So I marshaled then a major effort to revise completely the mental retardation system in Georgia. I did it successfully, I think. So that's the kind of contact to me that's very important. And under the zero-base budgeting technique, the instigation for change and for better delivery of services is deep within the department among people who actually deliver those services.

Vice Presidency

Q. *Is it possible to make the vice presidency a substantially important position? There's been certainly, with a strong White House staff, a constant tendency to downgrade the Vice President's role, to make sure that he gets neither the exciting nor credit-winning jobs,*

*and he's left with very heavily partisan duties or going to funerals in
other parts of the world. Do you think there's a way to prevent that
from happening?*
A. (Laughing) I think that's an inherent danger. I'm certainly determined to make the vice presidency a substantive position. I see no
reason for the President to be worried about challenge in public acceptance or public stature from the Vice President or anyone else. The
office of the presidency is so powerful and so much a center of attention that the idea of competition with a Vice President seems quite
remote. I hope to have the kind of Vice President, if I am elected, who
would share with me all the purposes of the Administration in an easy,
unrestrained way. And I think both the President and Vice President
are best served, no matter what their future aspirations might be, by
working in harmony. I think the people would react adversely to any
sort of disharmony or conflict. I think the country loses when a competent Vice President is deprived of an opportunity to serve in a forceful
way.

Q. *It's just that it seems to have happened every time, no matter
what everyone's intentions were at the start. Some people believe the
problem is so inherent that they say there should be no Vice President.*
A. I recognize that. That's why I laughed at first and said that it seems
to be inherent. But I'm determined to try.

Q. *Would the Vice President or another White House staff person
with direct access to you be given broad responsibility in the intergovernmental relations area?*
A. I intend to use the Vice President in major roles. It would depend
on the background and experience and knowledge of the Vice President, where the emphasis might be placed. And I have not made that
decision yet.

Q. *If not the Vice President, would another person have that role (in
intergovernmental relations), with direct access to you?*
A. Yes.

The Cabinet

Q. *Some of the experts on presidential leadership—Thomas E. Cronin in particular—say that there are really two Cabinets: the inner
Cabinet of Secretary of State, Attorney General, the Secretaries of
Treasury and Defense, and the outer Cabinet of Agriculture, Labor,
HEW, Transportation, etc. The latter are said, after a few weeks of
becoming Cabinet members, to become advocates of the special constituencies that they represent, and to become, as Vice President*

Charles G. Dawes once said, the natural enemies of the President because they're always trying to get more of the fiscal pie for their special concerns. Often Presidents do interpose staff members to fend off the outer Cabinet members. Do you think that's avoidable? Is there a way to treat your outer Cabinet as counselors rather than advocates?

A. I believe so. Of course the same situation, the same parallel exists in a state government. The best mechanism to minimize this problem is the establishment of long-range goals or purposes of the government and a mutual commitment to those goals by different Cabinet members, both so-called inner and outer Cabinet members. The preparation of the budget in accordance with the long-range goals of the nation would help to cement the different Cabinet functions to a common purpose. Another element is the relevant priorities of the President himself. HEW, for instance. President Johnson was probably more aggressive in trying to deal with human needs than even Secretaries of HEW were.

The same thing applied in other administrations, depending on the relative importance of different elements of government service to the President and his staff. In any instance when the President is laggard in meeting the needs of people, a given Cabinet member in that neglected area will probably be more of an advocate than a counselor. I think that's a good, built-in minor system of checks and balances. And I see nothing wrong with it.

Q. *You're saying that you will have no "oversecretaries of domestic affairs" in the White House to whom these Cabinet members speak. Are you making a pledge that if you're elected President these Cabinet members will have direct access to you?*

A. That's right. But I would certainly reserve the option of using the Vice President in a major role to be determined later. I would expect the Vice President to help carry out, in a generic sense, the commitments of my Administration and to deal directly with governors and other state officials, to work closely with the Congress and obviously work directly with the Cabinet members. I would not prevent, though, the governors, mayors, Congress and Cabinet members to have direct access to me.

Q. *What kind of people and qualities are you looking for in the Cabinet and other major policy-making roles? What kind of talent hunt method are you thinking of and what goals beyond just the brightest and best people in America—what types of directions are you looking in? How much would you be looking toward traditional establishment figures who've been in other administrations and have an understanding of federal policy making? How much fresh appeal?*

A. I think my inclination would be to go toward a new generation of leaders. I would put a strong emphasis on executive management capacity and sensitivity to people's needs. Obviously compatibility would be an important factor—not only with me but with other members of the Cabinet. I would ensure that those who are most dependent on government to meet their human needs would be reassured by the record and reputation and attitudes of the appointments I would make in the field of human rights, civil rights, justice, health, welfare, education, housing, transportation.

I would choose those in whom I have complete confidence to orient government services where services are the most needed—among the poor, deprived, the illiterate, and minority groups—and at the same time have the competence to deliver those services in an efficient, economical way.

I will probably continue to form my opinions about potential Cabinet members in the period following the convention when we start detailed preparation of legislation for issue analysis for the fall election. I will observe personally as much as possible the relative competence of the people who might be in the Cabinet in the future. I would deliberately seek advisers during the pre-election period with that as a major factor. If someone recommended to me a future Cabinet member, I'd be inclined deliberately to seek out that person as a working companion during the post-convention period so that I could become personally acquainted with him. I would seek the advice obviously of those who've served in previous administrations. I can't say I would never use somebody who had served in a previous administration. Obviously I will use some. But my inclination would be to go to a new generation.

Q. *Do you desire a high degree of independence among your Cabinet members?*
A. Yes.

Q. *Should a President tolerate Cabinet members who dissent from Administration policy as heavily as James R. Schlesinger did as Secretary of Defense?*
A. I believe I could prevent that disharmony occurring by being more heavily involved in the evolution of basic commitments. I always managed the affairs of Georgia on long-range goals, and I can't imagine a basic strategic difference developing between myself and one of my Cabinet members if the understanding were that we worked toward the long-range goals. There might be some difference on tactics. But I think I could tolerate the degree of independence shown by James Schlesinger—yes.

Q. *You recently stated that foreign and domestic issues are becoming more and more interrelated, and "we must develop a policy-making*

machinery that transcends narrow perspectives." *How would you propose to do that?*
A. Within the Cabinet structure, and within the process of evolving well-understood, publicly described, long-range policies in, for instance, economics and foreign political affairs, there's got to be some coordination. I would not make the Secretary of State the boss over his domestic counterparts. I think that the Secretary of the Treasury, the Secretary of Agriculture, the Secretary of Defense, Secretary of Commerce and others all inherently play a major role in the carrying out of matters that relate to foreign policy. Rather than make one of those leaders dominant over all the rest, the coordination has got to come from the President, I would say within the structure of the National Security Council, or perhaps some other Cabinet structure. But I think there ought to be a realization on the part of the Secretary of State that these are the long-range commitments that I've made in the fields of agriculture, commerce, Treasury, and so forth, and that the other Cabinet members have a similar awareness of the long-range commitments in foreign policy, and let me ensure, as President, through proper administrative mechanisms, that the disharmonies among these leaders be minimized.

Q. *Do you expect to continue both the Domestic Council and the National Security Council?*
A. I'm not yet ready to answer that question.

Q. *Would you pick many Cabinet or sub-Cabinet or key staff members from state and local governments?*
A. Yes.

White House Staff

Q. *Is it correct to assume that some of your long-term associates, including Hamilton Jordan and Jody Powell, would be members of your White House staff?*
A. That would be a good guess, but I think assumption is too strong a word. I've never discussed it with any of them. And I will reserve that judgment.

Q. *Do you have in mind what other type of persons you would seek for close-in staff—what kind of qualifications would you look for?*
A. I would guess that most of them would come from those who would help me following the convention in putting together plans for the election, for implementation of the platform, for working harmoniously with the Congress. There would certainly be some exceptions to that. But I would depend quite heavily for advice, at least for

the identification of staff members, on those with whom I've been associated during the campaign itself up through November.

Q. *Many past administrations have been heavily manned with former Capitol Hill staff, who were familiar with various areas of federal policy. Would that be true in your administration?*
A. Well I think "heavily" is the only word with which I would disagree. I certainly expect to have some representation within the White House staff from those who are familiar with the workings of Washington, and also working with Congress. But it would not be a dominant role.

Q. *Do you think the White House staff should be cut from its current level of 500 or 600?*
A. You can depend on it.

Q. *Do you think there's a need for a single White House chief of staff?*
A. I don't believe so. I did not have a single chief of staff as governor. I had, I would say, three or four persons who had equal responsibilities for different aspects of my own duties. And I would probably continue that approach as President.

Q. *How central a role would the Office of Management and Budget have in your administration? Do you see using it as the effective arm to manage the federal government?*
A. Yes. Not particularly management, but in planning and budgeting, yes. I favor a complete melding of the planning and budgeting process, using the monitoring of the expenditure of funds in the carrying out of programs as a basis on which to predicate decisions concerning the next year's budget.

In Georgia, we had a team made up always of planners and those evolving the next budget. And this was an extension of myself as governor. We never got the Office of Planning and Budget involved in the actual administration of programs, but in the monitoring of them, yes.

Congressional Relations

Q. *Would the consultation you talk of with Congress begin with key congressional figures in the formulative stages of legislation?*
A. Yes, it's already begun, as a matter of fact.

Q. *Would it extend to broad numbers of Senators and Representatives who are not in leadership positions?*
A. Yes. Not only in the actual work with key staff members, but also

during the campaign process itself in 1976. I would hope that with a very good Democratic Party platform, which we now have, that there would be a mutual commitment by myself and the 85 per cent of the Democratic Members of Congress who are running for re-election this fall that we would carry out the provisions of the platform. And at that very early stage, there would be a method by which they could cooperate.

Q. *Do you think there are circumstances under which a President should seek to influence the outcome of a competition for leadership posts in the House or Senate?*
A. No. I really don't think so. I attempted that a couple of times in Georgia as an ostensible demonstration of my strength. It was a mistake. And I don't intend to try to determine in the Congress who occupies positions of leadership.

Q. *Do you think the recent moves toward increased congressional independence—the War Powers Act and most particularly the new congressional budget process—will make it more difficult for a Democratic President to deal with a Democratic Congress?*
A. No. Not necessarily. I think it makes it much more incumbent on the President and Congress to share the responsibilities at the early stage of the evolution of foreign policy. I think the stronger the congressional budgeting process might be, the more sure the nation can feel that the final budget will be both proper, substantive and responsible. So I don't fear that at all. I'll prepare the executive budget, using the zero-base budgeting technique. I'll submit it to the Congress for final disposition. I'll reserve the right to use my influence within the Congress to prevail on recommendations in which I have a deep sense of conviction they're proper. But I don't see anything wrong with the Congress having a very strong, very competent, very responsible budgeting procedure. That's good.

Q. *Would you consider negotiation to set common budget goals with the Senate and House Budget Committees?*
A. I think consultation would be better than negotiation. I'll reserve the right to make the final decision on the executive budget recommendation. I'll reserve the right to determine how much consultation there ought to be. As the Congress considers the budget that I propose to them, then will come the time for negotiation and consultation in a much more in-depth manner.

Q. *When you were governor and consumer legislation was blocked in the legislature, you were openly critical of the special interest lobbies and the legislature's listening to them. Are there circumstances under which a major piece of legislation could be blocked in Congress, and you would feel compelled to make a similar statement as President?*

A. Yes. And I would not hesitate to do it.

Unfortunately for Georgia, I started working on consumer protection legislation too late. I was so wrapped up in complete reorganization of the government, mental health programs, prison reform, a new basic law on education, judicial reform, zero-base budgeting that I didn't start early enough in my administration on consumer protection, and the special interest groups prevailed on about half of it. I prevailed—rather the Georgia people prevailed—on the other half.

I would use that influence of going directly to the people and identifying special interest groups that block good legislation. And I believe the President's voice would be much more authoritative and much more clear than any governor's voice could be, because of the close attention paid to the President's statements by the news media—much more so than any governor.

Government Reform

Q. *Would you describe your opposition to incremental reform?*
A. Most of the controversial issues that are not routinely well-addressed can only respond to a comprehensive approach. Incremental efforts to make basic changes are often foredoomed to failure because the special interest groups can benefit from the status quo, can focus their attention on the increments that most affect themselves, and the general public can't be made either interested or aware.

Let's say welfare or tax reform or government reorganization is addressed, then a governor or a President can say "This is what we have now—quite often a terrible mess—this is what we can have—a much improved circumstance—and these are the steps to arrive at the change."

If it's clear, comprehensive and it's presented in such a way as to arouse the support of the people, then the special interests quite often back off because most of them don't want to be exposed to a public altercation against the people of a state or nation. So the comprehensive approach is inherently necessary to make controversial decisions.

Q. *Everyone says that in reorganization, you bird-tailed every detail, both in passage and implementation.*
A. I think I did. When the process was approaching a conclusion, I knew as much about the state government—its present form, the need for the changes—as anyone in Georgia. I also had a close enough relationship with the specialists in matters like personnel management, transportation, electronic data processing, printing, plus organizational structure, to speak with authority on the subject. But somebody has to understand the whole process in the comprehensive state.

If the person is a good manager and organizer, this can be done without interfering with the administrative responsibilities of the executive.

I recognize you can't as governor or President, you can't drop everything and just work on one item exclusively. . . . You don't drop everything else. But you have to let your workers know you're deeply interested and you have to let the persons who are deeply affected by the changes participate in the project from its inception.

Q. *Do you remain committed to seeking re-authorization of the executive branch reorganization authority that was enacted in 1949 but expired in 1973?*
A. Yes.

Q. *And are you going to ask Congress early in 1977 to grant that authority as an early priority?*
A. Yes. I might even ask them in 1976 during the campaign.

Q. *If this attempt to win reorganization authority were to fail, would the "sunset" bills now before Congress—which would put all federal programs on a five-year cycle and thus provide an opportunity for presidential leadership in what is extended and what not—be a logical fall-back position for you?*
A. I don't consider that a fall-back position, but I consider that a correlative commitment. The two are mutually exclusive. I don't believe that the sunset legislation or zero-base budgeting would be effective with the present conglomerate organizational structure. So I consider them to be separate considerations entirely, all of them almost mandatory: government reorganization, and either zero-base budgeting or the sunset approach. I personally favor zero-base budgeting, but they are related, one to another.

Q. *Both—sunset legislation and zero-base budgeting—could coexist, couldn't they?*
A. Yes, they could, certainly.

Q. *Would you expect reorganization, in addition to making the federal bureaucracy more rational and accessible, to cause the elimination of a substantial number of outmoded programs?*
A. Yes. The programs themselves are much more effectively eliminated through zero-base budgeting techniques. But as the programs become obsolescent, the major consideration is to detect that obsolescence and to act on it. I think that the proliferation of government agencies is quite often related to the number of programs, so that I don't believe it will be possible to separate the considerations.

Q. *Wouldn't any reorganization plan that you proposed be likely to encounter massive and perhaps crippling opposition from en-*

*trenched federal interest groups? I can name three: the government
employee unions, leery about any steps that might cut the number of
jobs; the so-called "poverty-industrial complex" of social workers
and others; and third, congressional chairmen and subcommittee
chairmen who are fearful of any departmental reorganization that
could render obsolete their chairmanships, power and patronage.*
A. All three of those are possible sources of opposition. Similar opposition is obviously a characteristic of state government. But the answer
to all those is to provide more effective government in the areas of life
that interest those groups.

When I demonstrated to the civil service employees in Georgia that
their professional careers could be more productive—the clear assignment of responsibility, clear delineation of authority, minimum of
red tape, minimum of paperwork, much more productive delivery of
services—they became strong supporters of reorganization. At first,
they were very afraid of it.

Secondly, the special interest groups. If we can combine comprehensive welfare reform, comprehensive national health care, better tax programs and tax reforms, this is the best way to assuage the
special interest groups that are interested in social programs.

The Congress is a key to the whole question. I believe that most of
the Members of Congress, and certainly all with whom I've discussed
this question, recognize the low esteem now of Congress in the eyes
of the public. I think they'll be very eager to share the credit for
government improvement. Their interest is the same as mine. I think
most Members of Congress want to do a good job. I don't think they
would put their own chairmanships above the public interest if that
public interest could be clearly identified.

The other factor is this: we will have made, during the campaign
this year, a commitment to the people to carry out these changes. I
hope that as many candidates for Congress as possible will have an
opportunity to express themselves on the subject. And if I should have
an ultimate disagreement with any of these groups, including the
Congress, I would take my case directly to the people and let them be
the ultimate forum. And I think they could prevail over public employees, they could prevail over the special interest groups, they
could prevail over the Members of Congress.

Q. *Can a President really control the permanent bureaucratic government in Washington? A corollary is: can the President use inspira-
tional leadership to motivate the civil service?*
A. The President can't control the bureaucracy if there's a dishar-
monious or combative relationship between the President and those
responsible for carrying out executive responsibilities. I don't intend
to have that kind of relationship. I'll consider the employees of the
federal government to be my allies, not my enemies, and try to work

intimately with them in the consummation of any changes that relate to their own public service. There's no other source of leadership of a comprehensive nature than the President. In the absence of that leadership, there is no leadership. . . .

Intergovernmental Relations

Q. *Would their understanding of intergovernmental relations be one reason for your intended choice of many key local officials for positions in your administration?*
A. Yes. And I also intend to adhere strictly to a rule of having representatives of state and local government help me in the evolution and consummation of major program changes, including the drafting of legislation. I want to make sure that the programs we put through Congress work at the delivery end. I think the best way to assure that is for governors, mayors and other officials of state and local government to be involved from the beginning.

Q. *Your statements and the Democratic platform indicate a desire for more federal aid to states and cities in the next years. If that issue is then put to the side, how do you feel about "New Federalism" in terms of devolution of authority to state and local governments? Do you favor more of it?*
A. Yes, I do. There are some programs that must be coordinated at the federal level just to provide equity. But whenever possible, I would give the authority to the local or state government to deliver services and to control the mechanism of delivery to meet the needs of the citizens of individual communities.

One area, to illustrate the point, would be in the field of education. I see a growing role for the federal government in financing education to eliminate discrepancies in the amount of local financing available in a community for the children who live there. But I would want to keep control of the school system as near as possible to the local government.

Q. *Are you concerned about federal funding reaching such levels that the impetus is lost for fundamental tax reforms on the state and local level, particularly the state level?*
A. I don't believe that's a danger. I would be much more inclined to give local governments financial relief than I would be to give states financial relief—for several reasons.

One is that the states have almost complete flexibility in their basic taxation and their rate of taxation. Second, the states have much more flexibility in the services that they deliver. Third, the states have a much greater authority to decide their own commitments than do local governments, because many of the local governments' decisions are made at the state legislative level. And fourth, the states have a much more progressive tax structure, based quite often on income tax, corporate tax, corporate and personal income taxes, whereas the local governments' tax base is most often restricted primarily to property taxes and sales taxes, which are inflexible and also fall more heavily on the low-income families. So for all those reasons, I would favor, when given a choice, the allocation of federal funds to local governments in preference to state governments.

Q. *Would some devolution of authority to state and local governments be part of your reorganization?*
A. I think that would come more naturally under the process of writing new programs in the field of education, health care, welfare reform, than under the reorganization of the federal government mechanism itself.

Foreign Policy

Q. *Would the heaviest priority of your administration be on foreign or domestic affairs?*
A. The number one responsibility of any President, above everything else, is to guarantee the security of his country—freedom from fear of attack or successful attack or blackmail, the ability to carry out a legitimate foreign policy. I would certainly place that aspect of life and world peace in a pre-eminent position. As far as the amount of time devoted to domestic or foreign affairs, I would guess that most of the time would be devoted to domestic affairs.

Q. *Some recent Presidents seem to have had a sickly fascination with foreign affairs—crisis management, the daily secret briefings, dealings with heads of state–all the while avoiding some hard domestic problems and slogging budget questions. Would you seek to avoid that type of diversion of time into foreign affairs?*
A. Yes, I would. I think a crucial prerequisite of an effective foreign policy is to restore the confidence and morale and commitment of our people in their own domestic affairs. So I would not use foreign affairs or foreign trips as an escape mechanism to avoid responsibilities on the domestic scene.

Q. *What type of qualities would you look for in a Secretary of State? What type of background and personal characteristics? Would you like to have someone who came out of the foreign-policy "establishment" and had been involved in foreign affairs over the years? Or someone who had been watching it in a more detached way?*

A. That's something I haven't yet decided, nor have I had to decide it. I would probably depend more upon my confidence in the intelligence and judgment and moral commitment of the person than I would on the particular environment that has shaped that person's knowledge of foreign affairs. I've got about 15 or 20 people in whom I have placed a lot of responsibility, and among that group I would seek advice before I made a final decision on Secretary of State. The main thing that's missing now is confidence by the Secretary of State in the sound judgment, common sense and integrity of the American people.

Q. *Would a Secretary of State in your administration be basically there to make foreign policy or to carry out the foreign policy that you make?*
A. Both. I would retain the responsibility of making the final decisions. I would insist on being clearly informed. And I would retain the role of being spokesman for this country. But I would consider the Secretary of State to be a partner with me, an adviser, an administrator of the complex foreign-affairs mechanism that falls within the responsibility of the Secretary of State. But I would be the ultimate one to make the decisions.

Q. *Do you see a model in any of the recent Secretaries of State— William Rogers, who was sort of a sword carrier, Henry Kissinger the policy maker, or perhaps Dean Acheson, who seemed to do it fairly cooperatively with the President?*
A. I think Dean Acheson, George Marshall would be two who did a superb job, in my opinion. I don't think there was ever any doubt in the minds of the American people about who was responsible ultimately. Even when those two very strong Secretaries of State were in office, it was the President. They were men of conviction, of sensitivity, of competence and authority. And they worked harmoniously with the President. And they carried out the responsibilities specifically designated to them by the President, on an individual basis of agreement. So I think those two would be the kinds of persons that I would admire very much.

Q. *In the foreign policy area, would your priorities be more East-West, dealing with traditional allies and the Soviet Union, or North-South, in planning for future relationships with the underdeveloped world?*
A. I really see three relationships. One is in our relationship with our natural allies and friends—the democratic, developed nations of the world: Canada, Western Europe, Japan, and others such as Australia, New Zealand, Israel. That's one solid base of strength, mutual purpose, consultation, and it must be maintained. It's been damaged severely, in my opinion, recently.

The second relationship would be the relationship between the democracies of the world and the socialist or Communist nations—our relationship with the Soviet Union and the People's Republic of China. Not a unilateral relationship between the United States and those nations, but as much as possible involving the other democracies of the world.

And third, of course, would be the relationship between the developed nations and the developing nations. And I would like to get as much as possible the OPEC [Organization of Petroleum Exporting Countries] countries and the Soviet Union, for instance, to join with the developed democracies of the world to share the responsibility for the less developed nations.

Defense

Q. *What qualities and experience would you look for in a Secretary of Defense?*
A. I would look on each Cabinet member to some degree as being an advocate for that department. And this would certainly include a Secretary of Defense who believes that we must always be able to defend our country without doubt. I would want one committed to the proposition of peace. I would want one to share my commitment that we should not become militarily involved in the internal affairs of another country unless our own security was directly threatened. I would want one who could withstand the pressures from special interest groups, including munitions manufacturers. I would want one who is an outstanding administrator, recognizing the complexities of the Defense Department organizational structure. I would want one who could reduce the involvement of the Defense Department in matters that can be equally well addressed by the civilian agencies of government, to remove the overlapping functions and singly address the Defense Department toward the capability to fight. I would want one who was willing to reduce waste in personnel allocations and also in unnecessary weapons systems that don't correlate with the long-range purposes of our own security and foreign policy. And one who could work harmoniously with the other Cabinet members. Those are some of the characteristics that come to mind at this moment.

Q. *Of the recent Secretaries of Defense, is there one that you have found you admire the most as a model for the job—Schlesinger, Melvin Laird, Clark Clifford or Robert McNamara?*
A. Well, I'm a little reluctant to choose one because of the implied criticism of the others. I think they all brought beneficial characteristics to the job—McNamara was coldly analytical, and I think operated

under very difficult circumstances in Vietnam. Laird was much better able to work harmoniously with the Congress. I think Schlesinger was a brilliant strategist who was very independent, who thought he didn't have quite close enough relationships with the President and the Secretary of State to avoid public disharmonies, but I think a very competent, brilliant man. I wouldn't want to say who was my favorite.

Q. *Will the Joint Chiefs of Staff have a veto over military policy?*
A. Well, the President of the United States is the commander-in-chief of the armed forces and makes the ultimate decisions. It would be a violation of the Constitution if the ultimate decisions in an incident of disagreement between the President and the Joint Chiefs was resolved by the Joint Chiefs. I think I have enough knowledge of the military and enough of an adequate concept of the presidency to avoid those conflicts. The Joint Chiefs would not be completely subservient to the President. They have a responsibility on their shoulders to testify openly and I presume aggressively before the committees of Congress, and the Congress would make the ultimate decisions on weapons of war and on organizational matters. But I, as President, would not defer to the Joint Chiefs if I thought that my opinion was in the best interests of our country.

Q. *Do you think the United States basically should look to buying enough military hardware for what is assessed as real strategic needs, or buy what's perceived as important in keeping up with the Soviets?*
A. I think the best approach is to buy what's necessary to meet the strategic security needs of our country and to meet our legitimate obligations to our allies.

The Judiciary

Q. *In Georgia, you established a judicial nominating commission and selected judges from a list that had been submitted. Would you do the same as President in nominating judges?*
A. Yes.

Q. *Would you seek Supreme Court nominees of a certain ideological persuasion or bent?*
A. Among the few best-qualified potential appointees that were available to me, I would probably choose the one that I thought was the most compatible with my own basic philosophy. That's the human thing to do, and I can't claim otherwise.

Q. *Would you look for Supreme Court Justices who had the same qualities of compassion and caring for people that you described for other types of appointees?*

A. Well, I think so. There's a great deal of injustice that still exists in this country, and I believe that the final arbiter of that injustice is the Supreme Court. So I would look for that as an ultimate characteristic compatible with the guarantees in the Constitution, which in my opinion are designed to correct those same injustices.

Q. *Do you favor reform of the federal judiciary and court system anywhere near as comprehensive as what you were able to effect during your four years as governor of Georgia?*
A. Well, I've only done an embryonic study of the federal judiciary, but the answer's yes. I believe that the speeches that have been made recently by Chief Justice Warren E. Burger are good indications that substantive reorganization is necessary. To the extent that it was appropriate, I would work closely with him and the other federal judicial leaders of the country in seeking far quicker trials, assured justice for equitable sentences, and a fair treatment of our people within the criminal justice system, without respect to wealth or social prestige or influence.

Civil Rights

Q. *The strong self-confidence in yourself that everyone comments on—does that stem in part from the lonely but ultimately vindicated position your family took on race relations in the 1950s in south Georgia?*
A. No, I don't think you could take a particular instance in our family life and ascribe one's self-confidence to it. We've always had a close-knit, I think competent, family group, who shared major problems and opportunities and with a mutual purpose. Any observer of the campaign itself would say that my family and the strong support I got from my home state were the two factors I had that gave me a decided advantage over all my opponents. It's a mistake to exaggerate—we were probably drawn together as a family because there was some degree of isolation there.

But then we had enough independence and enough stature in the community to prevent that isolation being a sacrifice or a danger. It wasn't a big factor of courage. I always felt Southern people even in those days were searching for some way to get past the racial question, even though publicly they weren't ready to accept the rulings of the Supreme Court or HEW or civil rights laws or integration of churches. They were looking for a few people in the South—perhaps like myself—who were in a position of influence to speak frankly. There was not that vicious reaction against us that might otherwise have been there. I think Southern people were ready for it.

PART TWO

The Presidency and American Politics

4. The Presidency and Its Paradoxes

Thomas E. Cronin

Why is the Presidency such a bewildering office? Why do presidents so often look like losers? Why is the general public so disapproving of recent presidential performances, and so predictably less supportive the longer a President stays in office?

The search for explanations leads in several directions. Vietnam and the Watergate scandals must be considered. Then, too, the personalities of Lyndon B. Johnson and Richard M. Nixon doubtless were factors that soured many people on the office. Observers also claim that the institution is structurally defective—that it encourages isolation, palace guards, "groupthink" and arrogance.

Yet something else seems at work. Our expectations of, and demands on, the office are frequently so paradoxical as to invite two-faced behavior by our presidents. We seem to want so much so fast that a President, whose powers are often simply not as great as many of us believe, gets condemned as ineffectual. Or a President often will overreach or resort to unfair play while trying to live up to our demands. Either way, presidents seem to become locked into a rather high number of no-win situations.

The Constitution is of little help in explaining any of this. The Founding Fathers purposely were vague and left the Presidency imprecisely defined. They knew well that the Presidency would have to provide the capability for swift and competent executive action; yet they went to considerable lengths to avoid enumerating specific powers and duties, so as to calm the then persuasive popular fear of monarchy.

In any event, the informal and symbolic powers of the Presidency today account for as much as the formal ones. Further, presidential powers expand and contract in response to varying situational and technological changes. Thus, the powers of the Presidency are interpreted in ways so markedly different as to seem to describe different offices. In some ways the modern Presidency has virtually unlimited authority for nearly anything its occupant chooses to do with it. In other ways, however, our beliefs and hopes about the Presidency very much shape the character and quality of the presidential performances we get.

The modern (post-Roosevelt II) Presidency is bounded and constrained by various expectations that are decidedly paradoxical. Presidents and presidential candidates must constantly balance themselves between conflicting demands. It has been suggested by more than one observer that it is a characteristic of the American mind to hold contradictory ideas simultaneously without bothering to resolve the potential conflicts between them. Perhaps some paradoxes are best left unresolved. But we should, at least, better appreciate what it is we expect of our presidents and would-be presidents. For it could well be that our paradoxical expectations and the imperatives of the job make for schizophrenic presidential performances.

We may not be able to resolve the inherent contradictions and dilemmas these paradoxes point up. Still, a more rigorous understanding of these conflicts and no-win or near no-win situations should make possible a more refined sensitivity to the limits of what a President can achieve. Exaggerated or hopelessly contradictory public expectations tend to encourage presidents to attempt more than they can accomplish and to overpromise and overextend themselves.

Perhaps, too, an assessment of the paradoxed Presidency may impel us anew to revise some of our unrealistic expectations concerning presidential performance and the institution of the Presidency and encourage, in turn, the nurturing of alternative sources or centers for national leadership.

A more realistic appreciation of presidential paradoxes might help presidents concentrate on the practicable among their priorities. A more sophisticated and tolerant consideration of the modern Presidency and its paradoxes might relieve the load so that a President can better lead and administer in those critical realms in which the nation has little choice but to turn to him. Whether we like it or not, the vitality of our democracy still depends in large measure on the sensitive interaction of presidential leadership with an understanding public willing to listen and willing to provide support when a President can persuade. Carefully planned innovation is nearly impossible without the kind of leadership a competent and fair-minded President can provide.

Each of the ten paradoxes following is based on apparent logical contradictions. Each has important implications for presidential performance and public evaluation of presidential behavior. A better understanding may lead to the removal, reconciliation, or more enlightened toleration of the contradictions to which they give rise.

1. The Gentle and Decent but Forceful and Decisive President Paradox

Opinion polls time and again indicate that people want a just, decent, humane "man of good faith" in the White House. Honesty and trustworthiness repeatedly top the list of qualities the public values most highly in a President these days. However, the public just as strongly demands the qualities of toughness, decisiveness, even a touch of ruthlessness.

Adlai Stevenson, George McGovern, and Gerald Ford were all criticized for being "too nice," "too decent." (Ford's decisive action in the *Mayaguez* affair was an exception, and perhaps predictably, his most significant gain in the Gallup Poll—eleven points—came during and immediately after this episode.) Being a "Mr. Nice Guy" is too easily equated with being too soft. The public dislikes the idea of a weak, spineless, or sentimental person in the White House.

Morris Udall, who was widely viewed as a decidedly decent candidate in the 1976 race for the Democratic nomination, had to advertise himself as a man of strength. He used a quotation from House Majority Leader Thomas P. O'Neill in full-page newspaper ads that read, "We need a Democratic president who's tough enough to take on big business. Mo Udall is tough." The image sought was unquestionably that of toughness of character.

Perhaps, too, this paradox may explain the extraordinary public fondness for President Dwight D. Eisenhower. For at one and the same time he was blessed with a benign smile and reserved, calming disposition and yet also was the disciplined, strong, no-nonsense five-star general with all the medals and victories to go along with it. His ultimate resource as President was this reconciliation of decency and decisiveness, likability alongside demonstrated valor.

During the 1976 presidential campaign, Jimmy Carter appeared to appreciate one of the significant by-products of this paradox. He pointed out that the American male is handicapped in his expressions of religious faith by those requisite "macho" qualities of overt strength, toughness, and firmness. Carter's personal reconciliation of this paradox is noteworthy: "But a truer demonstration of strength would be concern, compassion, love, devotion, sensitivity, humility—exactly the things Christ talked about—and I believe that if we can demonstrate this kind of personal awareness of our own faith we can provide that core of strength and commitment and underlying character that our nation searches for."

Thus this paradox highlights one of the distinctive frustrations for presidents and would-be presidents. Plainly, we demand a double-edged personality. We, in effect, demand the *sinister* as well as the *sincere*, President *Mean* and President *Nice*—tough and hard enough to stand up to a Khrushchev or to press the nuclear button; compassionate enough to care for the ill-fed, ill-clad, ill-housed. The public in this case "seems to want a softhearted son of a bitch," as a friend of mine, Alan Otten, aptly put it. It's a hard role to cast, a harder role to perform for eight years.

2. The Programmatic but Pragmatic Leader Paradox

We want both a *programmatic* (committed on the issues and with a detailed program) and a *pragmatic* (flexible and open, even changeable) person in the White House. We want a *moral* leader; yet the job forces the President to become a *constant compromiser*.

On the one hand, Franklin D. Roosevelt proclaimed that the Presidency is pre-eminently a place for moral leadership. On the other hand, Governor Jerry Brown aptly notes that "a little vagueness goes a long way in this business."

A President who becomes too committed risks being called rigid; a President who becomes too pragmatic risks being called wishy-washy. The secret, of course, is to stay the course by stressing character, competence, rectitude, and experience, and by avoiding strong stands that offend important segments of the population.

Jimmy Carter was especially criticized by the press and others for avoiding commitments and stressing his "flexibility" on the issues. This prompted a major discussion of what came to be called the "fuzziness issue." Jokes spread the complaint. One went as follows: "When you eat peanut butter all your life, your tongue sticks to the roof of your mouth, and you have to talk out of both sides." Still, his "maybe I will and maybe I won't" strategy proved very effective in overcoming critics and opponents who early on claimed he didn't have a chance. Carter talked quietly about the issues and carried a big smile. In fact, of course, he took stands on almost all the issues, but being those of a centrist or a pragmatic moderate, his stands were either not liked or dismissed as nonstands by most liberals and conservatives—especially purists.

What strikes one person as fuzziness or even duplicity appeals to another person as remarkable political skill, the very capacity for compromise and negotiation that is required if a President is to maneuver through the political minefields that come with the job.

Most candidates view a campaign as a fight to win office, not an opportunity for adult education. Barry Goldwater in 1964 may have run with the slogan "We offer a *choice* not an echo," referring to his unusually thematic strategy, but Republican Party regulars who, more pragmatically, aspired to win the election preferred "a *chance* not a *choice*." Once in office, presidents often operate the same way; the electoral connection looms large as an issue-avoiding, controversy-ducking political incentive. Most presidents also strive to *maximize their options*, and hence leave matters up in the air or delay choices. JFK mastered this strategy, whereas on Vietnam LBJ permitted himself to be trapped into his tragically irreparable corner because his options had so swiftly dissolved. Indeed, this yearning to maximize their options may well be the core element of the pragmatism we so often see when we prefer moral leadership.

3. The Innovative and Inventive yet Majoritarian and Responsive Presidency Paradox

One of the most compelling paradoxes at the very heart of our democratic system arises from the fact that we expect our presidents to provide bold, innovative leadership and yet respond faithfully to public-opinion majorities.

Walter Lippmann warned against letting public opinion become the chief guide for leadership in America, but he just as forcefully warned democratic leaders: Don't be right too soon, for public opinion will lacerate you! Hence, most presidents fear being in advance of their times. They must *lead us*, but also *listen to us*.

Put simply, we want our presidents to offer leadership, to be architects of the future and providers of visions, plans, and goals, and at the same time we want them to stay in close touch with the sentiments of the people. To *talk* about high ideals, New Deals, Big Deals, and the like is one thing. But the public resists being *led* too far in any one direction.

Most of our presidents have been conservatives or at best "pragmatic liberals." They have seldom ventured much beyond the crowd. John F. Kennedy, the author of the much acclaimed *Profiles in Courage*, was often criticized for presenting more profile than courage; if political risks could be avoided, he shrewdly avoided them. Kennedy was fond of pointing out that he had barely won election in 1960 and that great innovations should not be forced upon a leader with such a slender mandate. Ironically, Kennedy is credited with encouraging widespread public participation in politics. But he repeatedly reminded Americans that caution was needed, that the important issues are complicated, technical, and best left to the administrative and political experts. As Bruce Miroff writes in *Pragmatic Illusions*, Kennedy seldom attempted to change the political context in which he operated:

> More significantly, he resisted the new form of politics emerging with the civil rights movement: mass action, argument on social fundamentals, appeals to considerations of justice and morality. Moving the American political system in such a direction would necessarily have been long range, requiring arduous educational work and promising substantial political risk. The pragmatic Kennedy wanted no part of such an unpragmatic undertaking.

Presidents can get caught whether they are coming or going. The public wants them to be both *leaders* of the country and *representatives* of the people. We want them to be decisive and rely mainly on their own judgment; yet we want them to be very responsive to public opinion, especially to the "common sense" of our own opinions. It was perhaps with this in mind that an English essayist once defined the ideal democratic leader as an "uncommon man of common opinions."

4. The Inspirational but "Don't Promise More Than You Can Deliver" Leader Paradox

We ask our presidents to raise hopes, to educate, to inspire. But too much inspiration will invariably lead to dashed hopes, disillusionment, and cynicism. The best of leaders often suffer from one of their chief virtues—an instinctive tendency to raise aspirations, to summon us to transcend personal needs and subordinate ourselves to dreaming dreams of a bolder, more majestic America.

We enjoy the upbeat rhetoric and promises of a brighter tomorrow. We genuinely want to hear about New Nationalism, New Deals, New Frontiers, Great Societies, and New American Revolutions; we want our fears to be assuaged during a "fireside chat" or a "conversation with the President"; we want to be told that "the torch has been passed to a new generation of Americans . . . and the glow from that fire can truly light the world."

We want our fearless leaders to tell us that "peace is at hand," that the "only fear we have to fear is fear itself," that "we are Number One," that a recession has "bottomed out," and that "we are a great people." So much do we want the "drive of a lifting dream," to use Nixon's awkward phrase, that the American people are easily duped by presidential promises.

Do presidents overpromise because they are congenital optimists or because they are pushed into it by the demanding public? Surely the answer is an admixture of both. But whatever the source, few presidents in recent times have been able to keep their promises and fulfill their intentions. Poverty was not ended; a Great Society was not realized. Vietnam dragged on and on. Watergate outraged a public that had been promised an open Presidency. Energy independence remains an illusion just as crime in the streets continues to rise.

A President who does not raise hopes is criticized for letting events shape his Presidency rather than making things happen. A President who eschewed inspiration of any kind would be rejected as un-American. For as a poet once wrote, "America is promises." For people everywhere, cherishing the dream of individual liberty and self-fulfillment, America has been the land of promises, of possibilities, of dreams. No President can stand in the way of this truth, no matter how much the current dissatisfaction about the size of big government in Washington and its incapacity to deliver the services it promises.

William Allen White, the conservative columnist, went to the heart of this paradox when he wrote of Herbert Hoover. President Hoover, he noted, is a great executive, a splendid desk man. "But he cannot dramatize his leadership. A democracy cannot follow a leader unless he is dramatized."

5. The Open and Sharing but Courageous and Independent Presidency Paradox

We unquestionably cherish our three-branched system with its checks and balances and its theories of dispersed and separated powers. We want our presidents not only to be sincere but to share their powers with their cabinets, Congress, and other "responsible" national leaders. In theory, we oppose the concentration of power, we dislike secrecy, and we resent depending on any one person to provide all of our leadership. In recent years (the 1970s in particular), there have been repeated calls for a more open, accountable, and deroyalized Presidency.

On the other hand, we reject a too secularized Presidency. We reject, as well, the idea that complete openness is a solution; indeed, it has been suggested, instead, that the great presidents have been the strong presidents, who stretched their legal authority, who occasionally relied on the convenience of secrecy, and who dominated the other branches of government. This point of view argues that the country, in fact, often yearns for a hero in the White House, that the human heart ceaselessly reinvents royalty, and that Roosevelts and

Camelots, participatory democracy notwithstanding, are vital to the success of America.

If some people feel we are getting to the point where all of us would like to see a demythologized Presidency, others claim we need myth, we need symbol. As a friend of mine put it, "I don't think we could live without the myth of a glorified Presidency, even if we wanted to. We just aren't that rational. Happily, we're too human for that. We will either live by the myth that has served us fairly well for almost two hundred years or we will probably find a much worse one."

The clamor for a truly open or collegial Presidency was opposed on other grounds by the late Harold Laski when he concluded that Americans, in practice, want to rally round a President who can demonstrate his independence and vigor:

> A President who is believed not to make up his own mind rapidly loses the power to maintain the hold. The need to dramatize his position by insistence upon his undoubted supremacy is inherent in the office as history has shaped it. A masterful man in the White House will, under all circumstances, be more to the liking of the multitude than one who is thought to be swayed by his colleagues.

Thus we want our President not only to be both a lion and a fox, but more than a lion, more than a fox. We want simultaneously a secular leader and a civil religious mentor; we praise our three-branched system, but we place capacious hopes upon and thus elevate the presidential branch. Only the President can give us heroic leadership, or so most people feel. Only a President can dramatize and symbolize our highest expectations of ourselves as almost a chosen people with a unique mission. Note too that only the President is regularly honored with a musical anthem of his own: "Hail to the Chief." If it seems a little hypocritical for a semisovereign people deferentially to delegate so much hierarchical stature and semiautocratic power to their President, this is nonetheless precisely what we continually do.

We want an open Presidency, and we oppose the concentration of vast power in any one position. Still, we want forceful, courageous displays of leadership from our presidents. Anything less than that is condemned as aimlessness or loss of nerve. Further, we praise those who leave the Presidency stronger than it was when they entered.

6. The Taking the Presidency Out of Politics Paradox

The public yearns for a statesman in the White House, for a George Washington or a second "era of good feelings"—anything that might prevent partisanship or politics-as-usual in the White House. In fact, however, the job of a President demands that he be a gifted political broker, ever attentive to changing political moods and coalitions.

Franklin Roosevelt illustrates this paradox well. Appearing so remarkably nonpartisan while addressing the nation, he was in practice one of the craftiest political coalition-builders to occupy the White House. He mastered the art of politics—the art of making the difficult and desirable possible.

A President is expected to be above politics in some respects and highly political in others. A President is never supposed to act with his eye on the next election; he's not supposed to favor any particular group or party. Nor is he supposed to wheel and deal or to twist too many arms. That's politics and that's bad! No, a President, or so most people are inclined to believe, is supposed to be "President of all the people." On the other hand, he is asked to be the head of his party, to help friendly members of Congress get elected or re-elected, to deal firmly with party barons and congressional political brokers. Too, he must build political coalitions around what he feels needs to be done.

To take the President out of politics is to assume, incorrectly, that a President will be so generally right and the general public so generally wrong that a President must be protected from the push and shove of political pressures. But what President has always been right? Over the years, public opinion has been usually as sober a guide as anyone else on the political waterfront. Anyway, having a President constrained and informed by public opinion is what a democracy is all about.

In his re-election campaign of 1972, Richard Nixon in vain sought to display himself as too busy to be a politician: He wanted the American people to believe he was too preoccupied with the Vietnam War to have any personal concern about his election. In one sense, Nixon may have destroyed this paradox for at least a while. Have not the American people learned that we *cannot* have a President *above* politics?

If past is prologue, presidents in the future will go to considerable lengths to portray themselves as unconcerned with their own political future. They will do so in large part because the public applauds the divorce between the Presidency and politics. People naively think that we can somehow turn the job of President into that of a managerial or strictly executive post. (The six-year, single-term proposal reflects this paradox.) Not so. The Presidency is a highly political office, and it cannot be otherwise. Moreover, its political character is for the most part desirable. A President separated from, or somehow above, politics might easily become a President who doesn't listen to the people, doesn't respond to majority sentiment or pay attention to views that may be diverse, intense, and at variance with his own. A President immunized to politics would be a President who would too

easily become isolated from the processes of government and removed from the thoughts and aspirations of his people.

In all probability, this paradox will endure. The standard diagnosis
of what's gone wrong in an administration will be that the Presidency
has become too politicized. But it will be futile to try to take the
President out of politics. A more helpful approach is to realize that
certain presidents try too hard to hold themselves above politics—or
at least to give that appearance—rather than engage in it deeply,
openly, and creatively enough. A President in a democracy has to act
politically in regard to controversial issues if we are to have any
semblance of government by the consent of the governed.

7. The Common Man Who Gives an Uncommon Performance Paradox

We like to think that America is the land where the common sense
of the common man reigns. We prize the common touch, the "man of
the people." Yet few of us settle for anything but an uncommon performance from our presidents.

This paradox is splendidly summed up by some findings of a survey
conducted by the Field Research Corporation, a California public-
opinion organization. Field asked a cross-section of Californians in
1975 to describe in their own words the qualities a presidential candidate should have. Honesty and trustworthiness topped the list. But
one of the organization's more intriguing findings was that "while
most (72%) prefer someone with plain and simple tastes, there is also a
strong preference (66%) for someone who can give exciting speeches
and inspire the public."

It has been said that the American people crave to be governed by
men who are both Everyman and yet better than Everyman. The
Lincoln and Kennedy presidencies are illustrative. We cherish the
myth that anyone can grow up to be President—that there are no
barriers, no elite qualifications—but we don't want a person who is too
ordinary. Would-be presidents have to prove their special
qualifications—their excellence, their stamina, their capacity for uncommon leadership.

The Harry Truman reputation, at least as it flourished in the mid-
1970s, demonstrates the apparent reconciliation of this paradox. Fellow commoner Truman rose to the demands of the job and became an
apparent gifted decision-maker, or so his admirers would have us
believe.

Candidate Carter in 1976 nicely fitted this paradox as well. Local,
down-home farm boy next door makes good! The image of the peanut
farmer turned gifted governor and talented campaigner contributed

greatly to Carter's success as a national candidate, and he used it with consummate skill. Early on in his presidential bid, Carter enjoyed introducing himself as a peanut farmer *and* a nuclear physicist—yet another way of suggesting he was down-to-earth but cerebral as well.

A President or would-be President must be bright, but not too bright; warm and accessible, but not too folksy; down-to-earth, but not pedestrian. Adlai Stevenson was witty and clever, but these are talents that seldom pay in politics. Voters prefer plainness and solemn platitudes, but these too can be overdone. For instance, Ford's talks, no matter what the occasion, dulled our senses with the banal. Both suffered because of this paradox. The "catch 22" here, of course, is that the very fact of an uncommon performance puts distance between a President and the truly common man. We persist, however, in wanting both at the same time.

8. The National Unifier–National Divider Paradox

One of the paradoxes most difficult to alleviate arises from our longing for a President who will pull us together again and yet be a forceful priority-setter, budget-manager, and executive leader. The two tasks are near opposites.

Ours remains one of the few nations in the world that call upon their chief executives to serve also as their symbolic, ceremonial heads of state. Elsewhere, these tasks are spread around. In some nations there is a Monarch *and* a Prime Minister; in other nations there are three visible national leaders—the head of state, a Premier, and a powerful party head.

In the absence of an alternative, we demand that our presidents and our Presidency act as a unifying force in our lives. Perhaps it all began with George Washington, who so artfully performed this function. At least for a while, he truly was above politics and a near unique symbol of our new nation. He was a healer, a unifier, and an extraordinary man for all seasons. Today we ask no less of our presidents than that they should do as Washington did.

However, we have designed a presidential job description that impels our contemporary presidents to act as national dividers. They necessarily divide when they act as the leaders of their political parties, when they set priorities that advantage certain goals and groups at the expense of others, when they forge and lead political coalitions, when they move out ahead of public opinion and assume the role of national educators, and when they choose one set of advisers over another. A President, as a creative executive leader, cannot help but offend certain interests. When Franklin Roosevelt was running for a second term, some garment workers unfolded a great sign that said, "We love him for the enemies he has made." Such is the fate of a President on an everyday basis; if he chooses to use power he usually will lose the goodwill of those who preferred inaction over action. The opposite is, of course, true if he chooses not to act.

Look at it from another angle. The nation is torn between the view that a President should primarily preside over the nation and merely serve as a referee among the various powerful interests that actually control who gets what, when, and how and a second position, which holds that a President should gain control of government processes and powers so as to use them for the purpose of furthering public, as opposed to private, interests. Obviously the position that one takes on this question is relevant to how you value the Presidency and the kind of person you'd like to see in the job.

Harry S. Truman said it very simply. He noted that 14 million or 15 million Americans had the resources to have representatives in Washington to protect their interests, and that the interests of the great mass of other people, the 160 million or so others, were the responsibility of the President of the United States.

The President is sometimes seen as the great defender of the people, the ombudsman or advocate-general of "public interests." Yet he is sometimes (and sometimes at the same time) viewed as hostile to the people, isolated from them, wary of them, antagonistic to them, inherently their enemy.

This debate notwithstanding, Americans prize the Presidency as a grand American invention. As a nation we do not want to change it. Proposals to weaken it are dismissed. Proposals to reform or restructure it are paid little respect. If we sour on a President, the conventional solution has been to find and elect someone we hope will be better.

9. The "The Longer He Is There, The Less We Like Him" Paradox

Every four years we pick a President, and for the next four years we pick on him and at him, and sometimes pick him entirely apart. There is no adequate prepresidential job experience, so much of the first term is an on-the-job learning experience. But we resent this. It is too important a job for on-the-job learning, or at least that's how most of us feel.

Too, we expect presidents to grow in office and to become better acclimated to their powers and responsibilities. But the longer they are in office, the more they find themselves involved in crises with less and less public support. There is an apocryphal presidential la-ment that goes as follows: "Every time I seem to grow into the job, it gets bigger."

Simply stated, the more we know of a President, or the more we observe his Presidency, the less we approve of him. Familiarity breeds discontent. Research on public support of presidents indicates that approval peaks soon after a President takes office and then slides downward at a declining rate over time until it reaches a point in the latter half of the four-year term when it bottoms out. Thereafter it rises a bit but never attains its original levels. Why this pattern of declining support afflicts presidents is a subject of debate among social scientists. Unrealistic early expectations are, of course, a major factor. These unrealistic expectations ensure a period of disenchantment.

Peace and prosperity can help stem the unpleasant tide of ingratitude, and Eisenhower's popularity remained reasonably high in large part because of his (or the nation's) achievements in these respects. For other presidents, however, their eventual downsliding popularity was due nearly as much to the public's inflated expectations as to the presidents' actions. It was often as if the downslide in popularity would occur no matter what the President did. If this seems unfair, even cruel, it is, nonetheless, what happens to those skilled and lucky enough to win election to the "highest office in the land."

And all this occurs despite our conventional wisdom that the *office makes the man*—"that the presidency with its built-in educational processes, its spacious view of the world, its command of talent, and above all its self-conscious historic role, does work its way on the man in the Oval Office," as James MacGregor Burns puts it. If we concede that the office in part does make the man, we must admit also that time in office often unmakes the man.

10. The "What It Takes to Become President May Not Be What Is Needed to Govern the Nation" Paradox

To win a presidential election takes ambition, ambiguity, luck, and masterful public-relations strategies. To govern the nation plainly requires all of these, but far more as well. It may well be that too much ambition, too much ambiguity, and too heavy a reliance on phony public-relations tricks actually undermine the integrity and legitimacy of the Presidency.

Columnist David Broder offered an apt example: "People who win primaries may become good Presidents—but 'it ain't necessarily so.' Organizing well is important in governing just as it is in winning primaries. But the Nixon years should teach us that good advance men do not necessarily make trustworthy White House aides. Establishing a government is a little more complicated than having the motorcade run on time."

Likewise, ambition (in very heavy doses) is essential for a presidential candidate, but too much hunger for the office or for "success-at-any-price" is a danger to be avoided. He must have boldness and energy, but carried too far these can make him cold and frenetic. To win the Presidency obviously requires a single-mindedness, and yet we want our presidents to be well rounded, to have a sense of humor, to be able to take a joke, to have hobbies and interests outside the realm of politics—in short, to have a sense of proportion.

Another aspect of this paradox can be seen in the way candidates take ambiguous positions on issues in order to increase their appeal to the large bulk of centrist and independent voters. Not only does such equivocation discourage rational choices by the voters, but it also may alienate people who learn later, after the candidate has won, that his views and policies are otherwise. LBJ's "We will not send American boys to fight the war that Asian boys should be fighting" and Richard Nixon's "open Presidency" pledges come readily to mind. Their pre-presidential stands were later violated or ignored.

Political scientist Samuel Huntington calls attention to yet another way this paradox works. To be a winning candidate, he notes, the would-be President must put together an *electoral coalition* involving a majority of voters advantageously distributed across the country. To do this, he must appeal to all regions and interest groups and cultivate the appearance of honesty, sincerity, and experience. But once elected, the electoral coalition has served its purpose and a *governing coalition* is the order of the day. This all may sound rather elitist, but Harvard Professor Huntington insists that this is what has to be:

> The day after his election the size of his majority is almost—if not entirely—irrelevent to his ability to govern the country. What counts then is his ability to mobilize support from the leaders of the key institutions in society and government. He has to constitute a broad governing coalition of strategically located supporters who can furnish him with the information, talent, expertise, manpower, publicity, arguments, and political support which he needs to develop a program, to embody it in legislation, and to see it effectively implemented. This coalition must include key people in Congress, the executive branch, and the private-sector "Establishment." The governing coalition need have little relation to the electoral coalition. The fact that the President as a candidate put together a successful electoral coalition does not insure that he will have a viable governing coalition.

Presidential candidate Adlai Stevenson had another way of saying it in 1956. He said he had "learned that the hardest thing about any political campaign is how to win without proving that you are unworthy of winning." The process of becoming President is an extraordinarily taxing one that defies description. It involves, among other things, an unflagging salesmanship job on television.

Candidates plainly depend upon television to transform candidacy into incumbency. Research findings point out that candidates spend well over half their funds on radio and television broadcasting. Moreover, this is how the people "learn" about the candidates. Approximately two-thirds of the American public report that television is the best way for them to follow candidates, and about half of the public acknowledge that they got their best understanding of the candidates and issues from television coverage.

Thus, television is obviously the key. But the candidate has to travel to every state and hundreds of cities for at least a four-year period to capture the exposure and the local headlines before earning the visibility and stature of a "serious candidate." For the most part, it becomes a grueling ordeal, as well as a major learning experience. In quest of the Democratic nomination for President, Walter F. Mondale of Minnesota spent most of 1974 traveling some 200,000 miles, delivering hundreds of speeches, appearing on countless radio and television talk shows, and sleeping in Holiday Inn after Holiday Inn all across the country. He admits that he enjoyed much of it, but says, too, that he seldom had time to read or to reflect, not to mention having time for a sane family life. Eventually he withdrew on the grounds that he simply had neither the overwhelming desire nor the time, as an activist United States senator, to do what was necessary in order to win the nomination.

Mondale would later—in 1976—show that he is an extremely effective national campaigner, but his frustrations about his 1974 presidential bid are worth remembering:

> I love to ponder ideas, to reflect on them and discuss them with experts and friends over a period of time, but this was no longer possible. It struck me as being unfortunate and even tragic that the process of seeking the Presidency too often prevents one from focusing on the issues and insights and one's ability to express them, which are crucially important. I believe this fact explains many of the second-rate statements and much of the irrational posturing that are frequently associated with Presidential campaigns. In any case, after eighteen months I decided this wasn't for me. It wasn't my style and I wasn't going to pretend that it was. Instead of controlling events in my life, I was more and more controlled by them. Others have had an easier time adapting to this process than I did, and I admire them for it. But one former candidate told me, three years after his campaign had ended, that he *still* hadn't fully recovered emotionally or physically from the ordeal.

What it takes to *become* President may differ from what it takes to *be* President. It takes a near megalomaniac who is also glib, dynamic, charming on television, and hazy on the issues. Yet we want our presidents to be well rounded, careful in their reasoning, clear and specific in their communications, and not excessively ambitious. It may well be that our existing primary-and-convention system adds up to an effective obstacle course for testing would-be presidents. Certainly they have to travel to all sections of the country, meet the people, deal with interest-group elites, and learn about the challenging issues of the day. But with the Johnson and Nixon experiences in our not too distant past, we have reason for asking whether our system of producing presidents is adequately reconciled with what is required to produce a President who is competent, fair-minded, and emotionally healthy.

Conclusions

Perhaps the ultimate paradox of the modern Presidency is that it is always too powerful and yet it is always inadequate. Always too powerful because it is contrary to our ideals of a government by the people and always too powerful, as well, because it must now possess the capacity to wage nuclear war (a capacity that unfortunately doesn't permit much in the way of checks and balances and deliberative, participatory government). Yet always inadequate because it seldom achieves our highest hopes for it, not to mention its own stated intentions.

The Presidency is always too strong when we dislike the incumbent. On the other hand, its limitations are bemoaned when we believe the incumbent is striving valiantly to serve the public interest as we define it. For many people, the Johnson presidency captured this paradox vividly: Many who felt that he was too strong in Vietnam also felt that he was too weakly equipped to wage his War on Poverty (and vice versa).

The dilemma for the attentive public is that curbing the powers of a President who abuses the public trust will usually undermine the capacity of a fair-minded President to serve the public interest. In the nearly two centuries since Washington took office, we have multiplied the requirements for presidential leadership and made it increasingly difficult to lead. Certainly this is no time for mindless retribution against the already fragile institution of the Presidency. Neither presidents nor the public should be relieved of their respective responsibilities of trying to fashion a more effective and fair-minded leadership system simply because these paradoxes are pointed out and even widely agreed upon. It is also not enough to throw up our hands and say, "Well, no one makes a person run for that crazy job in the first place."

The situation analyzed in this essay doubtless also characterizes the positions of governors, city managers, university presidents, and even many corporate executives. Is it a new phenomenon, or are we just becoming increasingly aware of it? Is it a permanent or a transitory condition? My own view is that it is neither new nor transitory, but more comparative and longitudinal analysis is needed before we can generalize more systematically. Meanwhile, we shall have to select as our presidents people who understand these paradoxes and have a gift for the improvisation necessitated by their contrary demands. It is important for us to ask our chief public servants to be willing occasionally to forgo enhancing their own short-term political fortunes for a greater good of simplifying, rather than exacerbating, the paradoxes of the Presidency.

While the Presidency will surely remain one of our nation's best vehicles for creative policy change, it will also continue to be a hard-pressed office, laden with the cumulative weight of these paradoxes. We urgently need to probe the origins and to assess the consequences of these paradoxes and to learn how presidents and the public can better coexist with them, for it is apparent that these paradoxes serve to isolate a President from the public. Whether we like it or not, the growing importance of the Presidency and our growing dependence on presidents seem to ensure that presidents will be less popular, and more often handy scapegoats when anything goes wrong.

Let us ask our presidents to give us their best, but let us not ask them to deliver more than the Presidency—or any single institution—has to give.

5. Selecting and Electing Presidents

William R. Keech

Americans have perhaps the most popularly based methods of selecting chief executives of any nation in the world. Not only is the final choice highly responsive to popular preferences; the means of defining the final alternatives are highly responsive to them as well. Most democratic chief executives are not chosen by the mass publics but by legislators who are, in turn, selected by the people. The United States is fairly unusual in basing the final choice as directly on popular votes as it does, and it is quite unusual in the lengths to which it goes to ensure that the nominations are also popularly based. The American system even has a unique feature that can broaden the range of candidates from which the public chooses.

Whatever the limitations of the American presidential selection processes, they are second to few, if any, in the degree to which the people make the important choices. This does not mean that our system is perfect or even the best. It does suggest, however, that any inferiorities of the system are not likely to be due to insufficient democracy.

Securing the Republican or Democratic Nomination

There are two basic steps to the Presidency. The election stage is the final decision, and in that sense is the most important, but the most crucial step toward reaching the Presidency is achieving nomination by the Republican or Democratic Party. Those two parties have exclusively controlled access to the White House since 1860. Only once since then did someone other than the Republican or Democratic nominee rise as high as second place. That was in 1912, when Theodore Roosevelt, a former Republican President, ran as a Progressive and polled more votes than President William H. Taft.

While the election chooses between two serious candidates, the nominating stage does far more to narrow down the alternatives. When the Republicans and Democrats choose their presidential nominees, more individuals are ruled out than at the general election. This stage also determines how meaningful and how desirable the final alternatives will be. The 1972 election is a good example of a case in which the alternatives were sufficiently flawed that for many voters there was no desirable choice. The Republicans renominated a President who would only narrowly escape impeachment and would become the first President to be forced to resign from office. The Democrats chose a candidate who was deeply controversial in his own party and who would receive a smaller proportion of the votes from his fellow Democrats than any nominee since before Franklin Roosevelt's presidency.

Even when the candidates are not flawed as they were in 1972, some observers feel that the kinds of choices made by the Republican and Democratic parties narrow the range of policy alternatives to an undesirable degree. George Wallace has proclaimed loudly in recent years that there is not a "dime's worth of difference" between Republicans and Democrats, and in 1976 former Senator Eugene McCarthy, speaking from a far different political perspective, said that Republican and Democratic candidates are so similar that he would not care if his candidacy drained away enough votes from the Democrats to cost his former party the election victory.

The differences between a Carter and a Ford in 1976 may seem large or small depending on the observer. Recent efforts to increase the distinctions between the parties have been associated with shattering defeat in general elections. Barry Goldwater sought in 1964 to give the voters "a choice, not an echo" but was overwhelmingly defeated at the polls. George McGovern's candidacy was about as distinctively leftist as Goldwater's had been rightist, and he too was demolished at the polls. But before taking their experiences as definitive of what happens to ideologically distinct candidacies, we should recognize that both Goldwater and McGovern had unusually poor ratings from the voters as candidates, and that both ran against powerful incumbents whom many observers thought were unbeatable. Thus the prospects for ideologically distinctive candidates may be better than Goldwater's or McGovern's fortunes may suggest. In any case, it is the nominating process that largely determines the nature of the choices to be offered the voters, and whether the options are sharply distinct, as in 1964 and 1972, or only moderately different, as in 1960 and 1968.

The Nominating Process in the In-Party

The nominating process in the party controlling the White House is dominated by the incumbent President and usually results in the renomination of that incumbent. Only three times among the eleven nominations since 1936 was that not the case. One of these exceptions occurred in 1960, when President Dwight D. Eisenhower was completing his second full term at age sixty-nine. Even if Eisenhower had wished to run again, he would have been ineligible by virtue of the Twenty-second Amendment to the Constitution, which limits presidents to two terms. Eisenhower's Vice-President, Richard M. Nixon, became the early favorite for the nomination, and in spite of extensive preliminary activity in late 1959 by New York's Governor Nelson Rockefeller, Nixon was never seriously challenged.

The other two cases in which incumbents were not renominated were more complicated. In 1952 and 1968, Presidents Truman and Johnson had completed one full term in their own right after having been elevated from the Vice-Presidency on the deaths of Presidents Roosevelt and Kennedy, respectively. Both were presiding over unpopular wars in Asia, and both had become sufficiently controversial and unpopular that it was doubtful that they could win re-election. Nevertheless, it was widely assumed that each would run for renomination, since neither had withdrawn as the primaries began in March.

Both Truman and Johnson were challenged in the early primaries by candidates who were not thought to have much hope of success. Senator Estes Kefauver, who challenged Truman in the 1952 New Hampshire primary, and Senator Eugene McCarthy, who challenged Johnson there in 1968, were lightly regarded and not viewed as serious threats to the President. Nevertheless, Kefauver actually defeated Truman in the New Hampshire primary, and McCarthy did so much better than expected (41.9 percent to Johnson's 49.6 percent) that the result was considered a moral victory. Both Truman and Johnson withdrew from candidacy soon afterward.

It is tempting to conclude that these presidents withdrew because of their misfortunes in the primaries, but this would be a mistake. Truman had decided earlier that he did not want to run again, and he had sought unsuccessfully to persuade Chief Justice Fred Vinson and Governor Adlai Stevenson of Illinois to run. It was only because he did not have a candidate to back as his successor that he had not withdrawn already. Senator Kefauver, who defeated him in New

Major Party Nominees and Election Victors, 1936–76

Year	Preprimary Front-Runner	Leader of Final Poll of Party Rank and File	Nominee	Election Outcome
A. PARTY CONTROLLING PRESIDENCY				
1936	Roosevelt	Roosevelt	Roosevelt	won
1940	Roosevelt	Roosevelt	Roosevelt	won
1944	Roosevelt	Roosevelt	Roosevelt	won
1948	Truman	Truman	Truman	won
1952	Truman	Kefauver	Stevenson	lost
1956	Eisenhower	Eisenhower	Eisenhower	won
1960	Nixon	Nixon	Nixon	lost
1964	Johnson	Johnson	Johnson	won
1968	Johnson	Humphrey	Humphrey	lost
1972	Nixon	Nixon	Nixon	won
1976	Ford	Ford	Ford	lost
B. PARTY OUT OF POWER				
1936	Landon	Landon	Landon	lost
1940	?	Willkie	Willkie	lost
1944	Dewey	Dewey	Dewey	lost
1948	Dewey-Taft	Dewey	Dewey	lost
1952	Eisenhower-Taft	Eisenhower	Eisenhower	won
1956	Stevenson	Stevenson	Stevenson	lost
1960	Kennedy	Kennedy	Kennedy	won
1964	?	Goldwater-Nixon tie	Goldwater	lost
1968	Nixon	Nixon	Nixon	won
1972	Muskie	McGovern	McGovern	lost
1976	?	Carter	Carter	won

Hampshire, was not acceptable to him or to most of the leaders of the Democratic Party, largely because of the way the senator had handled some highly publicized investigations into organized crime. There is little doubt that President Truman could have won renomination if he had sought it.

President Lyndon B. Johnson also claimed that he had intended all along to withdraw, though there is less independent evidence of this, and he had not made any efforts to choose a successor. It was apparent that he did not favor Senators McCarthy and Robert Kennedy, and though he doubtless preferred Vice-President Hubert H. Humphrey to them, he took no active steps to support Humphrey's candidacy. As in Truman's case, there is little reason to believe that Johnson would have been defeated for renomination had he sought it. But in both cases renomination would have come only after a divisive battle that would have damaged the President's prestige and would have further reduced his already limited prospect of re-election.

Thus it would be a mistake to conclude that the New Hampshire primaries of 1952 and 1968 defeated these presidents or forced their withdrawal. More accurately, they increased the price of renomination at the same time that they reduced its value for the incumbent. Surely these primary setbacks reinforced any previous inclination the presidents had had to retire.

In all the remaining cases from 1936 on, the incumbent President was renominated. In fact, no incumbent was defeated for renomination since that happened to President Chester A. Arthur in 1884. This does not mean that incumbents since then were not vulnerable. The third-term issue made President Franklin D. Roosevelt vulnerable in 1940, but there was no very credible alternative to him. Truman's prestige was so low in 1948 that numerous prominent Democratic leaders sought to persuade General Eisenhower to run as a Democrat. The general declined, and again there was no credible alternative.

The nomination that best illustrates the power of the incumbency is that of Gerald R. Ford in 1976. Because of the unique way he had become President, on Nixon's resignation and without ever having been nominated for office by a national party convention, Ford was an unusually weak incumbent. Although his popularity was not as low as that of Truman in 1948, for example, he had the weakest electoral claim to the office of any President ever.

This unusual vulnerability was aggravated by the fact that President Ford was challenged by the strongest opponent any incumbent had faced since President Taft was challenged by former President Roosevelt in 1912. Ronald Reagan, formerly governor of California, was the most popular alternative Ford might have faced. A former actor and a skilled television performer, Reagan is one of the most effective speakers and campaigners in either party. In addition, he enjoys the deep loyalty and enthusiasm of the conservative wing of the Republican Party. Reagan was a far more formidable threat to the incumbent than Senators Kefauver and McCarthy had been.

Thus, while the incumbent President was renominated as usual in 1976, President Ford came closer to losing renomination than any incumbent since 1884. However, when we focus on the weakness of Ford's claim on the office, and the unusual strength of his challenger, the 1976 Republican nomination is the strongest testimony to the power of the incumbency since Taft beat Roosevelt in 1912. This fact is easier to grasp if we imagine a contest between former Governor Reagan and Congressman Gerald Ford. Although Ford had been House Minority Leader, he had never run for any elected office higher than membership in the House of Representatives, and he had never been thought of seriously as a potential nominee before Nixon elevated him to the Vice-Presidency on Spiro T. Agnew's resignation. Without the incumbency, Gerald Ford would not have been a very credible candidate for President, let alone the victor over as formidable an opponent as Reagan.

What happens when the incumbent President is not a candidate? There are too few recent examples to draw any meaningful generalizations, but clearly being Vice-President helps. Vice-President Nixon was nominated with ease in 1960 when Eisenhower was ineligible. Vice-President Humphrey was much advantaged by the office when he won in 1968. This is especially apparent when we compare his weakness when he ran for President as a senator in 1960. Vice-President Alben W. Barkley would have been a potent candidate for President in 1952 if he had not been seventy-five years old.

Popularity with the party rank and file also helps (and being Vice-President is a good way to become popular). Vice-Presidents Nixon and Humphrey led the polls of their parties' rank and file when they were nominated. In 1952, Senator Kefauver led the polls (Barkley was second and Stevenson third), but was unable to overcome the opposition of party leaders.

None of the three incumbents who were not candidates actively promoted his successor, for a variety of reasons, including the likelihood that such an effort would backfire. No one who was unacceptable to the President was chosen, and in Kefauver's case, the opposition of the President and party leaders was the central factor in his defeat. (However, with recent rules changes and reforms, it will be more difficult for party leaders to deny a popular candidate the nomination)[1].

The Nominating Process in the Out-Party

Nominations in the party out of power are not structured by the presence of a dominant figure such as an incumbent President. Accordingly, they are much more likely to involve open competition and division about who should be the nominee. However, until recently, many out-party nominations were rather similar to in-party nominations in that they were dominated by a single candidate from start to finish. Specifically, in five of the nine nominations from 1936 through 1968, a single candidate was identified as the front-runner before the first primaries began. Each of these five survived the primary season with his advantages and support intact and won the nomination. This is how the nomination was won by Governor Landon in 1936, Governor Dewey in 1944, Governor Stevenson in 1956, Senator Kennedy in 1960, and former Vice-President Nixon in 1968. In most of these cases the primaries did not play a very significant part in the selection process. These men won because they were the most popular candidates in the party, and because, as centrists, they were reasonably acceptable to most segments of the party. These advantages were apparent before the formal process began, and though some received more serious challenge than others, all survived the obstacles and achieved nomination on the first ballot.

Two other out-party nominations were somewhat similar in that the competition was highly structured from start to finish. In both 1948 and 1952 the Republicans had close races between two candidates with rather even chances to win, which were at the same time battles between the moderate and conservative wings of the party. Both times, Senator Taft was the candidate of the conservative wing, whereas in 1948 Governor Dewey represented the liberal or moderate wing and General Eisenhower did so in 1952. Both contests were hard-fought struggles from beginning to end, and both were won by the moderates, who were the candidates with the greatest support among rank-and-file Republicans, though not from all strata of party leaders. Each contest was very close: Dewey won on the third ballot, and Eisenhower was able to win on the first ballot only after Minnesota shifted its votes from Stassen to the General.

In spite of a reputation for importance in nominating politics, presidential primaries had very little to do with any of these nominations. In fact, during this period between 1936 and 1968, the primaries did not eliminate any candidate who was otherwise likely to win, nor were they instrumental in the victories of any candidate who was otherwise likely to lose. In 1940 and 1964, the contests were far less structured, but the first of these was won by Wendell Willkie, who had entered no primaries at all, and the second was won by Barry Goldwater, whose performance in the primaries was very mixed.

Beginning in 1972, however, the primaries were central to out-party nominating politics. In 1972, Senator Edmund S. Muskie was the preprimary front-runner, but his candidacy was so badly battered after he lost four of the first six primaries that he withdrew from active contention. Senator George S. McGovern, on the other hand, was seen before the primaries as an also-ran, but he used the primaries to develop a popular following and to amass a body of delegate votes that brought him the nomination. Senator McGovern certainly could not have won the 1972 nomination without the system of presidential primaries, and it is highly probable that Senator Muskie would have won it without them.

Again in 1976, the primaries were central. There was no preprimary front-runner like Muskie for the primaries to eliminate. Jimmy Carter was one of about a dozen candidates, and while he had shown some promise, the same could be said of several others. Before the first primary in New Hampshire, he had scarcely registered in the polls, but he was to win in New Hampshire and in all but three others of the first fourteen primaries. These victories helped to make him well known to voters all across the country and helped him to build a popular following. They also helped him to accumulate more than twice as many delegates as his nearest competitor, Senator Henry M. Jackson, who then withdrew, joining most of the other candidates who had originally declared.

These primaries established Carter as the man to beat and gave him a substantial lead in the ultimate currency of nominating politics— delegate votes. No resource is worth more in nominating politics than the number of delegate votes it can be translated into, and Jimmy Carter was far ahead in these. His performance in the remaining primaries was indifferent, bringing him only seven victories in the fifteen remaining primaries he contested. The only candidate who consistently defeated Carter in these late primaries was Governor Jerry Brown of California. But Brown had started too late. By the time he had started campaigning in earnest, Carter had built such momentum and such a delegate lead that Brown could not stop him. Also important to Carter's success was the fact that he regained some momentum on the final day of primaries with a very decisive and convincing win in the state of Ohio, which has a large number of delegate votes at a Democratic convention.

By this time several important party leaders had endorsed Carter, bringing him numerous delegate votes and increasing the breadth of his appeal. One of these leaders was Chicago's Mayor Richard Daley, the last of the old-time big-city organizational leaders who used to be viewed as President-makers. Someone like Daley could be expected to back a likely winner, but the most remarkable endorsement was that of Governor George Wallace, a notoriously divisive figure in the Democratic Party. Wallace had built a potent national following as a third-party candidate in 1968 and in the 1972 Democratic primaries, in part by exploiting division on explosive racial issues. Wallace's endorsement of a candidate who had been the major beneficiary of black support in the 1976 campaign was a very remarkable political development, and we may hope that it marks the ultimate defusing of the racial issue in American politics.

Some General Observations on the Nominating Process

Since their deeply divided convention in 1968, the Democrats have gone through two cycles of effort to reform procedures for nominating candidates for President. These efforts have led to numerous changes in party rules and many state-law changes that have also affected the Republicans. The most obvious and notable result has been the proliferation of presidential primaries, which have doubled in number to about thirty, and which now control the selection of some three-quarters of the delegates, as opposed to less than half previously. What difference has all this made?

Clearly it has made some. The belief that nominations are now more open and democratic seems to have attracted more candidates into contests for the out-party nomination, and the delegate votes are much more directly tied to popular preferences than before. These changes are surely also related to the increased importance of the primaries in defining the range of alternatives. Several times in the past, the primaries transformed previous unknowns in presidential politics into serious contenders, most notably Senator Kefauver in 1952 and Senator McCarthy in 1968. But before 1972, no person who owed his seriousness as a candidate to the primaries ever won the nomination. However, the primaries were central to the campaigns of both McGovern and Carter.

Yet it is easy to overestimate the importance of these changes. This is most apparent when we assess how democratic previous choices had been by the most relevant available standard: the polls of the party rank and file. Most nominees of both parties stood at the top of the final polls of their party's rank and file since the polls were first taken in 1936. (See the table on page 89.) This was as true before the reforms as after. There were several close cases, but only one in which a clear leader in the polls was denied the nomination. This was the 1952 Democratic nomination, when Senator Kefauver was turned back in spite of having far more popular support than any other candidate.

Under the reformed rules, it would be far more difficult now for party leaders to veto a candidate who had run successfully in most primaries as Kefauver did, but there are few other nominations that would obviously have turned out differently under different rules. The point is not that the new rules do not help ensure that the people's voice will be heard in nominating politics. The point is that it has long been heard and heeded. Party leaders may have been more influential in past nominations, but this does not mean that they did not support candidates who were popular. Leaders like to win elections, and it is easier to do so with popular candidates.

This is not to say that the leaders always prefer the candidate who is most popular with the rank and file. They obviously did not in the Democratic Party in 1952, and there are other examples. But the leaders do not always prevail over the rank and file when there are disagreements. For instance, George McGovern was chosen in spite of the opposition of most party leaders, but with the help of the rules changes. The most interesting example before the reforms was in the Republican Party in 1952: Taft was the choice of the lower echelon of party leaders such as the county chairmen, but Eisenhower was the choice of the rank and file and of the top echelon of leaders such as the party's governors. Eisenhower, of course, won.

Another kind of division within parties has received considerable attention in recent years. It has been repeatedly observed that the people who supported Goldwater for the Republican nomination in 1964 and those who supported McGovern for the Democratic nomination in 1972 were not representative of their parties' voters. Specifically, Goldwater's supporters were said to be more conservative than most Republicans and McGovern's supporters were said to be more liberal than most Democrats. Because partisans of relatively extreme views prevailed in these nominations, it is said, their parties could not appeal effectively for the votes of independents and partisans of the opposition, as is necessary in order to win elections.

There is much truth in these assessments, but it would be a mistake to conclude that this is the common pathology of nominating politics. Plainly, such activists of relatively extreme views are rarely so much in evidence as they were at these times, though similarities are to be found among the supporters of Senator Eugene McCarthy in 1968 and Governor Ronald Reagan in 1976. But Goldwater and McGovern were able to prevail not only because of their superior organizations of activist supporters but also because of the division in the remainder of their parties. McCarthy and Reagan failed largely because the rest of their parties were fairly united behind relatively viable candidates: Humphrey and Ford. Consequently, even though the nominations of Goldwater and McGovern were associated with their parties' most severe recent defeats, we need not view the events that led to their nominations as typical. Also, just as party leaders do not regularly disagree with the party rank and file, amateur activists do not always disagree either. Amateurs were unusually vocal in support of centrists Eisenhower, Stevenson, and Kennedy, as well as for Goldwater and McGovern.

The reforms have weakened the influence of party leaders and professionals and have enhanced somewhat the influence of amateur candidate enthusiasts. They have added to the directness of the influence of the party rank and file, but these party voters were indirectly influential before the reforms. Probably the more persistent characteristic of recent nominees before and after the reforms is that they usually have a better claim than any of their opponents to the support of their parties' voters.

In this respect, little change is needed (though the system could surely use simplifying and streamlining). A major innovation such as a national primary would usually lead to the same result as has otherwise occurred (except in the Democratic nominations of 1972 and 1976). But the present system has one feature that a national primary would not. The series of state primaries that begins with a few smaller states gives unknown challengers a chance to make themselves known and to develop a following. Only two such persons have won the presidential nomination (McGovern and Carter), but the possibility is a healthy one that is almost unique to our system.

Election

Once the Republican and Democratic parties have chosen their nominees, the choice is up to the voters, whose preferences are filtered through the Electoral College for the final decision. Most of the time, this involves a simple choice between two candidates wherein the winner of the largest number of popular votes is elected, but it is possible for the result to turn out otherwise. Because all the electoral votes of a given state go to the candidate who wins more votes there than any other candidate, a narrow victory in a large state like California can bring more than forty electoral votes, while an overwhelming victory in neighboring Nevada can bring only three. This phenomenon is likely to lead to electoral-vote totals that distort popular margins, and it is possible for the Electoral College to award the Presidency to someone who did not win the largest number of popular votes. This has not happened since 1888, however, when President Grover Cleveland received more popular votes than Benjamin Harrison but "wasted" many of them in big margins in the states he had already won while Harrison's votes were more evenly dispersed. Every President since Harrison has won a plurality of the popular vote as well as a majority in the Electoral College, but there is no guarantee that no popular vote winner will lose the Presidency in the Electoral College sometime in the future. Indeed, a very small shift of votes in Ohio and Hawaii could have cost Jimmy Carter the Presidency without denying him his popular vote majority.

Even though all presidents for more than a century have been nominees of the Republican or Democratic party, a minor-party candidate can have an impact on either the popular or the Electoral College outcome, or both. For example, Governor George Wallace ran in 1968 as an "American Independent" and received 13.5 percent of the vote. Because the contest between Nixon and Humphrey was so close (43.4 percent to 42.7 percent), these Wallace votes could easily have changed the popular-vote outcome. The best evidence seems to indicate that the majority of Wallace votes would have gone to Nixon had Wallace not been in the race, so the Alabamian seems not to have denied the victory to the candidate who would have won in a two-candidate race.

Nevertheless, this very nearly happened, because Humphrey had started the campaign far behind Nixon in the polls, and was still gaining when the election was held. If the election had been several days later, Humphrey might have won the popular vote. If he had, it would probably have been in substantial part thanks to Wallace for draining votes away from Nixon.

Only twenty years previously, in 1948, minor-party candidates also came close to denying a popular-vote victory to the likely winner of a two-man race. In 1948 there were two minor parties. Former Vice-President Henry A. Wallace was the Progressive candidate for President, and Governor Strom Thurmond of South Carolina (now a Republican senator from that state) ran as a Dixiecrat. While Wallace was to the left of President Truman and Thurmond was to the right, both were former Democrats, and most of their supporters were likely to be people who would otherwise have voted for Truman. To the surprise of most observers, however, the President won in spite of the votes he lost to Wallace and Thurmond.

Third-party candidates usually do not care very much what they do to popular-vote totals, which are not decisive in presidential elections. Some hope to concentrate their votes enough to win several states and deny victory to the major-party candidates in the Electoral College, where an absolute majority is required. This would throw the election into the House of Representatives, where each state would vote as a unit. This has not happened since 1824, but Governor Wallace was hoping to bring it about in 1968. Had Wallace been first instead of a respectable second in North Carolina, South Carolina, and Tennessee, Nixon would have won by only 1 of the 538 electoral votes. Of course, nobody knows what would have happened if the election had been thrown into the House of Representatives.

These peculiar possibilities in the Electoral College have led many people to favor a change to a direct popular vote for President and abolition of the Electoral College. This might well be a step forward, but as indicated, there is no guarantee that the most preferred candidate would win even under direct popular vote. This is because a third candidate might drain away enough votes from the most popular individual to deny him the popular majority. Accordingly, most proposals for direct popular elections provide for a runoff between the top two candidates if no one receives 40 percent of the vote. Thus the possibility that the "wrong" candidate may win is inherent when there are more than two candidates, and is not a peculiarity of either the Electoral College or the direct popular vote.

How Popular Votes Are Determined

Presidential elections have, overall, been quite competitive in recent years. Three times since World War II, the popular winner has received less than 50 percent of the vote (because of third-party candidates). And even though some of the other elections have been landslides, Republicans and Democrats have each held the Presi-

dency for sixteen of the last thirty-two years. This is true in spite of the
fact that Democrats outnumber Republicans by about a three-to-two
margin among the voters. Even though Republicans have been able to
elect majorities in Congress for only four of the last forty-four years,
they have been very competitive in presidential elections. Although
independents now outnumber Republicans, independents have favored Republican candidates in five of the last six elections, and
Democrats themselves have been increasingly likely to defect to Republican candidates.

The fact is that even though voters' party identifications may be the
most important single factor in presidential elections, these party
loyalties are declining in two ways. Fewer people identify with a
party, and those who do are less likely to support its candidates.
Short-term forces associated with a given election are more decisive
than before. The issues, the candidates, and the campaign decisively
influence election outcomes.[2]

In recent years, Republicans have regularly chosen presidential
candidates more preferred by the voters than Democratic candidates.
Among the years 1952–72, only in 1964, when President Johnson ran
against Senator Goldwater, was the Democratic candidate more favorably viewed by the voters than the Republican. Only in that year did
public perceptions of both candidates together help the Democrats
more than the Republicans. This observation is based on the unsur-
prising facts that Eisenhower was viewed more favorably than
Stevenson and that Nixon was seen more favorably than McGovern. It
is based also on the somewhat more surprising fact that Nixon was
more of an asset to the Republicans in 1960 than Kennedy was to the
Democrats. In spite of the decline in his reputation, and the controversial image that followed him throughout his political career, Nixon
was a distinct asset to the Republicans each of the three times he ran
for President.

Many commentators have deplored the facts that candidate image
and candidate personality are so important in electoral politics and
that issues do not count for more. Actually, candidate personality is a
perfectly legitimate and proper subject for voters to evaluate and
weigh. Presidents do far more than respond to the issue preferences of
the voters. They have enormous discretionary power, and their personalities can importantly affect the way they handle issues and decide public policy.

Thus, James David Barber argues that presidential personality has
been responsible for some major policy misfortunes.[3] He asserts that
personality was responsible for Woodrow Wilson's tenacious refusal
to compromise his version of the League of Nations treaty. This, in
turn, led to the failure of the United States to join the League, which
crippled that body's capacity to maintain peace. Barber writes that

personality was also responsible for Herbert Hoover's refusal to provide direct relief for the needy during the Depression, and for Lyndon Johnson's commitment to the Vietnam War long after it became apparent that our goals would not be achieved at reasonable cost. Barber also finds similar unfortunate personality characteristics to have been exhibited by President Nixon well before the Watergate affair ensured his demise.

While one may or may not agree with all of Barber's interpretation, personality doubtless can affect the way a President will behave in office. If personality can lead to tragedy, as Barber suggests, perhaps it should weigh more heavily and more systematically in public deliberations rather than less.

Apparently it is not easy for voters to make such judgments, however. Barber finds Johnson and Nixon to have had the most dangerous personalities among presidents since Hoover; yet as we have seen, both were regarded more favorably by the voters than their opponent(s). Both were re-elected as incumbents with landslide margins, only to be subsequently hounded from office.

Issues in Electoral Politics

Issues play a more complicated role in electoral politics than candidate personality. This is because issues are only indirectly involved in elections. Voters directly decide issues only in referenda, which do not occur in American national politics. Only the names of candidates and their parties are on the ballot in our national elections. Issues are important or are resolved only insofar as they become involved in the differences between the candidates, and there are many ambiguities in the ways that candidates and issues become associated.

Even when only a single issue is involved in an election, it may be ambiguously involved because the candidates may not clearly differentiate themselves with regard to it. Even if they do, the distinctions may not be clearly seen by the voters, or may not be decisive in many voters' choices. When many issues are involved in an election, as is typical, the complications are multiplied. Different issues may be salient to different voters, and candidates may find that they can gain more votes by appealing to minorities that care very much about an issue than by appealing to majorities that do not. Naturally, candidates who want to maximize their chances of victory will emphasize issues where they are advantaged and de-emphasize issues where they are not. This of course detracts from the clarity of the distinctions and contributes to the ambiguity with which elections handle issues. In addition, candidates sometimes mislead the people, deliberately or otherwise.

Involvement in a foreign war has been an issue in numerous elections, and has presented examples of several ways in which elections do not provide for precise popular control over the disposition of issues. Three times in this century, Democratic presidents have campaigned as peace candidates and subsequently involved us in war. In 1916, a key slogan of President Wilson's campaign was "He kept us out of war," but by 1917 America was involved in World War I. President Roosevelt promised in 1940 that "your boys are not going to be sent into any foreign wars" shortly before we became involved in World War II. Our entry into the Korean conflict did not follow any discussion of that issue in a campaign, but the sharpest escalation of our involvement in the war in Vietnam followed the 1964 presidential campaign, in which Goldwater seemed to be the hawk and Johnson the peace candidate who would not send American boys to fight an Asian war. We know that President Johnson's advantage over Goldwater in that election was enhanced by the fact that the President was seen as better able to handle foreign affairs.

How to get out of a war has been an important issue in modern campaigns, though again elections have not offered very precise control to the voters. In 1952, the Korean conflict was a great liability to the Democrats, and the Republicans were helped importantly by General Eisenhower's pledge to end the war. The general did not say much about how he would do it, but his personal prestige as a war hero and the fact that he was not identified with the incumbent administration lent credibility to his pledge. Whether or not it would have done so without his election, the war did end soon thereafter, leaving one of the better apparent examples of popular control of policy through the electoral process.

How to end the war in Vietnam was a central issue in the 1968 elections, but ironically, it had very little impact on the distribution of votes between the Republican and Democratic candidates.[4] This was because both Humphrey and Nixon were seen by the voters as very close to each other near the center of a hawk-dove continuum, and as very close to where most of the voters were. This did not provide the voters with much of a choice between the two candidates on this issue, but in one sense the voters could not lose: No matter which of the candidates won, the victor would be identified with a position that was close to that of most of the voters. If the candidates had distinguished themselves from each other more clearly, the voters might have had more of a choice, and perhaps some better options, but if we want publics to control policy, we cannot complain too much when the candidates identify themselves with the positions most preferred by the voters.

Vietnam was still an issue in the 1972 election, which provided a much clearer choice between an incumbent identified with an "honorable end to the war" and a challenger advocating an immediate end to the war, more or less regardless of the consequences in South Vietnam. President Nixon won decisively, and his handling of foreign affairs was a major factor in drawing votes to him. However, in spite of the electoral victory for him and his policies, in just over two years South Vietnam was taken over by the Communists, which was presumably not a result many people had in mind when they considered an "honorable end to the war." The Vietnam issue thus illustrates several great ironies about the role of issues in electoral politics.

Race is an issue in which elections have not always been constructive, though considerable strides have been made recently. After the end of Reconstruction, neither party did much to advance civil rights and racial equality. The blacks who could vote generally supported Republicans, apparently because Democrats were identified with white supremacy in the South and because the Republicans were identified with Lincoln, emancipation, and Reconstruction. After the Great Depression began, however, most blacks shifted to the support of the Democratic Party, not because it had embraced the cause of civil rights but, apparently, because it had become identified with economic underdogs, which included most blacks.

Harry Truman was the first twentieth-century President to make a sustained and direct appeal to black voters on civil-rights grounds. His proposal of civil-rights legislation and his executive orders to establish fair employment practices and to eliminate discrimination in the armed forces all served to identify Truman more directly with civil rights than any preceding twentieth-century President. Aside from Truman's egalitarian motives, it is well known that several of these moves were explicitly designed to help him appeal for black votes in his effort to win the 1948 election. These events also provide a good example of how efforts to appeal for votes can lead to constructive policy changes—though, of course, this is not always the case.

In the 1950s, the parties returned to a more ambiguous stance and to vaguer differences on civil rights. Neither Dwight D. Eisenhower nor Adlai Stevenson was clearly identified with a stance for or against civil rights. Both were considered moderates on the issue. Stevenson was the Northern candidate for the Democratic nomination who was most acceptable to the South, while Eisenhower was, on the one hand, distinctly cool to the *Brown* v. *Board of Education* school-desegregation decision and, on the other hand, the President who sent troops to Little Rock to enforce the law regarding school desegregation. Under the circumstances, it is not surprising that many voters found it hard in the 1950s to identify the party most likely to advance the cause of civil rights.

It was in the context of this ambiguity that the 1960 election took place. The differences between the candidates were marginal. John F. Kennedy had identified himself as slightly more pro civil rights by an important symbolic gesture, a telephone call to Mrs. Martin Luther King when Doctor King was in jail for civil-rights activities. Kennedy also criticized the Eisenhower Administration for not making a "stroke of the pen" to sign an executive order that would outlaw discrimination in public housing.

These things helped solidify black support behind Kennedy, but once he had been elected, he granted civil rights a low priority. He proposed no civil-rights legislation until 1963, after the Birmingham riots, and he himself did not make the stroke of the pen regarding public housing for almost two years after he took office.

The Civil Rights Act of 1964, the most important piece of legislation in this area since Reconstruction, was passed after Kennedy's death but during the term to which he had been elected. President Lyndon B. Johnson thoroughly identified himself with the law and campaigned in 1964 as an advocate of civil rights. During his subsequent administration, two other important civil-rights acts were passed.

From time to time presidents, once elected, violate expectations based on their previous careers or on what they have said in campaigns. This is, of course, sometimes to be deplored, but not always. In retrospect, it seems that President Johnson violated the promises he made in the 1964 election, with disastrous results. Few would now applaud his Asian policies, though soon after the election public support for his escalation of American involvement in Vietnam was high. In the short run, what turned people against Johnson was less that he involved them in a war after leading them to expect otherwise than that his policy was a failure. The cost in men, money, and time was far greater than anyone had expected, and the desired result was still not forthcoming.

President Richard Nixon did several things that were quite divergent from policies he had been identified with, and at least some were viewed positively. Although he had been viewed as a conservative in economic affairs, his policies included several things we might have expected Nixon himself to have criticized the Democrats for as being too liberal. The dollar was devalued in relation to foreign currency, and, though Nixon had long been a critic of government control over prices, he instituted a wage-and-price freeze with subsequent government regulation of increases. Nixon's Family Assistance Plan, which would have provided a guaranteed income to working poor families, was the most daring proposal for innovation in income-support policy since the Social Security Act of 1935, and in many ways he outflanked the Democrats with a proposal they might have feared was too liberal to propose.

The most daring and the most widely applauded of Nixon's policy innovations was surely his move to open and normalize official diplomatic contact with the People's Republic of China. Nixon had been associated with no policy more clearly than with a vigorous anti-Communism. He had been a strong defender of our association with Nationalist China, and veteran Nixon-watchers might have expected him to be the first to criticize a President who would normalize relations with the Communist Chinese. Surely it was easier for conservatives to accept this innovation from Nixon than it would have been for them to accept it from a Democrat or someone identified as a liberal.

Sometimes these turnabouts from previous expectations are applauded, as in the case of Nixon's China policy, and sometimes they are vilified, as in the case of Johnson's war policy. In either case, they are illustrations of the limitations of elections as instruments of popular control of public policy. Once elected, public officials have considerable freedom to create new policies that may be quite divergent from the expressed preferences of their supporters. Although there are times when this is to be deplored, there are others in which this seems to leave possibilities for creative leadership and innovation that would be far less likely to occur if the officials had to have the approval of voters in advance of their decisions.

In general, as this essay should make clear, elections are a blunt instrument of popular control. V. O. Key, Jr., once said that the voters' vocabulary is limited to two words, "yes" and "no." Insofar as this is true, one cannot expect voters to be able to provide very precise direction of the affairs of government. Nevertheless, American presidential nominations and elections are to a large extent popularly based, even though there remains room for reform. But many of the limitations of popular control over presidential politics are more directly rooted in the inherent limitations of elective and representative government than in the limitations of our own unique electoral institutions.

Notes

1. For more detailed analysis of these nominations and all others between 1936 and 1972, see William R. Keech and Donald R. Matthews, *The Party's Choice* (Washington D.C.: Brookings Institution, 1976).
2. For a more detailed analysis of American voting behavior, see Herbert Asher, *Presidential Elections and American Politics: Voters, Candidates and Campaigns Since 1952* (Homewood, Ill.: Dorsey Press, 1976), and Norman H. Nie, Sidney Verba, and John R. Petrocik, *The Changing American Voter* (Cambridge, Mass.: Harvard University Press, 1976).
3. James David Barber, *The Presidential Character* (Englewood Cliffs, N.J.: Prentice-Hall, 1972).
4. For a detailed analysis, see Benjamin I. Page and Richard A. Brody, "Policy Voting and the Electoral Process: The Vietnam War Issue," *American Political Science Review*, vol. LXVI (September 1972), pp. 979–95.

6. Lyndon Johnson's Political Personality

Doris Kearns

Lyndon Johnson's life took him through a succession of public institutions: the House of Representatives, the Senate, the vice-presidency, and the presidency. He first came to Washington when Herbert Hoover was still president; his public career spanned the depression, the New Deal, World War II, Korea, postwar economic expansion, the cold war, the Eisenhower years, the New Frontier, the Great Society, and Vietnam. He was a candidate for office from a fairly liberal congressional district with a populist tradition, then from a conservative state dominated by powerful economic interests, and, finally, his constituency was the entire nation.

This staggering diversity of historical circumstances and public institutions which constituted the changing environments of Lyndon Johnson's public life provides an unusual opportunity for understanding the interplay between personality and institutions in America. Lyndon Johnson's character, his favorite methods of acquiring power and of using that power, his personal strengths and weaknesses, can all be viewed in different contexts, thus providing an invaluable look at both the changeless dynamics of power and the changing structure of the American political system in the past forty years.

This article first examines Johnson's characteristic ways of dealing with the world, formed through his various experiences within his family and cultural setting. The study will then turn to a comparative examination of two of the major institutions Johnson encountered—the Senate and the presidency—in an attempt to assess the impact of personality on successful leadership in different settings.

Personality Development

The picture of Johnson's early life suggests a childhood torn between the irreconcilable demands of his mother—who hoped to find in his intellectual and cultural achievement a recompense of her dead father, unhappy marriage, and thwarted ambition—and those of his father, who considered intellect and culture unmanly pursuits. This may not, of course, be a wholly accurate or complete description, but the evidence we have—Johnson's recollections, his early letters to his parents, and his later behavior—supports this conclusion. His parents, most significantly his mother, seemed to bestow or withdraw approval on the basis of his behavior at home and, later, his accomplishments at school. All her expressions of satisfaction and love were related to something her son had done, just as his implied appeals for approval were accompanied by descriptions of all the good deeds he had accomplished.

Thus as Johnson grew up, he identified the success of his performance as the source of love. He could not allow himself to doubt that his mother loved him or that her praise was evidence and expression of her love. Unfortunately, however, words of admiration, praise, satisfaction, joy, even of love, which seemed a response to Johnson's activities in the many worlds through which he moved, could never truly fulfill his need for love. For the "love" whose experience, denial, or withdrawal is basic to the configuration of a given psychic structure must be, psychoanalysts tell us, perceived as a response to one's own being, unqualified by success or failure, by mental or physical defects, or by relationships to the external world. When this fundamental love is denied, or, as in Johnson's case, attached to external performance, then no recognition of personal qualities and gifts, such as integrity, warmth, energy, and talent can suffice to satisfy inward needs. Performance alone can prevent the sense of failure and that performance must be continually displayed since past effectiveness is swiftly erased and soon counts for nothing at all. Thus continual motion and limitless ambitions become the necessities of daily life.

Lyndon Johnson found the source of his achievement in the acquisition of power and control. Yet control is not the only road to success, even in public life. For Johnson, however, control fulfilled another need as well: mastery of the outer world was necessary to mastery of the self; controlling his home environment was the only means for reconciling the profound inward tensions imposed by the contradiction between his mother's demand for intellectual achievement and his father's notions of manly pride. And control of the external world was also the only way of containing the powerful mixture of hate, rage, and love he experienced at various times toward his mother, his father, and himself. Mastery of the outer world was necessary to mastery of the self. And the drive for control was a surrogate for his urgent childhood desires to control the earliest of his environments and change his position within his parental family, thus enabling him to compel love and prevent conditions that created inner conflicts, dangers, and fears.

This understanding of the inward forces that contributed to Johnson's pursuit of power should not diminish respect for his extraordinary achievements; on the contrary, it should increase our regard for the masterful way in which—most of the time—he was able to harness and direct his personal needs toward constructive, social ends. Why some men cope and others do not remains a mystery. While we are able to suggest a number of possible bases for Johnson's strength—his grandfather's reliability, his mother's early devotion, his father's interest and attention—we have no theory to connect these observations in a coherent pattern. The psychoanalytic literature is able to analyze sources of weakness better than sources of strength.

It is also important to recognize that, while the demands of psychic structure led Johnson to pursue power, they did not determine that politics would be the avenue for that pursuit. The larger social setting provided content for Johnson's ambitions. Had his father and his father's friends been engaged in business or finance, one can imagine Johnson pursuing a very different career. But the options for a poor boy from a poor place in central Texas were limited—practically, if not theoretically. Politics was the one profession that seemed to offer both a reasonable chance of entry and a limitless future. In short, the same drives set in a different society or in another age might have led to very different pursuits.

And one thing is certain: his childhood relationships, the manner in which he sought, out of necessity, to resolve conflicts, protect his identity, and find personal fulfillment, may have shaped and energized his ambitions, but they did not, and could not, ensure their realization.

Johnson's success and achievements—his performance—were made possible, to a very large extent, by his unusual capacities, his intellect, energy, talent, and insight into men and the nature of institutions, through which he developed techniques of incredible and intricate subtlety. To his knowledge and skill he applied an innovative genius to construct a large variety of instruments which increased the coercive powers that enabled him to impose his will. And that very success only strengthened and increased his ambition.

On the foundations of the basic elements of his psychic structure, Johnson constructed characteristic forms of behavior and conduct which he repeated constantly throughout the various stages of his career. Every time he entered an institution whose structure made such a relationship possible and productive, Johnson apprenticed himself to a man with superior power—Cecil Evans, the president of his college, Richard Russell, Senate leader of the southern bloc, even President John F. Kennedy; he became the invaluable helper, the deferential subordinate willing and able to perform a dazzling range of services for his master, until, step by step, the apprentice accumulated the resources that enabled him to secure the master's role.

But Johnson was not alone in playing the role of apprentice, a role marvelously suited to a political system marked at important institutional levels by seniority and gradual ascent. What distinguished his behavior from others' was the skill with which he managed to avoid remaining a completely loyal subordinate (a position that halted the ambitions of others), yet, even while changing his role, to retain his master's support. The skills he evidenced here resonated of ones he had shown much earlier in his life as he walked the even more treacherous path between his parents' conflicting demands. The boy's earliest relationship with his mother was shaped by the idea that she needed him, and the confidence that he was capable of fulfilling that need. But with his mother, more than with anyone else, the role of apprentice required a distance; nothing less than survival of the self was at stake. So Johnson instinctively reached for the only other base of power he knew: identification with his father provided the independence he needed to separate from his mother.

In the exercise of his power, Johnson used a related technique drawn from an old tradition: he obligated his followers by providing them with services or benefits which they desired or needed. But the line between obligation and coercion was often thin. In return for his gifts, Johnson demanded a high measure of gratitude, which could only be acceptably demonstrated by the willingness to follow his lead. Though with some colleagues (those not central to his pursuit of power) he was able to grant the leeway and independence he himself had demanded, his more typical pattern required a continuing proof of loyalty so extreme that their autonomy was endangered. These demands for submission invariably worked against him, insulating him from the give and take of an adversary proceeding. He seemed to fear that any relaxation of control, even in front of his closest colleagues, would open the door to unknown enemies.

Of course, this kind of behavior cannot be attributed solely to Johnson's inner needs. It was also a response to the nature of the political world. When every situation is translated into one of power lost or gained, all relationships, including friendships, are reduced to a series of shifting, undependable alliances. In such a world it is easy to succumb to the belief that even one's closest "friend" must be watched for signs of treason.

But the vicissitudes of the political career account for neither the urgency beneath Johnson's demands for submission nor the passions he projected onto his critics. These emotions can be understood only by recognizing the fears of illegitimacy and loss that plagued Johnson from his earliest experience with power (his position in his mother's home), where he knew that all the power he commanded, while momentarily great, was subject to instant removal the moment his father returned. And these fears of illegitimacy and loss were undoubtedly reinforced by the circumstances of a political career that depended over and over on death (in 1937, Congressman Buchanan's sudden death opened up the seat in the Tenth Congressional District; in 1948, Senator Morris Sheppard's death opened the second senatorship from Texas, and of course, in 1963, John Kennedy's assassination opened up the presidency) and political defeat (Lucas and McFarland, successive Senate Democratic leaders before Johnson, were defeated in the 1950 and 1952 elections). Nor was his sense of the precariousness of his power relieved by the narrow victory that launched his Senate career (eighty-seven votes).

Throughout his career, Johnson exhibited an unmatched capacity to persuade individuals in one-on-one or small private settings, coupled with a crippling incapacity to present himself effectively before large public audiences. This juxtaposition of traits has long served as a puzzle for Johnson watchers. Countless descriptions have been offered of his uncommon skill in personal encounters, his brilliant blend of calculation and instinct, his unmatched richness of language and tone. One can safely assert that no American political leader has ever equaled Lyndon Johnson in the capacity to know the motives, desires, and weaknesses of those with whom he dealt. He seemed to possess a wholly intuitive ability to perceive a man's nature so accurately and profoundly as almost to be unnatural. Yet this same man, forced to speak before a large public audience, invariably stiffened up, his words delivered in monotone voice, his smile frozen, his hands tightly gripping the lectern.

This contrast is partially accounted for by the recognition that formal settings were less suitable to Johnson's particular talents—crude and colorful metaphors are less appropriate in formal speeches, and the power of physical touch is obviously reduced when the speaker stands before an audience of ten thousand or sits alone in a bare television studio. And part of the explanation for the problem in his later years can be found in the concept of the president as a statesman above the fray, a concept that Johnson shared with many others.

Yet many of the skills involved in the one were applicable to the other, as Johnson's own successes showed. His best speeches were those in which he departed from the text, and by far his most effective television appearance as judged by a poll of viewers was a long, informal conversation with three reporters during which he alternately sat in his chair, roamed around the room, or stood beside his desk, raising and lowering his voice at will. After this appearance, the opinions of his advisers were unanimous: he must adapt his informal style to his public appearances. Johnson refused with a stubborn persistence that can only be understood by searching back in his past, to the contrast already mentioned between the rich and natural mode of talk he adopted from his father and his mother's very different standards of acceptability, which produced in him a measure of shame and a determination, at least in public, to meet his mother's ideal. Yet the son of the woman who taught elocution and debate was dismissed from his lessons in public speaking for mumbling too much—suggesting perhaps an unconscious impulse to take revenge on his mother—and he never conquered his terror of speaking before an audience.

Johnson's career was marked by a continuing effort to avoid confrontation and choice, to prevent passionate and emotional divisions over issues. This inclination can be understood as a response to his particular family situation. From his earliest days he had learned that if he chose his father, he might jeopardize the love and respect of his mother; if he chose his mother, his identity as a man would be in danger. The challenge then, as always, was to find a method of satisfying both—to shape an intermediate path, to find consensus. But Johnson's drive for consensus was not simply a product of inner need; its roots can be seen in the traditions and historical experience of his cultural environment, in the prevailing attitudes and ideals that comprised his view of the world.

The political heritage of Johnson's hill country was that of populism. There Johnson absorbed the established concept that government existed to help the ordinary citizen, and that the ordinary people's basic wants were essentially the same. He built his first campaign for the Congress on the promise that he alone could bring the benefits of the New Deal to the people of his district. And once elected he kept his promise: he brought water and electric power to the Tenth District; he developed a slum-clearance project for the poor; he focused on the problems of the Mexican-Americans. But the populism that influenced Johnson did not include a theory of class conflict. Johnson's family was poor, but it did not identify with the poor, choosing instead to identify with the great majority of Americans, who believed in the possibility of progress and quelled their resentments of the rich by the conviction that someday they, too, would be rich.

Over time, as Johnson stretched his ambition from the Tenth District to the state of Texas, he stretched his conception of "the people" to include the oil and gas men, the big ranchers, the big builders, and the cotton growers. Needing the support and the money of these powerful men, Johnson revised his definition of governmental responsibility to include help for the few as well as services for the many. He became a specialist in defense, a friendly agent ready to deliver any number of government contracts in return for campaign contributions and political support. He moved up in the world, but he never forgot the place where he had been born; he simply added new constituents to the ones he had originally served. Separate packages separately designed for separate groups—this was the winning strategy as Johnson defined it. Thus Johnson built his career on a series of disparate layers; he added one incompatible constituency on top of another; he juxtaposed contradictory ideas without choosing between them. This was a source of his personal strength in rising to power, but it also reflected the nature of a political system that rewards those capable of appealing to a variety of interests.

Johnson wanted many things, but among them, without doubt, that every American should have enough nourishing food, warm clothing, decent shelter, and a chance to educate his children; and later, as the presidency extended his reach, he wanted to restore nature, rebuild cities, even build a Great Society. He wanted to out-Roosevelt Roosevelt and, at the same time, thought that what he wanted, everyone wanted, or would want if only he could explain it to them.

So as President he took the course that was most congenial to his character, and probably the only course possible in 1963. He would persuade everyone—businessmen, union chiefs, bankers, politicians —that his goals were in their interest, an interest that he thought, perhaps naïvely, was buried somewhere in every man—the desire to contribute, to leave behind a mark of which he could be proud. This drive to avoid conflict was a source of his greatest achievements in using his power: his success in bringing the Senate to its peak of effectiveness in the 1950s and in forging a consensus on the Great Society that went beyond the splitting of differences. Yet the drive was also a source of weakness. The American political system, superb in developing the technique of consensus, proved less capable of providing direction. Where positive goals were lacking, consensus could not supply them. Where hard choices had to be made (between constituents and ideas), Johnson could not choose. He could not choose between the Great Society and Vietnam; not only when—as in 1965—that choice seemed unnecessary because of an expanding economy and a faith in technology, but, more revealingly, when the failure to choose was obviously destroying the Great Society, the prospects of the war, and Lyndon Johnson himself. Still refusing to face even the necessity of choice, Johnson evolved an elaborate and illusory system (statistics on the continuing progress of the Great Society, statistics on Vietnam proving that the war was indeed being won), which distorted his vision and limited his real options. But practical necessity could not shift his course; the fear of choice had its roots too deep in his character and experience.

Personality and Institutions

Experience would strengthen Johnson's capacities, modify and supplement his modes of behavior. Man's identity, as Erikson has pointed out, is not fixed; it continually evolves through different phases of life. Some experiences induce growth in character, others provoke regression or even mental disintegration. Johnson's life history shows that he could adapt his conduct to the requirements of different political settings, that his priorities and commitments could change with the circumstances of the time. But that adaptation was possible only within limits. Some of his techniques and his ways of dealing with the world were so deeply rooted in his character and his nature that alteration proved impossible, even when those techniques proved no longer effective.

Having examined these characteristic techniques, let us consider here two of the many institutions Johnson encountered—the Senate and the presidency—in order to assess the impact of personality in varying settings. In the present state of knowledge, it is not possible to describe the interaction of men and institutions in full and accurate detail. Institutions like individuals change over time; history moves on. The process itself cannot be frozen for inspection. The requisites for success in the same institution are different at different periods of time. This does not, however, make it impossible to analyze the interaction of men and events at a specific period of time and to draw conclusions, which I shall now attempt to do by examining the Senate first and then the presidency.

The Senate

When Lyndon Johnson became a senator, he entered an institution extremely well suited to his capacities, and at a time in the history of both Senate and country that made it possible for him to exert those capacities with great effect. No matter how great his abilities, Johnson's rise to power would not have been possible if the institutional conditions of the Senate had, like those of the House, not been favorable.

First, power in the Senate was less institutionalized than it was in the House. It was, for the most part, exercised by an informal group known as the "inner club"—the chairmen of important committees, mostly southerners and predominantly conservative—whose acknowledged leader was Richard Russell. The hierarchy was not rigid, nor did it attempt to extend control over all the details of Senate activity. The formal leadership positions had little actual authority, and were not sought by ambitious men who had invested years of service in anticipation of being selected; their occupancy was seen more as a duty than as a base of power. Moreover, as Truman's administration neared its close the Democratic party was in disarray, the president himself preoccupied with the Korean War, his influence dwindling. Thus there was no external party influence either on the current leadership or on the process of selection, as there might have been under a strong Democratic president and a united Democratic party.

All these factors contributed to a situation where Johnson was able by skillfully cultivating one man—Russell—to provide an entry for himself into the power structure without infringing on the authority and prerogatives of others. There was no need to displace existing leadership—happenstance opened the posts—or to fight the organized candidacies of others. He had simply to make himself both desirable to Russell and the inner club and at least acceptable to the northerners. And meeting the requirement, he played a skillful game: he apprenticed himself to Russell, performing all manner of tangible and psychic services, yet he avoided being placed in an ideological category that would have made him totally unacceptable to the other senators. Thus he was prepared for the leadership opportunity when it came—through the successive vacancies of the offices of party whip and minority leader.

Once he became minority whip and leader, Johnson was able to accumulate power by exploiting institutional vulnerabilities—some the very ones that had made his selection possible—and the changing conditions of national and political life. Slack in the system was perhaps the most important condition. The inner club exercised its power only over those matters it considered important or of special interest. In other areas there was no real authority, nor was there any leadership concerned with the interest of the Senate as a whole. Moreover, the inner club tended to exercise its power along ideological lines, enforcing interests and attitudes that were generally conservative and southern. Its members were not concerned with the inevitable resentments of other senators who did not share their convictions, because their power was based not on majority vote but on control over committees and tacit acknowledgment of their right to authority. Nor did the inner club try to placate the inevitable resentment of an increasing number of new senators who felt that the established customs, leadership, and procedures barred them from a significant role in the legislative process, diminishing their opportunity to perform as they wanted and as their constituents expected.

Yet, if resentments smoldered and needs went unmet, there was no organized or coherent effort on the part of any group to displace the present leadership with a majority leadership of its own. The formal discipline that would have been required for such a revolt was hard to find in a body characterized by independent bases of power for each of its members. Each senator had interests distinct from those of every other—derived primarily from the necessities of his own political career. While a senator's concern for the effective functioning of the Senate as a whole was not absent, it was not generally a priority concern compared to his relationship with his constituents. Thus the alternatives history provided—strong, elective party leaders with party caucuses to bind votes and men—seemed even less appealing than a disorderly, uninstitutionalized Senate.

The situation was ripe for a personal leadership style: one that could lessen the tensions resulting from the southerners' tight control, concern itself with the smoother operation of the Senate, gather central resources to help individuals, but always remember that a senator's relationship with his constituency was the primary concern.

So upon taking over, Johnson assumed some burdens of leadership that had not previously been exercised—allotment of office space, scheduling of legislation, appointments to committee delegations. Able to comprehend the current structure of the Senate as a whole, he formed a mental picture of a different structure and moved toward it with such skill that he managed to bring everyone along with his changes, even those who would potentially lose power under the new system. He began by persuading the inner club to relax seniority just a little, to provide more seats on important committees to new members as a token means of quelling incipient resentment and as a way of making the Senate function more effectively. By this move, however, he obligated the freshmen senators to him; he established the appearance that his authority was the source of their ability to do their work effectively. At the same time, the small size of the Senate allowed him to gather information about every senator: what he was going to do, was likely to do, or might be persuaded to do. Over time, Johnson became the only source of authoritative information on the Senate as a whole. Thus he became useful, and often indispensable, to other senators who were forced to rely upon his judgment about, for example, the chances of passing legislation in which they were interested, or what form of compromise could bring agreement, or when they could take a trip without missing a crucial vote. In addition, he made it impossible for others to separate the appearance of power from its reality. If, for example, he told a senator that he would make sure of a favorable vote on his bill and the bill passed, one could not know whether Johnson had exerted his authority or whether he had already known what the result would be. In this way he secured obligations not only by rendering real services and rewards but by seeming to produce results that were not, in fact, of his doing.

The insulation of the cloakroom, where much of the Senate's business occurred, allowed Johnson to impose his will separately on each senator and in such a way as to reduce awareness of the coercive nature of his leadership. Had there been collective forums of decision in which he had forced individuals to go his way, the coercive nature of his tactics would have been all too clear. And, in fact, Johnson drained the collective organs, the caucus and the conference, transforming most of the Senate's business to his own office, where his relations were seen as bargaining. And, true, his capacity to bargain and persuade was undoubtedly an important element in his leadership. Yet the process was essentially coercive; over time, Johnson's power became increasingly necessary to the capacity of others to sustain and exercise their own authority. Every time he bargained there was always the implicit threat—never voiced, but inherent in the very disproportion of power and rewards—that failure to go along might have damaging consequences. And in most cases the senators yielded, except, of course, on matters of fundamental concern to their constituencies—a limit Johnson understood and respected. When he anticipated failure, he didn't try to persuade—a fact that only enhanced his reputation as a leader who accomplished what he set out to do.

The disguise was essential. For no senator could afford to let others know he was being compelled to act by another, that he was submitting to Lyndon Johnson's will. The nature of the Senate required unanimous acceptance of the mask—continual recognition of the majority leader's skills, his brilliance in argument, his effectiveness in conducting the business of the Senate, his genius at compromise—but not of his power to enforce his will. It is true that Johnson disliked, even feared, direct and open confrontation. But he was essentially a coercive personality, working in a situation in which bargaining and persuasion were the necessary forms for the acquisition of power and the exercise of control. Such forms were also more congenial to his personal qualities, reducing the possibility of failure, since one could not be defeated in a discussion or defied and overcome by another's inability to understand the wisdom of one's advice and arguments.

If institutional process and structure made the most important contribution to Johnson's power and the manner of its use, he was also helped by historical conditions and political circumstances, which—and partly because they were so congenial to his own character—in turn, influenced his conduct in the Senate. It is, for example, difficult to imagine Johnson's achieving a similar concentration of power in the Senate of Daniel Webster or John Calhoun. He came to Senate leadership during a time of relative quietism. The economy was doing well, and occasional recessions seemed nothing more than transient interruptions in the steady growth of personal affluence. There were no passionate issues of the kind that led to deep and irreconcilable divisions along lines of fundamental interest or ideology.

And the political circumstances were also congenial: a president uninterested in social reform, whose popularity restrained most Democrats from too open or strong opposition, permitted Johnson to avoid disruptive debates whose outcome he could not control. And that same president, because he was a Republican, made it unnecessary for Johnson to subordinate his conduct to the White House as he might have had to do with a strong Democratic leader.

Let us now turn to the influence of his power on the structure of the institution and on national events. Clearly, he had achieved more power as leader than any other leader in decades. And he had built that power from the qualities and structure of the institution. But he had not created institutionalized power. His powers had not, with a few exceptions, been incorporated into the formal authority of the majority leader. He had transformed a position of limited significance into one of great power. But he had used the majority leadership and not transformed it. His system depended on his capacities, knowledge, and command over a variety of procedures which he enforced but did not establish. As a result, when he left, the Senate had no centralized structure of leadership—unless it could find another Lyndon Johnson, which seemed unlikely, since it had waited two centuries for the first one.

Despite the failure to institutionalize his power, we must conclude that Johnson did bring the Senate during his reign to unprecedented heights of effective function. Legislation was moved from introduction to committee to floor and then enacted smoothly and with dispatch. Conflicts were reduced and respect for the Senate increased. Johnson's leadership is also responsible for speeding up the process through which the powers of the conservative southern coalition were redistributed to the Senate as a whole, a process made inevitable by population shifts and the loss of a one-party South, and for reducing some of the inequalities resulting from the seniority system. The old system had rested on accepted traditions and procedure, informal alliances based both on common outlook and mutual interest and on established procedure—seniority—for the acquisition of authority. Once that system had changed, then the belief that the way things were was the only way they could be was shattered. Nor was it likely that any new group of senators would now deliberately grant authority to a group of committee chairmen dominated by southern authority.

· Yet the powers once held by the inner club were not, after Johnson, lodged in a new leader; they were simply fragmented to the benefit of individual senators. These senators have since developed a stake in the existing system of leadership. Any change now would entail a transfer of power, a probability that familiar modes of conduct would be changed; the ultimate consequences are uncertain and thus appear as risk. This is precisely why structures of power in the Senate are not codified, but, instead, continually evolve over a long period of time with changes in the nature of the Senate membership. Johnson's rise was exceptional in this regard. The Senate would never have voted to give him the powers of leadership that they so often praised. Nor are they likely to bestow the same powers on any other majority leader or on the position itself. That would require a sense of devotion to the Senate as a whole, which would only be possible in an institution that was a collective body—that is, in a different institution.

Johnson's system of power and leadership influenced not only the Senate as an institution but national conditions and events. For one thing, he inhibited the development of effective and coherent opposition on domestic issues. There were serious national problems—persisting poverty, inadequate health care, recurrent recession, and unemployment—along with questions of defense policy and foreign affairs. There was debate on these issues, both in the country and, later, during the 1960 presidential campaign. But the Senate was potentially the most important forum for the expression of opposition. It could influence the national dialogue, many of its members were themselves significant political figures, and with a Democratic majority could force a confrontation. Historically, it had often taken this role (congressional opposition during the later New Deal, the great and partly decisive debate over the Marshall Plan, etc.). This does not mean that the Senate could have substituted its policies for those of Eisenhower, but it abdicated the possibility even of stimulating national debate; of influencing, if not decisively changing, the course of events and those administration policies that needed senatorial acquiescence. Yet the days of the Senate's involvement with legislation had been steadily waning even before Johnson, and on the other side of the ledger is the fact that Johnson's leadership was vital to the passage of the first civil rights act since 1867, and in forcing the government to initiate a large-scale space program. And there were other accomplishments. Nevertheless, we must conclude that while Johnson's leadership style—his avoidance of issues and his fear of confrontation—may have increased his power over the Senate, it lessened the influence of the Senate on the country.

Under Johnson's reign, floor debate was substantially reduced in importance, and with it, the role of the Senate in foreign policy. Again we must acknowledge an institutional evolution toward increased executive authority in foreign policy. Yet in the decades before, Congress had felt free to debate—often along partisan lines—to oppose, and occasionally to act against the president's foreign policy. Since then, the felt requisites of unity in the difficult period of the cold war had worked to reduce open debate. But Johnson led in a time of peace, in a time when the Senate might have—as Senator Joseph Clark repeatedly suggested—moved to increase its supply of information without threatening executive authority. But Johnson refused, preferring always to resolve issues by private compromise followed by public agreement, and thus contributed to the general weakening of the Senate's role.

And once the traditional responsibilities were abandoned, there was little move to reclaim them. Because Senate constituencies had little interest in most matters of foreign policy, the most important incentive to action was missing. And the irony was that Johnson's own performance in the presidency would itself be seriously influenced by this weakening of the Senate—by reducing an important check that might well have constrained his decisions on Vietnam in ways helpful to him as well as to his country.

The Presidency

In 1963 Johnson entered an arena vastly different from the Senate. Yet for the first twelve months the circumstances of the transition period and the election allowed him to conduct his presidency in a manner consistent with his previous efforts to acquire and exercise power.

Upon his succession to the presidency, Johnson confronted a dual problem: he had to guide the country through a traumatic and uncertain moment and work to ensure his nomination at the Democratic Convention, which was only eight months away.

The course he chose to meet the first objective—the theme of continuity—was natural to his character and to the need of his time. Moreover, he was helped in this endeavor by the institutionalized process of succession—established by constitutional and historical precedent—which immediately placed in his hands all the powers, institutional authority, symbolic functions, and impressive trappings of the American chief of state—a transfer that was more than a transfer, but rather a replacement thought so necessary and appropriate that not a single dissenting voice marred the population's unquestioning acknowledgment of its legitimacy.

The circumstances of the public mood even allowed Johnson while in the presidency to assume his accustomed role of the faithful follower—this time of the memory of a dead president. Now, unlike the vice-presidency, where he had nothing to give, he could, as he had done with Russell, provide a significant service (the enactment of the dead man's program) and then reap the rewards that would enable him to consolidate his power.

This was possible because he had come into the legislative cycle at the ideal moment for his particular talents. Kennedy had already articulated the goals—most of the issues on Kennedy's agenda were suspended between formulation and approval—leaving the new president the familiar task of mobilizing congressional support.

Moreover, 1964 was a year of relative tranquillity in foreign policy, while the country itself experienced relative economic stability, and there were no serious or turbulent manifestations of domestic distress. Serious and visible crises would have required him to devote attention to unaccustomed responsibilities. In their absence, the enormous resources and elaborate machinery of the modern presidential institution—bureaucracies, established hierarchies of authority and decision, experts, a White House staff large and specialized enough to exercise some form of White House jurisdiction over every activity of importance and make decisions in his name—could ensure that the activities of government were continued, decisions made, foreign leaders placated, etc., without compelling him to divert his attention to unfamiliar matters or to consider and resolve problems unrelated to his immediate objectives: legislative achievement and election.

In the election, too, the circumstances created an ideal situation for Johnson. He had always sought to avoid campaigns based on divisions over issues, trying instead to focus attention on his performance. Now his performance would be the main issue—a transition performance whose circumstances allowed him to combine a deferential dignity with a dazzling display of effectiveness, which brought first relief, then approval and even admiration from the press and the general public. Indeed, his display of large abilities and presidential stature was so significant that he could, even though he had been in office for only a few months, run on the record; and the shortness of his incumbency enabled him to define that record as a demonstration of stature and performance rather than of the substance and directions of his policies, which would obviously be more divisive.

To these conspicuous and influential circumstances was added the nomination of Goldwater, reflecting the culmination of an evolution—a shift part ideological, part geographical—of power within the Republican party. Goldwater's candidacy—his insistence that he was truly ideological, the nature of some of his support for the nomination, and some of his speeches—gave the impression that he wanted to eliminate many of the programs and institutions established in the decades since Roosevelt took office, which had come to be viewed by moderates and many conservatives not as liberal experiments or intrusions but as part of the established order. The same interests who had opposed Social Security and government regulation of business activity had no desire to tear apart a structure they were now accustomed to, had conformed their activities to, and under which, moreover, they were doing better than before.

One can hypothesize a moderate to liberal Republican candidate who could have made a serious issue of Johnson's already expressed intentions and their implication of greatly increased federal activity and spending, who might have accused him of dangerous incapacities in foreign policy, or have debated the Democratic party's intention—already manifested by the actions of Kennedy and Johnson—to reverse Eisenhower's refusal to intervene militarily in Indochina; a debate that would have permitted the Republicans to exploit the public's recollection of Truman and Korea and the vague identification of the Democratic party as the party of war. Instead, however, the Republicans nominated a candidate whose campaign imposed upon his candidacy the most serious traditional vulnerabilities of both parties.

This made possible the kind of campaign most congenial to Johnson's own temperament. His election was in everybody's interest: to the conservative, complacent, or fearful, he was the protector of the system; to a people whose enthusiastic response to the Test Ban Treaty had surprised even Kennedy, he was the man of peace who would meet crises with restraint; to the poor and the blacks, he offered not only understanding but a demonstrated capacity for effective action; to the middle class, he could appear as both a guarantor of increasing affluence and, without seeming inconsistent, as one who understood and would try to alleviate many of the sources of middle-class discontent—the state of the environment, pollution, the conditions of urban life. He was under no compulsion to set forth a coherent program, which might have revealed the difficulties of fulfilling such diverse and often conflicting expectations, whose content and potential consequences would have increased opposition. The unusual conditions of political life in 1964 allowed him to rely, instead, on general statements of purpose, principle, and intention. His opponent not only did not challenge him from the middle, but made *himself* and not Johnson's policies the issue (McGovern was to perform a similar service for Nixon in 1972). Johnson was, therefore, in the fortunate circumstance of being able to combine elements of the kind that contributed to the disparate appeal of both Eisenhower and Roosevelt.

So everywhere he went huge crowds assembled to greet his arrival, attend his movements through the streets. Millions of people he hadn't met, didn't know, whose motives and interests he had not calculated in order to decide how best to impose his will, cheered, almost screaming, often jumping excitedly, in their enthusiasm at his presence. No advance men or organization could have produced such multitudes or intensities. He had accomplished some significant things, but less than several other presidents, far less than he intended, yet he was hailed as if he were a national conqueror. And even if he didn't understand and only half-trusted it, he couldn't get enough of it, traveling from place to place, descending into every crowd, touching the few he could reach as if to reassure himself it was really happening, and more obviously out of an uncontrollable and understandable exuberance. And who could blame him? It was the closest he could come to feeling loved, and who would not express— in his own manner and to the extent he could—exultance at the unexpected approach toward satisfaction of this universal longing?

The election of 1964, both the victory and its size, changed the nature of Johnson's political constituency. The Democratic party itself was no longer a factor in the exercise of power or its renewal. His election left the party apparatus in his hands, and he would soon move to eliminate any remnants of independent authority or access to resources that the Kennedy White House had left intact. As an incumbent, his renomination, if he wanted it, was assured—or so he had every right to assume, and must have assumed. It was, therefore, no longer necessary to direct efforts or policies to cultivate the support of groups because of their potential influence on the party. Their importance to Johnson now depended on their potential influence on the outcome of a national election, and—of more immediate and pressing significance—on the extent to which they could help or obstruct the achievement of his objectives, mostly the passage of legislation.

After the 1964 election, Johnson found himself in command of an institution very different from the institutional and political settings in which he had spent virtually his entire life, and through which he had pursued his ambitions with enormous, if not uninterrupted, success. He had great powers whose acquisition he could now regard as the consequence of his own abilities and that could, therefore, be exercised for his own purposes. However, it is unlikely that he fully understood the extent of the differences in function and structure between the presidency and the earlier settings for his activity and ambition, nor the extent to which presidential powers were not only greater but of a different nature.

In the presidency, unlike in the Senate, the standards of achievement had to be established in relation to accomplishments external to the presidential institution. Here Johnson's own skill and natural inclination, reinforced by the experience of the transition, led him to establish standards of achievement based on his success in designing and enacting a program of domestic reform. Moreover, institutional relationships between the president and Congress required that he must also determine the substance of that program—the general policies and the content of the legislation he would propose. Here Johnson could benefit from the ideas of a liberal tradition institutionalized in his agencies and the Bureau of the Budget, which for twenty years had been proposing legislation that had never passed; now their time had come and they had a ready agenda.

However, neither Johnson's own ambitions and convictions nor the ready agenda would have prevailed under adverse conditions. But in 1965 conditions could not have been more auspicious for domestic reform. Sustained economic growth combined with a relative stability of prices had strengthened a conviction that affluence was inevitable. Moreover, there was still a general desire for the reestablishment of some form of shared national purpose: a sentiment that had formed the theme of Kennedy's successful 1960 campaign. The absence of paramount domestic divisions made it unnecessary for him to take positions that would have aroused the kind of opposition that would have extended beyond the issues themselves to him and his administration. Economic conditions and, even more, established economic expectations made it possible to convince people that the poor and disadvantaged could be helped and that national problems— conditions of urban life, disintegration of the natural environment, transportation facilities, etc.—could be resolved without requiring any group to sacrifice income or significant interests.

Finally, there was the influence of Johnson's own leadership—his natural capacities and unequaled knowledge of Congress, which enabled him to confound the traditional relationship between president and Congress, mixing the two so that both branches were involved in the acts of proposing and disposing. Moreover, the familiar resources of the presidential institution enabled him to provide a great variety of benefits and services that would create obligation and various degrees of dependency. Most importantly, as president Johnson could now bargain directly with leaders of powerful interest groups—business executives, leaders of financial communities, union chiefs, the acknowledged spokesmen for minority groups, etc. As president, he could virtually command their presence, allowing him to exert his formidable personal powers. Even more significantly, every important group in the society was affected by the activities of the federal government, especially by the executive branch Johnson commanded. Thus every encounter also involved an awareness—rarely, if ever, expressed—of mutual interest more direct and specific than their shared patriotism and belief in the American dream. Thus Johnson was able to enlist support, or, at the least, mute potential opposition, from those interest groups whose views could influence the decisions of Congress. They were important, not just because of their wealth or numbers, but because there was no member of Congress whose political base was not subject to the influence of one or more of them. As president, Johnson could thus do what he could not do in the Senate—extend his reach to the foundation and source of office.

Of course, without general public support this would have been to no avail. But the aspect of consensus politics that made effective performance possible was a consensus among a limited number of special groups, whose leaders could be identified, making possible the personal contact that was the medium through which Johnson could make the most effective use of his personal powers and tangible resources—to persuade, convince, bargain, obligate, or coerce. As long as the objective was congressional action—the passage of legislation—the presidential institution enormously increased the effectiveness of behavior that had been successful in other contexts.

In particular, in the area of civil rights Johnson's legacy is clear: his position on racial issues was more advanced than that of any other American president; had he done nothing else in his entire life, his contributions to civil rights would have earned him a lasting place in the annals of history.

But if the modern presidency permitted Johnson an unparalleled authority in domestic affairs for the successful exercise of his qualities and abilities, modes of conduct and methods of exercising power, it also permitted an equally unparalleled failure when those same qualities and patterns of behavior were applied where all Johnson's talents and skills were not merely inadequate but irrelevant and, even more, counterproductive.

Lyndon Johnson did not create the framework within which his country defined its commitment to South Vietnam. That framework, developed in the space of more than twenty years by three previous presidents and their many advisers, rested on a series of assumptions derived from historical experience: the experience of World War II and the events that precipitated it; the initial confrontations between the Soviet Union and the United States; the fear of making concessions to adversary powers; the identification of the potentially dangerous power—the Soviet Union—with the ideology of communism, an identification which required that any political leader or insurgent chief who called himself a Communist was simply an extension of Soviet power.

Of course, experience was not all so one-sided. We had resigned ourselves to the "loss" of Eastern Europe and China, accepted stalemate in Korea, refused to intervene in Indochina; in other words, had shown that our policies, the underlying convictions, and their sometimes violent expression by leaders such as John Foster Dulles had not destroyed our ability to assess realities, and to accept limits imposed by the calculation of practical possibilities.

But the institutional structure Johnson inherited in 1963-1964 narrowed access to the information and perceptions that might have placed Vietnam in one of the above categories. All Johnson's principal advisers agreed on the critical nature of the goal of a non-Communist Vietnam, on the interpretation of the internal struggle as a struggle against communism, and on the possibility of achieving that goal with gradual escalation short of large-scale war.

Clearly, Johnson's own qualities influenced his initial decision to escalate. In domestic affairs, particularly in the passage of legislation, he was used to grasping practical realities first and then adapting his goals to those realities. But his lack of intimate knowledge about foreign policy and Vietnam led him to rely, instead, on the goals and principles themselves, losing sight of the question of available means. The failure to ask "Will it work?" was reinforced by a pristine concept of foreign policy as an arena of choice that should be removed from ordinary political consideration. Therefore his means were subordinated to his ends; his ends *became* his means. Lack of experience and confidence also produced in Johnson an unquestioning acceptance of the "experts'" advice, something he would never have accorded to anyone in domestic affairs. Moreover, Johnson's adversary in Vietnam—unlike nearly all his opponents at home—was unwilling to bargain. Even if Johnson had been able to sit down with Ho Chi Minh, there was nothing to talk about so long as the goals of the two countries remained irreconcilable. So, faced with a situation he could not control and an adversary who was unwilling to bargain, Johnson would force him to bargain. And since he could not compel in his usual way—the denial of rewards or necessities—he was forced to act more directly, in this case with the only instrument of compulsion he had: military force. And, given his character, that force would be exercised in graduated degrees (thus avoiding the even more uncontrollable situation of all-out war).

To say Johnson's qualities were expressed in the decision to escalate is not, however, to say that his character caused that decision. On the contrary, in late 1964 and early 1965, as we have seen, all the relevant elements of the governing process moved in the same direction, making it impossible to filter out the particular weight of personality. Indeed, given the momentum, the necessity of choice—since at this point not choosing would have meant turning South Vietnam over to the Communists—and the consistency of advice from almost every corner, it is easy to imagine many other presidents, acting under very different internal compulsions, making the same decision.

The influence of Johnson's personality on the decision making in Vietnam is easier to observe in his conduct of the war—in the decision to conceal its nature and extent from the American people. Here the advice was not unanimous; indeed, most of Johnson's principal advisers recommended a different course from the one Johnson chose, urging him to go to the Congress, declare a state of emergency, and put the economy on a wartime footing. Johnson refused, opting instead to hide the costs of the war in the Defense Department budget, keeping the pretense of a peacetime economy, and letting the public know as little as possible about the nature and extent of the war—all of which he assumed would allow the Great Society to continue on course.

This decision was Lyndon Johnson's decision. It is easy to imagine another president, less concerned with domestic reform, more capable of choosing between goals, less confident of his ability to move in contradictory directions at the same time, less experienced in the arts of secrecy, deciding differently. Indeed, this decision seems almost to sum up the character of the man. The very qualities and experiences that had led to his political and legislative success were precisely those that now operated to destroy him. His tendency to resolve conflict instead of accepting it—responsible for his rise to power and his success in the Senate—now led him to manipulate and orchestrate the political process in order to shape a formula that could accommodate both the Great Society and Vietnam. Years of experience in gaining and exercising power had taught Johnson that the leader could move in contradictory directions at the same time as long as he compartmentalized everything he did and kept his dealings with one group secret from those with the next. Finally, the bipartisan tradition in foreign policy, responsible for producing consensus behind World War II and the Marshall Plan, now led to the conclusion that complicated decisions of foreign policy should be left in the hands of the leaders; the people would only be hurt by knowing too much.

As it turned out, however, the people were not hurt by knowing too much; Lyndon Johnson was hurt by knowing too little. The loss of public debate on the war lessened the possibilities of judgment, depriving Johnson of the chance to test various responses to different policies and of the opportunity to dispel misconceptions. Nor, in the absence of any clear understanding of the goals in Vietnam, could he expect to sustain the public's support.

He had hoped that a middle course at home and abroad would secure his place in history as a leader of war and a leader of peace. Instead, halfway measures on both fronts produced a condition of half-war and half-peace which satisfied no one and created resentments on all sides.

Moreover, the failure to increase taxes produced inflation, which produced, in turn, a squeeze on moneys for the Great Society instead of the steadily expanding supply of resources Johnson had originally promised. (At this stage of the Great Society, the difficulties Johnson experienced on questions of implementation were similar in nature to those that plagued him on Vietnam. Here, too, because he was so sure of the ends and because the persons involved in implementing the means were so far away, he underestimated the problems of making his programs work.) Furthermore, diversion from the Great Society was not only a question of economic resources; the war drained time, energy, and attention as well.

As the Great Society crumbled and the war continued with no end in sight, Johnson's popularity began to drop. The effective performer was no longer performing effectively, and once that measure of favorable judgment was gone, there was nothing else on which to base his relations with the people—except all those qualities he had never trusted: public advocacy, personal integrity, credibility.

Gradually, and for almost the first time, Johnson now found himself amid events and men he could not master: Vietnam and the Kennedys, and, later, the press, Congress, and even the public whose

approval was all he could experience of love. One could have anticipated the result. As his defenses weakened, long-suppressed instincts
broke through to assault the carefully developed skills and judgment
of a lifetime. The attack was not completely successful. The man was
too strong for that. Most of Johnson—the outer man, the spheres of
conscious thought and action—remained intact, for most of the time.
But in some ways, increasingly obvious to his close associates, he
began to crumble; the suspicions congenital to his nature became
delusions; calculated deceit became self-deception, and then matters
of unquestioned belief.

Moreover, Johnson was aided—or, more accurately, hurt—in this
process of deception by the nature of the institutional relationships
around him. The White House itself—as opposed to the Senate—was
not manned by individuals with independent political bases and formal authority. Here Johnson was in command, and, expectedly, the
coercive aspects of his nature manifested themselves. He could impose his will much more directly upon colleagues—members of his
staff and of his cabinet—whose positions and power within the government rested primarily on him. Of course, he, in turn, depended on
the abilities of these men, but that meant that the only hold they had
was the right to resign. And it was not much of a hold. For Johnson
knew that few men easily relinquished their high positions in government. Both Johnson and his subordinates knew that resignation
involved forfeiting recognized status and power in return only for
escape. Under these conditions, the independence of the cabinet
members and of those in charge of the most important White House
functions was gradually reduced. The president's will, once expressed, was not challenged. Advisers began to anticipate his reactions before they said or did anything; self-deceptions multiplied in
this hall of distorting mirrors. The more Johnson's energies turned to
his critics, the more obsessed he became with the need to discredit his
opponents, the less anyone tried to stop him.

Nor did the president have to listen to the Congress so long as it
continued, out of tradition, habit, and deference, to appropriate funds
for the war, and so long as it refused to take a single vote on the war
itself. Nor—for three years—did any other external force break
through. Surrounded by the White House staff, cocooned in an institutional framework protecting him from the outside world (his schedule,
secretaries, planes, and cars), Johnson effectively insulated himself
from information he did not want to hear.

But there was a limit to Johnson's insulation and his self-defeating
belief in the possibility of turning the corner in Vietnam. The Tet
offensive and the presidential primaries changed the framework
within which Johnson had to work. Finally, the checks and balances
of the political system came back into play.

Forced to confront a precipitous drop in his public standing, a sharp shift in editorial reaction, and the loss of support from key interest-group leaders, Johnson finally accepted the fact that he was in a situation he could no longer control and that further escalation would produce only more uncontrollability. Faced at the same time with loss of love and gratitude on what seemed an irretrievable scale, Johnson had no choice but to withdraw. Nor did he have any choice but to believe, since he had to believe it in order to survive, that eventually his withdrawal would make possible even more control over and more love from history—the only constituency that really mattered in the end.

Conclusions

Lyndon Johnson's public career, with the exception of a single election defeat, was one of uninterrupted and unparalleled success in the accumulation of power and—although with less consistency—in the use of power to achieve practical results. This implies that varied repositories of public authority share common elements of structure, which are, moreover, relatively resistant to rapid historical change. Our examination of Johnson's leadership proved to be a study not only of particular institutions but of attributes and vulnerabilities which are common to several institutions, and which, therefore, probably derive from the more comprehensive institutional processes of politics and government.

I offer these general observations more by way of suggestion than conclusion, but useful, perhaps, in framing questions that might enable us to understand better the relationship between leaders and the qualities of leadership, events and historical circumstances, and institutional structure. I offer these as only a few possibilities. The reader hopefully will see many more.

First: Different institutions reward different qualities—although what constitutes "reward" depends not only on the institution but upon the nature of the individual leader's ambitions. Neither John Kennedy nor Richard Nixon wanted to become a great Senate leader; to them the Senate was a useful platform, though not the only one possible, to advance their careers. Of equal importance, the abilities and characteristic modes of conduct of both men kept them from attempting to become powerful Senate leaders, and would have kept them from accomplishing such an objective.

Johnson, on the other hand, in psychic nature, modes of conduct, and natural abilities, possessed all the qualifications required by the structure in the Senate as it existed at a particular moment for becoming an enormously powerful leader. The institution rewarded his qualities, and that reward was the object of his ambitions. Of course, he, too, had higher aspirations. But his qualities, forms of conduct, the demands and fears that were an aspect of his nature seemed to foreclose other routes. He had to depend, as he always had, upon effective performance—which meant controlling his institutional environment. He was further restrained by the fact that this performance not only was his means of advancing his ambition but was also an end in itself, and he was not capable of risking it for actions that might seem to enhance his chances for more significant power in another institution.

In fact, the qualities the Senate rewarded were not adapted to the institutional process of presidential nomination nor, probably, to that of presidential election, for it was unlikely that Johnson could have moved from majority leader to election as president on his own.

Not only do institutions reward different qualities, but their demands are often contradictory. The same qualities and capacities that make success probable in one setting may be inconsistent with success in another setting. Johnson was fortunate that conditions in 1964 and 1965 permitted him to use many of the abilities and qualities with which he had mastered the legislative process to conduct his presidency with some success. However, when circumstances changed, these capacities proved ill-suited to the presidency, which was a vastly different institution. He could not lead or inspire the nation by secret deals; he did not understand foreign policy; he could not deal with conflicts taking place in a setting where he could not establish personal detailed knowledge of the problems and the participants; and the same search for control that gave such force and direction to his legislative career caused him now to move toward coercive action and to transform the executive branch into a personal instrument, and a weapon for concealing facts and policies from other branches of government and the people.

Of course, Johnson was unique, as was his career. However, that career suggests that many of the qualities that make for success in the legislative branch—compromise, avoidance of conflict, secrecy, the effort to submerge personal responsibility for success or failure in a collective body, the vision of law as the end of the process, etc.—may be contradictory to those required for effective national leadership: indeed, that a career in the legislative process may inculcate modes of behavior or strengthen existing qualities inconsistent with the nature of the presidential institution. This conjecture, which I believe to be true, is of special importance at a time when the Congress has become a significant platform for presidential candidates.

However, it demonstrates the fact that talent for public life is not a unity, but that there are distinct, often contradictory, talents, which are relevant to success in one area of public life and not in another. This is important in assessing not only whether a leader is likely to achieve his ambitions in a particular setting, but—more significantly—whether his leadership to likely to benefit or damage the country.

Second: Johnson demonstrated hitherto unsuspected powers in the executive branch. There was, as many have observed, a growing evolution toward concentration of power in that branch. However, Johnson did not merely continue this evolution. He gave it a new dimension. Previous evolution had rested on changing circumstances, e.g., federal intervention in economic policy and problems of public welfare, the growing significance of foreign policy, the size of the defense establishment, involvement in war, etc. For the most part, this expanding power was exercised with the knowledge and acquiescence of Congress and the informed public. Johnson discovered that the resources of the presidency allowed him to conceal much of the exercise of power; that presidential authority could be exerted on the basis of undisclosed information and the private interpretation of information; indeed, that in many cases even presidential actions and decisions could be concealed. Of course, the effect of many such decisions would eventually become visible, thus revealing the decision itself. But not all. Moreover, concealment of the decision-making process shut out the opportunity for public discussion that is an essential part of the institutional process in our representative democracy. Johnson's actions became known because they were directed toward public goals, their objectives were of a public nature, and, hence, their effects would inevitably be revealed. Nixon illustrated how this power of concealment could be used for other kinds of objectives so that the probability of continuing concealment was increased. The development or discovery of a capacity to exercise substantial executive power in secret is not simply an increase in the power of the presidency; it represents a change in the relationship of institutions within the constitutional framework, a change which, in some part, has the potential of moving the presidential institution outside the framework itself.

Third: This aspect of institutional change, developed under Johnson, and reinforced by the fate of the Nixon administration, suggests that the most effective checks on presidential power are not the institutions that form the constitutional system of "checks and balances." They are the media and public opinion, catalyzed, in Johnson's case, by the presidential primaries. In both administrations these nongovernmental institutions were more effective restraints on presidential actions and usurpations than established governmental institutions.

Fourth: Johnson's career also helps to reaffirm the significance, probably the necessity, of consensus politics to effective presidential leadership. Historically, the only exceptions have been under special conditions—depression under Roosevelt, shifts and growth of population under Jackson—which produced large popular majorities whose interests were opposed to those protected by the dominant structure of economic and political power. Jefferson, after all, moved to placate the Federalists, even at the cost of disappointing some of his Republican followers, while Theodore Roosevelt took steps to placate his business supporters even while establishing a reputation as a trust buster. Johnson, however, showed that consensus could be a foundation for an extensive program of domestic reform even at a time when there were no serious class hostilities nor any economic crisis. That accomplishment requires a modification of what is meant by "consensus," or, rather, a recognition that the term is susceptible to different definitions. Eisenhower's consensus consisted of the fact that a large popular majority was satisfied with his policies, and no substantial proportion of the population was urging him in another direction. Under Johnson as well, there was no significant movement for domestic reform (with the exception, for a time, of the civil rights movement). He himself was the initiating force. Admittedly, the absence of serious division, and favorable economic conditions, made it possible for him to initiate such a program. However, he also saw that consensus did not require him to marshal public enthusiasm and support. He would achieve consensus among groups of special interests and concerns, usually organized and with identifiable leaders, who could influence congressional action directly. And each program required a different kind of appeal to different kinds of groups. By persuading religious and educational associations, he could remove obstacles to a program for aiding education. Certain programs of public welfare required union support and the willingness of business groups to, at least, withdraw opposition. Thus, in a manner similar to the way in which he imposed his will in the Senate, he constructed a consensus from an assembly of particular groups and interests, most of them led by individuals with whom he could deal directly. He created an interlocking web of services and obligations. Finally, many were willing to support particular programs about which they had reservations because they believed that, on the whole, Johnson's program was good for them and for the country. It was a pluralistic consensus, an agreement among groups of limited, often contradictory interests. This consensus, Johnson knew, would shape the actions of Congress. Popular support, that other form of consensus, would be a consequence of achievement, not its source.

We cannot determine, however, the extent to which Johnson had developed a method for public action that can be applied in other situations, and how much its effectiveness depended upon his unique qualities and capacities. And of course, events during the last years of his administration showed that even a consensus built on majority support and the desire for action cannot survive serious public divisions.

Fifth: Johnson's career also provides further evidence that the basic qualities of a leader do not change when he assumes new and larger responsibilities. It is more a metaphor than an accurate description to say, for example, that a man "grows" in office. Of course, individuals do learn from experience—some better than others, and some become more skillful. But basic abilities, ambitions grounded on inner needs, modes of conduct, and inclinations of behavior are deeply and permanently embedded. It may be that these qualities cannot be displayed in a particular setting, or are not suited to achievement within a particular institutional framework and/or under certain historical conditions; yet in another place they can be the basis of accomplishments and actions that others would not have anticipated. One thinks of Truman. Or it may be that the widened constituency of the presidency allows a broadening of goals. Yet, while Johnson's landslide victory did stretch his aspirations, it did not change the essential elements of his behavior. Even his possession of the most powerful office in the country did not diminish his need to extend control or increase his capacity to deal with certain kinds of conflict or resistance. All his newly acquired ability to command did not reduce his drive to coerce. And under the right conditions, these qualities, which many had seen in him previously, were bound to emerge. And just as great office could magnify, if not change, his strength, so it could disastrously extend the consequences of his flaws. So, too, we discovered that the new Nixon was the old Nixon with much more power.

Therefore, the best evidence of what can be expected of a candidate for high office—especially the presidency—can better be found in an examination of his pattern of activity at other stages of his public life than in his statements or goals, and particularly in situations of stress, when he was confronted with difficult decisions that were bound to affect his ambitions, his leadership, and his concept of himself.

Sixth: The dilemma of the modern presidency is not as simple as the contemporary talk of the imperial president suggests. Admittedly, the presidential institution has widened in power, as has the capacity of the president to concentrate that power in his own hands—a consequence less of tyranny than of the steady weakening of the various institutions designed to check the president—the cabinet, the Congress, and the party. But the same centralization of resources that allows an almost unconstrained initiation of policies in some areas (the making of war and peace) and the exercise of almost unilateral authority in others (the dropping of bombs) incapacitates implementation of both domestic and foreign programs and eventually weakens the president's ability to lead. With a weakened cabinet, the president has less chance of controlling his vast bureaucracy; with a shattered party and diminished Congress, he is unable to command that restrained public support essential for the continued viability of both his policies and his leadership. Thus the concentration of resources is at once enabling and constricting; the analytical problem is to understand not only where the president is too strong but also where he is too weak; to delineate what is meant by strong and weak and to describe the curious relationship between the two.

Seventh: The president's ability to focus national attention upon his every word and deed—which is made possible, and almost inescapable, by the nature of the national media—is a source of both power and illusion. And the same can be said of the enlarged White House staff and the use of a technological apparatus unparalleled in history. For five years, between 1963 and 1968, Lyndon Johnson dominated public life in Washington to such an extent that the cabinet was *his* cabinet, the Great Society *his* program, the Congress *his* instrument. With every technological innovation at his disposal, he could tape his own television shows, tell his pilots ten thousand miles away where and when to bomb, talk with the Soviet premier on a moment's notice, and fly around the world in less than two days. But the man in the center when things are good remains in the center when things go bad, and the resources technology provides are often illusory, substituting the sense of control for real control. Thus the war in Vietnam became Lyndon Johnson's war; he personally was dropping the bombs, disrupting the economy, making prices rise, setting back the progress of black and poor. Obviously, neither image—villain or hero—is valid; historical circumstances and institutional conditions were vital to both success in the Great Society and failure in Vietnam. And this understanding is of more than intellectual interest, for exaggeration of the president's personal powers (both self-induced and media propelled) is an inevitable source of frustration as the president's actions invariably fall short of expectations, producing a destructive cycle for the man, the office, and the nation.*

*This article is based primarily on extended conversations I held with Lyndon Johnson about his childhood and his political career and on Johnson's personal papers.

7. Presidential Autocracy in America

F. G. Hutchins

The tyranny of the legislature is really the danger most to be feared, and will continue to be so for many years to come. The tyranny of the executive power will come in its turn, but at a more distant period.

Thomas Jefferson, *letter to James Madison, March 15, 1789.*

The American Presidency has today become the "tyranny" that Jefferson foresaw. The executive branch, the Cinderella of the Constitution of 1789, which fell into such disrepute and inconsequence in the nineteenth century that Lord Bryce felt compelled to explain "Why Great Men Are Not Elected President," has in the twentieth century come into an inheritance greater than that ever enjoyed by her two sister branches of government.

The triumph of the Presidency was accomplished without constitutional alteration, because the federal government, from the beginning, was a system of separation of power, but fusion of function. Each of the separate branches of government—the Congress, the Presidency, the Supreme Court—was assigned legislative, executive, and judicial functions. The "strengthening of the Presidency" has resulted not simply from the growth in the importance of executive authority in an increasingly complex, developed society, but, more importantly, from the fused growth of the legislative, executive, and judicial authority of the Presidency. This has not appeared to involve usurpation of functions from the other two branches, because the constitutional framework did give the Presidency a foothold in all three areas from which to develop.

The image of the President as an elective monarch had been present in the minds of the Founding Fathers from the beginning. Monarchy—enlightened or otherwise—was the normal pattern of governance in the eighteenth century, and the availability of a suitable candidate in the person of George Washington made the notion of elective monarchism—articulated most forcefully by Alexander Hamilton—the pattern of the constitutional Presidency. This idea, latent in the Constitution, never died completely. For the time being, however, the expansion of presidential power was eclipsed in 1801, when Jefferson, a presidential minimalist, succeeded Adams. Jefferson was effective as President, but his *purpose* as President was to further the independence of individuals rather than to establish and consolidate an autocratic form of government.

Lincoln expanded the powers of the Presidency in practice; but this expansion did not survive, because Lincoln did not develop a rationalization for the retention of these expanded powers. Lincoln expanded his powers because the nation was threatened by an emergency; he increased the *executive* powers of the Presidency because decisions needed to be centralized in wartime. Lincoln was willing to do almost anything to save the Union. But the Union Lincoln wanted to save was a land of free yeomen, and in this land there was no room for an institutionalized monarchy. Lincoln viewed his actions as extraordinary. He took extreme measures under the press of circumstances without trying to build these actions into permanent presidential prerogatives, and without conducting himself as licensed, in his representative capacity, to articulate newly discovered general principles. The Emancipation Proclamation was viewed as exceptional by Lincoln himself, and its moralistic phraseology was urged upon him by others.

The methodical consolidation of presidential supremacy required more than monarchical instincts or the *de facto* expansion of powers under the press of emergency. The institutionalization of presidential supremacy required a theory, and this was not developed until the twentieth century, when the Progressives concluded that the President could wield best all three of the traditional functions of government.

The legislative, executive, and judicial powers of the President have not only been expanded but also used to justify one another. Enthusiasts stress the representative character of the Presidency; the role of presidential leadership in foreign and domestic affairs; and the judgmental power of the President, who, because of his special representativeness and responsibilities, as well as his special advantages of position and access to advice, is able to arbitrate issues in a uniquely judicious way. The Presidency, in short, is three branches in one. The definition that the Presidency gives to each of these functions is not, however, identical with the definition of these functions traditionally upheld by the other branches. The President's apologists have defined the prime functions associated with the other branches in ways that make it appear that the President is better suited to pursue them than the originally constituted branch.

The most grandiose conception of the President's representativeness was that first articulated by Woodrow Wilson, that the President represents all the people. If the Presidency could be made to seem more truly representative of the "people" than was the Congress, where arguably only "interests" were represented, then the Presidency could, in the name of the people, exercise ultimate power with righteous vigor. If the President really, effectively represents everybody, then the Congress, in opposing the President, may seem to represent nothing more than selfishness. Legislators have themselves helped strengthen this impression by their willingness to accept a role as little more than lobbyists for their constituents, exerting influence in the bureaucratic labyrinth on behalf of their constituents, thereby appearing, in fact, to represent nothing that cannot be rightfully subordinated to a larger national interest. If the President is the only true representative institution, or even only a representative institution that is somewhat preferable to Congress, there is logically no reason why the President should feel bound by Congress; the moral pressure, indeed, moves in the opposite direction.

In 1885, Woodrow Wilson, in his book *Congressional Government*, argued that America needed majestic leadership, and that Congress was not supplying it. At this time, with the power of the American President at its nadir, and with the brilliant parliamentary duels of Gladstone and Disraeli fresh in Wilson's mind, the remedy for the sorry state of Congress that recommended itself to Wilson was a form of cabinet government for America on the British model. It was only later, after Theodore Roosevelt had demonstrated in practice the Presidency's potential as a platform for strong leadership, that Wilson finally found the proper solution for America. In 1908, he paired his denunciation of Congress with a eulogy for the President:

> The nation as a whole has chosen him, and is conscious that it has no other political spokesman. His is the only national voice in affairs. Let him once win the admiration and confidence of the country, and no other single force can withstand him, no combination of forces will easily overpower him. His position takes the imagination of the country. He is the representative of no constituency, but of the whole people. When he speaks in his true character, he speaks for no special interest. If he rightly interprets the national thought and boldly insists upon it, he is irresistible; and the country never feels the zest for action so much as when its President is of such insight and calibre.[1]

The Wilsonian conception of the Presidency has triumphed far beyond Wilson's wildest imaginings. The President, representing all the people, can act in his executive capacity in response to his representative capacity. He need not think of himself as the executive of Congress; he is the executive of the people. He does not need a law upon which to base his actions. Actions can be justified by reference to the President's "constitutional powers," which means, in effect, his direct representativeness. In 1973, President Richard M. Nixon, for example, defended his bombing of Cambodia as an exercise of his "inherent authority" as Commander in Chief and pointed to his re-election margin of 1972 to refute the apparent constitutional requirement of congressional authorization for military initiatives. Originally, the President's constitutional powers meant little more than the power to enforce the laws approved by Congress. Being Commander in Chief did not seem initially a license to use force if the President, exercising his personal judgment, deemed it necessary. Now, the President's constitutional power is defined to mean the power to make and enforce decisions in response to a direct popular mandate. Congress is frequently urged to pass laws that amount to little more than the authorization of administrative discretion in new areas. Many other laws passed by Congress contain saving clauses stating that they can be set aside by the President in response to some "emergency." The President, in fact, is considered derelict by the public if he does not himself initiate the bulk of legislation placed before Congress. The President may use Congress's laws with discretion and further has innumerable direct discretionary powers.

Most recent presidents have seemed to take literally the Wilsonian aspiration to "represent all of the people all of the time." John F. Kennedy, however, while still a senator, defended the election of the President by the Electoral College against the proposal that the College be abolished in order to ensure a more representative Presidency, on the grounds that the President represented the industrial North to a greater extent than other parts of the country, under the present arrangement, and that this was desirable because other parts of the country were better represented in other parts of the government. Because Congress was a stronghold of Southern strength, the slight advantage the North had in the contest for the Presidency was important to preserve, in Kennedy's eyes. This argument implied a conception of representation that included the entire government, in which the Presidency was seen as a competing representative institution representing a part of the whole, while the Congress represented another part.

While few presidents have advanced such an explicit argument as Kennedy made, all presidents feel representative of a primary constituency as well as of the people as a whole. One's primary constituency may be only characterized vaguely as the "forgotten man" or the "silent majority," or its existence may be denied altogether. The significant consideration, however, is that the direct, fractional representativeness of the President is not thought to make it impossible for him to be, when necessary, also the representative of all. The President may feel that the better half of the nation that supports him is also more representative of the nation's future, and that, in responding to it, he is thereby responding to the interests of all, properly and prospectively defined.

The representativeness of the Presidency is inherent and desirable. What and whom the President actually represents are important and affect the decisions he makes. It is consequently possible to argue about the impact of the President's constituency on his decisions. The President's ability, in individual cases, to decide whether or not to act as a representative of his constituency, and to alter the definition of the group he will consider himself representative of, suggests the other half of the story: The President is a representative not only of the people but also of the inherent power of the Presidency in his dealings with the people.

The complexity of the meaning of the Presidency, answerable and yet not answerable to the people, is similar to the complexity inherent in the medieval concept of dual sovereignty, according to which sovereignty resided both in the King and in the people. The King was both God's representative on earth and the representative of all the people. The "confusion" of legal texts on the issue of sovereignty, as perceived by later, more logical generations, was no more than the confusion of reality, a complex balance in which neither the King nor the people claimed exclusive rights. It was only the eventual breakdown of this confused but viable system that necessitated the location of sovereignty in either King or Commons, in the seventeenth century. The medieval King ruled by virtue of his divine position, but only in the way in which a divinely sanctioned monarch was supposed to rule. Beyond the bounds of conventionally sanctioned behavior, the King might seem to be acting nakedly, without the divinity that hedged him—but also hedged him in. The people could not rule without the King, but a bad King could be replaced, though, of course, only to be followed by another King.[2]

The people might have a role in protesting the conduct of the King, or the state of the kingdom, but once the act of confirming a new King had been completed, the people were expected to settle down and watch the new King address himself to the country's problems. The people could hope that the new King would remedy their problems and be different from his predecessor, but all they could do was wait and see. And the active process of selecting a new King determined nothing about the set of personal advisers he might choose—quite possibly the same ones who had surrounded his hated predecessor.

The new King might have witnessed the old King's fate but have concluded that the hatred directed against him was now expended and that it would be safe for him to act in precisely the same way— certainly safe for a period.

The practice in America is not too different. The President is chosen by the people, more or less, and can be removed by the normal process of election, by the extraordinary process of impeachment and conviction for high crimes and misdemeanors, or by the illegal action of assassination. Once chosen, however, he is the President. There is only one President at a time. Certain things can be done only by presidents. Thus, as in the Middle Ages, the exercise of popular sovereignty is circumscribed.

The American people are involved in the exhausting process of substituting one President for another. But the range of substitutes available is limited, and the degree of popular control that can be exercised on the President in the day-to-day performance of his duties is also limited. The new President may choose as his deputies the same people, or the same kind of people, used by his predecessor. The Constitution provides that the Senate, representing the people, should have a role in the screening of presidential advisers, but even the formality of Senate confirmation is now frequently evaded by the utilization of special presidential assistants not subject to Senate approval for duties once performed by Cabinet officers.

Some feel that the President, though freed from most congressional and popular restraints, is nonetheless still effectively controlled by the groups who helped put him in office. This is true only with qualification. Presidential candidates are selected by powerful coalitions in American society who hope to sustain their power by association with a person who may become the legitimate President of all Americans. Every four years competing coalitions offer alternative candidates, and the acquisition of the largest number of votes is accepted as proof of constitutional legitimacy. The President is then able, if he acts with circumspection, to dispense with the services of the coalition behind him. Once in office the office is his, and he belongs to the office, not to his backers. Only the sustained opposition of the nation as a whole—not the withdrawal of the support of his backers—can bring him down. He is now motivated by his own sense of who he is—a person placed in a historic office who will be judged in retrospect in terms of his ability to radiate the full majesty of that office. The President tries to act as the legitimate spokesman of an entire people. As a spokesman, he speaks not only to the people but also to history. By history, he means the court of future public opinion that will assign him his rank. Speaking to the court of history, the President is speaking to his own moral conscience, to his own conviction that certain values will be shared by future generations. In speaking for the people, the President also hopes to retain his legitimacy in the eyes of the present generation of voters, from whom he must secure re-election.

Being above politics is the best, the only politics for a legitimate President. If being above politics means that the President must dissociate himself from some of those who put him in office, he will do so.

Once installed, a President is hedged by the divinity of his office. Although selected by a coalition and elected by the people, once sworn in he is also the representative of the Constitution, from which stems the presidential line. The President must safeguard the source of his legitimacy by identifying himself with his precursors in this office, an office which only its holders, so they say, can understand. By convention there are areas in which the President's sole responsibility is respected; in recent decades, foreign policy has been championed as one such. By convention there are other areas—primarily domestic—in which the President is conceived as relatively helpless. In these areas, continual defeats for the President will not damage his dignity, because here the dual sovereignty of the people is recognized. The people, through Congress, have a right to settle directly for themselves certain matters affecting their fate, just as the President has a right to the unfettered exercise of his power in certain other matters, not so directly affecting people in his country. When the President ventures beyond the hedge of his office, he is naked. Defeats within the hedge will not damage his image; victories beyond it may be ruinous.

The Presidency's insulation from popular pressure in specified areas has not discouraged presidents from trying to expand their room for maneuver by pushing the hedge of their divinity outward. Presidents, like others, create wishing worlds. Presidents may find themselves, for example, tantalized by the thought that the deference they inspire in a self-selected circle of sycophants abroad might be replicated at home.

A supposedly representative leader is naturally interested in appearing to be responding to "demands" in taking a given action, even if this means orchestrating the demands to order. If a demand comes from a source beyond the immediate familiarity of those the President is addressing, they will not know how to refute the assertion that a demand has been received from this other source. A President may make a claim to be responding to invisible parts of the electorate or to the higher imperatives of the office he holds, just as he may pretend to be responding to foreign obligations—and to have no choice but to do so. A President elected in the purest democratic manner with no evident way of pretending to be the representative of any group other than the electorate will be tempted to build up foreign alliances to create obligations to which he may respond if he wishes to act in opposition to a popular mandate. Such obligations, the electorate will be told, are obligations of the presidential office, and hence of the nation as a whole; failure to fulfill them would disgrace the nation. In reality, they may have been created by presidential pump-priming and may be used to disguise arbitrary actions the President wishes to take for his own purposes.

Presidents who grasp the potential of their office have seldom had difficulty being re-elected, even if opposed on specific issues by a majority of the people. The President can easily hold out against transitory opposition. A President may not even claim to represent more than a plurality; even if he claims to represent the people as a whole, he will not think of himself simply as their representative, with no choice but to bend to every public pressure. The President thinks of his representativeness as an attribute compatible with, but subordinate to, his other attributes, as leader and rational decision-maker. The President, as a representative institution, wants to be representative enough to be re-elected; but as an executive institution, he wishes to do grand things worthy of his office.

Montesquieu contended that the governing principle of a constitutional monarchy is honor, whereas that of a republic is virtue. The leader of a republic, Montesquieu suggested, is satisfied with the existence in it of many individually virtuous men. A monarchy, whether elective or hereditary, is concerned with grandeur, with putting all its subjects to tasks of appropriate magnitude, with justifying the awe in which it is held abroad by acting in accordance with the dignity of its power.[3] In advocating a step-up in military activity in Vietnam, presidential adviser McGeorge Bundy, for example, argued that America's power imposed an obligation. In a memorandum to President Lyndon B. Johnson written on February 7, 1965, Bundy noted "that in all sectors of Vietnamese opinion there is a strong belief that the United States could do much more if it would, and that they are suspicious of our failure to use more of our obviously enormous power."[4]

The concentration of power in the President's hands, which has permitted him to indulge in international exploits in a manner befitting a powerful monarch, was first urged, ironically, by liberals attempting to replace conflict for conflict's sake with regulation for regulation's sake. Governing institutions, standing above others, it was felt, would not need to engage in petty competition with those below them and would be able to govern in the interest of all. The Presidency was to be the one place where all competing interests would be viewed from a superior "vantage point," to use Lyndon Johnson's phrase. Since no one had his perspective, no one could be entirely sure that the President's judgment was flawed; everyone consequently ought to be expected to give the President the benefit of the doubt. But the President's liberal eulogists did not succeed in placing above the chaos of competition a single individual who was liberated from the ambitions that drove men placed lower. Rather, they succeeded in elevating a single man driven by the same passions as others into a position in which the only way he could gratify his passions was in a vastly more dangerous arena. The man who was supposed to act in the public interest, because it was at his personal disposal, became a man who could subordinate the public interest to his personal drive for glory. It was, in fact, tempting to the man exalted above others to endeavor to fulfill his particular drive for recognition by utilizing all his citizens in a competition with powerful enemies. James MacGregor Burns has noted that "for a man with Theodore Roosevelt's need for personal fulfillment it was a sort of tragedy that he had no war—not even a Whiskey Rebellion."[5] President Kennedy referred to the week of the Cuban missile crisis as a week in which he "really earned his pay." This was pre-eminently the week in which Kennedy felt that his conception of his proper activity as President of all Americans was fulfilled; the power of all Americans was pitted against a worthy antagonist in a way that permitted him to test his leadership ability. Kennedy saw the Presidency as a position of great power; he defined his personal challenge as the holder of that office as the grasping of opportunities to exemplify "grace under pressure." In planning the strategy of the Vietnam conflict, Lyndon Johnson felt that a large group "with 100 people sitting around was not the place . . . to build a military effectiveness. . . . I want to put it off as long as I can, having to make these crucial decisions. I enjoy this agony."[6]

Ruling, as President, as a neutral arbiter of lower conflicts among his subjects has not afforded equal gratification. Only Dwight D. Eisenhower, of recent presidents, has come close to the conception of a neutral Presidency, and this was clearly a reflection of his life stage, as a man of proved skill in grand combat now in semiretirement.

Montesquieu was right: If you make a man a King, he will begin to think in terms of glory. How could proponents of the enhancement of presidential power not have anticipated that a great leader armed with great discretion would seek glory rather than goodness? They failed to anticipate this result because they had also written into the drama a role for themselves. The President, subordinating representativeness to the imperatives of executive leadership of a great power, in turn was to subordinate executive leadership to the directives of a "rational" decision-making process. A judicious President, exercising discretion wisely, would be guided at every juncture by the expert advisers at his side.

The original purpose of the Constitution was to give necessary power to officials hamstrung by legal strictures. As Herman Melville put it, "If there are any three things opposed to the genius of the American Constitution, they are these: irresponsibility in a judge, unlimited discretionary authority in an executive, and the union of an irresponsible judge and an unlimited executive in one person."[7] The rule of laws, not men, meant that, though men would rule, they could not rule as idiosyncratically as they would wish. Implicit in the contemporary vision of presidential government, in contrast, is a vast role for discretion. Centralized action is obviously more efficient; if it can be claimed that it is also more just, the old fears of the Founding Fathers can be dismissed as out of date.

A judicious President, it is argued, can act with speed and flexibility on the basis of expert advice. Is not the President the best-informed person, the best-situated person to make a decision? Actually, the availability of expert advice has served to isolate the President. Whether advised by an elite of independently accomplished men, or by specialists on his own payroll, the President is trapped by those trying to help him. The President may be the worst-informed person in the country if he is systematically shielded from the normal experience and outlook of citizens. Akbar the Great of India and Henry V of England used to disguise themselves as ordinary men and wander freely among their subjects to learn what was really going on. Surrounded by sycophants and specialists, these monarchs went to their lowly subjects in search of unbiased views on the needs of the kingdom. A President who honors his advisers with the highest possible praise—his trust that their presentation of his country's needs makes him well informed—is the most pathetic of captives, a bear on a string.

The myth of the judicious President is not only factually inaccurate, it is deeply destructive of the character of the occupant of the office. The President, we are told, is a different sort of person from the generality of Americans. As he has a special nature, so he has special duties. He alone, for example, can determine when his political opponents are endangering "national security" and giving "comfort to America's enemies." His special duties necessitate his possession of special privileges—picture phones, jet airplanes, summer and winter palaces, and a prescriptive right to impound the consciences of the highest and lowest members of his realm. The Watergate affair demonstrated graphically that a surprising number of Americans of high patriotism felt unable to refuse a request from the "White House" that they break the law of the land.

A structure wrought to ensure rational decision-making has instead hopelessly entangled private whims with national needs. A President, freed to do as he wishes, is expected to be right; in fact, he is permitted no defense against his own fallibility. He is routinely tempted by the logic of false determinism; having made a decision, he is likely to say, and come to believe, that he had "no choice" but to make the decision he did. George Reedy has argued that, with the possible exception of Franklin D. Roosevelt, recent presidents have been ordinarily unable to profit from their mistakes. In Reedy's view, a person who enters the Presidency with normal, or even above-normal, intelligence and political sensitivity will soon start making political blunders which would make a ward heeler blush.[8] Together, the forces around and within the President are likely to destroy even the elementary political sensitivity of a man who showed enormous subtlety in his march to the throne.

No person can rule without help; no sane person can come to believe he is infallible without frequent testimony to that effect from others. The President is unlikely to experience a rude awakening at the hands of his staff. In fact, the greater effort he makes to surround himself with apparently distinguished, independent, accomplished professionals with standing in their own fields, the greater may be the resulting delusion that their praise is accurate. Independent American intellectuals have offered their services to the President to ensure the rationality of his decisions; ironically, their willingness to serve negates the goal they seek. Their availability feeds the vanity of the President and offers no obstacle to his ability to toy with them for his own purposes, while they remain subject to the delusion that the President values them for their wisdom. A King and his courtiers feed one another's vanity. Pride in servility for the adviser, pleasure in adulation for the King—both are satisfied by a mutually corrupting relationship.

Many observers have been puzzled by the reluctance of the President's "independent" advisers to resign when the President disregards their advice. Yet, if they sense their impotence within the inner circle, they also realize that they would be even more powerless outside of it, capable only of making appeals to "public opinion." A class of notables may put pressure on the person they advise if, as a class, they possess independent bases of power and regulate admission to their class—and if the class is not very large. If a group of would-be advisers lacks cohesion, the task of selecting favorites who will identify with the King rather than the class from which they are drawn will be child's play. A regulating class, such as the barons at Runnymede or, on rare occasions, the British Prime Minister's Cabinet colleagues, even in the best of circumstances, purchases its power of regulation at a high price. It can only perform a restraining function, pinning the King down. It cannot actively advise the King on the positive manner in which he should conduct his affairs in those areas which remain his prerogative. Its preference for defiance is a self-denying ordinance, preventing its accepting a position as a trusted ally of the King. An adviser can only influence an autocrat in a positive manner by presenting himself as a person who presumably advises the autocrat to do what is in his own interest—who claims to be putting the interest of his master above the retention of his class affiliation. He may use his class identity to present himself to the autocrat as an analyst of his class, an interpreter of the way in which it can be best exploited by the autocrat, but he cannot act as a spokesman for his class. In a sense, the most salient question is the simplest: Who rewards his services?[9]

A President needs different sorts of advisers from different backgrounds. A President's advisers are drawn from many sources—business, the professions, politics, the bureaucracy. In their new role, however, they become the President's agents in his dealings with these estates, and they probably will remain in this role, even if they formally return to the estates from which they came. A high government official who returns to his bank or airplane factory or university may well remain informally a member of the President's staff, even though he is now only engaged in a rear-guard action of defending his past actions.

The King's men are not likely to provide him with the corrective advice that might shake his confidence. Even the designation of a devil's advocate within the inner circle may only reinforce the impression that all possible objections have been anticipated and can be coped with. Beyond the circle of presidential appointees, however, there remain the great bureaucratic establishments, which have, on occasion, been portrayed as an immovable "fourth branch of government," fiercely resistant to presidential prodding. In fact, this tenured establishment can only rarely provide a corrective to the President. Bureaucrats have even less independence than private advisers. The bureaucrat is an employee who must look up to the President and his agents as the embodiment of the public interest he has sworn to serve. In this sense, even a merit bureaucracy becomes, to a degree, a personal household staff. The bureaucrats' job is not to analyze reality, but to make their presentation of reality one that will appeal to their superiors. The simple fact that a bureaucrat is right is no guarantee of his credibility in the eyes of his superiors. The bureaucracy is not a class capable of limiting the President's freedom of action; it is a group of servants dependent on his attention.

A sizable bureaucracy is naturally difficult to control, but by making careful appointments and promotions, the President can usually drive opposition underground, whatever the organizational structure of the bureaucracy may be. In dealing with obstructive agency heads, he can threaten the creation of competing policy-making units within the White House. The State Department in recent years, for example, far from "influencing" the President, has had to acquiesce in the concentration of foreign policy–making in the White House. This lesson has not been lost on other bureaucratic establishments. It has seemed far safer to be accommodating than to oppose and then be circumvented. Even those apparently indispensable and autonomous specialized agencies, the CIA and the FBI, have found it difficult to withstand pressure to perform unwelcome tasks set by the White House when threatened with the possible establishment of competing units within the White House. J. Edgar Hoover—a uniquely powerful bureaucratic fixture—did prevent the creation of a White House "crime" unit desired by President Nixon, but lesser men have ordinarily been unwilling to risk their agencies' prospects by defying clear White House preferences. Far from encouraging open deliberation on policy alternatives, the President's elevation has only intensified presidential arrogance and bureaucratic servility.[10]

What, finally, can be said of the effect of the myth of the judicious President on the morale of the public at large? The President's superhuman prerogatives ultimately rest on the assumption that it is in the interest of all of us to have a person who is pure and high-minded, and who consequently must be presented publicly as such even if there are good grounds for believing differently. The feeling persists that something dreadful would happen to all of us, and to the entire structure of government from which we benefit so substantially, if anybody acted publicly on the basis of his private knowledge of the personal character of the President. If all avert their eyes, the President will not be in danger of damaging his image by walking around naked. The myth of the Presidency is the creation of people who know better but who are appalled by the prospect of having to consider the alternatives. We cling to the hope that a person, even though an ordinary man to all appearances, when supplied with a magical apparatus, can bring about a complete change in the entire polity. The irony is, we know that the President's magic is manufactured and maintained by our own efforts and that a man riding on a wish is not really a magician; he is a confidence artist. We supply him with the confidence that makes him look like an artist. You can't fool all the people all the time, but can all the people fool themselves all the time?

The myth of the magical President is of relatively recent origin. The contemporary phenomenon of presidential autocracy was created by the strengthening of one of the three constituted branches of government, a strengthening resulting not from necessity but from choice, the considered preference of idealists for a kind of decision-making that somehow seemed more just because it was made on high by one man. Today many people recognize that the system has not worked as hoped but are uncertain why that is, and how it might be remedied. The most natural response is to assume that there is nothing wrong with the basic approach but that the faults lie in its implementation. The easiest argument is that all that is lacking for the system to function as planned is the right individual. If all our troubles can be said to stem from the tragic unsuitability of the individuals catapulted into office by a series of historical accidents, why is it not reasonable to hope that all will be set right through one more swing of the pendulum?

As in the Middle Ages, so in America today, much political discourse ranges between two poles, from romantic optimism to grim pessimism, from hope for the succession to the throne of a truly good King to tyrannicide. This discourse, as in the Middle Ages, is limited by the assumption that the extent of political change possible is to replace one monarch with another—by natural or surgical means. Such a preoccupation with the possibility that the replacement of one man with another will produce a total transformation in the policy and posture of government is as intense as it would be in any divine-right monarchy; the basis for such a preoccupation is so fragile as to be pathological. Like any entrenched pathology, it is an effort to adjust to the presence in the organism of a searing disease and may consequently be stabilizing in the short run. Since the effort to adjust cannot halt the progress of the disease, however, the effort at adjustment only makes things worse in the long run. Intense hope in the magical transformation that a change of regime will produce turns to appalling disillusionment when that change occurs and nothing happens. The engine of hope is once again revved up. Attention focuses once again on the next succession and the high-minded, pure people whose elevation will make all the difference. And yet, as the cycles of hope and disillusionment expand their duration and intensity, they begin to overlap, and people become increasingly aware of the similarity between the new vain hope and the last blasted hope.

The answer lies not in pursuing the present course to the end but in changing course. Instead of attempting to remove the human need to demonstrate adequacy by wielding power, one should attempt to neutralize the danger of wielding power by restricting the scope of possible conflicts. Placing men above ambition simply releases them from normal restraints and forces them to invent new and more reckless forms of moral testing. To attempt to institutionalize virtue is to guarantee disaster.

The President should be respected for what he is—a man representative of the forces that put him in office—not what it is hoped he may become once in office, through the magic of disinterestedness or the brilliance of his advisers. If the President ceases to pretend that he does not represent some more than others, he will be a more candid, more effective person. He will be less deferential to his predecessors in office, who represented other coalitions, and by his candid partisanship, he will make it easier for ordinary citizens to recognize him for the significant, partial person that he is. A series of presidents with alternating constituencies would make it possible for each President to pursue an active policy of representing primarily the interests of some, with the implicit understanding that others would have their turn. This could be said to be the situation currently in existence in Great Britain, where the representative and executive functions are formally consolidated in one man, the Prime Minister. The Prime Minister, in fact, represents little more than one-half of the electorate, and the country is governed by two halves, each taking turns at the exercise of substantial, directly representative executive power.

A second alternative would be to establish a purer division of legislative and executive power, in which Congress decided policies and the President merely implemented them. Firm lines of division between functions embodied in separate institutions do not offer much promise on the basis of past performance. The classic example of a clear-cut division between executive and legislative bodies is in the meeting of the French Estates-General, which led to the outbreak of the French Revolution. The monarchy and the Estates-General were so completely out of touch that inevitably each was driven to try to govern without resort to the other. First the monarchy tried to get along without the Estates; then the Estates tried to get along without the monarchy. The American system has never been characterized by the separation of legislative and executive powers ascribed to it, and there seems little reason to hope for improvement by making that separation a practical reality. The balance of *power* between legislative and executive branches should be redressed more favorably to Congress, but a viable system would retain fused functions in each of the branches of government. Congress thus should increase its legislative and executive roles, while those of the Presidency should be diminished.

One should be cautious, in strengthening Congress, that one is, in fact, strengthening it in the name of an alternative vision of government functioning. There is an ominous tendency, for example, to speak of the strengthening of Congress by providing congressmen with longer terms and more staff and amenities. It is possible that Congress might, in consequence, be strengthened in relation to the President, and that both these branches would then be even more isolated from the citizenry. Congress should not be strengthened to make it more like the present Presidency; the current appeal of Congress is in the fact that it shares many of the hardships experienced by ordinary citizens. Television viewers of the Senate's Watergate hearings saw a disorderly, contradictory human spectacle—in contrast to the cut-and-dried imperial pronouncements from the closed presidential suite to which the American public had become so accustomed. The Senate's hearings were accessibly, persuasively inefficient.

The main direction of congressional reform should be to bring Congress even closer to the ordinary citizen, by eliminating the rigidities in the internal structure of Congress that make it most representative of the public opinion of twenty or thirty years ago. A strict seniority system for selecting committee chairmen is ludicrous in a body such as the House of Representatives that the Constitution directed should be freshly elected once every two years.

One may safely assume that the main structural outlines of the American political system will remain: that an individual will continue to be selected by powerful coalitions and accepted by the general public as a legitimate ruler because of its minimal role in his final ratification. One may safely assume that the uniqueness of the office will continue to hold a fascination for its occupant, and that he will never be simply a creature of those who put him in a position where he can dispense with their services. There is no great reason to hope for significant change from the assembling of a new coalition of interests for the purpose of putting a new man into this unique office. The only hope of significant change in the nature of presidential conduct lies in the alteration of the expectations a President is supposed to live up to, an alteration in the constraints on his actions in office rather than in the obligations he may assemble on his way to the office. Such constraints would have to be reflected in popular expectations of what a good President would be like. Such expectations would have to be clear and deep enough to impress every President with the belief that they will still be around when history puts him in his place.

What constitutes greatness in a President? Is a great President one who permits the gigantic bureaucracy he heads to occupy itself in vindicating his special privileges and powers? Is a great President one who patterns his personal life and public conduct after those of Louis XIV? Is a great President one who, like monarchs of the past, engages in warfare to preserve personal vanity, to avoid, for instance, being the first President to lose a war? (Countries can usually survive the loss of a war; presidents cannot.) Can one not conceive of a country that insisted that its President did not have a special nature, did not have a special wisdom stemming from his vantage point and number of advisers? Such a country's President would not be permitted to pretend to infallibility; if he spoke with pious smugness or implied that his policy was inevitable, he would be laughed at.

Citizens are too sensible to want to concern themselves all the time with everybody else's business, but the President in Washington should be made aware that citizens want public men directing the polity politically, with the force of argument, not administratively, with the assistance of advertising. Citizens should demand responsible leaders and not settle for covert controllers.

Notes

1. Woodrow Wilson, *Constitutional Government in the United States,* quoted in James MacGregor Burns, *Presidential Government* (Boston: Houghton Mifflin, 1965), p. 96.

2. See Donald Hanson, *From Kingdom to Commonwealth* (Cambridge, Mass.: Harvard University Press, 1970).

3. Baron de Montesquieu, *The Spirit of the Laws,* trans. Thomas Nugent (New York: Hafner, 1962).

4. *The Pentagon Papers* (New York: Bantam Books, 1971).

5. Burns, *op. cit.,* p. 66.

6. *The Pentagon Papers,* p. 496.

7. Herman Melville, *White-Jacket* (New York: Russell and Russell, 1963), p. 178.

8. George Reedy, *The Twilight of the Presidency* (New York: New American Library, 1970). This book provides an excellent insider's account of the "court" atmosphere of the contemporary White House.

9. For a heroic but ultimately unpersuasive effort to formulate a procedure that will encourage "rational" presidential decision-making by a rearrangement of the President's advisory establishment, see Alexander George, "The Case for Multiple Advocacy in Making Foreign Policy," *American Political Science Review,* September 1972.

10. Concerning Hoover's opposition to Nixon, see Nixon's statement, *New York Times,* May 23, 1973. The Watergate hearings turned up elaborate evidence of White House pressure on the CIA and the post-Hoover FBI and of the reluctance of their senior officials to oppose or report to the public illegal requests made by White House aides.

PART THREE

The Institutionalized Presidency Reappraised

8. White House Staffing: The Nixon-Ford Era

Dom Bonafede

It is hardly coincidental that the swelling of the White House staff complex over the last four decades paralleled the growth of the monarchical Presidency: In a symbiotic union, the two fulfill each other's needs and are mutually dependent for their survival.

As government became more pervasive and society more complex, modern presidents, hard pressed to control a meandering federal bureaucracy and sustain their political position, have broadened their area of executive authority and delegated an increasing amount of responsibility to their White House aides. Today, these subordinates represent a new mandarin class within the government hierarchy. Operating under the light of their benefactor, they are endowed with princely powers and privileges. They stand as both a symbol and reflection of the President. They act in his image. They revel in his glory. If necessary, they take refuge under his protection. Neither elected nor confirmed, they are entrusted with jurisdictional domains over which they exert more influence than all but the most powerful department heads and members of Congress. Their prestigious rank was perceived long ago by Charles Dawes, the first Budget Director, who wrote in his diary that he told President Franklin D. Roosevelt, "If I could take any office I would not want the position of Secretary of Treasury but that of an assistant secretary to the President."*

*Recognition of the influence of presidential aides is not an exclusive manifestation of the modern Presidency, as commonly believed. A July, 1902, issue of *World's Work* magazine carried an article on "The President's Business Office," which noted, "The Secretary to the President accordingly is now regarded in Washington as an official of fully as much consequence as a Cabinet member and the formerly almost unheard of positions of the assistant secretaries are correspondingly important."

As Theodore C. Sorensen observes, the quality of his assistants tells us more about the President than about them. "A President," Sorensen writes, "must be judged in part on whom he is willing to take into his house, there to invoke his name and use his telephone—and affect our lives."[1]

Notwithstanding his dominance, the President and his official family are so closely interrelated that one cannot be studied without the other. Neither the man who presides over the Oval Office nor his lieutenants can be viewed in a solitary context.

In essence, the executive branch is the President. He determines the rhythm and pattern of his administration. But members of his supporting cast greatly determine the level of his performance in his numerous roles as chief executive, Commander in Chief, party leader, legislative initiator, and chief of state. Ideally, his White House aides refine his style, interpret his policies, and husband his time. To a great degree, they also serve as a mirror of his political philosophy, set the moral tone of his office, facilitate his decision-making, and help fix the standard of his national leadership. They cannot, however, cross the constitutional line and assume his responsibilities or make policy judgments. At most, they help develop policy options, sort out problems, recommend priorities, and offer political and public-relations advice. Their work is merely complementary to the President's larger task. As his lieutenants assigned to specific areas of delegated authority, their job is to lighten the President's work load and prepare decisions that conform with established policy, thus conserving his time and energy for more vital matters. "Upon this I insisted," President Dwight D. Eisenhower writes in his memoirs. "Whenever I had to make a decision that properly belonged to a subordinate I admonished him once, but if he failed again it was time to begin looking for a replacement."[2]

As Eisenhower implies, even the most senior presidential assistant is, in reality, simply an adjunct, serving at the pleasure of the President. His authority is wholly derived from the President, whom he represents as a trustee. The best are keenly sensitive of their station for, as Patrick Anderson remarks, "The President has been elected to lead the nation; they have been selected only to serve his convenience."[3]

Yet, in the heady atmosphere of the White House, reality gives way to illusion. White House aides carry the appearance of power and are festooned with those mystical qualities that are often associated with the Presidency. They are courted and celebrated as members of the political aristocracy—Roosevelt's Harry Hopkins, Eisenhower's Sherman Adams, Kennedy's Ted Sorensen, Johnson's Joe Califano, Nixon's Bob Haldeman and John Ehrlichman. Protocol is rigidly observed within the White House. Ranking presidential assistants are feted by social lions and fussed over by maitre d's; they enjoy an array of luxurious prerogatives, including a fleet of chauffeured limousines, a White House office with custom-made furniture, and a personal staff. They have access to the White House tennis court and swimming pool, as well as the White House dining mess, which is split into sections reserved for senior and junior executives, in recognition of a tacit caste system, and serviced by about ninety Filipino employees.* All this, not unexpectedly, contributes to the imperialization of the Presidency. With only slight exaggeration, Jack Valenti described working in the White House as the "ultimate seduction."[4]

Historical Perspective

The unchecked growth of the White House staff is generally dated from the implementation in 1939 of recommendations made to President Roosevelt by the Committee on Administrative Management, headed by Louis Brownlow. But while the Brownlow Committee did suggest that the President's immediate staff be enlarged, that an Executive Office of the President be established, and that the Budget Bureau be brought directly under White House jurisdiction, it did not intend that these innovations should foster the usurpation and concentration of executive authority. The committee members specified that the President's aides "would have no power to make decisions or issue instructions in their own right . . . would not be interposed between the President and the heads of his departments . . . would not be assistant Presidents in any sense . . . their effectiveness in assisting the President will, we think, be directly proportional to their ability to discharge their functions with restraint. They would remain in the background, issue no orders, make no decisions, emit no public statements."

One need only contrast those legitimate objectives with the subsequent expansion of the White House staff structure and the exercise of excessive presidential powers, culminating in the extralegal transgressions committed during the Nixon Administration, to see how far we have departed from the word and spirit of the Brownlow Commit-

---

*Blessed with the wisdom of hindsight, John Ehrlichman, who was convicted in connection with the Ellsberg burglary and the Watergate cover-up and was once so addicted to power he tried to have television newsman Dan Rather fired from CBS and urged that acting FBI Director Pat Gray be left "twisting in the wind," told me two years after leaving the White House that special privileges accorded presidential aides encourage a hermetic existence, stimulate their egos, and remove them from the world of reality. "You can spend twenty hours at the White House and not see anybody from outside," he commented. "There is something to be said about getting out in the morning and wiping ice off your car windows. It brings you back into the real world."

tee's recommendations. This was pointed up in a report issued in 1974 to the Senate Select Watergate Committee by a panel of government specialists drawn from the National Academy of Public Administration, who maintained, "Centralization of power in the Presidency has increased over the years to the present extreme situation in which the prevailing view is that the whole government should be run from the White House. The role of the principal assistants to the President has been virtually transformed to one of 'assistant Presidents.' "

The emergence of the presidential establishment, evolving into the equivalent of a special branch of government, has been called, without hyperbole, an "institutional phenomenon."[5] The White House Office budget alone since 1969 has escalated from $3.2 million to about $17 million, and the White House staff, notwithstanding the Nixon Administration's "honest count" in 1970, has doubled its numbers to five hundred or more. Not included are outside consultants and specialists from other federal agencies who are detailed to the White House for indeterminate periods—a practice that continues despite periodic assurances to Congress that it will be curtailed.

Also, the galaxy of offices, councils, and agencies that comprise the Executive Office of the President includes more than two thousand employees, with a total budget in excess of $108 million. A congressional report in 1972 observed that "over 50 percent of the increase in the Executive Office of the President has occurred since 1970."[6] The report further noted, "There is an inherent contradiction between the expansion of the Executive Office of the President, having policy guidance over all the executive departments, and a concomitant increase in executive personnel within the departments. It makes little sense to have executive growth in both areas since they are fundamentally performing the same tasks." Although they did not so state, the authors of the report were presumably aware that most recent Presidents have considered the White House Office and the Executive Office as their private army, with which to deal with an often recalcitrant and unsympathetic permanent government and promote their political interests.

No matter what its organizational arrangement, the modern presidential complex, composed mainly of the White House Office and the Executive Office of the President, is a multitiered schematic structure, as elaborate in design as any corporate conglomerate, with various divisions and subdivisions. The principal sections are concerned with domestic policy, national security, economic policy, congressional relations, press and public relations, legal counseling, and special-interest constituencies.

Included are such special units as, for instance, the White House Office of Communications, created by Nixon and perpetuated by Ford as a public-relations and propaganda clearing house for the administration. There are transitional agencies, such as the Special Office for

Drug Abuse Prevention and the Office of Consumer Affairs, which are established and nurtured by the White House, mainly in response to public concern over current issues, before being absorbed by the federal bureaucracy. Other offices are considered permanent extensions of the Presidency, including the National Security Council, the Council of Economic Advisers, the Office of Management and Budget, and the Domestic Council.

Inevitably, executive fiefdoms become ensconced, each with its advocates, who compete against each other for the attention of their benefactor, the President. Bigness dilutes accountability and encourages bureaucratic cannibalism whereby each agency seeks to fatten its role and extend its responsibility at the expense of another. And delusions of grandeur among petty princes who sit at the right hand of power lead to autocratic practices.

Whereas presidents from George Washington to FDR governed with but a handful of personal aides, their successors are surrounded—and catered to—by a "royal court" that tends to shield and isolate them: The result is an inflexible and impersonal White House. Accordingly, many White House aides in recent administrations have wielded profound influence on national policy and become prominent figures in their own right. The notion, all too often proposed, that presidential advisers are impartial in their counsel is more idealistic than realistic. A cliché often sounded by presidential assistants, including H. R. Haldeman under Nixon and Donald Rumsfeld under Ford, is that they are "honest brokers," who simply set out a platter of options before the President, allowing him to select the one that most appeals to him. That, of course, is a simplistic view. For the most part, senior White House aides are pragmatic, politically oriented, and personally ambitious. Not surprisingly, they attempt to sell their individual points of view, either directly or indirectly.

One of the reasons they are chosen for the job is that it is believed that their judgment will be of value to the President; hence, a philosophical eunuch would be of little use in complex policy negotiations. Carl Kaysen, former deputy special assistant to President Kennedy, observed, "Every adviser is a little bit of an advocate, he has some interest in what he proposes." Clark M. Clifford, onetime Defense Secretary and adviser to Presidents Truman, Kennedy, and Johnson, further noted that White House advocates will often recruit colleagues of similar persuasion to their side in hopes of winning the President's approval. "Among themselves," Clifford said, "the advocates ask, 'Is he one of us?' "*

Additionally, it should be mentioned that the President's decisions

*The comments by Kaysen and Clifford were made at a Princeton University Conference on "Advising the President," October 31–November 1, 1975. During the conference, James David Barber remarked, "Presidential advisers have their own ambitions; they are hustlers to a degree and follow the Irish maxim 'Don't get mad; get even.' "

are largely, though not entirely, based on information he receives
from his staff aides. They act as a conduit through which the information, collected from numerous sources in and out of government, is
filtered, in the process of which it may be edited or even blocked.
Frequently, the President will ask his aides for their opinions or they
may offer suggestions in the never ending stream of memorandums
that circulates throughout the White House.

Access to the Oval Office carries both prestige and the potentiality
for power. The fact that outsiders *believe* that a White House official
has influence within the President's inner circle is, in itself, a form of
power. Nevertheless, out of either modesty or fear of provoking the
President, White House aides continue to give voice to the "honest
broker" myth.

In part, at least, the Watergate scandal can be attributed to the
attitude of noblesse oblige that prevailed in the White House. Ultimately, it led to the exposure of secret activities and corrupt practices
within the White House and focused national attention on the lack of
constraints on presidential favorites, while raising legal and ethical
questions regarding their official status.

Yet, aside from President Nixon's misleading use of literary allusion
in saying that it has merely "grown like Topsy," a convincing argument can be offered to justify the growth of the White House staff.
Wars (hot and cold), economic crises, increased federal regulation, the
complexity of national and international issues, the encroachment of
Washington on new areas (such as environmental concerns), the
broadening role of government in social policy, the inclusion of new
managerial and evaluation functions—all have contributed toward the
institutionalization and alleged legitimization of the outsized Presidency.

Still other reasons for the ballooning of the White House establishment include the need by Presidents to coordinate interagency issues
and resolve jurisdictional conflicts; the increasing trend toward the
appointment of presidential aides as protective counterpoises to un-
cooperative departmental bureaucracies; and the creation of internal
units to deal with special interests, such as minority groups, women,
youth, labor, and business, and such problem areas as foreign trade
and tariffs and energy and environment. Consequently, as noted by
Thomas E. Cronin, the White House is becoming a "miniaturization
of important government agencies."[7]

Congress, too, must accept some of the blame for the proliferation of
the White House staff because of its past willingness to abdicate its
responsibilities in deference to the executive branch. During a congressional hearing in 1975, Democratic Representative Tom Steed of
Oklahoma, chairman of the appropriations subcommittee concerned
with the White House budget, stated, "Every time we create a new

function for the President, he has got to have somebody to help him do it. If we are going to keep on imposing all these functions on his office, it seems to me the least we could do would be a little less touchy about the manpower he has to have to carry out all these functions."

Steed is a staunch proponent of the rule of comity, a hoary political courtesy whereby one branch of government respects the wishes of another in return for a similar consideration. Referring to legislative proposals that would impose a ceiling on White House personnel, Steed, in blatant disregard of his oversight function, declared:

> I am sorry that we continue to have these harassing problems in connection with this because I think it really serves no useful purpose and does in effect belittle the Congress. I think it is not to our credit that we can nit-pick in this particular place. . . . I wouldn't want the President to tell me what I should have and who I should have, any more that I want to tell him. I don't think the members of Congress really understand that they demand and get this same prerogative in their own affairs that some of them now would deny the President of the United States under almost identical circumstances.

A classic example of the quid pro quo principle operating at the highest levels of government.

Claims have been made that allowing five hundred or more personal aides to the President, who presides over the largest enterprise yet conceived by man, is not an ostentatious extravagance. After all, many of our big corporations have more executives on their payrolls. However, as Christopher Lasch and other students of government have noted, a huge, elaborately structured White House staff has "the effect of isolating the office not simply from criticism but from the intrusion of everyday reality." Rather than act as his "eyes and ears," the palace guard has "rendered the President deaf and dumb, dangerously oblivious to ordinary facts."[8]

Concern over a White House bloated with power and personnel is rightly a public issue in these politically conscious times. There is no denying that the President needs personal assistants, including economists, management counselors, publicists, administrators, business experts, and political, legal, and legislative specialists. But the crux of the debate should revolve less on the number of White House aides who can crowd into the Oval Office than on defining the limitations of their jurisdiction and guaranteeing their accountability, because they now operate in a twilight zone of executive privilege. Assurance of maximum efficiency within a legal framework, to assist the President in his duties, is more crucial than the setting of a magic number.

Admittedly, the President has the right, as well he should, to exercise his prerogatives and rearrange his executive staff to his liking, in a manner he finds most comfortable and helpful in carrying out his responsibilities. But by creating a gargantuan superstructure and appointing a cadre of power brokers around him, he stifles debate, blocks off fresh ideas, and prevents dissenting opinions from reaching him. Somewhat like the situation of a maharaja and his food-tasters, nothing is put before him without first being sampled and approved. An overprotective in-house bureaucracy sees that he is not contaminated by complaints, opposing briefs, and unsolicited recommendations. Such incestuousness leads to a dryness of spirit, a withering homogeneity, and a blandness of thought.

The Nixon White House

Characteristically, few American presidents enter the White House with administrative experience. Except for an occasional Eisenhower, most come from the legislative arena, with little training in running any organization larger than their offices or campaign staffs. Usually, they have gratefully left their office operations in the hands of a trusted aide rather than become involved in messy staff interrelationships, often marked by personal feuds and jurisdictional battles. Nixon, as we now know, possessed a congenital distaste for dealing with all but a few select aides, those with whom he felt at ease.* In talks with author John Hersey, Ford acknowledged that one of his saddest duties as President was being called upon to mediate staff disputes.

Perhaps, then, it should be expected that modern presidents prefer that a chief of staff reign over their government households. The last President to serve as his own chief of staff was Harry S. Truman. He assumed the responsibility for delegating authority and controlling his official family, just as Franklin D. Roosevelt had before him. FDR believed there should be a distinction between "personal" and "institutional" staffs, those who worked in the White House directly under his purview and those who worked in the executive agencies on administration matters.

Today, the distinction is blurred and the two thousand or so employees of the Executive Office of the President invariably identify themselves as White House staff members. They consider it a cachet of their office to use White House stationery and make telephone calls saying, "This is the White House calling."

---

*Alexander Butterfield, whose duties at the White House required him to see the President several times daily, bringing papers into the Oval Office for him to read and sign and seeing that he kept to his schedule, reported in an interview that it was several months before Nixon called him by name. Butterfield subsequently disclosed the existence of the White House tapes.

If incoming presidents are ill-equipped as staff administrators, their personal aides, in many instances, are even less experienced in the business of government. There is no blueprint to guide presidents in the design of their staff organizations; the requirements and working habits of each are different. Furthermore, there are no criteria for the appointment of White House aides. Most are invited to join the President's staff not because of their intellectual skills or personal capabilities but because they had previously served under him or had worked in his campaign or were fortunate enough to be acquainted with him or one of his senior assistants.

Ironically, a GS-5 in the government bureaucracy must pass a qualification test, but not a presidential aide. All are novices when they enter White House service. Failure to learn the limitations of their rank may result in an arrogance of power, such as that associated with the Nixon White House.

Early in his administration, President Richard M. Nixon envisioned a White House that would be lean in size and open in its operations. His aides would be generalists and not power-hungry specialists interfering in the affairs of federal departments. Authority would be decentralized. Members of his Cabinet, all men of "extra dimension," would be given an active role in the formulation of policy. There would be no "assistant President" acting in his name as chief of staff. Nixon would be his own spokesman, and no one would hold the title of Press Secretary. "I don't want a government of yes-men," he proclaimed. That these promises raised false expectations and were never kept is one of the tragedies of the Nixon Administration.

Nixon had a keen appreciation of the value of patronage and the need to surround himself with aides who were compatible with his political philosophy and loyally dedicated to his cause. From his preinauguration headquarters at the Hotel Pierre in New York City, he announced ninety-nine personnel appointments, including thirty-five to the White House and Executive Office. Three days after his inauguration on January 20, 1969, he withdrew all nominations pending from the Johnson Administration, thus seizing an opportunity to appoint Republicans to posts slated for Democrats. In Nixon's defense, his aides argued that President Kennedy had taken similar steps after assuming office.

Nixon's initial White House appointments were mostly drawn from loyalists on his campaign staff. More than thirty members of the White House staff were thirty years old or younger. Few had government experience. Most had roots in California, and many had come from the illusion-filled world of advertising, where the printed or spoken word is viewed as a selling tool rather than a means by which to communicate the truth.

Almost all appointments, including those to the federal agencies, were made without consultation with, or approval by, party or congressional leaders. Under Nixon's recruitment program, Peter M. Flanigan was given the assignment of finding prospects for executive positions in the administration and Harry S. Flemming, for lower-level slots. Appointees were selected largely on the basis of whether they satisfied Nixon's personal and political specifications and less on grounds of talent. Hiring of non-Republicans by agency heads had to be justified in writing.

More than most recent presidents, Nixon recognized the value of organization in the exercise of power. During the formative period of his administration, he broadened the jurisdictional operations of the Executive Office by establishing the Urban Affairs Council, the Office of Intergovernmental Relations (to act as liaison between the administration and state and local officials), the Rural Affairs Council, and the Council on Environmental Quality. He also upgraded the National Security Council as the "principal forum for consideration of policy issues requiring presidential determination" and appointed the Advisory Council on Executive Organization, headed by industrialist Roy L. Ash, to conduct an overall review of the organizational apparatus of the executive branch.

Within the White House itself, Haldeman stood astride a pyramidal staff structure, with Ehrlichman at one side as domestic czar and Henry A. Kissinger, assistant to the President for national security, on the other as the dominant figure in foreign policy. It soon became apparent that talk of the decentralization of power was nothing more than political rhetoric, that Nixon, in countervailing action, was actually tightening the reins of authority within the White House.

In other reorganization moves, Nixon created the White House Office of Communications, named investigative reporter Clark R. Mollenhoff as a special counsel with the primary function of being the White House's troubleshooter, and designated Martin Anderson to be a special consultant for systems analysis. As such, Anderson was to dissect federal programs and determine their cost-effectiveness.

Certainly one of the most significant reorganization schemes of the Nixon Administration was the establishment in July 1970 of the Domestic Council and the remodeling of the Budget Bureau into the Office of Management and Budget. Nixon eagerly embraced the plan, recommended by the Ash Council, because it fitted in with his concept that authority should reside in the White House and that lines of information leading to the Oval Office should be few, clearly designated, and uncluttered.

In a message to Congress regarding the plan, Nixon declared, "There does not now exist an organized, institutionally staffed group charged with advising the President on the total range of domestic policy." The Domestic Council, he said, would fill that need and further be charged "with integrating the various aspects of domestic policy into a consistent whole." The reorganization, he added, "will not only improve the staff resources available to the President, but will also strengthen the advisory roles of those members of the Cabinet principally concerned with domestic affairs." As it turned out, Nixon was only partly correct—the influence of the domestic departments was not strengthened but diminished.

Basically, the Domestic Council replaced Nixon's Urban Affairs Council and was patterned on the National Security Council model. In addition to its formal members—each of the Cabinet secretaries with the exception of those at State and Defense and any other members the President may designate—it was given a permanent, institutional staff, all of whose members were politically appointed. Fear that the staff would dominate the Domestic Council operations and loom as a shield between the federal agencies and the President was promptly manifested.

Democratic Representative Chet Holifield of California, then chairman of the House Government Operations Committee, maintained that the new presidential agency "sets up a council of political appointees, who, in effect, are doing the work, making the policy determinations, and setting the priorities which heretofore had been made by the various Cabinet departments and the Bureau of the Budget." Holifield also objected to the lack of accountability that would cloak the staff members.

It was immediately clear that Nixon relied considerably more on Ehrlichman and the Domestic Council staff than on his Cabinet for the initiation and implementation of domestic policy. The Domestic Council's Cabinet members seldom met as a body. Task-force committees that included Cabinet officers were run mostly by a Domestic Council staff aide. And there was little doubt that Ehrlichman was Nixon's lead man in domestic affairs.

Operating in tandem, Ehrlichman and Haldeman were Nixon's most intimate advisers. By their style, demeanor, and character, they came to symbolize the fortress-like Nixon White House, and they were variously referred to by reporters as the "Berlin Wall," the "Prussians," and the "Katzenjammer Kids." During moments of relaxation, Ehrlichman could occasionally be an outgoing, gracious companion. He often chatted with visitors in his second-floor White House office with his coat off and his feet propped on a coffee table. Haldeman, however, always gave the impression of being a self-contained and rigidly disciplined private person. Even to White House aides he remained an aloof, coldly unemotional figure. As an exponent of the presidential options system, Haldeman downplayed his personal involvement in policy-making, preferring to describe himself as a "devil's advocate, to see whether all the input is there and whether it is put together to give the President the full picture, with all the pros and cons."9

However, as the White House tapes revealed, Nixon seldom made a major decision without consulting Haldeman, whose influence was truly enormous, albeit more passive than active, more custodial than creative, and more private than public. He guarded the portals of the Oval Office with the ferocity of a wounded bull, and to paint him as a glorified usher is to distort vastly his real role as White House major-domo and confidant of the President. He and other members of the Nixon White House possessed almost no concept of the shared powers of government, and ultimately their elitist delusions led to Watergate and their downfall.

In the beginning, Watergate offered Nixon an opportunity to re-place the secretive way of conducting national business with an open and more even-handed style more in keeping with the American tradi-tion. Instead, undaunted by criticism from outside the administration and disaffection from within, he sought to consolidate further his executive authority. Fortified by what he interpreted as an over-whelming popular mandate in his 1972 re-election, he created what became known as the "supercabinet," or "consular" system.

From his mountaintop hermitage at Camp David Nixon announced on November 27, 1972, that he was reorganizing the executive branch as a means to generate new ideas, give greater voice to Cabinet mem-bers, and decentralize the White House decision-making process. Surely, these were noble ideals, worthy of a beneficent conqueror who has scored a historic triumph. Unhappily, Nixon's loudly trum-peted personnel shake-up bore less the spirit of sincere reformation than the flesh of political machination.

Glossed over was the fact that during the election campaign he had spoken in glowingly Napoleonic tones of his subalterns in govern-ment service. They were members of a "winning team" who had been to Peking and Moscow with him, had helped forge his economic guidelines, and had fought by his side in legislative skirmishes with Congress.

But to the victor belong the spoils, and he was now prepared to discard many of his companions, like a pampered debutante shedding last summer's beaus. As one of the first moves in his effort to "stream-line the federal government," the President ordered a litmus-test re-evaluation of some two thousand appointees, with loyalty to the ad-ministration as the prime criterion for rejection or reinstatement. Such mavericks and free thinkers as Housing and Urban Development (HUD) Secretary George Romney and Commerce Secretary Peter G. Peterson were eased out. None too gently dropped were revisionists such as the Reverend Theodore M. Hesburgh, chairman of the Civil Rights Commission, Social Security Administrator Robert M. Ball, and

Geoffrey H. Moore, Bureau of Labor Statistics Commissioner. Others, seeing the handwriting on the wall, as did Richard P. Nathan, assistant secretary of Health, Education, and Welfare (HEW) and onetime Budget Bureau whiz kid, silently slipped away, leaving their resignations behind them.

Meanwhile, tried and trusted Nixon acolytes were transplanted like vital organs into the Cabinet departments as overseers of administration policy. They included three Domestic Council deputy assistants: John C. Whitaker as under secretary of Interior; Egil Krogh, Jr., as under secretary of Transportation; and Edward L. Morgan as assistant secretary of the Treasury. Alexander Butterfield was elevated to Administrator of the Federal Aviation Administration, and Lewis Engman, another Domestic Council official, was handpicked by Nixon to be Chairman of the Federal Trade Commission. A White House advance man, Ronald H. Walker, was appointed Director of the National Park Service over the objections of conservation spokesmen. Control over the Park Service was especially coveted by the White House because the agency helps designate lands for park use, an invaluable pork-barrel item, and lets contracts for concessions at federal recreational centers.

Previously, the appointment of officials at the assistant-secretary level in the Cabinet departments had fallen within the prerogative of the secretary, but now they were being selectively chosen by the White House. Remarked a White House aide, "They will know who hired them. In effect, they will carry commissions from the President, not the secretary. Regardless of who announces it, they'll see something hanging on their walls with Richard M. Nixon on it. There will be no more assistant secretaries saying, 'I don't work for Nixon; I work for the Secretary.' If he's hired, he will know why and by whom. There will be less disloyalty and more direction and guidance."

The White House brotherhood cult and its extermination methods were graphically illustrated in the peremptory sacking of Peter Peterson. To the Nixon White House, Peterson was an anomaly who, on occasion, broke out of the mold and exhibited a flair in his life-style that was considered alien to his administration colleagues.

Peterson had performed with distinction as the first Director of the President's Council on International Economic Policy. He was one of the early advocates of the "doctrine of equivalence," whereby economic factors are weighed as peer elements with diplomatic factors in the fashioning of U.S. foreign policy. As such, he battled with State Department careerists, representatives from foreign governments, and lobbyists for special-interest groups but managed to emerge unscathed. It was internecine scrapping with the White House wolf pack that was to do him in.

Contributing to Peterson's fall from grace was his well-known friendship with prominent columnists, his association with Republican liberal Senator Charles H. Percy, of Illinois, and his fondness for publicity. He also displayed an addiction to jokes, sometimes at the expense of the administration. ("When the President offered me the Commerce job he should have explained it was a secret mission.")

Peterson's independence marked him as a man to be watched, not unlike an apostate at the Vatican. His heretical tendencies, in the view of White House loyalists, surfaced during the 1972 campaign. Despite the entreaties of White House political directors, he repeatedly refused in campaign speeches to make personal attacks against Senator George McGovern, the Democratic nominee. A former aide to Peterson recalled, "Chuck Colson's office would keep sending material, telling him what to say and what the line of the week was and he would ignore it. Then they would call up and want to know what the hell was going on and he still did nothing about it." This attitude of benign disobedience put Peterson high on the White House's most-wanted list and led to his eventual departure.

Nixon's crowning glory, a move reminiscent of the court of Louis XIV, was the erection of a protective wedge of vice-regents around the President, its purpose being to grease the transmittal of White House policies through the bureaucracy without meddlesome dissidents kicking sand in the pathways. Fundamentally, the reorganization scheme consisted of two tiers of policy manipulators at the top of the White House hierarchy. On the uppermost rung were five presidential assistants, each with a special area of responsibility: Haldeman, White House staff; Kissinger, foreign affairs; Treasury Secretary George P. Schultz, economic affairs; Roy Ash, budget and executive management; and Ehrlichman, domestic affairs. Directly below Ehrlichman were three Cabinet secretaries who had been given the additional title of counselor to the President and were responsible for coordinating interagency matters in broadly defined operational areas of domestic concern: HEW Secretary Caspar W. Weinberger, human resources; Agriculture Secretary Earl L. Butz, natural resources; and HUD Secretary James T. Lynn, community development. Presumably, Nixon, intent on tightening his hold on the federal bureaucracy, made the move because Congress refused to act on his proposal to merge "seven outmoded, constituency-oriented departments" into "four streamlined, goal-oriented departments."

The counselor structure, however, never got off the ground. It was disbanded after about four months when Ehrlichman and Haldeman resigned on April 30, 1973, in connection with charges growing out of the Watergate affair. Shortly afterward, Nixon announced that General Alexander M. Haig, Jr., a former Kissinger deputy, would succeed Haldeman as White House chief of staff. Thereafter, Haig presided over the White House in a holding operation until the final days of Nixon's personal and political disintegration.

To a degree, the oligarchic form of government spawned under Nixon encouraged the Watergate crimes and stimulated the siege mentality indigenous to the cover-up. Most of Nixon's chief advisers were as cloistered as their patron. Like fireflies, they flitted and fluttered in the dark until by a strange turn of events they burst upon the public's consciousness.

The Nixon penchant for privacy, however, should not be confused with the "passion for anonymity" once upheld as a prerequisite for presidential aides. The era of faceless White House viceroys faded with the introduction of instant communications and the increased centralization of power in the White House. We now know that the presidential establishment, like any organism, needs a certain amount of light to function properly and honestly. Harold J. Laski reminds us, "Anyone today who is in the continuous service of the White House is, in the nature of things, news . . . the more we know of the men who actually assist in the shaping of policy, the more honest that policy is likely to be."[10]

The Ford White House

A few days before succeeding to the Presidency, Gerald R. Ford spoke meditatively to a reporter about the kind of staff he preferred. "I want them to be a working staff," he said. "I want them to have a good public image because what they do reflects on me, good or bad. I want them to conduct themselves as I try to conduct myself in a friendly, personable way. I want them to be loyal to me. I want them to be a working unit, not individuals. . . . I want them to reflect my personality, and I think my personality is open and candid."[11] Those conditions roughly served as the criteria he followed in assembling his presidential staff.

Like earlier Vice-Presidents who ascended to the Presidency at a moment's notice, Ford entered office without the luxury of time to collect his own staff. The course of government cannot be interrupted, and Ford, like Lyndon B. Johnson and Harry S. Truman before him, had to rely on holdover personnel to assist in the transition from one administration to another. They inherited not only their predecessor's staff but his operational system as well.

In Ford's case, the situation was even more acute. As an "appointed President," he was, in a sense, indebted to a banished benefactor. From the beginning, his administration was inhibited by ghosts of the past regime. Yet, it was imperative that he restore trust and dignity to institutional government as seen through the prism of the White House. Occupants immediately preceding him had discredited the White House, publicly perceived as the heart and spirit of the American democratic process, and Ford's first priority was to restore it to its rightful place of honor.

Upon taking office, Ford indicated his administration would be one of reformation and restoration. He promised there would be substantive changes in style and operations at the White House, that the Cabinet would be returned to the policy-making councils of government, and that the coequal relationship between the executive and legislative branches would be revived. "I want to be a good President," he told Congress.

To assist him in putting together a staff organization, Ford established a four-man transition team comprised of Donald Rumsfeld, then U.S. Ambassador to the North Atlantic Treaty Organization; John O. Marsh, Jr., former Democratic member of Congress whom Ford had named presidential counselor; Interior Secretary Rogers C. B. Morton; and former Pennsylvania governor William W. Scranton.

The expected overhaul, nonetheless, was slow in coming, and Ford came under increasingly heavy criticism for failure to take action and create a White House distinctively his own. According to aides, he was reluctant to initiate a wholesale purge, preferring out of compassion to move at a measured pace.

Recalling those tumultuous early days of the Ford Administration, White House aide James E. Connor said:

> During a normal transition, the bureaucratic machinery slows down. . . . Issues have been attended to and dealt with by a President on a day-to-day basis. An agenda has been set. But when a President takes office under circumstances Ford did, there are problems in grabbing hold of the beast in full flight. . . . Ford could have used a terrible swift sword and purged the Nixon appointees, regardless of their competence or integrity or what it did to them personally and he would have been entitled to do it. Instead, he stressed continuity and set out to make the system function, both in foreign affairs and in the management of government. It was a conscious decision to calm down a frenetic situation.

More than two months after Ford took office, a *National Journal* survey showed that about 60 percent of the White House senior staff were holdovers from the Nixon Administration. This did not include Nixon appointees who remained on the public payroll but were relieved of any responsibilities, or those engaged in pursuits on behalf of the former President. Nor did it take into account members of the various units of the Executive Office or the Cabinet and sub-Cabinet ranks, almost all of which remained intact during the transition.

In twenty-one White House offices surveyed, 69 of 108 aides had worked in the Nixon Administration. The odd coupling of Ford appointees and Nixon holdovers resulted in a divided White House, affecting morale and overall efficiency. As might be expected, this was a sore point with the early Ford White House. Rumsfeld, who replaced Haig as White House chief of staff and was himself a holdover,

insisted, "This is a Ford White House, not a Nixon White House." Be
that as it may, many Nixon appointees, including Jerry H. Jones, William J. Baroody, Jr., Max Friedersdorf, David Gergen, Brent Scow-
croft, Michael Duval, and James Cavanaugh, were retained by
Ford—most of them to the very end.

During the first year of his administration, Ford showed little inclination to redesign the organizational structure of the Executive Office.
With relatively minor changes, he retained the model left by Nixon.
He pledged to reduce the size of the White House staff by at least 10
percent; yet it continued at its former level.

Some areas of the White House, such as the press-communications,
public-liaison, and lobbying sectors, were expanded by Ford. He also
continued the President's news summary, originated by Nixon and
considered a luxurious frill by many in and out of the White House.
And notwithstanding Ford's reputation as an amiable, commonsensi-
cal man, the imperial trappings of the White House remained untouched.

The most significant innovations by Ford were the establishment of
the Council on Wage and Price Stability, a monitoring agency proposed by Nixon just before he resigned; the dismantling of the Special
Action Office for Drug Abuse Prevention; the reinforcement of the
Economic Policy Board and the Federal Energy Administration; the
de-emphasis on the functions of the Office of Telecommunications
Policy; and the reinstitution of the Office of Science and Technology,
abolished earlier by Nixon.

Overall, Ford possessed less of an appreciation than Nixon of the
institution of the Presidency as an organic body that must constantly
be revised and revitalized to serve effectively as a mechanism to obtain information, act as the President's agent in his official relationships, and allow him to see that his policies are carried out. Unfortunately, Nixon had misused and distorted the machinery he had
crafted. Ford took a more conventional approach to the art of governing, perhaps mindful of the fate that overcame the Nixon White
House.

With Rumsfeld aboard as chief of staff—a title he eschewed because
of its autocratic implications and the memories it provoked of the
Haldeman-Haig era—the Ford White House gradually began to assume a semblance of form. Rumsfeld installed longtime aide William
N. Walker as director of the presidential personnel office, and in short
order the appointments process was speeded up.

With some overlapping, the Ford White House could be perceived
as being composed of four concentric circles:

1. The Old Boy Network, mostly associates of Ford's during his
years in the House, including presidential counselors Robert T.

Hartmann and John Marsh, CIA Director George Bush, and William Scranton, United States Ambassador to the United Nations

2. The Grand Rapids Crowd, longtime friends of Ford's whom he invited to Washington after becoming President—notably, Philip W. Buchen, counsel to the President, and L. William Seidman, assistant for economic affairs

3. The New Wave, those appointees who were young, energetic, and in highly responsible positions, including Richard B. Cheney, who succeeded Rumsfeld as White House chief of staff, press secretary Ron Nessen, and Frank Zarb, Director of the Federal Energy Administration

4. The New York Set, led by Vice-President Nelson Rockefeller and two of his aides who were initially placed in charge of the Domestic Council—James M. Cannon and Richard L. Dunham

Such diversity may be viewed as beneficial because it stimulates an intellectual interplay among several sources. However, it also incites power struggles and personal feuds among staff aides, thereby polluting the atmosphere surrounding the President. A classic example was the battle for supremacy as the President's favorite between Rumsfeld and Hartmann. In a trivial yet significant incident reflecting bureaucratic gamesmanship, Rumsfeld had Hartmann removed from a small but coveted office adjoining the President's to one farther down the corridor on the first floor of the West Wing of the White House, between suites occupied by Kissinger and himself.

Finally, in a move to assert mastery over his own house, President Ford, on December 18, 1974, announced a revised staff alignment. At a White House press briefing, Rumsfeld made it clear that the plan had actually been in force for several weeks and that it was decided to unveil it to counter criticism that Ford was slow in cleaning out Nixon appointees and putting his own stamp on the White House.

In obvious contrast to the pyramidal structure of the Nixon White House, which featured a chief of staff at the apex controlling all lines of communication to the President, the reconstructed Ford organization was rectangular in shape, with nine senior aides at the top level, each with an assigned area of jurisdiction, a backup deputy, and a supporting staff. The nine were Rumsfeld, assistant to the President for administration and coordinator of operations; Hartmann, counselor, in charge of speech-writing and other editorial functions and chief political adviser; Buchen, counsel to the President; Marsh, counselor, supervisor of congressional relations and public liaison; Kissinger, Secretary of State and assistant to the President for national-security affairs; Seidman, assistant for economic affairs; Nessen, press secretary; Roy Ash, Director of the Office of Management and Budget; and Kenneth R. Cole, Jr., Domestic Council Director and assistant for domestic affairs. Ostensibly, the nine were peers with equal access to the President. In reality, Rumsfeld, who played down the staff-restructuring as "probably imperfect" and subject to continual change, was plainly more equal than the others.

Access to the President is a traditional measurement in Washington of an official's influence and status, and Rumsfeld saw and consulted with the President far more than any other White House aide. He also was in charge of the White House Secretariat and the advance and scheduling offices. He ruled on the "perks" granted White House aides, such as use of limousines and White House mess privileges. He had the final "sign-off" on prospective presidential appointments. Although not the sole arbiter as to who and what went into the Oval Office, he did exercise influence over the flow of activity. At his urging, a Cabinet Secretariat was established in the White House and placed under the direction of James Connor, who reported directly to Rumsfeld.

While discussing the new White House staff system, Rumsfeld sometimes seemed to speak with two voices. He said the organizational structure would ensure an "orderly decision-making process." At another point, he acknowledged that presidential decision-making is an untidy process and added, "There is no formula for how a presidential decision gets made." The remark recalled an observation by W. Averell Harriman, erstwhile adviser to several presidents, who once said, "You cannot organize wise decisions."

A separate part of Ford's reorganization program involved the attempted rejuvenation of the Domestic Council. Since its establishment in 1970 as an executive arm of the Presidency to coordinate domestic policy, the agency has run an erratic course. Its responsibilities have alternately been expanded and contracted, the size of its staff has fluctuated from thirty to almost eighty, and its impact has been both great and small. Once a significant partner in the formulation of domestic policy, the Domestic Council became just another service unit in the presidential establishment after John Ehrlichman's resignation in 1973. When Ford became President, the agency's institutional role remained undefined, and its performance had yet to match its promise.

At a "Salute to the Vice-President" dinner in New York on February 13, 1975, Ford announced that he had decided to "redefine and broaden the function and responsibility of my Domestic Council." He reported that Vice-President Rockefeller would serve as operating director of the Council in his capacity as vice-chairman and that two of Rockefeller's associates would be put in charge of the agency, James M. Cannon as executive director and Richard L. Dunham as deputy director. Probably never before had a President granted a Vice-President so much operational authority in a major policy area.

Rockefeller, apparently perceiving the Domestic Council role as a means for injecting himself into White House policy deliberations, personally lobbied for it in talks with Ford, who gave his approval despite objections from several of his principal advisers, including Rumsfeld. A few days later, Philip E. Areeda, White House counsel, who reportedly was in line to become the Council's Executive Director before the job was given to Cannon, quit to teach at Harvard.

By underscoring Rockefeller's Domestic Council authority, Ford confirmed his decision to restore the agency to its former prominence. But in less than a year, it became evident that the Vice-President's experimental involvement in domestic policy was less than a success, and he asked to be relieved of the assignment.

Rockefeller, one of a succession of vice-presidents who yearned to become active participants in administration affairs, failed because of several factors: the natural antipathy between the White House and vice-presidential staffs, budgetary restrictions that precluded the enactment of new domestic programs, constitutional limitations on the Vice-Presidency, and the lack of a political base and a supportive constituency. Also, Rockefeller hoped to concentrate on long-range academic studies of the country's domestic needs, unaware that much, if not most, of the Domestic Council's work is involved with current problems that demand prompt presidential decisions. Thus, the Vice-Presidency of Nelson Rockefeller, launched with fanfare and high expectations, ended in disappointment, offering further proof that a Vice-President is bound by the Constitution and other political forces and cannot easily extend his mandate to that of an aide to the President.

As Ford's Cabinet secretary observed, White House aides must realize their power is totally derivative and not try to project themselves as major actors in the government; they work for one man only and must subdue their own egos. "They must," he said, "adopt perspectives that are not necessarily their own—that is, try to conceive problems from the principal's perspective. The White House staff ought to be what the President wants it to be. And do only what the President wants it to do."

In a dramatized affair, President Ford, on November 3, 1975, announced a "major staff shake-up," which included the replacement of Defense Secretary James R. Schlesinger with Donald Rumsfeld, the nominations of George Bush as CIA Director and Elliot L. Richardson as Commerce Secretary, the withdrawal of Secretary of State Kissinger's dual post as assistant to the President for national security, and the appointment of Richard Cheney as White House chief of staff. Ford stressed that he made the personnel changes in accord with every President's prerogative to assemble his own "team" and that the action was taken without political or personal implications. "These are the guys that I wanted," Ford declared.

Despite his reputation for candor, Ford's explanation tended to strain his credibility because the reshuffling introduced not a single new face: All those affected were, in fact, Nixon holdovers and already members of the administration. Furthermore, it was no secret that Ford was dissatisfied with Schlesinger because of policy differences, particularly one involving the administration's espousal of detente with the Soviet Union. Hence, Ford was simply following presidential tradition: Almost every President comes into office welcoming "honest dissent" within his official family, insisting he does not want "yes-men" as aides—yet, before long, he becomes less enchanted with dissenting opinions, and the dissenters are weeded out. All of which underlines the frailties of presidents and the fact that their relationships with their staffs are based on human as well as political factors.

Summary

As this is being written, President-elect Jimmy Carter is in the midst of designing and staffing his administration in what is recognized as the most elaborately orchestrated transition in presidential history. In numerous interviews and public statements by the President-elect and his aides, a Carter White House was portrayed as being smaller in size than that of its predecessors; there would be no chief of staff to guard the Oval Office portals; presidential aides would have equal access to the President; in all probability, some units of the Executive Office of the President, such as the Domestic Council and the Council on International Economic Policy, would be reduced or even dismantled; Cabinet secretaries would have autonomous supervision over their departments without interference from White House aides; perquisites available to White House aides would be cut back; and the Vice-President would be given a substantive policy role.

Most, if not all, of these proposals have been made by other presidents, without ringing success. There is little guarantee that Carter will fare much better, mainly because the White House, like the federal bureaucracy, has become an institutionalized giant, impervious to presidential demands.

At the height of the Watergate investigation, numerous suggestions were made to constrict presidential powers and keep the White House staff within bounds. These included proposals for institutional changes to correct the "imbalance of power" between the executive and legislative branches by reestablishing oversight and investigatory responsibilities in Congress, limiting the White House budget, and requiring the confirmation of senior presidential aides and making them more accountable for their actions and decisions.

Some reformers advocated a complete overhaul of the executive departments with a view toward reinforcing Cabinet authority. Others favored government by a "presidential committee." Still others called for the remodeling of the Presidency, making the holder of the office a "manager" rather than a chief executive.

In the Senate Watergate Committee's final report, Senator Lowell P. Weicker, Jr., contended, "The issue at stake is the exercise of potentially awesome presidential power." The committee, however, declined to get into the issue except in a marginal sense—an omission that has since been recognized as one of its most glaring deficiencies.

Executive authority, nonetheless, may be constrained through legislative and administrative remedies available under the present system. This entails a repair operation, not a dismantling project that could leave us worse off than before. Proposed changes concerning White House aides might include:

- A redefinition of executive privilege as it applies to presidential-staff members
- A method of accountability that would provide public disclosure of their areas of jurisdiction and official functions
- A prohibition against allowing presidential aides to serve in a dual capacity as department heads, in which case their responsibilities and loyalties are diffused to the decided advantage of the White House
- Closer congressional scrutiny of the White House and Executive Office budgets, particularly as to staffing, the "borrowing" of personnel from federal agencies, and the perquisites made available to presidential personnel
- Restoration of the prestige and authority traditionally reserved to the executive departments, recognizing they have obligations to both the President and Congress and are not political instruments solely at the disposal of the White House
- A check on the infiltration of the government career service by presidential patronage, as well as a limitation on White House control over agency appointments below a defined grade level

These and other modifications might temper the movement toward a super Presidency, yet allow the President the flexibility he needs to govern, for ours is a presidential government.

Notes

1. Theodore C. Sorensen, *Watchmen in the Night* (Cambridge, Mass.: MIT Press, 1975), p. 158.
2. Dwight D. Eisenhower, *Waging Peace: The White House Years 1956–61* (New York: Doubleday, 1965), p. 632.

3. Patrick Anderson, *The Presidents' Men* (New York: Doubleday, 1969), p. 480.
4. Jack Valenti, *A Very Human President* (New York: W. W. Norton, 1975), p. 61.
5. Emmet John Hughes, *The Living Presidency* (New York: Coward, McCann & Geoghegan, 1972–73), p. 138.
6. *A Report on the Growth of the Executive Office of the President*, prepared under the direction of Representative Morris K. Udall and submitted to the House Committee on Post Office and Civil Service, April 24, 1972.
7. Thomas E. Cronin, in prepared testimony before the House Select Committee on Committees, July 12, 1973.
8. Christopher Lasch, "Paranoid Presidency," *Center Magazine*, March–April 1974.
9. *National Journal*, March 6, 1971.
10. Harold J. Laski, *The American Presidency* (New York: Harper & Bros., 1940), pp. 260–61.
11. *National Journal*, August 10, 1974.

9. The President and the Press

Daniel P. Moynihan

As his years in Washington came to an end, one President wrote a friend, *"I really look with commiseration over the great body of my fellow citizens, who, reading newspapers, live and die in the belief that they have known something of what has been passing in the world in their time."* A familiar presidential plaint, sounded often in the early years of the Republic and rarely unheard thereafter. Of late, however, a change has developed in the perception of what is at issue. In the past, what was thought to be involved was the reputation of a particular President. In the present, what is seen to be at stake, and by the presidents themselves, is the reputation of government—especially, of course, presidential government. These are different matters and summon a different order of concern.

There are two points anyone would wish to make at the outset of an effort to explore this problem. First, it is to be acknowledged that, in most essential encounters between the Presidency and the press, the advantage is with the former. The President has a near limitless capacity to "make" news that must be reported, if only by reason of competition between one journal, or one medium, and another. If anything, radio and television news is more readily subject to such dominance. Its format permits of many fewer "stories." The President-in-action almost always takes precedence. The President also has considerable capacity to reward friends and punish enemies in the press corps, whether they be individual journalists or the papers, television networks, news weeklies, or whatever these individuals work for. And, for quite a long while, finally, a President who

174

wishes can carry off formidable deceptions. (One need only recall the barefaced lying that went with the formal opinion of Roosevelt's Attorney General that the destroyer–naval base deal of 1940 was legal.)

With more than sufficient reason, then, publishers and reporters alike have sustained, over the generations, a lively sense of their vulnerability to government coercion or control. For the most part, their worries have been exaggerated. But, like certain virtues, there are some worries that are best carried to excess.

The second point is that American journalism is almost certainly the best in the world. This judgment will be disputed by some. There are good newspapers in other countries. The *best* European journalists are more intellectual than their American counterparts, and some will think this a decisive consideration. But there is no enterprise anywhere the like of the *New York Times*. Few capitals are covered with the insight and access of the *Washington Post* or the *Washington Evening Star*. As with so many American institutions, American newspapers tend to be older and more stable than their counterparts abroad. The *Hartford Courant* was born in 1764, twenty-one years before the *Times* of London. The *New York Post* began publication in 1801, twenty years before the *Guardian* of Manchester. What, in most other countries, is known as the "provincial" press—that is to say, journals published elsewhere than in the capital—in America is made up of a wealth of comprehensive and dependable daily newspapers of unusually high quality.

The journalists are in some ways more important than their journals—at least to anyone who has lived much in government. A relationship grows up with the reporters covering one's particular sector that has no counterpart in other professions or activities. The relationship is one of simultaneous trust and distrust, friendship and enmity, dependence and independence. But it is the men of government, especially in Washington, who are the more dependent. The journalists are their benefactors, their conscience, at times almost their reason for being. For the journalists are, above all others, their audience, again especially in Washington, which has neither an intellectual community nor an electorate, and where there is no force outside government able to judge events, much less to help shape them, save the press.

That there is something wondrous and terrible in the intensities of this relationship between the press and the government is perhaps best seen at the annual theatricals put on by such groups of journalists as the Legislative Correspondents Association in Albany or the Gridiron in Washington. To my knowledge, nothing comparable takes place anywhere else in the world. These gatherings are a kind of ritual truth-telling, of which the closest psychological approximation would be the Calabrian insult ritual described by Roger Vailland in his novel

The Law, or possibly the group-therapy practices of more recent origin. The politicians come as guests of the journalists. The occasion is, first of all, a feast: the best of everything. Then, as dinner progresses, the songs begin. The quality varies, of course, but, at moments, startling levels of deadly accurate commentary of great cruelty are achieved. The politicians sit and smile and applaud. Then, some of them speak. Each one wins or loses to the degree that he can respond in kind; stay funny and be brutal. (At the Gridiron, John F. Kennedy was a master of the style, but the piano duet performed by Nixon and Agnew in 1970 was thought by many to have surpassed anything yet done.) A few lyrics appear in the next day's papers, but what the newspapermen really said to the politicians remains privileged—as does so much of what the politicians say to them. The relationship is special.

How is it, then, that this relationship has lately grown so troubled? The immediate answer is, of course, the war in Vietnam. An undeclared war, unwanted, misunderstood, or not understood at all, it entailed a massive deception of the American people by their government. Surely a large area of the experience of the 1960s is best evoked in the story of the man who says, "They told me that if I voted for Goldwater there would be 500,000 troops in Vietnam within a year. I voted for him, and, by God, they were right." The story has many versions. If he voted for Goldwater, we would be defoliating the countryside of Vietnam; the army would be sending spies to the 1968 party conventions; Dr. Spock would be indicted on conspiracy charges; and so on. By 1968, Richard Rovere described the capital as "awash" with lies.

The essential fact was that of deceit. How else to carry out a full-scale war that became steadily more unpopular with none of the legally sanctioned constraints on the free flow of information that even the most democratic societies find necessary in such circumstances? This situation did not spring full-blown from the involvement in Southeast Asia. It was endemic to the cold war. At the close of World War II, official press censorship was removed, but the kinds of circumstances in which any responsible government might feel that events have to be concealed from the public did not go away. The result was a contradiction impossible to resolve. The public interest was at once served and disserved by secrecy, at once disserved and served by openness. Whatever the case, distrust of government grew. At the outset of the U-2 affair in 1960, the U.S. Government asserted that a weather plane on a routine mission had been shot down. The *New York Times* (May 6, 1960) reported just that. *Not* that the U.S. Government *claimed* it was a weather plane, but simply that it was. Well, it wasn't. Things have been the same since.

But there are problems between the Presidency and the press that have little to do with the cold war or with Vietnam, and which—if this analysis is correct—will persist or even intensify as those conditions recede, or even dissolve, as a prime source of public concern. The problems flow from five basic circumstances that together have been working to reverse the old balance of power between the Presidency and the press. It is the thesis here that, if this balance should tip too far in the direction of the press, our capacity for effective democratic government will be seriously and dangerously weakened.

I

The first of these circumstances has to do with the tradition of "muckraking"—the exposure of corruption in government or the collusion of government with private interests—which the American press has seen as a primary mission since the period 1880–1914. It is, in Irving Kristol's words, a "journalistic phenomenon that is indigenous to democracy, with its instinctive suspicion and distrust of all authority in general, and of concentrated political and economic power especially." Few would want to be without the tradition, and it is a young journalist of poor spirit who does not set out to uncover the machinations of some malefactor of great wealth and his political collaborators. Yet, there is a cost, as Roger Starr suggests in his wistful wish that Lincoln Steffens's *The Shame of the Cities* might be placed on the restricted shelves of the schools of journalism. Steffens has indeed, as Starr declares, continued "to haunt the city rooms of the country's major newspapers." The question to be asked is whether, in the aftermath of Steffens, the cities were better or merely more ashamed of themselves. Looking back, one is impressed by the energy and capacity for governance of some of the old city machines. Whatever else, it was popular government, of and by men of the people. One wonders: Did the middle- and upper-class reformers destroy the capacity of working-class urban government without replacing it with anything better, so that half a century later each and all bewail the cities as ungovernable? One next wonders whether something not dissimilar will occur now that the focus of press attention has shifted from City Hall to the White House. (And, yet, a miracle of American national government is the almost complete absence of monetary corruption at all levels, and most especially at the top.)

The muckraking tradition is well established. Newer, and likely to have far more serious consequences, is the advent of what Lionel Trilling called the "adversary culture" as a conspicuous element in journalistic practice. The appearance, in large numbers, of journalists shaped by the attitudes of this culture is the result of a process whereby the profession thought to improve itself by recruiting more and more persons from middle- and upper-class backgrounds and trained at the universities associated with such groups. This is a change but little noted as yet. The stereotype of American newspapers is that of publishers ranging from conservative to reactionary in their political views, balanced by reporters ranging from liberal to radical in theirs. One is not certain how accurate the stereotype ever was. One's impression is that, twenty years and more ago, the preponderance of the "working press" (as it liked to call itself) was surprisingly close in origins and attitudes to working people generally. They were not Ivy Leaguers. They now are or soon will be. Journalism has become, if not an elite profession, a profession attractive to elites. This is noticeably so in Washington, where the upper reaches of journalism constitute one of the most important and enduring *social* elites of the city, with all the accoutrements one associates with a leisure class. (The Washington press corps is not leisured at all, but the style is that of men and women who *choose* to work.)

The political consequence of the rising social status of journalism is that the press grows more and more influenced by attitudes genuinely hostile to American society and American government. This trend seems bound to continue into the future. On the record of what they have been writing while in college, the young people now leaving the Harvard *Crimson* and the Columbia *Spectator* for journalistic jobs in Washington will resort to the Steffens style at ever escalating levels of moral implication. They bring with them the moral absolutism of George Wald's vastly popular address, "A Generation in Search of a Future," that describes the Vietnam war as the "most shameful episode in the whole American history." Not tragic, not heartbreaking, not vastly misconceived, but *shameful*. From the shame of the cities to the shame of the nation. But nobody ever called Boss Croker any name equivalent in condemnatory weight to the epithet "war criminal."

II

An ironical accompaniment of the onset of the muckraking style directed toward the Presidency has been the rise of a notion of the near omnipotence of the office itself. This notion Thomas E. Cronin describes as the "textbook President." Cronin persuasively argues that, in the aftermath of Franklin Roosevelt, a view of the Presidency, specifically incorporated in the textbooks of recent decades, was developed that presented seriously "inflated and unrealistic interpretations of Presidential competence and beneficence," and which grievously "overemphasized the policy change and policy accomplishment capabilities" of the office. Cronin cites Anthony Howard, a watchful British commentator:

For what the nation has been beguiled into believing ever since 1960 is surely the politics of evangelism: the faith that individual men are cast to be messiahs, the conviction that Presidential incantations can be substituted for concrete programs, the belief that what matters is not so much the state of the nation as the inspiration-quotient of its people.

In his own researches among advisers of Kennedy and Johnson, Cronin finds the majority to hold "tempered assessments of presidential determination of 'public policy.'" Indeed, only 10 percent would describe the President as having "very great impact" over such matters.

Working in the White House is a chastening experience. But it is the experience of very few persons. Watching the White House, on the other hand, is a mass occupation, concentrated especially among the better-educated, better-off groups. For many, the experience is one of infatuation followed much too promptly by disillusion. First, the honeymoon—in Cronin's terms, the "predictable ritual of euphoric inflation." But then the "Camelot of the first few hundred days of all Presidencies fades away. . . . Predictably, by the second year, reports are spread that the President has become isolated from criticism." If this is so, he has only himself to blame when things go wrong. And things do go wrong.

If the muckraking tradition implies a distrust of government, it is nonetheless curiously validated by the overtrusting tradition of the "textbook Presidency," which recurrently sets up situations in which the Presidency will be judged as having somehow broken faith. This is not just the experience of a Johnson or a Nixon. Anyone who was in the Kennedy Administration in the summer and fall of 1963 would, or ought to, report a pervasive sense that our initiative had been lost, that we would have to get re-elected to get going again.

Here, too, there is a curious link between the Presidency and the press. The two most important *presidential* newspapers are the *New York Times* and the *Washington Post* (though the *Star* would be judged by many to have the best reporting). Both papers reflect a tradition of liberalism that has latterly been shaped and reinforced by the very special type of person who *buys* the paper. (It is well to keep in mind that newspapers are capitalist enterprises that survive by persuading people to buy them.) Theirs is a "disproportionately" well-educated and economically prosperous audience. The geographic areas in which the two papers circulate almost certainly have higher per capita incomes and higher levels of education than any of comparable size in the nation or the world. More of the buyers of these two papers are likely to come from "liberal" Protestant or Jewish backgrounds than would be turned up by a random sample of the population; they comprise, in fact, what James Q. Wilson calls the "Liberal Audience." Both the working-class Democrats and the conservative Republicans, with exceptions, obviously, have been pretty much driven from office among the constituencies where the *Times* and the *Post* flourish. It would be wrong to ascribe this to the influence of the papers. Causality almost certainly moves both ways. Max Frankel of the *Times,* who may have peers but certainly no betters as a working journalist, argues that a newspaper is surely as much influenced by those who read it as vice versa.

The readers of the *New York Times* and the *Washington Post,* then, are a special type of citizen: not only more affluent and more liberal than the rest of the nation, but inclined, also, to impose heavy expectations on the Presidency, and not to be amused when those expectations fail to be met. Attached by their own internal traditions to the "textbook Presidency," papers like the *Times* and the *Post* are reinforced in this attachment by the temperamental predilections of the readership whose character they inevitably reflect. Thus, they help to set a tone of pervasive dissatisfaction with the performance of the national government, whoever the Presidential incumbent may be and whatever the substance of his policies.

III

A third circumstance working to upset the old balance of power between the Presidency and the press is the fact that Washington reporters depend heavily on more or less clandestine information from federal bureaucracies, which are frequently, and in some cases routinely, antagonistic to presidential interests.

There is a view of the career civil service as a more or less passive executor of policies made on high. This is quite mistaken. A very great portion of policy ideas "bubble up" from the bureaucracy, and, just as importantly, a very considerable portion of the "policy decisions" that go down never come to anything, either because the bureaucrats cannot or will not follow through. (The instances of simple inability are probably much greater than those of outright hostility.) Few modern presidents have made any impact on the federal bureaucracies, save by creating new ones. The bureaucracies are unfamiliar and inaccessible. They are quasi-independent, maintaining, among other things, fairly open relationships with the congressional committees that enact their statutes and provide their funds. They are usually willing to work with the President, but rarely to the point where their perceived interests are threatened. Typically, these are rather simple territorial interests: not to lose any jurisdiction, and, if possible, to gain some. But, recurrently, issues of genuine political substance are also involved.

At the point where they perceive a threat to those interests, the bureaucracies just as recurrently go to the press. They know the press;

the press knows them. Both stay in town as presidential governments come and go. Both cooperate in bringing to bear the most powerful weapon the bureaucracies wield in their own defense, that of revealing Presidential plans in advance of their execution. Presidents and their plans are helpless against this technique. I have seen a senior aide to a President, sitting over an early morning cup of coffee, rise and literally punch the front page of the *New York Times*. A major initiative was being carefully mounted. Success depended, to a considerable degree, on surprise. Someone in one of the agencies whose policies were to be reversed got hold of the relevant document and passed it on to the *Times*. Now everyone would know. The mission was aborted. There was *nothing* for the Presidential government to do. No possibility of finding, much less of disciplining, the bureaucrat responsible. For a time, or rather from time to time, President Johnson tried the technique of not going ahead with any policy or appointment that was leaked in advance to the press. Soon, however, his aides began to suspect that this was giving the bureaucracy the most powerful weapon of all, namely, the power to veto a presidential decision by learning of it early enough and rushing to the *Times* or the *Post*. (Or, if the issue could be described in thirty seconds, any of the major television networks.)

What we have here is disloyalty to the Presidency. Much of the time what is involved is no more than the self-regard of lower-echelon bureaucrats who are simply flattered into letting the reporter know how much *they* know, or who are just trying to look after their agency. But just as often, to repeat, serious issues of principle are involved. Senator Joseph McCarthy made contact with what he termed the "loyal American underground"—State Department officials, and other such, who reputedly passed on information to him about Communist infiltration of the nation's foreign-policy and security systems. President Johnson made it clear that he did not trust the Department of State to maintain "security" in foreign policy. Under President Nixon, the phenomenon has been most evident in domestic areas, as OEO warriors struggle among themselves to be the first to disclose the imminent demise of VISTA, or HEW functionaries reluctantly interpret a move to close some fever hospital built to accommodate an eighteenth-century seaport as the first step in a master plan to dismantle public medicine and decimate the ranks of the elderly and disadvantaged.

It is difficult to say whether the absolute level of such disloyalty to the Presidency is rising. One has the impression that it is. No one knows much about the process of "leaking" except in those instances where he himself has been involved. (*Everyone* is sooner or later involved. That should be understood.) The process has not been studied, and little is known of it. But few would argue that the amount of clandestine disclosure is decreasing. Such disclosure is now part of the way we run our affairs. It means, among other things, that the press is fairly continuously involved in an activity that is something less than honorable. Repeatedly, it benefits from the self-serving acts of government officials who are essentially hostile to the Presidency. This does the Presidency no good, and, if an outsider may comment, it does the press no good, either. Too much does it traffic in stolen goods, and it knows it.

This point must be emphasized. The leaks that appear in the *Post* and the *Times*—other papers get them, but, if one wants to influence decisions in Washington, these are clearly thought to be the most effective channels—are ostensibly published in the interest of adding to public knowledge of what is going on. This budget is to be cut; that man is to be fired; this bill is to be proposed. However, in the nature of the transaction, the press can publish only half the story—that is to say, the information that the "leaker" wants to become "public knowledge." What the press *never* does is say who the leaker is and why he wants the story leaked. Yet, more often than not, this is the more important story: that is to say, what policy wins if the one being disclosed loses, what individual, what bureau, and so on.

There really are ethical questions involved here that have not been examined. There are also serious practical questions. It would be my impression that the distress occasioned by leaks has used up too much Presidential energy, at least from the time of Roosevelt. (Old-time brain-trusters would assure the Johnson staff that nothing could compare with FDR's distractions on the subject.) The primary fault lies within government itself, and one is at a loss to think of anything that might be done about it. But it is a problem for journalism as well, and an unattended one.

IV

The fourth of the five conditions making for an altered relation between the Presidency and the press is the concept of objectivity with respect to the reporting of events and, especially, the statements of public figures. Almost the first canon of the great newspapers, and by extension of the television news networks that, by and large, have taken as their standards those of the best newspapers, is that the "news" will be reported whether or not the reporter or the editor or the publisher likes the news. There is nothing finer in the American newspaper tradition. There is, however, a rub, and it comes when a decision has to be made as to whether an event really is news or simply a happening, a nonevent staged for the purpose of getting into the papers or onto the screen.

The record of our best papers is not reassuring here, as a glance at the experience of the Korean and the Vietnam wars will suggest. Beginning a bit before the Korean hostilities broke out, but in the general political period we associate with that war, there was a rise of right-wing extremism, a conspiracy-oriented politics symbolized by the name of Senator Joseph McCarthy and directed primarily at the institution of the Presidency. There was, to be sure, a populist streak to this movement: Yale and Harvard and the "striped-pants boys" in the State Department were targets, too. But to the question "Who promoted Peress?" there was only one constitutional or—for all practical purposes—political answer, namely, that the President did. McCarthy went on asking such questions, or rather making such charges, and the national press, which detested and disbelieved him throughout, went on printing them. The American style of objective journalism made McCarthy. He would not, I think, have gotten anywhere in Great Britain, where, because it would have been judged he was lying, the stories would simply not have been printed.

Something not dissimilar has occurred in the course of the Vietnam war, only this time the extremist, conspiracy-oriented politics of protest has been putatively left-wing. Actually, both movements are utterly confusing if one depends on European analogues. McCarthy was nominally searching out Communists, but his preferred targets were Eastern patricians, while his supporters were, to an alarming degree, members of the Catholic working class. The Students for a Democratic Society, if that organization may be used as an exemplar, was (at least in its later stages) nominally revolutionist, dedicated to the overthrow of the capitalist-imperialist-fascist regime of the United States. Yet, as Seymour Martin Lipset, Nathan Glazer, and others have shown, its leadership, and perhaps also its constituency, was disproportionately made up of upper-class Jewish and Protestant youth. By report of Steven Kelman, who lived as a contemporary among them at Harvard, the SDS radicals were "undemocratic, manipulative, and self-righteous to the point of snobbery and elitism." Peter Berger, a sociologist active in the peace movement, has demonstrated quite persuasively—what others, particularly persons of European origin like himself have frequently seemed to sense—that, despite the leftist ring of the slogans of the SDS and kindred groups, their ethos and tactics are classically fascist: the cult of youth, the mystique of the street, the contempt for liberal democracy, and the "totalization of friend and foe [with] the concomitant dehumanization of the latter," as in the Nazi use of *Saujuden* ("Jewish pigs").

In any case, the accusations that . . . filled the American air during the period of Vietnam [were] no more credible or responsible than those of McCarthy during the Korean period, and the tactics of provocation and physical intimidation [were,] if anything, . . . more disconcerting. Yet, the national press and, especially, television . . . assumed a neutral posture, even at times a sympathetic one, enabling the neofascists of the Left to occupy center stage throughout the latter half of the 1960s with consequences to American politics that have by no means yet worked themselves out. . . .

If the press is to deserve our good opinion, it must do better in such matters. And it should keep in mind that the motivation of editors and reporters is not always simply and purely shaped by a devotion to objectivity. In the course of the McCarthy era, James Reston recalled the ancient adage that, translated from the Erse, proposes that, "If you want an audience, start a fight." This is true of anyone who would find an audience for his views or simply for himself. It is true also for anyone who would find customers for the late city edition. T. S. Matthews, sometime editor of *Time*, retired to England to ponder the meaning of it all. In the end, all he could conclude was that the function of journalism was entertainment. If it is to be more—and that, surely, is what the Rosenthals and Bradlees and Grunwalds and Elliotts want—it will have to be willing, on occasion, to forgo the entertainment value of a fascinating but untruthful charge. It will, in short, have to help limit the rewards that attend this posture in American politics.

V

The final, and by far the most important, circumstance of American journalism relevant to this discussion is the absence of a professional tradition of self-correction. The mark of any developed profession is the practice of correcting mistakes, by whomsoever they are made. This practice is, of course, the great invention of Western science. Ideally, it requires an epistemology that is shared by all respected members of the profession, so that, when a mistake is discovered, it can be established as a mistake to the satisfaction of the entire professional community. Ideally, also, no discredit is involved. To the contrary, honest mistakes are integral to the process of advancing the field. Journalism will never attain to any such condition. Nevertheless, there is a range of subject matter about which reasonable men can and will agree, and within this range American journalism, even of the higher order, is often seriously wide of the mark. Again Irving Kristol: "It is a staple of conversation among those who have ever been involved in a public activity that when they read the *Times* the next morning, they will discover that it has almost never got the story quite right and has only too frequently got it quite wrong."

Similar testimony has come from an editor of the *New York Times* itself. In an article published some years ago in the Sunday *Times Magazine*, A. H. Raskin had this to say:

No week passes without someone prominent in politics, industry, labor or civic affairs complaining to me, always in virtually identical terms: "Whenever I read a story about something in which I really know what is going on, I'm astonished at how little of what is important gets into the papers—and how often even that little is wrong." The most upsetting thing about these complaints is the frequency with which they come from scientists, economists and other academicians temporarily involved in government policy but without any proprietary concern about who runs the White House or City Hall.

This is so and, in part, is unavoidable. Too much happens too quickly: That the *Times*, the *Post*, or the *Star* should appear once a day is a miracle. (Actually, they appear three or four times a day in different editions.) But, surely, when mistakes are made, they ought to be corrected. Sometimes they are, but not nearly often enough. It is in this respect that Kristol is right in calling journalism the "underdeveloped profession."

In the wake of so lengthy an analysis, what is there to prescribe? Little. Indeed, to prescribe much would be to miss the intent of the analysis. I have been hoping to make two points—the first explicitly, the second largely by implication. The first is that a convergence of journalistic tradition with evolving cultural patterns has placed the national government at a kind of operating disadvantage. It is hard for government to succeed. This theme echoes from every capital of the democratic world. In the United States, it is hard for government to succeed and just as hard for government to appear to have succeeded when, indeed, it has done so. This situation can be said to have begun in the muckraking era with respect to urban government; it is now very much the case with respect to national government, as reflected in the "national press," which primarily includes the *New York Times*, the *Washington Post*, *Time*, *Newsweek*, and a number of other journals.

There is nothing the matter with investigative reporting; there ought to be more. The press can be maddeningly complacent about real social problems for which actual countermeasures, even solutions, exist. (I spent a decade, 1955–65, trying to obtain some press coverage of the problem of motor-vehicle design, utterly without avail. The press, from the most prestigious journals on down, would print nothing but the pap handed out by the automobile companies and wholly owned subsidiaries, such as the National Safety Council.) The issue is one not of serious inquiry but of an almost feckless hostility to power.

The second point is that this may not be good for us. American government will only rarely and intermittently be run by persons drawn from the circles of those who own and edit and write for the national press; no government will ever have this circle as its political base. Hence, the conditions are present for a protracted conflict in which the national government keeps losing. This might once have been a matter of little consequence or interest. It is, I believe, no longer such, for it now takes place within the context of what Nathan Glazer has so recently described as an "assault on the reputation of America . . . which has already succeeded in reducing this country, in the eyes of many American intellectuals, to outlaw status." In other words, it is no longer a matter of this or that administration; it is becoming a matter of national morale, of a "loss of confidence and nerve," some of whose possible consequences, as Glazer indicates, are not pleasant to contemplate.

Some will argue that, in the absence of a parliamentary question time, only the press can keep the Presidency honest. Here, we get much talk about Presidential press conferences and such. This is a serious point, but I would argue that the analogy does not hold. Questions are put in Parliament primarily by members of an opposition party, hoping to replace the one in office. Incompetent questions damage those chances; irresponsible questions damage the office. Indeed, British politicians have been known to compare the press lords to ladies of the street, seeking "power without responsibility." It would, of course, be better all around if Congress were more alert. Thus, the *Times* has reported that the GNP estimate in the 1971 Budget Message was not that of the Council of Economic Advisers but, rather, a higher figure dictated by the White House for political purposes. This is a profoundly serious charge. Someone has a lot to explain. It could be the administration; it could be the *Times*. Congress should find out.

Obviously, the press of a free country is never going to be, and never should be, celebratory. Obviously, government at all levels needs, and will continue to get, criticism, and some of it will inevitably be harsh or destructive, often enough justifiably so. Obviously, we will get more bad news than good. Indeed, the content of the newspapers is far and away the best quick test of the political structure of a society. Take a morning plane from Delhi to Karachi. One leaves with a sheaf of poorly printed Indian papers filled with bad news; one arrives to find a small number of nicely printed Pakistani papers filled with good news. One has left a democracy and has entered a country that is something less than a democracy.

Nonetheless, there remains the question of balance. Does not an imbalance arise when the press becomes a too willing outlet for mindless paranoia of the Joseph McCarthy or New Left variety? Does it not arise when the press becomes too self-satisfied to report its own mistakes with as much enterprise as it reports the mistakes of others?

Norman E. Isaacs, a working journalist, has written thoughtfully about the possibility of establishing a "national press council." This, in effect, was proposed by Robert M. Hutchins's Commission on

Freedom of the Press in 1947: "A new and independent agency to appraise and report annually upon the performance of the press." There are press councils in other democratic countries, which hear complaints, hand down verdicts, and even, as in Sweden, impose symbolic fines. There is a case to be made here, but I would argue that to set up such a council in this country at this time would be just the wrong thing to do. There is a statist quality about many of the press councils abroad: Often as not, they appear to have been set up to ward off direct government regulation. Freedom of the press is a constitutional guarantee in the United States. How that freedom is exercised should remain a matter for the professional standards of those who exercise it. Here, however, there really is room for improvement. First, in the simple matter of competence: The very responsibility of the national press in seeking to deal with complex issues produces a kind of irresponsibility. The reporters aren't up to it. They get it wrong. It would be astonishing were it otherwise.

Further, there needs to be much more awareness of the quite narrow social and intellectual perspective within which the national press so often moves. There are no absolutes here; hardly any facts. But there *is* a condition that grows more, not less, pronounced. The national press is hardly a "value-free" institution. It very much reflects the judgment of owners and editors and reporters as to what is good and bad about the country and what can be done to make things better. It might be hoped that such persons would give more thought to just how much elitist criticism is good for a democracy. Is this a shocking idea? I think not. I would imagine that anyone who has read Peter Gay or Walter Laqueur on the history of the Weimar Republic would agree that there are dangers to democracy in an excess of elitist attack. A variant of the Jacksonian principle of democratic government is involved here. Whether or not ordinary men are capable of carrying out any government task whatsoever, ordinary men are going to be given such tasks. That is what it means to be a democracy. We had best not get our expectations too far out of line with what is likely to happen, and we had best not fall into the habit of measuring all performance by the often quite special tastes, preferences, and interests of a particular intellectual and social elite. (Perhaps most importantly, we must be supersensitive to the idea that, if things are not working out well, it is because this particular elite is not in charge. Consider the course of events that led to the war in Indochina.)

As to the press itself, one thing seems clear. It should become much more open about acknowledging mistakes. . . . Doubtless, the bane of any editor is the howling of politicians and other public figures claiming to have been misquoted. But often they *are* misquoted. At the very least, should not more space be allotted to rebuttals and exchanges in which the issue at hand is how the press performed?

Another possibility is for each newspaper to keep a critical eye on itself. In the article previously cited that he did for the Sunday *Times Magazine,* A. H. Raskin called for a "Department of Internal Criticism" in every paper "to put all its standards under re-examination and to serve as a public protection in its day-to-day operations." The *Times* itself has yet to establish such a department, but the *Washington Post* has recently set a welcome example here by inaugurating a regular editorial-page feature by Richard Harwood entitled "The News Business." Harwood's business is to check up on what his paper runs, and he is finding a good deal to check up on. (To all editors: *Please* understand there is nothing wrong with this. It is a routine experience of even the most advanced sciences. Perhaps especially of such.) Harwood has made a useful distinction between mistakes of detail—the ordinary garbles and slips of a fast-moving enterprise— and mistakes of judgment about the nature of events:

> The mistakes that are more difficult to fix are those that arise out of our selection and definition of the news. Often we are unaware of error until much time has passed and much damage has been done.
>
> In retrospect, it seems obvious that the destructive phenomenon called "McCarthyism"—the search in the 1950s for witches, scapegoats, traitors—was a product of this kind of error. Joseph McCarthy, an obscure and mediocre senator from Wisconsin, was transformed into the Grand Inquisitor by publicity. And there was no way later for the newspapers of America to repair that damage, to say on the morning after: "We regret the error."

Which will turn out, "in retrospect," to seem the obvious errors of the 1960s? There were many, but they are past. The question now is what might be the errors of the 1970s, and whether some can be avoided. One Richard Harwood does not a professional upheaval make, but he marks a profoundly important beginning. All major journals should have such a man in a senior post, and very likely he should have a staff of reporters to help him cover the "news business."

As for the government itself, there is not much to be done, but there is something. It is perfectly clear that the press will not be intimidated. Specific efforts like President Kennedy's to get David Halberstam removed as a *Times* correspondent in Vietnam almost always fail, as they deserve to do. Nonspecific charges, such as those leveled by Vice-President Agnew, get nowhere, either. They come down to an avowal of dislike, which is returned in more than ample measure, with the added charge that, in criticizing the press, the government may be trying to intimidate it, which is unconstitutional.

What government can do and should do is respond in specific terms to what it believes to be misstatements or mistaken emphases; it should address these responses to specific stories in specific papers, and it should expect that these will be printed (with whatever retort the journal concerned wishes to make). Misrepresentations of government performance must never be allowed to go unchallenged. The notion of a "one-day story" and the consoling idea that yesterday's papers are used to wrap fish are pernicious and wrong. Misinformation gets into the bloodstream and has consequences. . . .

In the end, however, the issue is one not of politics but of culture. The culture of disparagement that has been so much in evidence of late, that has attained such an astonishing grip on the children of the rich and the mighty, and that has exerted an increasing influence on the tone of the national press in its dealings with the national government is bad news for democracy. Some while ago, the late Richard Hofstadter foresaw what has been happening:

> Perhaps we are really confronted with two cultures (not Snow's), whose spheres are increasingly independent and more likely to be conflicting than to be benignly convergent: a massive adversary culture on the one side, and the realm of socially responsible criticism on the other.

But, given what has been happening to the press in recent years and what is likely to go on being the case if current trends should continue on their present path, where is such "socially responsible criticism" to come from? Or, rather, where is it to appear in a manner that will inform and influence the course of public decision-making?

Editors' Note: This essay aroused much comment and some lengthy rebuttals when it was first published. See especially White House correspondent Max Frankel's letter to the editor in the July 1971 issue of *Commentary* and a later analysis of White House press relations by veteran *New York Times* reporter John Herbers, *No Thank You, Mr. President* (New York: W. W. Norton, 1976). A book that presents even more evidence to support Moynihan's interpretations is James Keogh, *President Nixon and the Press* (New York: Funk & Wagnalls, 1972). On the other hand, the best-seller *All the President's Men* (New York: Simon & Schuster, 1974) by Carl Bernstein and Bob Woodward well illustrated some of the important contributions to be made by investigative reporters with some of the old-fashioned muckraking perspective. See also, on the role of the press and the limits of the press during a presidential campaign, Timothy Crouse, *The Boys on the Bus: Riding with the Campaign Press Corps* (New York: Random House, 1973).

10. On the Isolation of Presidents

George E. Reedy

It has probably never been so difficult to assess the place of the Presidency in the view of the American people as at this writing. It is possible to draw certain impressionistic—and probably valid—conclusions. The office has undoubtedly lost the imperial grandeur of the last decade. It no longer has the power to evoke the "my President right or wrong" response from its constituency. Significant boundaries have been set around the chief executive's heretofore unchecked power to deploy armed forces as an instrument of foreign policy. But whether these factors represent a temporary lapse in the onward march of the office or whether they signal a radical turn in the development of our government is unclear.

The problem is that we are viewing the Presidency in the wake of two disastrous administrations and at the end of that of a man who has been appointed to the job through machinery that did not exist a few years ago. Even for abnormal times, these are abnormal circumstances in which perspectives are necessarily distorted. Events have moved too rapidly to be digested. The moth-eaten cliché that "the people have been stunned" may, for once, be a literal description of the state of mind of large parts of our population, at least when they direct their attention to questions of government. The unusually low voting turnouts in 1976 probably reflect more than anything else a desire not to think about the presidential election.

Nevertheless, the Presidency is still *there* whether people think about it or not. It remains the only structure for the conduct of our national affairs and the only human symbol of our national unity. It has not been replaced, and there has not been, nor is there now, a substantial effort to devise an alternative method of doing business. The fundamental sources of a President's power have not been altered. He (perhaps, in a few years, she) remains the only official elected to office by a national vote, the only official who can speak as "the United States" to other nations, the only official who can give ultimate orders to the armed forces, the only official who can come close to mobilizing the total economic, social, and political power of the nation. At the moment, no prudent chief executive would try to exercise these powers to the same extent as his predecessors of the past forty-five years. But the inhibitions are less a function of checks on the President than they are of a national desire for a lower degree of activity in the international field. Americans simply do not want to send troops anywhere at the present time.

In short, the Presidency has survived its critics. It will remain the focal point of our national life. The issue before us is not whether it is an adequate focal point as contrasted to alternatives but whether what has happened to the office has opened the door to improvements in terms of fostering a higher degree of national unity and greater coherence in problem-solving. No conclusive answer can be given at this point. We can only speculate. In my judgment, the most important area for speculation is that of presidential isolation. Have there been developments that have broken down the walls that separated the President from the American people?

On the surface, it would appear that a change *has* taken place. Our recent President, Gerald R. Ford, gave every appearance of enjoying an easy and human relationship with his fellow Americans. As a person, he is liked even by severe critics who questioned his competence, and there was no evidence that he succumbed to the temptations inherent in the White House for a man to reign rather than govern. If the Presidency is a monarchy, he was in the pattern of Louis Philippe, the "Citizen" King rather than Louis XIV, the Sun King.

Although Jimmy Carter seems aware of the isolation problem and may even be going too far in his efforts to democratize the Presidency, we will not know whether his efforts will be successful until he has settled into the office. For the time being, the only solid evidence we have is the conduct of President Ford. However, two factors must be taken into consideration that render a judgment very hazardous at this time.

First, Ford was originally appointed, rather than elected, to the job. He was a caretaker, and he knew it. He did not have the mystic ordination that comes from a popular ballot in which the "voice of the people" expresses a choice. The real test will be in the conduct of an *elected* President, and it is possible that even Ford could have become quite regal as the possessor of a national mandate.

Second, a major portion of Ford's appointive term was spent preparing for the 1976 elections. There is nothing that brings a politician so close to the people as an election campaign. Anxiety for votes sharpens sensitivities marvelously and has a remarkable influence in fostering humility. The real test, again, will come in the conduct of a President who can look back to an election with satisfaction rather than forward to an election with apprehension.

It should be clearly understood that I am not implying in the preceding two paragraphs that there has been no change. In fact, I believe there have been within the past few years developments that may have opened important channels of communication between the President and the American people. Whether this belief is valid or merely wishful thinking, however, cannot be determined at the present time. All I can do is suggest certain promising avenues to explore and watch carefully.

Before discussing the developments, however, it would be well to define the trends that led to the isolation of presidents. Basically, they rested upon factors that were built into the office by the Constitution but did not assume serious proportions until the advent of a truly mass society, with its overriding requirement for a decision center that can react quickly to emergencies entailing the possibility of catastrophe. In a simpler age, the aloofness of the chief executive was probably a positive virtue. It served as an offset to the intransigent sectional passions that in the highly individualistic atmosphere that persisted even after the closing of the frontier were quite capable of tearing the nation to pieces unless checked. Furthermore, until quite recently, the isolation of the office from popular pressures was not truly dangerous. The United States could survive four—or even eight—years of bad leadership; the President did not have at his command instruments of social control that would make possible the institution of genuine dictatorship; and the time interval between a decision and its effectuation was sufficiently long to permit the operation of the checks and balances built into our system.

The social and economic interdependence that characterizes modern life changed the factors upon which the conclusions in the preceding paragraph are based. The exact point at which the change took place cannot be stated with any degree of certainty, but it is useful to consider, as an important milestone, the advent of the New Deal, with its successful assertion of the principle that it is legitimate to use federal power as an engineering instrument to enhance the public welfare. That principle is now accepted by all except the extreme right and the extreme left, and any argument over it is moot, even though it has become apparent that the "public welfare" is rather difficult to define. Nevertheless, the practice of the concept involves consequences with which we must deal, and they have not been considered sufficiently.

The first consequence is that enhancing the public welfare necessarily requires an increasing amount of interdependence and the surrender of a degree of individuality. It also means a higher degree of social vulnerability to individual action and, consequently, a sharper reaction from more stable elements in society to nonconformists who threaten, or appear to threaten, economic and social stability. This has brought about a type of polarization we have not had before. On the one hand, young people who have no memories of the economic horrors of the Depression and minorities who have not shared in the economic gains of the past forty years find the conformity that goes with interdependence to be oppressive. On the other hand, those who have participated in the advance regard dissidence as the opening wedge for a return to the dark days of economic insecurity. Under these circumstances, the problem of sustaining national unity takes on new dimensions. It is not resolved merely by maintaining national symbols. Instead, a very subtle form of political brokerage—the art by which leaders assure highly diverse elements in the population that they are getting a fair hearing—is needed. It is an art that can be practiced successfully only by sensitive politicians.

In the second place, social engineering requires social controls and the application of mass information techniques that tend to treat people as roughly comparable units rather than individual human beings. Even so humane an act as the establishment of a social-security system calls for the registration of citizens in the mass. Furthermore, the conscious change of institutions necessitates the use of forms of coercion ranging all the way from incentives to outright policing. The necessity for such devices increases directly with the degree of interdependence in a society, and it is rather obvious that we can look forward to an era of ever increasing controls unless we fall into social disintegration. In addition to these factors, the international tensions of the past twenty-five years have brought about the maintenance of permanent military forces so large and so well organized that the concept of an armed citizenry capable of resisting an oppressive government is obsolete. Thus, we have a situation in which previously unforeseen instruments of power have been placed in the hands of a chief executive at the same time that events are forcing him to make basic decisions with less time for reflection and under circumstances that force him to focus his attention upon masses of statistics rather than individual human beings.

In the third place, severe strains have been placed on the checks-and-balances system of the Constitution. This is largely a function of the necessity for quick reaction time—a necessity that enhances the power of the initiative inherent in the Presidency and permits the chief executive to commit irrevocable acts before his decision processes can be subjected to outside scrutiny. At all times, he has sufficient money available to carry out military operations to a point where competing branches of government must rally to his support. Legal interpretations of the interstate-commerce and public-welfare clauses of the Constitution have become sufficiently broad that he can exercise federal police powers even to the extent of coercing industry into observing his pricing policies in fields where no specific law governs. Nearly four decades of experience have produced a rough form of parallelism between the executive and the judiciary, and court decisions in modern times are more likely to sustain than overturn national policy.

All of these factors have altered the shape of the Presidency. They cannot be regarded as mere accretions of power. They have actually changed the relationships between the branches of government and the people as these relationships were understood by the Founding Fathers. Careful study of the changes is urgent.

Past studies of the Presidency have focused generally on the question of what the man has done to, or with, the job. The subject raised here is the direct opposite—what the job does to the man, and the consequences for our society. There is a personal quality to political leadership that ultimately overrides all other considerations, and, whatever may be the components that enter into a man's individual psychology, his relationship to other human beings is a determining factor in what he will do. In this respect, the basic factor in the President's position is that he can shape his immediate environment to his liking to a greater degree than any other citizen of the United States. His immediate environment is the executive branch of the government, with more than 2.5 million civilian employees and a like number of men and women in uniform, and annual budgets inching up toward $500 billion despite stern efforts to hold them down.

Naturally, there are limitations to his power, and there would be limitations even should the President bring the nation into what is generally described as an absolute dictatorship. But, with the passage of time, these limitations appeared more and more as frustrations that must be surmounted rather than elements that must be taken into account in resolving political problems. For a lengthy period of time, the major preoccupation of the White House was finding ways to bypass both Congress and the courts in carrying out presidential designs.

Circumstances surrounded the Presidency with an atmosphere of adulation, composed of both sycophancy and genuine respect for the office, which has had parallels only in divine-right monarchies. This was no trivial matter. Every man has a tendency to interpret the universe in terms of his immediate environment, and everything surrounding a President was designed to please him. Personal, adversary relationships in which he must come to terms with others on a day-to-day basis were absent, and virtually all the information he received was presented by people who desired to retain his favor. This situation had two deleterious effects. First, the information that reached the White House had gone through a filtering process that may not have altered facts (though even this was possible) but had stripped those facts of the unpleasant nuances and the controversial passions that are essential to valid political judgments. Second, the atmosphere of the White House itself tended to dull the sensitivities of the politician to the emotions of other people. These are both situations that tend to isolate a man from the realities of democratic politics, which basically consist of resolving differences between contentious people and persuading them to work together, in some kind of harmony, toward national goals.

Isolation from reality is inseparable from the exercise of power. It is inherent in the positions of industrial leaders, labor leaders, intellectual leaders—any people who can bid others to do their will. But there is always a question of degree. Only the President achieves an ultimate of power in our society (or at least an approximation to an ultimate). All other leaders have peers who can speak to them on a one-to-one basis without any sense of awe or subordination. This is the one office that can be almost totally isolated from the necessity most human beings face of accommodating themselves to the desires of others.

This does not mean that a President can be shielded completely from unpleasant comment or attack. Senators and representatives can make blistering speeches from the floors of their respective chambers. Unfortunately, these rarely coincide with the tone of what they say within the executive mansion, and thus the chief executive is frequently left with the impression that he is the victim of duplicity. Newspaper editorials and television commentaries can be bitter. But these enter the White House as mechanical contrivances, which can be cut off, and there is a very human tendency to ascribe such criticism to a conspiracy rather than to genuine feeling. The ultimate cushioning, however, is the realization that the Presidency is the summit of political ambition, and that there is nowhere else to go. Under such circumstances, a man who does not expect to serve in public office again can easily persuade himself that he can safely ignore his critics because he will be vindicated by the verdict of history and that his detractors will look very small in the long view.

It is too much to expect a man to make sensitive judgments on the enduring will and tolerance levels of the people whom he has been commissioned to lead under such circumstances. He has available to him the methods of modern, scientific polling, which have been brought to a relatively high degree of accuracy. But, at best, they reflect only a crude majority, which can be broken up very easily, and in addition, they reflect only *where* that majority stands—not *why* it stands and what must be done to lead people instead of just going along with them. Government by poll can be a stagnant proposition, indeed.

The effects of this situation on our national life are readily apparent. Without entering into an argument on the substantive merits of Southeast Asian policy, it is quite clear that overoptimistic reports on the balance of forces in Vietnam and overoptimistic assessments of the reaction of the American people to the war led us into a bitter divisiveness with few precedents in our history. And it is equally clear that the Nixon Administration failed totally to open up some channels of communication with dissident elements in our population that may have been in a minority but were quite capable of tearing our nation apart or—more likely—provoking repression that could put an end to democracy. We survived, owing either to the intercession of a Divine Providence, the soundness with which the Founding Fathers constructed our institutions, or, more probably, a little bit of both.

An interesting feature of our survival, however, is that it demonstrated strengths and flexibilities in our system of which we had been unaware. Congress, which had been virtually impotent for many years, did find and exercise checks on executive power. The courts, which had been approving most adventures in executive activity, did uphold the principle that even the President is not above the law. And the people discovered that it was possible, however difficult, to rid themselves of an intolerable President before the end of his term. Precedents have been established that will not quickly go away.

It is significant, for example, that Gerald R. Ford decided to go to Congress and seek authority to aid the anticommunist forces in Angola. It is doubtful whether his predecessors would have taken such a step. The mere presence of Cuban troops in the country would have been enough. Some document that could be interpreted as an American commitment would have been found, and the marines would have been on their way even while the explanatory report to Congress was in the process of preparation. What is even more important than the President's request for authority, however, is the precedent that was set when Congress turned him down. Such actions can be habit-forming. The post–World War II pattern was based on the assumption that the legislative branch of the government will always support a chief executive who moves against communism. The record now says that there are times when Congress will not grant such support under certain circumstances, and future Presidents must take this record into account before moving.

The courts shattered an important wall of insulation when Nixon was compelled to surrender the tapes of his conversations in the White House. Again, this is not the place to discuss either the circumstances under which the compulsion took place or the legal niceties of the doctrine of executive privilege. Whatever the lawyers may have thought, recent presidents have operated on the assumption that, as a practical matter, they could withhold any or all documents in the White House from other branches of the government and could prevent testimony before Congress and the courts on the internal life of the White House. Future presidents will no longer be able to eliminate from their calculations the possibility of adversary scrutiny of their private words and adversary questioning of their trusted assistants. They may not know the circumstances under which such adversary proceedings can take place, but the uncertainty will merely add to their discomfort.

Finally—and most important—no President in the future can operate in confidence that he will serve out his term, barring death in office. The American system demonstrated that it can rid itself of even so determined a man as Richard M. Nixon without waiting for an electoral end to his administration. This may be the most important legacy of Watergate.

Legally, it was always possible to unseat a President through the impeachment process. But no substantial body of thought in Washington, D.C., before 1974 regarded impeachment as a practical possibility. It was considered a dead provision of the Constitution, one that had been tried once against a President under dubious circumstances and had failed. It was a power that had fallen into disuse even in its application to judges and lower officials. The basic assumption was that presidents were—and should be—untouchable in their tenure.

The fact that Nixon resigned before the impeachment process could run its course does not alter the precedent that has been set. A basic tenet of monarchy is unchallengeable tenure. The Watergate case proved that unchallengeable tenure no longer exists. It is exceedingly difficult—and should be—to oust a sitting President, *but it is possible*. A line has been drawn over which the chief executive cannot step, and the uncertainty of the precise location of that line probably strengthens its value as a boundary to conduct.

When all these factors are viewed together, it becomes apparent that very important *possibilities* have been opened for breaking the political isolation under which the presidents of recent years have operated. The isolation was, more than anything else, a function of the unchecked (or seemingly unchecked) powers of the chief executive. It had come to be taken for granted that the President's judgment was *final* in the field of foreign affairs, that his judgment was virtually final in all but a few domestic matters, and that he could not be called to account for his actions, short of the election process. No one can exercise final judgments without eventually becoming isolated from his fellow human beings.

What happened to us is that our presidents lost the most important of all political skills—the ability to take other viewpoints into account.

It is not surprising that this happened. Presidents are politicians, and politicians are men and women under constant bombardment from opposing points of view. Out of the sheer necessity of setting some form of priorities over what they will or will not listen to, they become accustomed to considering only those views that are backed by political strength with which they must negotiate. A President lives under the illusion that he need not negotiate with anyone other than the heads of foreign powers. The creation of this illusion has been the real mischief of the atmosphere of the office.

It is now clear that there are other factors that presidents must take into account. They must, at least for the time being, negotiate with Congress in the field of foreign, as well as domestic, policy. They must conduct their operations in the realization that all of them can be spread on a public record. And they must also realize that they are no longer untouchable.

There are other things that should be done. It would be well to devise means of reducing the size of the White House staff. A sharper definition of which staff members are, and which are not, entitled to executive privilege would be helpful. It is urgent that Congress devise checks upon such agencies as the CIA.

Nevertheless, there are now precedents that can—if they are continually pressed—bring our presidents back into the world of political reality. This is a "consummation devoutly to be wished." It may not lead to "better government" in the sense of problem-solving. But it could lead to a higher degree of national unity on a democratic basis and to a higher degree of confidence in our free institutions.

PART FOUR

The Imperial Presidency Reappraised

11. Congress and the Making of American Foreign Policy

Arthur Schlesinger, Jr.

The problem of the control of foreign policy has been a perennial source of anguish for democracies. The idea of popular government hardly seems complete if it fails to embrace questions of war and peace. Yet, the effective conduct of foreign affairs appears to demand, as Tocqueville argued long ago, not the qualities peculiar to a democracy but "on the contrary, the perfect use of almost all those in which it is deficient." Steadfastness in a course, efficiency in the execution of policy, patience, secrecy—are not these more likely to proceed from executives than from legislatures? But, if foreign policy becomes the property of the executive, what happens to democratic control? In our own times, this issue has acquired special urgency, partly because of the Indochina war, with its aimless persistence and savagery, but more fundamentally, I think, because the invention of nuclear weapons has transformed the power to make war into the power to blow up the world. And, for the United States, the question of control of foreign policy is, at least in its constitutional aspect, the question of the distribution of powers between the Presidency and the Congress. . . .

The war power has historically involved a competition between the power of the Congress to authorize war and the power of the President as commander in chief. It is important to state the issue with precision. The issue is not the declaration of war in a strict sense. Long before Under Secretary Katzenbach startled the Senate Foreign Relations Committee, in 1967, by pronouncing the declaration of war "outmoded," Hamilton had written, in the 25th *Federalist*, "The ceremony of a formal denunciation of war has of late fallen into disuse." One study of European and American wars shows that, between 1700 and 1870, hostilities began in 107 cases without declaration of war; in only ten cases was there a declaration of war in advance of hostilities. Though the United States has engaged in a number of armed conflicts in the last two centuries, it has only made five formal declarations of war (of which four—all but the War of 1812—recognized the prior existence of states of war).

The real issue is congressional authorization—whether or not by declaration of war—of the commitment of American forces in circumstances that involve or invite hostilities against foreign states. One aspect of this issue emerged clearly during the undeclared naval war with France in 1798–1801. Mr. Katzenbach injudiciously testified that "President John Adams' use of troops in the Mediterranean" (by which he presumably meant Adams's use of the fleet in the Atlantic) was "criticized at the time as exceeding the power of the Executive acting without the support of a congressional vote." Others, before and since, have cited this conflict as an early precedent in the cause of Presidential warmaking. In fact, when trouble with France began, Adams called Congress to meet in special session "to consult and determine on such measure as in their wisdom shall be deemed meet for the safety and welfare of the said United States." In due course, Congress turned more belligerent than the President and, in the spring of 1798, passed some twenty laws to encourage Adams to wage the war. Adams's Attorney General described the conflict as a "maritime war *authorized* by both nations," and, in 1800, the Supreme Court, called up to define the conflict, drew a distinction between "perfect" and "imperfect" wars. As it concluded, in a unanimous decision, if war

> be declared in form, it is called solemn, and is of the perfect kind. . . . But hostilities may subsist between two nations, more confined in its nature and extent; being limited as to places, persons, and things; and this is more properly termed imperfect war. . . . Still . . . it is a war between two nations, though all the members are not authorized to commit hostilities such as in a solemn war.

Both sorts of war, whether solemn or nonsolemn, complete or limited, were deemed to require some mode of congressional authorization. When John Marshall assumed leadership of the Court in 1801, he reinforced the point in a second case arising out of the trouble with France. "The Congress," he ruled, "may authorize general hostilities . . . or partial war."

Jefferson similarly acknowledged the congressional right to license hostilities by means short of a declaration of war, while, at the same time, he affirmed the right of the executive to repel sudden attack.

When an American naval schooner was fired on by a Tripolitanian cruiser in the Mediterranean, it repulsed the attack with signal success; but, Jefferson instructed Congress, its commander was "unauthorized by the Constitution, without the sanction of Congress, to go beyond the line of defense," so the enemy vessel, having been "disabled from committing further hostilities, was liberated with its crew." Jefferson went on to ask Congress to consider "whether, by authorizing measures of offense also, they will place our force on an equal footing with that of its adversaries." Again, fearing incursions into Louisiana by the Spanish in Florida in 1805, he declined to broaden defense against sudden attack into defense against the threat of sudden attack and said in a special message: "Considering that Congress alone is constitutionally invested with the power of changing our condition from peace to war, I have thought it my duty to await their authority for using force. . . . The course to be pursued will require the command of means which it belongs to Congress exclusively to yield or to deny."

In this case, Congress chose to deny. But, half a dozen years later, a more belligerent Congress led a more reluctant President into war. In 1812, Madison, now that he was the executive and the War Hawks of the legislature were demanding hostilities with Britain, may well have reflected ruefully on his argument of 1798 about the supposed greater interest of the executive in war.

When the Seminole Indians were conducting raids into American territory in 1818, President Monroe chose not to consult Congress before ordering General Andrew Jackson to chase the raiding parties back into Spanish Florida, where Jackson was soon fighting Spaniards and hanging Englishmen. But tangling with foreigners was incidental to Jackson's ostensible objective, which was punishing Indians. We would now call the principle on which he and Monroe acted "hot pursuit." Where direct conflict with a foreign state was the issue, Monroe was more cautious. When he promulgated his famous Doctrine, he neither consulted with Congress nor sought its subsequent approval; but, when Colombia requested U.S. protection under the Monroe Doctrine, John Quincy Adams, Monroe's Secretary of State, carefully replied that the Constitution confided "the ultimate decision . . . to the Legislative Department."

Jackson himself, as President, meticulously respected this point. Though he enlarged the executive power with relish in other areas, on the question of the war-making power he followed not his own example of 1818 but Jefferson's of 1801. Thus, in 1831, after ordering an armed vessel to South America to protect American shipping against Argentine raiders, he said, "I submit the case to the consideration of Congress, to the end that they may clothe the Executive with such authority and means as they deem necessary for providing a force adequate to the complete protection of our fellow citizens fishing and trading in these seas." When France persisted in her refusal to pay long-outstanding claims for damage to American shipping during the Napoleonic wars, Jackson, instead of moving on his own, took care to ask Congress for a law "authorizing reprisals upon French property, in case provision shall not be made for the payment of the debt." (Albert Gallatin observed that this "proposed transfer by Congress of its constitutional powers to the Executive, in a case which necessarily embraces the question of war or no war," was "entirely inconsistent with the letter and spirit of our Constitution," and Congress turned Jackson down.) When Texas rebelled against Mexico and sought U.S. recognition as an independent republic, Jackson referred the matter to Congress as a question "probably leading to war" and therefore a proper subject for "previous understanding with that body by whom war can alone be declared and by whom all the provisions for sustaining its perils must be furnished."

Still, the executive retained the ability, if he so desired, to contrive a situation that left Congress little choice but to give him a declaration of war. James K. Polk demonstrated this in 1846, when, without congressional authorization, he sent American forces into disputed land, where they were attacked by Mexican units who, not unreasonably, considered it Mexican territory. Polk quickly obtained a congressional declaration of war, but many members of Congress had the uneasy feeling that the President had put something over on them. Two years later, with the war still on, the House resolved by a narrow margin that it had been "unnecessarily and unconstitutionally begun by the President of the United States." Perhaps so; but, unlike some later presidents, Polk did have behind him not just a congressional or U.N. resolution, but a formal declaration of war by the Congress. In any case, this was the situation that provoked Congressman Lincoln of Illinois into his celebrated attack on presidential war-making:

> Allow the President to invade a neighboring nation, whenever *he* shall deem it necessary to repel an invasion . . . and you allow him to make war at pleasure. Study to see if you can fix *any limit* to his power in this respect. . . . If, today, he should choose to say he thinks it necessary to invade Canada, to prevent the British from invading us, how could you stop him? You may say to him, "I see no probability of the British invading us," but he will say to you, "Be silent; I see it, if you don't."

The prevailing view in the early Republic, it has been suggested, was that congressional authorization was clearly required for the commitment of American forces overseas in circumstances that involved or invited hostilities against foreign states. But what if the hostilities contemplated were not against foreign governments but were in protection of American honor, law, lives, or property against

Indians, slave traders, pirates, smugglers, frontier ruffians, or foreign disorder? Early presidents evidently decided, as a practical matter, that forms of police action not directed against a sovereign nation did not rise to the dignity of formal congressional concern. These were mostly trivial episodes; and, when Senator Goldwater, with such fugitive engagements in mind, said "We have only been in five declared wars out of over 150 that we fought," he was stretching the definition of war in a way that could comfort only those who rejoice in portraying the United States as incurably aggressive throughout its history.

Jackson in Florida was an early example; but the commitment of armed force without congressional authorization was by no means confined to North America or to the Western Hemisphere. American naval ships in these years took military action against pirates or refractory natives in places as remote as Sumatra (1832, 1838, 1839), the Fiji Islands (1840, 1855, 1858), and Africa (1820, 1843, 1845, 1850, 1854, 1858, 1859). As early as 1836, John Quincy Adams could write, "However startled we may be at the idea that the Executive Chief Magistrate has the power of involving the nation in war, even without consulting Congress, an experience of fifty years has proved that in numberless cases he has and must have exercised the power."

Adams, who in any case (at least till the Mexican War came along) regarded the power of declaring war as an "Executive act," mistakenly turned over by the Founding Fathers to the Congress, somewhat exaggerated. Still the spreading employment of force overseas by unilateral presidential decision, even if not yet against sovereign governments, was a threat to the congressional monopoly of the war power. In the meantime, the demonstration by Monroe of the unilateral presidential power to propound basic objectives in foreign policy, the demonstration by Polk of the unilateral presidential capacity to confront Congress with *faits accomplis*, the demonstration by Pierce of the unilateral presidential power to threaten sovereign states (as when he sent Commodore Perry and a naval squadron to open up Japan in 1854)—all these further diminished the congressional voice in the conduct of foreign affairs. Congress continued to fight back, particularly on the question of the war power. It took, for example, special pleasure in rejecting half a dozen requests for the authorization of force from the punctilious Buchanan, who believed that "without the authority of Congress the President cannot fire a hostile gun in any case except to repel the attacks of an enemy."

Perhaps it was Buchanan's strict constructionism that led to the drastic expansion of presidential initiative under his successor; for Lincoln may well have delayed the convocation of Congress till ten weeks after Fort Sumter lest rigid constitutionalists on the Hill try to stop him from doing what he deemed necessary to save the life of the nation. In this period of executive grace, he reinforced Sumter, assembled the militia, enlarged the army and navy beyond their authorized strength, called out volunteers for three years' service, disbursed unappropriated moneys, censored the mail, suspended habeas corpus, and blockaded the Confederacy—measures that, as he said, "whether strictly legal or not, were ventured upon under what appeared to be a popular demand and a public necessity; trusting then as now that Congress would readily ratify them." He added that it was with deepest regret he thus employed what he vaguely called the "war power"; however, "he could but perform this duty, or surrender the existence of the Government."

No President had ever undertaken such sweeping actions in the absence of congressional authorization. No President had ever confronted Congress with such a massive collection of *faits accomplis*. Benjamin R. Curtis, who had been one of the two dissenting justices in the Dred Scott case, wrote that Lincoln had established a "military despotism." But Congress gave retroactive consent to Lincoln's program; and, two years later, the Court, in the Prize cases, found constitutional substance (narrowly; the vote was 5–4) for his idea of the "war power" by attaching it to his authority as commander in chief and to his right to defend the nation against attack. Throughout the war, Lincoln continued to exercise wide powers independently of Congress. The Emancipation Proclamation, for example, was a unilateral executive act, pronounced under the war power without reference to Congress. But Lincoln's assertion of the war power took place, it should not be forgotten, in the context of a domestic rebellion and under the color of a most desperate national emergency. There is no suggestion that Lincoln supposed he could use this power in foreign wars without congressional consent.

The presidential prerogative has not grown by steady accretion. Nearly every President who has extended the reach of the White House has provoked a reaction toward a more restricted theory of the Presidency, even if the reaction never quite cuts presidential power back to its earlier level. When Lincoln expanded presidential initiative, Congress took out its frustrations by harassing him through the Committee on the Conduct of the War, impeaching his successor, and eventually establishing a generation of congressional government. In this period of relative military quiescence (there were only 17 instances of American military action abroad in the twenty years after the Civil War as compared to 38 in the twenty years before the war), the locus of conflict shifted from the war power to the treaty power. The Senate's constitutional right to consent to treaties—even though it had long since lost to George Washington its claim for a voice in negotiations and to his successors its power to confirm the appointment of negotiators—turned out to be more solidly embedded in the structure of government than the constitutional right of the Congress to declare war.

In the years after the Civil War, the Senate freely exercised its power to rewrite, amend, and reject treaties negotiated by the President. Indeed, it ratified no important treaty between 1871 and 1898. Writing in 1885, Woodrow Wilson observed that the President was made to approach the Senate "as a servant conferring with a master. . . . It is almost as distinctly dealing with a foreign power as were the negotiations preceding the proposed treaty. It must predispose the Senate to the temper of an overseer." Wilson grimly noted that the treaty-making power had become the "treaty-*marring* power"; and, a dozen years later, John Hay told Henry Adams that he did not believe "another important treaty would ever pass the Senate."

Secretaries of State regarded the assertion of senatorial prerogative as the mindless expression of institutional jealousy. As Secretary of State Richard Olney observed in one case, "The Treaty, in getting itself made by the sole act of the executive, without leave of the Senate first had and obtained, had committed the unpardonable sin. It must be either altogether defeated or so altered as to bear an unmistakable Senate stamp . . . and thus be the means both of humiliating the executive and of showing to the world the greatness of the Senate." Hay regarded the one-third veto as the "original," the "irreparable" mistake of the Constitution, now grown to "monstrous shape," and wrote, "The attitude of the Senate toward public affairs makes all serious negotiations impossible."

Ways had to be found to evade the veto. One was the use of the joint resolution, which required only a majority of the Congress as against two-thirds of the Senate; by such means Texas was annexed in 1845 and Hawaii in 1898. Another was the use of agreements entered into directly by the President with foreign states. The "executive agreement" had the legal force of a treaty; and, though largely confined, in the nineteenth century, to technical matters, it could be the vehicle of large purposes. It was, for example, the means by which Britain and the United States agreed, in the Rush-Bagot accord of 1817, to disarm the Great Lakes and by which the United States, in 1898–99, developed the policy of the Open Door in China.

Still, Congress remained in the saddle. As Henry Adams put it in a famous complaint:

> The Secretary of State exists only to recognize the existence of a world which Congress would rather ignore; of obligations which Congress repudiates whenever it can; of bargains which Congress distrusts and tries to turn to its advantage or to reject. Since the first day the Senate existed, it has always intrigued against the Secretary of State whenever the Secretary has been obliged to extend his functions beyond the appointment of Consuls in Senators' service.

But, just as executive domination had produced a shift in power over foreign policy toward Congress after the Civil War, so congressional domination was beginning to produce a shift back to the Presidency. And, in clamoring for war with Spain, Congress became its own executioner. Writing in 1900, Wilson eloquently portrayed the impact of that war upon the lodgment and exercise of power within the federal system. When foreign affairs dominate the policy of a nation, he said, "its Executive must of necessity be its guide: must utter every initial judgment, take every first step of action, supply the information upon which it is to act, suggest and in large measure control its conduct. The President of the United States is now . . . at the front of affairs, as no president, except Lincoln, has been since the first quarter of the nineteenth century."

Oddly, Congress, in its salad years, had not asserted itself on the question of the war power, perhaps because it so generally agreed with the use the executive made on his own motion of American forces abroad. Victory over Spain now made the United States a world power; and, in 1900, President McKinley set the tone for the new century by sending 5,000 American troops to China. The pretext was the protection of American lives and property; in fact, the Americans joined an international force, besieged Peking, and helped put down the Boxer Rebellion. This was done without reference to Congress and without serious objection from it. The intervention in China, resulting, among other things, in the exaction of an indemnity from the Chinese Government, marked the start of a crucial shift in the use of the armed forces overseas. Where, in the nineteenth century, military force committed without congressional authorization had been typically used in police actions against private groups, now it was beginning to be used against sovereign states. In the next years, Theodore Roosevelt and Taft sent American forces into Caribbean countries and, in some cases, even installed provisional governments—all without prior congressional sanction.

In 1912, in an effort to meet the constitutional problem, J. Reuben Clark, the Solicitor of the State Department, offered a distinction between "interposition" and "intervention." Interposition meant simply the insertion of troops to protect lives and property; it implied neutrality toward the government or toward contesting forces within the country; and, since it was a normal exercise of international law, it did not, Clark argued, require congressional approval. Intervention, on the other hand, meant interference in sovereign affairs; it implied an act of war and required congressional authorization.

Whatever merit this distinction might have had in the nineteenth century when the United States was a small power, by the twentieth century a great power could hardly interpose anywhere without intervening in sovereign affairs. On the other hand, it could be argued that the superior force of the United States was now so great, relative to the Caribbean states, that intrusion, whether interposition or intervention, did not invite the risk of war and therefore did not require congressional consent. Still, whatever the nuances of arguments, limitations were evaporating. The executive was becoming habituated to the unconstrained deployment of American forces around the world, and Congress chose not to say him nay. Though Wilson received retroactive congressional approval for an incursion into Mexico in 1914 and the approval of the Senate for another in 1916, he did not seek congressional authorization when he sent troops to Siberia after World War I. Congressional resolutions of protest perished in committee.

The revival of presidential initiative under Theodore Roosevelt and Wilson provoked the predictable reaction. The Senate, reasserting its prerogative, rejected the Versailles Treaty (though, when the elder Henry Cabot Lodge claimed, in his second reservation, that Congress had the "sole power" to "authorize the employment of the military or naval forces," his fellow isolationist William E. Borah called it a "recital which is not true"). By the 1930s, the Congress, regarding World War I as the malign consequence of presidential discretion in foreign affairs, imposed a rigid neutrality program on the executive and remained generally indifferent when Germany and Japan set out on courses of aggression. The reassertion of the presidential prerogative in the years since must be understood, in part, as a criticism of what happened when Congress tried to seize the reins of foreign policy in the years 1919–39.

The outbreak of war, in 1939, found the President restrained both by the neutrality laws and by the balance of power in Congress from doing what he deemed necessary to save the life of the nation. Roosevelt responded, as Lincoln had eighty years before, by pressing to the utmost limits of presidential power. But, though doubtless encouraged by Justice Sutherland and the Curtiss-Wright decision, he did this without grandiose claims of executive authority. When he exchanged American destroyers for British bases in an executive agreement [in] 1940—Senators Fulbright and Church have both said that Roosevelt "usurped the treaty power of the Senate"—he did not found his action on novel authority claimed as commander in chief nor as inherent powers of the Presidency, but on the construction of laws passed by Congress in 1917 and 1935. Nor did the transaction involve promises of future performance, and Roosevelt's circle of prior consultation included even the Republican candidate for President.

When, in 1941, he sent American troops to Greenland and later to Iceland, this was done in agreement with the Danish Government in the first case and the government of Iceland in the second; moreover, the defense of Greenland and, less plausibly, Iceland could be considered as part of hemisphere security. Senator Robert A. Taft declared that Roosevelt had "no legal or constitutional right to send American troops to Iceland" without authority from Congress. Few of his colleagues echoed this protest. The Selective Service Act of 1940 had contained a provision that draftees could not be used outside the Western Hemisphere (except in American possessions); but the younger Lodge, who sponsored this provision, evidently doubted its force and called it a "pious hope."

In instituting a convoy system and issuing the "shoot at sight" order to the navy in the North Atlantic, Roosevelt was bringing the nation, without congressional authorization, into undeclared naval war with Germany. Senator Fulbright has latterly charged that he "circumvented the war powers of the Congress." But the poignant character of Roosevelt's dilemma was made clear when, in August, 1941, the House of Representatives renewed the Selective Service Act by a single vote. If Congress came that close to disbanding the army at home, how could Roosevelt have reasonably expected congressional support for his forward policy in the North Atlantic? His choice was to go to Congress and risk the fall of Britain to Hitler or to proceed on his own with measures that, "whether strictly legal or not, were ventured upon under what appeared to be a popular demand and a public necessity; trusting then as now that Congress would readily ratify them."

Roosevelt did not, like later presidents, seek to strip Congress of powers in the name of the inherent authority of the commander in chief. The most extraordinary prewar decision—Lend-Lease—was authorized by Congress following intensive and exacting debate. After America entered the war, Roosevelt asked Congress for authority to send military missions to friendly nations. Both Roosevelt and Hull, remembering the fate of Wilson, made elaborate efforts to bring members of Congress from both parties into the discussion of postwar policy through the Advisory Committee on Postwar Foreign Policy and through congressional representation at Bretton Woods, San Francisco, and in the delegations to the United Nations. The United Nations Participation Act of 1945 took express care to protect the war powers of Congress.

The towering figure of Franklin Roosevelt, the generally accepted wisdom of his measures of 1940–41, his undisputed powers as commander in chief after Pearl Harbor, the thundering international agreements pronounced at wartime summits of the Big Two or the Big Three—all these factors, combined with the memory of the deplorable congressional performance in foreign affairs during the years between the wars, gave Americans, in the postwar years, an exalted conception of presidential power. Moreover, Roosevelt's successor, a man much read in American history and of doughty temperament, regarded his office, in the words of his last Secretary of State, as a "sacred and temporary trust, which he was determined to pass on unimpaired by the slightest loss of power or prestige." Dean Acheson himself, though an eminent lawyer, was impatient with what he saw as constitutional hair-splitting and encouraged the President in his stout defense of high prerogative. Nor were they alone. As early as 1945, Senator Vandenberg was asserting that the "President must not be limited in the use of force" in the execution of treaties; and, when Vandenberg asked the retired Chief Justice, Charles Evans Hughes, whether the President could commit troops without congressional approval, Hughes replied, "Our Presidents have used our armed forces repeatedly without authorization by Congress, when they thought the interests of the country required it." It must be added that American historians and political scientists, this writer among them, labored to give the expansive theory of the Presidency due historical sanction.

Above all, the uncertainty and danger of the early cold war, with the chronic threat of unanticipated emergency always held to require immediate response, with, above all, the overhanging possibility of nuclear catastrophe, seemed to argue all the more strongly for the centralization of the control over foreign policy, including the use of armed forces, in the Presidency. And the availability of great standing armies and navies notably enlarged presidential power; before World War II, presidents (Lincoln excepted) could call on only such limited force as was already in existence. Where Truman required congressional consent either because of the need for appropriations (the Marshall Plan) or for treaty ratification (NATO), he rallied that support effectively. But he decided not to seek formal congressional approval for the commitment of American forces to hostilities in Korea (though he consulted congressional leaders informally before American troops went into action) lest he diminish the presidential prerogative. This was followed by his decision, also proposed without reference to Congress, to send four divisions to reinforce the American army in Europe. These initiatives greatly alarmed conservative members of Congress. On January 3, 1951, Congressman Frederic Coudert of New York introduced a resolution declaring it the sense of the Congress that no "additional military forces" could be sent abroad "without the prior authorization of the Congress in each instance." Two days later, in a full-dress speech before the Senate, Taft returned to the argument he had made against Roosevelt ten years earlier. "The President," he said,

> simply usurped authority, in violation of the laws and the Constitution, when he sent troops to Korea to carry out the resolution of the United Nations in an undeclared war. . . . I do not believe the President has the power without congressional approval to send troops to one country to defend it against a possible or probable attack by another country.

Tom Connally, the Chairman of the Senate Foreign Relations Committee, responded with a stirring assertion of high prerogative. "The authority of the President as Commander in Chief to send the Armed Forces to any place required by the security interests of the United States," he said, "has often been questioned, but never denied by authoritative opinion." Secretary of State Acheson went even further:

> Not only has the President the authority to use the Armed Forces in carrying out the broad foreign policy of the United States and implementing treaties, but it is equally clear that this authority may not be interfered with by the Congress in the exercise of powers which it has under the Constitution.

Acheson added irritably: "We are in a position in the world today where the argument as to who has the power to do this, that, or the other thing, is not exactly what is called for from America in this very critical hour."

The debate also divided scholars. Henry Steele Commager wrote, "Whatever may be said of the expediency of the Taft-Coudert program, this at least can be said of the principles involved—that they have no support in law or in history." The present writer, with a flourish of historical documentation and, alas, hyperbole, called Taft's statements "demonstrably irresponsible." In reply, Professor Corwin, who had studied the constitutional position of the Presidency for many years with sardonic concern, pronounced Commager and Schlesinger (with some justice) "high-flying prerogative men" who ascribed to the President a "truly royal prerogative in the field of foreign relations . . . without indicating any correlative legal or constitutional control to which he is answerable."

The Great Debate of 1951 ended inconclusively in the passage of a "sense of the Senate" resolution in which the Senate approved the sending of Truman's four divisions but asserted that no additional ground troops should be sent to Western Europe "without further congressional approval." The administration opposed this ceiling; Senator Nixon of California was among those who voted for it. Where Acheson noted that the resolution was "without force of law" and "had in it a present for everybody," Taft applauded it as a "clear statement by the Senate that it has the right to pass on any question of sending troops to Europe to implement the Atlantic Pact." Both were right; and since no subsequent President has tried to increase the American army in Europe, the resolution has never been tested.

In areas more clearly dependent on the appropriations power, notably in foreign aid, Congress neither then nor later hesitated to tie up executive programs with all manner of hortatory prescriptions, rigid stipulations, and detailed specifications, often against executive desire. In 1948, it forced an additional $400 million in aid to China; in 1950, over strong executive objection, it imposed a mandatory loan to Spain. Nor did it hesitate, in 1951–52, to go beyond the administration in using economic aid to encourage not only economic cooperation but political integration in Western Europe. This congressional effort to shape foreign policy through appropriations did not relent in subsequent years; and the greatest dependency of foreign policy on appropriations has meant that, in this sector at least, the Presidency has lost power to Congress. When Monroe issued the Monroe Doctrine, he did not seek congressional assent, but when Kennedy called for the Alliance for Progress, he was at the mercy of Congress every step along the way.

The postwar argument between the Congress and the Presidency spilled over to the treaty power as well. Members of Congress feared that the executive agreement, which had started out (with notable exceptions like Rush-Bagot) as a vehicle on minor matters, was now threatening to supersede the treaty as the means of major commitment. In December, 1950, when Prime Minister Attlee came to Washington, a resolution sponsored by, among others, Senator Nixon declared it the sense of the Senate that the President not only report in full to the Senate on his discussions but refrain from entering into any understandings or agreements. The Secretary of State dismissed this as "plainly . . . an infringement of the constitutional prerogative of the President to conduct negotiations." Still, the resolution received thirty votes. Concern over the abuses of the executive agreement, already set off by hysteria among conservatives about the Yalta accords, soon flowed into the movement for the Bricker Amendment.

This amendment went through a succession of orchestrations; but the pervading theme was that treaties and executive agreements should become effective as internal law only through legislation valid in the absence of a treaty. This would mean not only that a treaty could not authorize what the Constitution forbids but that action by the House of Representatives and, in some cases, by state legislatures might be necessary to give it full effect. One version specifically empowered Congress "to regulate all executive and other agreements with any foreign power or international organization." When moderate conservatives joined with liberals to resist the amendment, Senator Knowland plucked out the section on executive agreements and offered a bill requiring that all such agreements be transmitted to the Senate within sixty days of their execution. Though the Senate passed this bill, in July, 1956, the House failed to act. In 1972, when Senator Case of New Jersey, a liberal Republican, revived the Knowland idea, the Senate, with liberals in the lead, passed it almost unanimously, and a liberal Democrat, Senator Pell of Rhode Island, recently remarked that the Bricker Amendment, "if put up today, would be voted overwhelmingly by all of us."

The congressional protest subsided, in part because the election of a Republican President, in 1952, seemed to promise a period of executive restraint and congressional influence, and in part because Congress, no less than the executive, accepted the presuppositions of the cold war. Moreover, as so often, the acquisition of power altered perspectives. Secretary of State Dulles opposed the Bricker Amendment as strongly as any Democrat; and, while the Eisenhower Administration was active in seeking joint resolutions at times of supposed vital decision in foreign affairs, it did so not because it thought Congress had any authority in the premises but because the resolution process, by involving Congress in the takeoff, would incriminate it in a crash-landing (this valuable aerial metaphor had been invented by Harold Stassen in 1946). The resolution process now became a curious ceremony of propitiation in which presidents yielded no claims and Congress asserted few, but which provided an amiable illusion of partnership; it was in domestic terms what someone had said of the Briand-Kellogg Pact—"an international kiss."

Sometimes, even members of Congress considered such resolutions superfluous. When President Eisenhower, recalling Truman's omission in 1950, asked, in 1955, for a resolution to cover possible American military activity around Formosa, Sam Rayburn, Speaker of the House and presumably an incarnation of the congressional prerogative, said, "If the President had done what is proposed here without consulting the Congress, he would have had no criticism from me." The Formosa Resolution at least contained language by which the President was "authorized to employ the Armed Forces," however lightly the executive regarded that language, but Congress loosened even that pretense of control by adding that he could use these forces "as he deems necessary" in the defense of Formosa and the Pescadores. When Eisenhower sought a Middle East Resolution in 1957, the Senate Foreign Relations Committee this time deleted the idea of congressional authorization. Senator Fulbright even expressed the fear that any resolution might limit the President's power as commander in chief to defend the "vital interests" of the nation. And when Eisenhower, in what in retrospect seems a mysterious and, indeed, hazardous mission, sent 14,000 troops to Lebanon the next year, he cited as authority for this action, not at all his own resolution but the now capacious presidential prerogative.

On the other hand, Eisenhower had acknowledged the practical importance of congressional support when, in 1954, he yielded to congressional (as well as British) opposition and declined to commit American force to the relief of Dien Bien Phu. At the same time, however, he reduced the significance of the troop-commitment issue by confiding an increasing share of American foreign operations to an agency presumed beyond the reach of Congress, the Central Intelligence Agency. In the Eisenhower years, the CIA became the primary instrument of American intervention overseas, helping to overthrow governments in Iran (1953) and Guatemala (1954), failing to do so in Indonesia (1958), helping to install governments in Egypt (1954) and Laos (1959), organizing an expedition of Cuban refugees against the Castro regime (1960). Congress had no oversight over the CIA. It even lacked regular means of finding out what it was up to. There was a joint congressional committee on atomic energy but none . . . on secret intelligence operations.

The cold war created both a critical environment and an uncritical consensus; and these enabled even a relatively passive President, a "Whig" like Eisenhower, to enlarge the unilateral authority of the executive. Nor did either the President or the Congress see this as a question of usurpation. During the 1950s, and much of the 1960s, most of Congress, mesmerized by the supposed need for instant response to constant crisis, overawed by what the Senate Foreign Relations Committee later called the "cult of executive expertise," accepted the "high-flying" theories of the presidential prerogative. In early 1960, Senator John F. Kennedy observed that, however large the congressional role in the formulation of domestic programs, "it is the President alone who must make the major decisions of our foreign policy." As late as 1961, Senator Fulbright contended that "for the existing requirements of American foreign policy we have hobbled the President by too niggardly a grant of power." While he found it "distasteful and dangerous to vest the executive with powers unchecked and unbalanced," the question, he concluded, was "whether we have any choice but to do so." Republicans were no less devoted to the crisis of executive supremacy. "It is a rather interesting thing," Senator Dirksen, then Republican leader, told the Senate in 1967, "—I have run down many legal cases before the Supreme Court—that I have found as yet no delimitation on the power of the Commander in Chief under the Constitution." "I am convinced," said Senator Goldwater, "there is no question that the President can take military action at any time he feels danger for the country or, stretching a point, for its position in the world."

In this state of political and intellectual intimidation, Congress forgot even the claim for consultation and was grateful when the executive bothered to say what it planned to do. ("The distinction between solicitation of advice in advance of a decision and the provision of information in the wake of a decision would seem to be a significant one," the Senate Foreign Relations Committee finally commented in 1969. Pointing out that, in the cases of the Cuban missile crisis and the Dominican intervention, congressional leaders were informed what was to be done only a few hours before the decisions were carried out, the Committee added dryly, "Such acts of courtesy are always to be welcomed; the Constitution, however, envisages something more.") In this mood, too, Congress acquiesced in national commitment through executive agreement—as, for example, in the case of Spain, where the original bases agreement of 1953 was steadily escalated by official pronouncement through the years until the Foreign Relations Committee could conclude, in 1969, that the sum of executive declarations was a virtual commitment on the part of the United States to come to the aid of Spain. Senator Fulbright recently remarked a little bitterly, "We get many treaties dealing with postal affairs and so on. Recently, we had an extraordinary treaty dealing with the protection of stolen art objects. These are treaties. But when we put troops and take on commitments in Spain, it is an executive agreement."

The case of Thailand is equally astonishing. In 1962, Secretary of State Rusk and the Thai Foreign Minister expressed, in a joint declaration, "the firm intention of the United States to aid Thailand . . . in resisting Communist aggression and subversion." While this statement may have been no more than a specification of SEATO obligations, the executive branch thereafter secretly built and used bases and consolidated the Thai commitment in ways that would still be unknown to Congress and the electorate had it not been for the indomitable curiosity of Senator Symington and his Subcommittee on Security Arrangements and Commitments Abroad. The Subcommittee also uncovered interesting transactions involving the executive branch with Ethiopia (1960), Laos (1963), and South Korea (1966). The case of Israel is even more singular. Here a succession of executive declarations through five administrations have produced a virtual commitment without the pretense of a treaty or even an executive agreement.

In this mood, also, Congress accepted the Americanization of the Vietnam war in 1965. "If this decision was not for Congress under the Constitution," Professor Bickel has well said, "then no decision of any consequence in matters of war and peace is left to Congress." As for the Tonkin Gulf Resolution, though President Johnson liked to flourish it as proof that Congress had indeed made a decision, he himself really did not think, as he later put it, that the "resolution was necessary to do what we did and what we're doing." As he unfolded his view of Presidential power in 1966: "There are many, many, who can recommend, advise and sometimes a few of them consent. But there is only one that has been chosen by the American people to decide."

Listing twenty-four statutes facilitating the fighting in Vietnam, Senator Goldwater said, in 1971, "Congress is and has been involved up to its ears with the war in Southeast Asia." The argument that Congress thereby "authorized" the war, especially by voting appropriations, has a certain practical strength up to the point (as Judge

Frank Coffin put it in a 1971 decision of the First Circuit Court) where Congress asserts a conflicting claim of authority, which it has not done. But, also as a practical matter, it is rare indeed for parliaments to deny supplies to fighting men, and too much cannot be inferred from the refusal to punish the troops for the sins of those who sent them into the line. It is true that members of the British Parliament voted against supply bills during the American Revolution, but this was before the Reform Acts had created constituencies broad enough to include large numbers of relatives of men in combat. At the height of his opposition to the Mexican War, Congressman Lincoln said, "I have always intended, and still intend, to vote supplies." Still, though Congress has placed restrictions on troop deployment, it had not, by the middle of 1972, interposed a decisive obstacle to presidential escalation of the war.

If President Johnson construed the high prerogative more in the eighteenth-century style of the British king than of the executive envisaged by the Constitution, his successor carried the inflation of presidential authority even further. In asserting that his power as the commander in chief authorized him to use American ground troops to invade Cambodia—and to do so without reference to, or even the knowledge of, Congress—President Nixon indulged in presidential war-making beyond a point that even his boldest predecessors could have dreamed of. Those who had stretched the executive war power in the past had done so in the face of visible and dire threat to national survival: Lincoln confronted by rebellion, Roosevelt by the Third Reich. Each, moreover, had done what he felt he had to do without claiming constitutional sanction for every item of presidential action.

But, in justifying the commitment of American troops to war in a remote and neutral country, Nixon cited no emergency that denied time for congressional action, expressed no doubt about the total legality of his own initiative, and showed no desire even for retroactive congressional ratification. All he was doing, he told the Senate Republican leader in June, 1970, was fulfilling the "Constitutional duty of the Commander in Chief to take actions necessary to protect the lives of United States forces." This was no more, he implied, than the routine employment of presidential power; it required no special congressional assent, not even the fig-leaf, shortly repealed and abandoned, of the Tonkin Gulf Resolution. William Rehnquist of the Department of Justice, himself soon escalated by the President to the Supreme Court, called it a "valid exercise of his constitutional authority as Commander in Chief to secure the safety of American forces"—a proposition that might not have deeply moved the Nixon Administration had it been advanced by the Presidium to explain why the Red Army was justified in invading a neutral country to secure the safety of

Russian forces. "The President's authority to do what he did, in my view," Rehnquist concluded, "must be conceded by even those who read executive authority narrowly." It was, in fact, challenged by even those who read executive authority broadly.

The government thus committed armed forces to hostilities, first in Cambodia, then in Laos and North Vietnam (for the air force remains a part of the armed forces), on the basis of a theory of defensive war so elastic that a President could freely and on his own initiative order armed intervention in any country housing any troops that might in any conceivable circumstance be used in an attack on American troops. If this seemed an extraordinary invasion of the congressional war power, there seemed a comparable invasion of the appropriations power when Henry Kissinger informed Hanoi, in secret negotiation, that the United States "could give and undertake, a voluntary contribution by the President, that there would be a massive reconstruction program for all of Indochina, in which North Vietnam could share to the extent of several billion dollars."

Congress appeared increasingly impotent in the face of the size and momentum of the postwar institutions of American foreign policy—an institutional array spearheaded by an aggressive Presidency and supported by a military and intelligence establishment virtually beyond congressional reach. Indeed, large sections of the electorate were coming to feel that foreign policy had escaped from democratic control, and that the institutions would have their way however the voters might vote.

Excess, as usual, invites reaction; and the Senate, with due timidity, reacted. What Versailles had done to the congressional prerogative, Vietnam now did to the presidential prerogative. But Congress did not react by frontal attack on the means by which the President continued the war, though various members of Congress urged this course on their colleagues. The Senate reacted rather by passing, in June, 1969, by 70 to 16, the National Commitments Resolution, described by the Senate Foreign Relations Committee as an "invitation to the executive to reconsider its excesses, and to the legislature to reconsider its omissions in the making of foreign policy." Neither invitation was accepted.

The Senate also reacted, in April, 1972, by passing a War Powers bill, from the workings of which Vietnam was specifically exempted. This bill, conceived and bravely promoted by Senator Javits, has, from some views, substantial defects. Had it been on the statute books in past years, it would surely have prevented Roosevelt from responding to Hitler in the North Atlantic in 1941 and would surely not have prevented Johnson from escalating the war in Vietnam (for Johnson would have received—indeed, did receive—overwhelming congressional support for escalation at every point till the middle of 1968). If passed by the Congress, the bill might be more likely to become a means of inducing formal congressional approval of warlike presidential acts than of preventing such acts.* Moreover, the principle on which the bill is based—that the President must carry out the policy directives of Congress in the initiation and prosecution of military hostilities—might itself have bellicose consequences the next time War Hawks dominate the legislative branch. Still, the Senate's passage of the bill—especially by the impressive margin of 68 to 16— might have been expected to have some cautionary influence in reminding the President that Congress, in its pathetic way, thought it had some voice in the determination of peace and war. It had no such effect. A fortnight after its passage, President Nixon, again without reference to Congress, threw the American air force into devastating attacks on North Vietnam.

If there is an imbalance of powers, if Congress has lost authority clearly conferred on it by the Constitution, it can only be said that Congress has done little to correct the situation. Its complaints have been eloquent; its practical action has been slight. Its problem has been less lack of power than lack of will to use the powers it has—the power of appropriation; the power to regulate the size of the armed forces; the power, through joint resolutions, to shape foreign policy; the power to inform, investigate, and censure. As late as the summer of 1972, the Senate, in declining Senator Cooper's amendment to the aid bill, which proposed to cut off funds for American troops and bombing in four months, relinquished, in the words of the *Washington Post*, the "only opportunity it has ever dared afford itself to make an independent and conclusive judgment of the war."

In the present as in the past, Congress has preferred to renounce responsibility—which is why the Presidency has retained power. "We may say that power to legislate for emergencies belongs in the hands of Congress," said Justice Jackson in the Steel Seizure case, "but only Congress itself can prevent power from slipping through its fingers." The situation today, for all the wails of congressional self-pity, is much the one that Lincoln feared in 1848: "Allow the President to invade a neighboring nation [or, today, a nation on the other side of the world], whenever *he* shall deem it necessary to repel an invasion . . . and you allow him to make war at pleasure. Study to see if you can fix *any limit* to his power in this respect."

*Arthur Schlesinger's views here are developed more extensively in his *The Imperial Presidency* (Houghton Mifflin, 1973). After his essay was published, Congress attempted to assert itself. Thus, the War Powers Resolution of 1973, which is described and discussed in detail by Graham Allison in Selection 12. Also, in May 1976, after twenty years of various legislative efforts in this direction, the U.S. Senate established a permanent Select Committee on Intelligence with legislative and budgetary authority over the CIA and other federal agencies.—Eds.

The Abraham Lincoln who had thus challenged the presidential prerogative of Polk was the same Abraham Lincoln who, a dozen years later, gave the Presidency greater powers over war and peace than ever before, as the Andrew Jackson who showed such deference to Congress in the 1830s was the same Andrew Jackson who, a dozen years earlier, had charged without congressional authority into Spanish Florida. This is a critical point in understanding the nature of the issue. For nothing has been more characteristic of the perennial debate than the way in which the same people, in different circumstances and at different points in their lives, have argued both sides of the issue.

Richard M. Nixon had one set of views in 1951 on the question of whether Congress could control troop commitments and executive agreements. By 1971, he had an opposite set of views. Senator Fulbright, moving in the reverse direction, has long since repented his belief that the President needs more control over foreign policy. Professor Corwin's "high-flying prerogative men" of twenty years ago have zoomed downward on this question in recent times. Professor Commager has, in effect, accepted the Taft-Coudert case in his testimony in favor of the War Powers bill; and this writer, while remaining skeptical about the War Powers bill, would freely concede that Senator Taft had a much more substantial point than he supposed twenty years ago. But, to make that point, Senator Taft had to explain away the views of *his* father, the Chief Justice, who had written, in 1916, that the President as commander in chief "can order the Army and Navy anywhere he will, if the appropriations furnish the means of transportation." And, while the younger Senator Taft has followed his father rather than his grandfather, such heirs of Taft as Goldwater and Rehnquist are today very high-flying prerogative men. For that matter, Professor Corwin's own record was not all that immaculate. While he defended the congressional prerogative in 1951, in 1940 he had raised the question "whether the President may, without authorization by Congress, take measures which are technically acts of war in protection of American rights and interests abroad," and replied: "The answer returned both by practice and by judicial doctrine is yes." Even as late as 1949, Corwin described the power "to employ without congressional authorization the armed forces in protection of American rights and interests abroad wherever necessary" as "almost unchallenged from the first and occasionally sanctified judicially."

There are several reasons for this chronicle of vacillation. For one thing, the issues involved are ones of genuine intellectual difficulty, about which reasonable men may well find themselves changing their minds. For another, power usually looks more responsible from inside than from outside. For another, general questions often assume different shapes in different lights. It is agreeable to claim constitutionality for policies one supports and agreeable, too, to stigmatize policies one opposes as unconstitutional. All these reasons tend toward a single conclusion: that the problem we face is not primarily constitutional. It is primarily political. History offers the lawyer or scholar almost any precedent he needs to sustain what he may consider, in a concrete setting, to be wise policy. There is simply no absolute solution to the constitutional issue. This is no doubt why the Supreme Court has been so skittish about pronouncing on the problem. In our long and voluble judicial history, the decisions bearing even marginally on the question can be numbered on the fingers of one hand, and the illumination they provide is, at best, flickering if not dim.

If this is so, we must restrain our national propensity to cast political questions in constitutional terms. Just as in other years we went too far in devising theories of spacious presidential power because we agreed with the way one set of presidents wanted to use this power, now we are likely to go too far in limiting presidential power because we disagree with the projects of another set of presidents. We must take care not to convert a passing historical phase into ultimate constitutional truth. Professor Bickel has even suggested that "Congress should prescribe the mission of our troops in the field, in accordance with a foreign and war policy of the United States which it is for Congress to set when it chooses to do so. And Congress should equally review and settle upon an appropriate foreign policy elsewhere than in Vietnam, and reorder the deployment of our forces accordingly." There is no great gain in replacing high-flying presidential men by high-flying congressional men, nor is James Buchanan necessarily the model President.

As the guerrilla war between the Presidency and the Congress for control over foreign policy has dragged along through our history, the issue is sometimes put as if one or the other were the safer depository of authority. Congressional judgment, Adolf Berle once argued, "tends to lag behind the facts in an international case to which the President must address himself. . . . Defense means seeing trouble in advance and moving to prevent it. The President's estimates of what will happen have usually been better than those of men who do not live with the problems." Senator Goldwater opposed the War Powers bill because, as he said, "I would put more faith in the judgment of the Office of President in the matter of warmaking at this time than I would of Congress." But Senator Fulbright, who in 1961 feared the "localism and parochialism" of Congress, now believes the "collective judgment of the Congress, with all its faults, could be superior to that of one man who makes the final decision, in the executive."

History does not support any general assignment of superior virtue to either branch. In spite of Madison, the Congress is not always a force for restraint (as he himself discovered in 1812) nor the executive always a force for bellicosity. One need go back no further than the Cuban missile crisis to recall, as Robert Kennedy has told us, that the congressional leaders, including Senators Russell and Fulbright, "felt that the President should take more forceful action, a military attack or invasion, and that the blockade was far too weak a response." Those of us who hate the Indochina war may see more hope today in the Congress than in the Presidency; just as those who grew up in the days when Congress rejected Versailles and promulgated the neutrality acts saw more hope in the executive. But it would be folly to regard either presidential or congressional wisdom as a permanent condition. Neither branch is infallible, and each needs the other—which is, I guess, the point the Founding Fathers were trying to make.

There is no worse fallacy than to build final answers on transient situations. The questions of the war power and the treaty power are, and must remain, political questions. This is not a zone of clear-cut constitutional prescription. It is rather what Justice Jackson, in his brilliant opinion in the Steel Seizure case, described as

> ...a zone of twilight in which [the President] and Congress may have concurrent authority, or in which its distribution is uncertain. Therefore, congressional inertia, indifference or quiescence may sometimes, at least as a practical matter, enable, if not invite, measures on independent presidential responsibility. In this area, any actual test of power is likely to depend on the imperatives of events and contemporary imponderables rather than on abstract theories of law.

While the Constitution sets outer limits on both presidential and congressional action, it leaves a wide area of "joint possession." Common sense, therefore, argues for congressional participation as well as for presidential responsibility in the great decisions of peace and war.

To restore the constitutional balance, it is necessary in this period to rebuke presidential pretensions, as it has been necessary in other periods to rebuke congressional pretensions. Perhaps Tocqueville was not so profound after all (for once) in his theory of the antagonism between democracy and foreign policy. Perhaps Bryce (for once) was more to the point when he argued that the broad masses are capable of assessing national interests and of sustaining consistent policies. So far as judging the ends of policy is concerned, Bryce said, "History shows that [the people] do this at least as wisely as monarchs or oligarchies, or the small groups to whom, in democratic countries, the conduct of foreign relations has been left, and that they have evinced more respect for moral principles."

We are still told about the supposed structural advantages of the executive as portrayed in the *Federalist*—unity, secrecy, superior sources of information, decison, dispatch. These advantages seem less

impressive today than they must have been 180 years ago. Our sprawl-
ing executive branch is often disunited and is chronically incapable of
secrecy. Its information is no longer manifestly superior and is often
manifestly defective. The need for decision and dispatch has been
greatly exaggerated; apart from Korea and the Cuban missile crisis, no
postwar emergency has demanded instant response. Moreover, there
was far more reason for unilateral executive action in times when
difficulties of transport and communication could delay the convening
of Congress for weeks than there is in our age of the telephone and the
jet aircraft. What remains to the President is his command of the institutions of war and his undeniable ability to create situations that
will make it hard for Congress to reject his request. Here, it might be
well to recall the warning of the *Federalist*: "How easy would it be to
fabricate pretenses of approaching danger."

But, in demythologizing the Presidency, we must take care not to
remythologize the Congress. If it is extreme to say that the President
can send troops anywhere he pleases without congressional authorization, it is equally extreme to say he cannot do so short of war without
congressional authorization (even Senator Taft proposed no limitations on presidential deployment of the navy and air force). In this
area, John Norton Moore and Quincy Wright have proposed a test
worth careful consideration: that the President must obtain prior congressional authorization in all cases where regular combat units are
committed to what may be sustained hostilities, or where military
intervention will require congressional action, as by appropriations,
before it is completed. This would leave the President with independent authority to deploy forces short of war (and, of course, to
repel attack), while it would assure congressional authority to limit or
prohibit presidential commitment when war impends. But this provision, however attractive, would not have stopped escalation in Vietnam, where President Johnson would have had no difficulty in getting
the necessary authorization. The War Powers bill, though excessively
rigid in its definition of situations where the President is authorized to
act and unconvincing in its reliance on a thirty-day deadline, contains
valuable provisions for presidential reporting to the Congress once
hostilities begin. Congressman Jonathan Bingham has proposed a
simpler approach, which would avoid the rigidities of the War Powers
bill but retain its affirmation of congressional control of undeclared
hostilities. Citing the Executive Reorganization Act as a precedent, he
would give either house of Congress power to terminate such hostilities by resolution. Some declaration of congressional power in this
area would serve as a useful check on presidents.

As for the treaty power, Senator Case's efforts to bring executive
agreements within congressional purview and to induce the executive
to submit major agreements in the form of treaties are long overdue.

But the notion that executive agreements must be rigorously confined to minor matters, and that all important international undertakings must be subject to senatorial veto, would bring us back to the frustrations of Olney and Hay. Does anyone seriously suggest that every time a President meets another chief of state their understandings can be extinguished by one-third of the Senate? Would even high-flying congressional men contend that the Monroe Doctrine, the Emancipation Proclamation, the Fourteen Points, and the Atlantic Charter were cases of presidential usurpation? And in the period ahead, with the bipolar simplicities of the cold war giving way to the shifting complexities of a multipolar world, the executive simply cannot operate just on the leading strings of Congress. There has to be a middle ground between making the American President a czar and making him a puppet.

Senator Fulbright once distinguished between two kinds of power involved in the shaping of foreign policy—that pertaining to its direction, purpose, and philosophy; and that pertaining to the day-to-day conduct of foreign affairs. The former, he suggested, belonged peculiarly to Congress, the latter to the executive. The trouble was that Congress was reversing the order of responsibility. "We have tended to snoop and pry in matters of detail, interfering in the handling of specific problems in specific places which we happen to chance upon. . . . At the same time we have resigned from our responsibility in the shaping of policy and the defining of its purposes, giving away things that are not ours to give: the war power of the Congress, the treaty power of the Senate and the broader advice and consent power." Perhaps it would be well to recall the hope expressed by Senator Vandenberg in 1948 that the habit of senatorial intervention in foreign affairs would not become "too contagious because . . . only in those instances in which the Senate can be sure of a complete command of all the essential information prerequisite to an intelligent decision should it take the terrific chance of muddying the international waters by some sort of premature and ill-advised expression of its advice to the Executive."

Vandenberg was everlastingly right in his emphasis on information; for a flow of information to Congress is indispensable to a wise use of both the war and the treaty powers. And in no regard has Congress, until very recently, been more negligent than in acquiescing in executive denial of information. As Woodrow Wilson said long ago,

> Unless Congress have and use every means of acquainting itself with the acts and the disposition of the administrative agents of the government, the country must be helpless to learn how it is being served; and unless Congress both scrutinize these things and sift them by every form of discussion, the country must remain in embarrassing, crippling ignorance of the very affairs which it is most important that it should understand and direct.

In Wilson's judgment, "The informing function of Congress should be preferred even to its legislative function." The executive has devised no more effective obstacle to the democratic control of foreign policy than the secrecy system that has grown to such appalling proportions since World War II.

It is time for Congress to reject the "if you only knew what we knew" pose by which the executive deepens the congressional inferiority complex. Members of Congress, at least those who read the *New York Times*, know more than they think and, in general, would not receive blinding illumination if they read Top Secret documents, too. While the executive, through its diplomatic, military, and intelligence operatives, has an abundance of short-run information not easily available to Congress, experience shows that this information is seldom essential to long-run judgments. Nor is executive information all that infallible; one has only to recall the theory prevailing in the executive bureaucracy a few years back that Hanoi and the Vietcong were the spearhead of a system of Chinese expansion in Southeast Asia. If the executive "had been subjected more quickly and more closely to the scrutiny of informed public and congressional opinion," Senator McGovern has said, "it may not have fallen prey to its own delusions and fantasies."

And, as former government officials readily concede, there is no reason, in most cases, why Congress should be denied classified information. Thus George Ball: "I think there is very little information that Congress should ever be denied"; McGeorge Bundy: "I do not believe most of what is highly classified . . . should be kept from responsible members of the Congress at all. Indeed I believe the opposite." Nor should members of Congress be denied the opportunity to interrogate public officials presently shielded from them by the promiscuous invocation of executive privilege. Ball, calling executive privilege a "myth, for I find no constitutional basis for it," contends it should be invoked only when the President makes the decision himself and communicates that decision to Congress. George Reedy would even take the position "that the President has no executive privilege whatever in any public question." This is going a little far. The executive branch must retain the capacity to protect its internal processes of decision, and the President must, on occasion, assert a power to resist the disclosure of information against what he seriously believes to be the public interest. But Senator Fulbright's bill to restrain the flagrant abuse of executive privilege surely deserves enactment.

If Congress really wants to reclaim lost authority, it can do little more effective than to assure itself a steady and disinterested flow of information about foreign affairs. More than ever, information is the key to power. That is why the MacArthur hearings were so valuable in 1951; why the hearings conducted in recent years by the Senate

Foreign Relations Committee under Senator Fulbright's leadership have done more to turn opinion against the Vietnam war than other, more tangible weapons in the congressional arsenal. Perhaps the flow of information could be usefully institutionalized—as in Benjamin V. Cohen's proposal for the establishment by Congress of a commission of eight: two from the House, two from the Senate, four from the executive branch, empowered to exchange information and views on critical questions of foreign affairs.

Structural change can effect only limited improvements. The greater hope, perhaps, lies in increasing sensitivity to the problem of "joint possession" of constitutional powers. Greater awareness of the problem, to which so many for so long were oblivious, has recently led serious men into serious consideration of the issues of constitutional balance. In the future, such awareness may both restrain conscientious presidents and reinvigorate responsible Congresses.

Nor can structural change save us from the exasperations of choice. We must recognize both that our government must operate within constitutional bounds and that, within this spacious area, questions involved in the control of foreign policy are political rather than constitutional. If we do this, we will perhaps stop turning passing necessities, or supposed necessities, into constitutional absolutes. For a self-styled strict constructionist, President Nixon has gone very far, indeed, in anointing manifest excesses with the lotion of constitutional sanctity.

In this regard, he compares unfavorably with such presidents as Jefferson, Lincoln, and Franklin Roosevelt. Faced with infinitely more genuine emergencies, they had considerably more excuse for expansion of the presidential prerogative. But they did not claim that they were doing nothing more than applying routine presidential authority. Lincoln, particularly, in his troubled justification for the suspension of habeas corpus, said, "Would not the official oath be broken if the government should be overthrown, when it was believed that disregarding the single law would tend to preserve it?" Jefferson put the case more generally:

> To lose our country by a scrupulous adherence to written law, would be to lose the law itself, with life, liberty, property and all those who are enjoying them with us; thus absurdly sacrificing the end to the means. . . . The line of discrimination between cases may be difficult; but the good officer is bound to draw it at his own peril, and throw himself on the justice of his country and the rectitude of his motives.

A conscientious President must distinguish between the exception and the rule. Emergency may compel him to abandon the rule in favor of the exception; but he must not pretend—as Jefferson, Lincoln, and

Roosevelt declined to pretend and as Johnson and Nixon have pretended—that the exception *is* the rule. Rather, like Lincoln in 1860, the executive may, at his own peril, undertake measures about whose strict legality he may be in doubt, and do so not under an illusion of constitutional righteousness but in terms of a popular demand and a public necessity. In the end, he must rest such acts on the assent of Congress, the justice of his country, and the rectitude of his motives. Only presidents who distinguish emergency from normality can both meet emergency and preserve the constitutional order. As Justice Jackson said in the Korematsu case, "The chief restraint upon those who command the physical forces of the country, in the future as in the past, must be their responsibility to the political judgments of their contemporaries and to the moral judgments of history."

12. Making War: The President and Congress

Graham T. Allison, with the assistance of Richard Huff

The Barbary Pirates. In the summer of 1801, newly inaugurated President Thomas Jefferson learned that a declaration of war had been issued against the United States by Tripoli, one of the four kingdoms of the Barbary Coast. Congress was not in session and was not scheduled to reconvene for several months. Jefferson was acutely aware that only Congress had the power to declare war. What to do?

Jefferson was already familiar with the Barbary situation. For centuries, these states had been running a "protection racket" of sorts against the European nations whose ships plied the Mediterranean's waters: capturing ships, enslaving seamen or holding them for ransom, and exacting tribute from European governments in return for a promise to refrain from such harassment. After U.S. independence, American ships no longer enjoyed British protection, and several were captured. As U.S. Ambassador to France during the 1780s, Jefferson had tried unsuccessfully to secure the release of the crewmen of those ships. Moreover, he had attempted to organize a multilateral naval force to police the Mediterranean against such piracy, but to no avail. Having no alternative, the United States had followed European practice and negotiated with the four Barbary states treaties calling for annual tribute payments.

When Tripoli declared war on the United States, in hope of a higher rate of payment, President Jefferson decided that the United States had had enough. He dispatched four ships of the U.S. Navy to protect American shipping in the area, but—in the absence of congressional authorization—ordered them to take only defensive measures. When Congress reconvened that fall, he asked for specific authority to prosecute the war more vigorously, which he promptly received. The combined action of the U.S. Navy and Marines forced Tripoli to sue for peace in 1805, and by 1830 the Barbary pirates had been driven from the sea.[1]

War with Mexico.   No President added more territory to the United States than James K. Polk. A firm believer in U.S. expansionism, he tapped latent sources of power within the Presidency to achieve his territorial goals— powers that had previously remained untouched, most notably the President's control over the deployment and stationing of U.S. troops.

In 1845, the United States annexed Texas, despite the strong opposition of Mexico, which had never conceded the independence of its breakaway province. To protect this new acquisition, Polk sent American troops to defend Texas against a potential Mexican invasion. But the border was ill-defined, and as the American troops advanced into the disputed area, Mexico attempted to repel this alleged invasion of its territory. Polk then used its attack as a pretext for seeking a congressional declaration of war, which he was speedily granted. But many members of Congress were aghast at what they saw as a presidential usurpation of the war-making power. Former President John Quincy Adams, then a member of the House of Representatives, fumed that Polk's actions had created "an irreversible precedent . . . that the President of the United States has but to declare that War exists, with any Nation upon Earth . . . and the War is essentially declared." Adam's colleague Representative Abraham Lincoln held similar views: "Allow the President to invade a neighboring nation, whenever he shall deem it necessary to repel an invasion . . . and you allow him to make war at pleasure."[2]

The Cuban Missile Crisis.   For thirteen days in October 1962, the United States and the Soviet Union stood "eyeball to eyeball," each with the power of annihilating the other. The United States was firm but forebearing. The Soviet Union looked hard, blinked twice, and then withdrew without humiliation.

Lincoln had written that "no one man" should have the power to involve the nation in war. Yet in the missile crisis, with the nation on the brink of the most destructive war in history, one man did wield that power, perhaps necessarily. The demands of the missile crisis—the need for unity, secrecy, flexibility, and dispatch—made congressional consultation impractical. There was time for Congress to pass a resolution authorizing or endorsing whatever actions Kennedy felt it necessary to take. Indeed, Congress only two weeks earlier had enacted the Cuban Resolution of 1962, expressing the "determination of the United States to prevent the Marxist-Leninist regime in Cuba, by whatever means may be necessary, including the use of force of arms, from extending its aggressive or subversive activities to any part of the Hemisphere" and "to prevent the creation of an externally supported military capability there endangering United States security."[3] But there could be only one hand on the nuclear trigger. In this instance, command authority over U.S. forces and decision authority for war or peace were inseparable.

Yet, President John F. Kennedy did not make his decisions alone. His "ExCom," the group of men who advised him during the crisis, represented one of the most impressive collections of experience, wisdom, and expertise ever assembled in the White House. No members of Congress were included in the ExCom, or even asked for their advice. Is it likely that they could have improved upon the array of options presented to the President, options ranging from doing nothing at all to an invasion of Cuba? Could the presence of a few individual members of Congress have conferred the *institutional* approval of that body upon the President's decision? Although the Constitution assigned to Congress the authority to declare war, technology and time have, it appears, amended the Constitution. Kennedy's ExCom served as a partial equivalent of the constitutional intent.

Vietnam.   Arthur Schlesinger, Jr., writes, "Kennedy's action [in the missile crisis], which should have been celebrated as an exception, was instead enshrined as a rule. . . . The very brilliance of Kennedy's performance appeared to vindicate the idea that the President must take unto himself the final judgments of war and peace. . . . But one of its legacies was the imperial conception of the Presidency that brought the Republic so low in Vietnam."[4]

After a Viet Cong assault on a U.S. base at Pleiku on February 9, 1965, President Lyndon B. Johnson ordered the initiation of regular air strikes against North Vietnam, the beginning of the most intensive aerial bombardment in history. One month later, the first American combat troops landed in South Vietnam, and America's longest war — already four years old by official estimate — had entered its costliest and bloodiest phase.

Who authorized this undertaking? President Johnson claimed that the responsibility was his alone. The previous August, Congress had passed the Tonkin Gulf Resolution, in which it declared its support for the "determination of the President, as Commander in Chief, to take all necessary measures to repel any armed attack against the forces of the United States and to prevent further aggression."[5] Yet Congress, Johnson claimed, was not delegating its authority in the resolution but merely approving the President's actions. "We stated then," he said in 1967, "and we repeat now, we did not think the resolution was necessary to what we did and what we're doing."[6] Nor did his successor. Presidential war reached its zenith during the administration of Richard Nixon, who asserted that his constitutional authority as Commander in Chief gave him virtually unlimited discretion over the deployment of U.S. troops.*

Each of these vignettes describes a case in which the United States faced the question of whether or not to make war. In each case, the nation's decision was affected by a large number of broad factors: the deeper values and current views of the President, the values and views of Congress, the prevailing consensus in the country about the U.S. role in international affairs in general and the merits of the specific case in question. In each case, the decision was also importantly affected by the specific constitutional division of war-making

*Nixon claimed that the "legal justification" for the invasion of Cambodia, for example, "is the right of the President of the United States under the Constitution to protect the lives of American men. . . . As Commander-in-Chief, I had no choice but to act to defend those men."[7]

powers among politically responsible officials, as interpreted by practice, custom, and associated law.

This essay focuses on the last cluster of factors: constitutional and legal arrangements for war-making. Our purpose is to examine these "constitutional" issues in their concrete *political* dimensions—identifying effects of alternative divisions of powers, responsibilities, and associated procedures on probabilities of action, and exploring criteria for selecting a preferred division of powers between the President and Congress on this vital issue. The War Powers Act of 1973 serves as our central test case.

Constitutional and Political Developments

The American Constitution is a product of the eighteenth century. Its authors were men of the Enlightenment and also men of action—political philosophers, mostly at second hand, with firsthand practical experience. They were intensely conscious of what we have called elsewhere the "paradox of rulership."* On the one hand, the common good required that political power be placed in some human hands. Only by yielding considerable discretion to a central public authority could citizens secure the common defense, law, order, and personal liberties. But on the other hand, to establish a powerful public authority was to create enormous risks of the misuse of power. As so often before, the rulers, being human and thus fallible, might choose unwisely, or might implement their choices clumsily, at awful cost. Our Constitution's framers aimed at an effective central government, else they would not have come to Philadelphia. But they sought to minimize the risks.

The product of their work had four distinctive features. One of these was limited authority: The federal Bill of Rights and its state counterparts were meant to wall off civil liberties, including private property, from arbitrary government action. A second feature was shared powers: Federal and state governments had overlapping functions, and within the federal structure, so did the President, House, Senate, and Supreme Court. A third feature was separated institutions: Each power-sharing body had a separate base of political accountability, hence constituency, and these were kept distinct from one another. A fourth feature was legitimation by the symbols of popular sovereignty: The people replaced the monarch, and this was done in such a way as to clothe institutions with their status while yielding little to direct democracy.

*The section that follows draws heavily on the "Afterword" to Robert F. Kennedy, *Thirteen Days* (New York: Norton, 1971), by Graham T. Allison and Richard E. Neustadt.

Throughout the underlying theme was checks and balances: rights hedging authority, powers checking powers, and separate institutions in enforced collaboration, with political accountability divided and legitimacy dispersed. No one man was entrusted with unlimited prerogatives; neither was the mob. Instead, a goodly group of men, each with a piece of power, backed by a constituency, would scrutinize each other, balancing each other, as they tried to fit their pieces into governance. As Justice Brandeis noted, the separation of powers "was adopted by the convention of 1787 not to promote efficiency but to preclude the exercise of arbitrary power. The purpose was not to avoid friction, but by means of the inevitable friction incident to the distribution of the governmental powers among three departments, to save the people from autocracy."[8]

Then as now, the ultimate expression of authority was war, and there this general pattern was applied with special care. The model evidently was the English royal prerogative as modified by Parliament's control over the purse. Our Constitution-makers modified it further. Congress as a substitute for Parliament could also declare war. The Senate as a parliamentary body was to share in making treaties of alliance or of peace. Our President, as substitute for the King, had no prerogative to do these things alone. What he retained, alone, was actual command of such armed forces as congressional enactments gave him leave to raise and keep. Mindful of the problems caused by the Continental Congress's attempts to direct the conduct of the Revolutionary War, the framers sought to protect the President from such harassment. As Alexander Hamilton explained in the seventy-third *Federalist*, "of all the cares or concerns of government, the direction of war most peculiarly demands those qualities which distinguish the exercise of power by a single hand." But it was the intention of the framers that recourse to war require a *collaborative* judgment by the whole body of men in national elective office. Presidents could not declare war; Congressmen could not deploy troops. On this as on all lesser issues, these men were to check and balance one another.

Law must square with reality in order to be effective. Reality is inevitably complex: What constitutes a "war" requiring congressional declaration or authorization? The framers clearly intended that the President be empowered to defend the United States against sudden attack. But the line between defense and offense, never entirely clear at the outset of American history, grew increasingly hazy as America's contacts with the outside world proliferated. Virtually from the start of our development under the Constitution, presidents have employed U.S. military forces abroad to protect American lives, property, or other interests without declarations of war, and often without congressional authorization. By various counts, there have been one hundred to two hundred such incidents in American history.*[9] Moreover, of the conflicts known to us as "wars," three of the four most costly in both lives and money—the Civil War, Korea, and Vietnam—were undeclared and waged largely on presidential authority, with Congress at best an after-the-fact ratifier of presidential initiatives. Most of these one hundred to two hundred incidents were small-scale affairs, limited in duration, involving few, if any, U.S. casualties. In many, prior consultation with Congress would have been impractical or impossible. But, unfortunately, no sharp line divided such "incidents" from major wars.

Moreover, the idea that small-scale uses of U.S. military force (however defined) need no congressional authorization[10] raises several troublesome issues when thinking about preferred constitutional and legal processes for making decisions about war. The first is moral: Most of these actions were directed against the "half-assed nations" of the world, as Senator Goldwater uncharitably described Cambodia during the *Mayaguez* affair. But should the United States employ one allocation of war-making power in its relations with strong nations and quite another with weak ones?† The second issue is legal: If the President is empowered to use military force where the costs, duration, and scope of the action are likely to be limited, what legal restrictions are there on his authority in such cases? May a President legally occupy Botswana or Burundi merely because resistance is likely to be slight?‡ That question leads to a third, more practical one: If the probable cost of a potential military action is the principle that determines whether congressional authorization is necessary, how are those costs to be ascertained beforehand? And, more to the point, who

*Among the more important were Polk's occupation of the Mexican border territory, Wilson's interventions in Mexico and Siberia, and intervention in the Dominican Republic by no fewer than four presidents.

†As Professor Henry Steele Commager pointedly testified during the Senate Foreign Relations Committee's hearings on the war-powers bill, "It is a sobering fact that we do not rush in with the weapons of war to bring Britain, France, Italy, Russia, or Japan to heel. Would we have bombarded Southampton to collect a debt? Would we have sent an expedition into Rome to protect Americans against a threat from a fascist government? Would we have precipitated a war with Britain over a boundary dispute in Maine? Would we have landed marines in France if customs collectors did not behave themselves? Would we bomb Siberia for years if shots were fired—without any hits—at an American vessel? And does it really comport with the honor and dignity of a great nation to indulge its Chief Executive in one standard of conduct for the strong and another for the weak?" (*War Powers Legislation*, hearings before the Committee on Foreign Relations, U.S. Senate, 92d Cong., 1st sess., 1971, pp. 25–26.)

‡As, for example, President Wilson occupied Haiti in 1915. That occupation, which lasted until 1934, was formalized by a treaty ratified by the Senate in February 1916, but the first six months of the occupation were conducted under presidential authority alone. (*War Powers Legislation*, 1973, p. 139.)

is to ascertain them? It is not always clear just how extensive a military conflict will be before the first shots are fired; in fact, it rarely is. Historically, governments have repeatedly embarked on "splendid little wars" only to have them turn into long, drawn-out disasters. The Constitution rests on the assumption that collaborative judgments of the President and Congress will, on the average, produce the most accurate assessments of the probable costs of war and whether they are justified by the potential benefits. If Congress cannot be persuaded that the United States should engage in military or paramilitary operations in Angola, for example, one must presume on constitutional principles that it is in fact not in America's best interest to do so.

The applicability of the constitutional guidelines for the allocation of authority over war-making has been complicated by yet another factor, the so-called "Lockean prerogative." Locke, the philosophic progenitor of the American Constitution and intellectual champion of limited government, had acknowledged that in times of dire necessity "the laws themselves should . . . give way to the executive power."[11] This view of the necessity for emergency powers was shared by all of the framers of our Constitution; even Jefferson admitted that "on great occasions, every good officer must be ready to risk himself in going beyond the strict line of the law, when the public preservation requires it."[12] But while the framers agreed that crisis situations might require that the customary checks upon executive effectiveness be released, they were extremely uncomfortable with the idea, for they were only too aware of the danger that a temporary dictatorship might become a permanent one. As the expanse of government power increased, so did the danger of its abuse.

Undoubtedly the clearest example of the exercise of such emergency authority in our nation's history was set by Lincoln. Upon taking office in March 1861, he faced America's gravest crisis. Congress was not in session and was not scheduled to reconvene until the following December. Lincoln immediately called for a special session, but he delayed the opening of that session until July, giving him four months in which to act unilaterally to meet the growing crisis. He ordered a blockade of Southern ports, spent public funds without congressional appropriation, expanded the army and navy, suspended habeas corpus, and declared martial law throughout the land. These actions, he told that special session of Congress, "whether strictly legal or not, were ventured upon under what appeared to be a popular demand and a public necessity; trusting then as now that Congress would readily ratify them."[13] And Congress did ratify them, retroactively authorizing all of his unilateral initiatives. So, too, did the Supreme Court, though in a much more limited way. In the *Prize Cases*, it upheld Lincoln's unilaterally imposed blockade, finding that the outbreak of war had created a situation to which the President was legally justified in responding "without waiting for Congress to baptize it with a name."[14] Lincoln himself was uncertain of the legality and constitutionality of his actions. He inclined to the view that, though some of his actions might not be legal, the necessity of the situation justified them; thus he vowed privately that "I will violate the Constitution, if necessary to save the Union."[15] At other times he asserted that the very necessity legalized those actions: "Measures otherwise unconstitutional," he wrote, "might become lawful by becoming indispensable to the preservation of the Constitution through the preservation of the nation."[16] But whether or not his actions were legal, there is no doubt that they were politically legitimate, at least in retrospect, though controversial at the time. After his death, however, Congress reasserted its authority, and the nation entered a period of "congressional government" that was to last until the end of the century. But the questions raised by Lincoln's four years as President remained: What circumstances justify the exercise of such emergency presidential powers? And who is to be the judge? Ultimately, these are political questions of the highest order.

Many parallels have been drawn between the presidencies of Abraham Lincoln and John F. Kennedy. One of the more intriguing concerns the forceful action taken by each on his own authority to meet a grave military threat to the nation. In the Cuban missile crisis, Kennedy held the life of the nation in his hands. He was assisted in his ordeal by some of the ablest men of the day, but ultimately the decision was his alone. Why did Kennedy hold the decision so close to his own chest? The answer is not hard to find. The need to preserve *secrecy* and *flexibility* of action, the *uncertainty* of Soviet intentions, the extreme *complexity* of the diplomatic and military maneuvering, and *time*, or the lack thereof—taken together, these factors, above all, time, limited the circle of men with whom the constitutional Commander in Chief could engage in meaningful consultation. To maximize the prospect of a wise and viable choice, some interests could not be excluded. In the missile crisis, the issue was preeminently a matter of *defense* and *diplomacy*; it depended throughout on the capability of our *intelligence* and posed the possibility of *military* action. As constituted, the Executive Committee of the National Security Council (ExCom) ensured representation of these interests. Natural parochialism, stemming from the government positions of these men, guaranteed that considerations of defense, diplomacy, intelligence, and military action would be voiced. But potentially, the life of the nation was at stake. How was this interest represented? By the President himself, with aides of his own choosing, not least his brother Robert F. Kennedy.

Time made the presidential mind the only source available from which to draw politically legitimated judgments on what, broadly speaking, can be termed the political feasibilities of contemplated action vis-à-vis our antagonists: judgments on where history was tending, what opponents could stand, what friends would take, what officials would enforce, what men in the street would tolerate— judgments on the balance of support, opposition, and indifference, at home and abroad. As Richard E. Neustadt observes, "Technology has modified the Constitution: the President, perforce, becomes the only man in the system capable of exercising judgment under the extraordinary limits now imposed by secrecy, complexity, and time." In addition to his traditional roles, the President has become, in Neustadt's term, "the nation's Final Arbiter."[17]

Where was Congress? What about those other minds legitimated by election? They were out of play, except to have their leadership informed at the last moment. Earlier consultation offered nothing indispensable. Congress, to be sure, could add legitimacy, but of this the President conceived he had enough. As a nationally elected officer, he was, himself, more representative than all of them together. Besides, command decisions rested constitutionally with his office, not theirs. So he decided first and told them after.

Since the Soviet Union's entry into the nuclear club, the scenario of nuclear confrontation has dominated most political thinking about the allocation of war-making authority between the President and Congress. Coupled with the memory of the debilitating effects of congressional isolationism before World War II, this has allowed postwar presidents a degree of freedom and autonomy over the disposition of U.S. military forces enjoyed by few presidents before Franklin D. Roosevelt. Indeed, the belief in executive authority was so strong that when President Dwight D. Eisenhower asked for a congressional resolution endorsing and authorizing whatever military action he might order to defend Formosa, "Mr. Congress" (Sam Rayburn) feared that the resolution might imply that Eisenhower did not already possess such authority.[18]

Eisenhower also used his executive authority to send several hundred U.S. military advisers to assist the regime of President Ngo Dinh Diem of South Vietnam; nobody challenged his right to do so. President Kennedy vastly expanded the American contingent there, and no one questioned his authority either. But after Lyndon Johnson turned the American commitment into a full-scale war, the whole ideology of presidential prerogative in military affairs came under increasingly bitter attack.

What Johnson did in Vietnam he did on his own authority. After sharply escalating America's role in the war in the first half of 1965, Johnson could have asked Congress to ratify his policies and to authorize further operations. Although there is little doubt that his request would have been granted, Johnson refused to do so, perhaps fearing to acknowledge publicly that the United States had entered into large-scale hostilities likely to last several years. Johnson did, of course, have the 1964 Tonkin Gulf Resolution in his pocket. Formally, it was a sweeping affirmation of support for whatever the President might choose to do in Southeast Asia; in it, Congress declared that the United States was "prepared, *as the President determines*, to take all necessary steps, including the use of armed force, to assist any member or protocol state of the Southeast Asia Collective Defense Treaty requiring assistance in defense of its freedom."[19] Politically, however, it was a flimsy shield. As the scale and intensity of the war steadily increased, it became more and more clear that—whatever the resolution actually said—Congress had not intended for it to be taken quite so literally. In considering it initially, the Senate had rejected an amendment stating that Congress did not endorse "extension of the present conflict"; this followed Senator Fulbright's assurance that such an amendment was needless. As the war progressed, or failed to, the legitimacy of the resolution as an expression of congressional sentiment faded.

Once the war had expanded, congressional disillusion was fueled by a feeling of having been duped. Having never committed themselves to an American war in Vietnam, members of the Senate and House felt free to attack "Johnson's war." Attacks by congressmen helped to legitimate dissent in the country, encouraging others, especially in universities and the media. Moreover, the character of congressional criticism gave some credibility to charges that the war was not only senseless and immoral but also illegal and, therefore, illegitimate.

Vietnam's cost, both human and material, and its duration, coupled with the absence of agreed success or even agreed purpose, aroused an opposed perspective to the nuclear-inspired doctrine of presidential prerogative. Through its long and painful history, Vietnam undermined the simple confidence in each of the arguments that had traditionally supported congressional deference to the President in the area of foreign affairs: unity, secrecy, superior expertise, superior sources of information, decision, dispatch. Indeed, as the neutrality acts of the 1930s sapped the self-confidence of Congress with regard to its role in foreign affairs, and discredited congressional control in the eyes of the public, so Vietnam, compounded by Watergate, may have similar effects on the Presidency for years to come.

The early 1970s, therefore, saw new impetus behind a search for a functional equivalent of the Constitution's intent, namely, that the body of elected men on Capitol Hill share in White House decisions at the time warfare begins. The power of the purse evidently did not suffice: Withholding funds from forces in the field proved not to be a practicable course for most elected politicians. Congressional search, therefore, focused on ways of giving Congress a voice before those forces got committed beyond recall. From this search emerged the War Powers Act of 1973.

The War Powers Resolution

The War Powers Act did not leap full-blown from any single mind. Rather, Congress considered a number of alternative proposals of varying scope and intensity for restoring the constitutional balance between Congress and the Presidency in war-making. In the summer of 1973, with U.S. forces finally withdrawn from Vietnam, each chamber approved its own version of a war-powers bill.

The Senate bill was most notable in that it attempted to define quite precisely the only circumstances in which a President would be legally authorized to commit U.S. forces to hostilities in the absence of a declaration of war. These circumstances were (1) to repel, retaliate against, or forestall an armed attack on the United States, its territories and possessions; (2) to repel or forestall an attack on U.S. troops abroad; (3) to protect while evacuating, under specific circumstances, U.S. citizens and nationals whose lives are under direct and imminent threat; and (4) pursuant to specific statutory authorization. The Senate bill also required that the war be terminated after 30 days unless Congress voted to continue it, though it did allow the President an additional 30 days to continue the war if "unavoidable military necessity" forced him to do so.

The House version contained no specific delineation of the contingencies that would justify a presidential commitment of U.S. armed forces into battle. Its time period was 120 days, but it allowed for no 30-day extension similar to the Senate's bill. It also attempted to strengthen congressional control over the deployment of U.S. troops overseas, while providing that Congress could terminate the war at any time by concurrent resolution, not subject to veto.

The final version of the resolution, passed over the veto of President Nixon on November 7, 1973, combined elements of both versions. The Senate's legally binding delineation of the only circumstances to which a President could respond militarily was replaced by a general policy statement without similar force. The President was required to report to Congress within 48 hours of the initiation of hostilities on the causes for such action, and to terminate American involvement unless Congress approved the action within 60 days (allowing him a final 30-day extension). The conference version required that the President report to Congress on the progress of an undeclared war at least every six months, and that Congress vote to continue or terminate the war within 60 days of each such report.[20]

The War Powers Act, naturally, aroused a good deal of emotion both pro and con. President Nixon charged that it was "clearly unconstitutional" and that it would "seriously undermine this nation's ability to act decisively and convincingly in times of international crisis."[21] Then Vice-President Gerald R. Ford complained that it "has the potential for disaster."[22] Arguing against the bill from the opposite perspective was Senator Thomas Eagleton, who believed that the Senate version's legally binding delineation of the President's war powers was the essence of the bill; he called the compromise version a "horrible mistake" that would grant the President "unilateral authority to commit troops anywhere in the world for 60 to 90 days."[23] Similarly, Senator Abourezk decried it as a "blank check which will implicate Congress in whatever aggressive warmaking a President judges to be necessary."[24] On the other hand, Senator Javits, who cosponsored the Senate bill, claimed, "this is a very real, substantive check upon the President so that he must, with any kind of practicality, seek the concurrence of Congress in what we prescribe."[25]

Was the War Powers Act really a "turning point in the continuing struggle to restore the American constitutional system of checks and balances," as the *New York Times* editorialized?[26] Was it the "disaster" that Ford predicted? Or was it a measure with a good deal less significance than both its proponents and its detractors ascribed to it?

Criteria for Evaluation

On what basis is one to judge constitutional-legal arrangements for making war? Focusing specifically on the War Powers Act, how is one to decide whether the arrangements it defines for war-making are to be preferred to the arrangements that preceded passage of the bill, or to other alternative arrangements—for example, a modern-day version of the Ludlow Amendment that would require a national referendum to declare war or to engage in warfare overseas? Or to take a more timely example, what are the merits and possible effects of the proposal recently advanced by Senate aide Michael J. Glennon[27] to attach a statutory funding prohibition to the existing War Powers Act in order to deny funding for any activities outside the three conditions set forth in the resolution's "Purpose and Policy" section?* What about the resolution introduced by Senator Alan Cranston that would prohibit

*Section 2(c) of the War Powers Act states: "The constitutional powers of the President as Commander-in-Chief to introduce United States Armed Forces into hostilities, or into situations where imminent involvement in hostilities is clearly indicated by the circumstances, are exercised only pursuant to (1) a declaration of war, (2) specific statutory authorization, or (3) a national emergency created by attack upon the United States, its territories or possessions, or its armed forces."

the first use of nuclear weapons by the United States unless the President obtains the consent of a majority of a committee composed of the Speaker of the House and the Minority Leader, the Majority and Minority leaders of the Senate, and the chairmen and ranking minority members of both Armed Services committees, the Foreign and International Relations committees, and the Joint Committee on Atomic Energy?[28] And what might be the effects of a bill passed in January 1976 by the Senate allowing the President to call up to fifty thousand reservists to active duty for up to 90 days without a declaration of war or national emergency? While procedures are far from all-important, they do have some effect. In trying to evaluate the War Powers Act, it is necessary to weigh at least seven clusters of complex considerations:

1. What is the prospect for "good" decisions on war, or the avoidance of war, under the distribution of power and rules of the game envisaged by the resolution? Does it offer the highest probability among possible alternatives for getting the nation into wars its proponents want it to enter, and keeping it out of the wars they prefer it to avoid? Obviously, Americans differ on this issue, some glad of U.S. participation in World War II, Korea, and Vietnam alike, some wishing we had stayed out of all three, and many drawing distinctions between them. It is well to recall that in 1812 and again in 1898 Congress, rather than the President, took the lead in forcing war upon the country. Indeed, the Spanish-American War might have been fought five years earlier had not President Cleveland made it plain that he would not wage it even if Congress declared it.

2. However one answers the first question "on the average," what about the next case, say in the Middle East? Under the War Powers Act, as compared to other possible alignments of power, what are the prospects for "appropriate" choice? Again, there is obvious disagreement among Americans on what may be appropriate.

3. How does the resolution fare as a mechanism for resolving differences among Americans over the decision to enter war? What are its prospects for producing politically viable decisons about war? Is the process it codifies one that most citizens recognize as legitimate for making such important decisions about issues on which the nation may be sharply divided?

4. What effects will the resolution have on the conduct of any given war the United States enters? Will strategy, tactics, and the overall administration of the war be affected by the provisions of the resolution, and, if so, how?

5. How will the resolution affect prospects for the termination of a war? How will it influence the U.S. negotiating position? Under its terms, what role will Congress play in the war's conclusion?

6. How will the resolution affect the overall balance of power be-

tween the President and Congress during wars or other military actions?

7. What of unintended side effects? These are the bane of constitutional reforms adopted to keep some contemporary problem from ever recurring. The Twentieth Amendment is a classic case. In order to avoid, forevermore, the crisis that ensued in the four months from FDR's election to his inauguration, we so shortened the learning time for presidents-elect as to invite fiascos like the Bay of Pigs invasion.

The War Powers Act in Perspective

The War Powers Act was intended to prevent "another Vietnam," at least to the extent that no future President would be able to exercise the kind of unilateral authority that, it was claimed, Presidents Johnson and Nixon had wielded during the course of American involvement in Indochina. But what effect would it have had on U.S. policy during our last Vietnam? "Historical replays" call for difficult judgments. As a point of departure for broader argument, we offer our judgments—making explicit use of the criteria just listed:

1–2. *Effect on U.S. entry into the war.* Would the resolution have prevented the massive Americanization of the war that occurred in 1965? The answer is a clear no. Despite the popularity of President Johnson's 1964 campaign pledge that "American boys should not do the fighting for Asian boys," most Americans supported the war effort in 1965. Opposition was confined to relatively small segments of public and congressional opinion, and it seems fairly certain that, if President Johnson had reported to Congress—as required by the resolution—shortly after the initiation of sustained U.S. bombing of North Vietnam or the introduction of regular U.S. combat troops in South Vietnam, Congress would have speedily authorized a continuation of the war. (Indeed, as argued above, if he had wanted a formal declaration of war, he would have gotten it.)

3. *Effect on consensus and legitimacy.* Assuming Johnson had eschewed a formal declaration of war, going the War Powers Act route instead, repeated congressional authorizations of the war, long after the Tonkin Gulf Resolution had ceased to command any real respect, would certainly have served to legitimize the war and the decision-making process governing it. No longer would it have been so starkly "Johnson's (or Nixon's) war"; Congress would have been on record as a willing accomplice. But it is not at all clear how this process of semiannual reauthorization of the war would have affected public opinion on this divisive issue. On the one hand, with Congress officially "on board," an important forum for legitimizing dissent on the war might have been denied antiwar forces. Congressional complicity

in the war-making process might have stifled congressional dissent. Politicians are notoriously reluctant to publicly admit that they have been wrong—repeatedly wrong—on an important issue. It is one thing for senators and congressmen to admit that they were wrong (or had been deceived) five or six years ago; it is quite another for them to stand up and say, "I was wrong on this six months ago. Now I'm going to vote differently." Without the vigorous criticism that flowed through the halls of the Capitol, it might have been possible for the administration to isolate dissenters from the mainstream of public opinion, to brand them as unpatriotic extremists.

Yet opposition to the war sprang far more from its frustrating failure than its apparent illegality, and it is doubtful that this dissent would have been perpetually stifled by the knowledge that Congress had acquiesced in the war's continuation. Indeed, the requirement that Congress periodically renew its approval of the war might well have provided a focal point for dissent on the war, a target at which antiwar groups could have directed their efforts. These efforts, in addition to the counterefforts of the administration and its supporters, might have further polarized public opinion on the war instead of creating a consensus.

4. *Effect on the conduct of the war.* In a very real sense, the Vietnam War was fought out in America's living rooms. It was America's first televised war, probably the most intensively reported war in history. Above all, it was a struggle for the hearts and minds of the people: the American people as well as the Vietnamese. Both sides realized this and planned their strategies accordingly—the communists gambling (successfully, as it turned out) that their staying power would outweigh American firepower, the Americans churning out reams of statistics purporting to prove that they were somehow winning the war: body counts, targets destroyed, and villages pacified. Rarely has "PR" been such an important military weapon.

Had it been in effect, the War Powers Act could only have intensified this Madison Avenue aspect of the conduct of the war. American strategy in Vietnam was importantly affected by the presidential campaigns of 1964, 1968, and 1972. According to some reports, John Kennedy had hoped to withdraw from Vietnam after the 1964 elections. After becoming President, Lyndon Johnson postponed the sustained bombing of North Vietnam until he had been elected in his own right. In 1968, Johnson apparently tried to boost the candidacy of Hubert Humphrey by ordering a complete halt to the bombing of North Vietnam only a few days before the election. And in 1972, peace suddenly became "at hand" with the election only a few weeks away. The War Powers Act would have forced the administration to tailor its strategies more closely to the need to obtain congressional approval every six months. It thereby raises the issue of congressional interference in the President's role as Commander in Chief. The Stennis hearings on the air war during the summer of 1967—which concluded with the ringing declaration, "It is high time, we believe, to allow the military voice to be heard in connection with the tactical details of military operations"[29]—were at least partially responsible for President Johnson's decision to escalate the bombing further later that year. The resolution's semiannual reauthorization process might therefore have provided a lever for increased congressional influence over U.S. tactics and strategy in Vietnam.

It also would have strengthened the argument of those who favored a more rapid escalation of the war against that of the proponents of the "slow squeeze" approach adopted in 1965. Time was an important factor in the war. In many respects, the American strategy was one of buying time until the South Vietnamese could "hack it." On the other hand, the administration could not rely on indefinite public and congressional support for the war effort. The War Powers Act would have raised the specter of a Congress eventually refusing to renew its authorization of the war in the absence of tangible results, thus strengthening the hand of administration hawks.

5. *Effect on the war's termination.* It is interesting to speculate on just when the war would have ended if the War Powers Act had been in effect. This would have depended upon how the war had been conducted under the resolution, the efficacy of the administration's salesmanship, the willingness or reluctance of congressmen to reverse their votes on the issue, the effectiveness of antiwar groups in persuading or electing congressmen to vote against the war, and other intangible factors that cannot be weighed with any precision. Yet, given the rising tide of opposition to the war, especially after the Tet offensive of 1968, it is at least arguable that at some point before January 1973, Congress would have refused to renew its approval of the war. This is particularly true because the resolution would have conferred jurisdiction over the resolutions reauthorizing the war to the Foreign Affairs* and Foreign Relations committees, bodies that were notably more dovish than the Armed Services and Appropriations committees, which handled the bulk of Vietnam-related legislation.

Had Congress actually gone so far as to declare war on North Vietnam in 1965, congressional approval would have been required for the peace agreement that terminated that state of war. What would have happened if the Paris agreement had come before the Senate as a treaty? Most likely, it would have been speedily ratified; whatever misgivings individual senators may have had about the agreement would have been subordinated to their overwhelming desire to end the war officially.

6. *Effect on balance of power between the President and Congress.*

*Now International Relations.

A war President is a powerful President, and his powers do not stop at the water's edge. Inevitably, the requirements of war enlarge his influence over domestic policy too. But, if Congress had been required to give its seal of approval to the war, those members of Congress who were able to deliver the votes might have enjoyed a vast influence. A legislative leader as powerful as Rayburn or Johnson might have been able to trade his influence on a war authorization for administration support of his own preferred policies in another realm; an Albert or a Mansfield, perhaps less so. Moreover, because the resolution alters the structure of power within Congress, providing additional leverage to its more dovish members, the bargaining position of Congress as a whole might have been strengthened. In any event, the need for a President during the Vietnam involvement continually to bargain with Congress in order to gain approval for "his" war might have forced him to make significant concessions on other fronts and thus might have reduced his unilateral authority.

7. *Side effects*. The principal side effects of the War Powers Act on the Vietnam War would seem to have been those listed above: pressure for more rapid escalation, effects on dissent from both hawks and doves, possible greater stage-managing of the war effort in order to win congressional approval. Most importantly, though, the resolution would have changed the political structure of the debate on the war in this country. The war was a critical factor in presidential politics every four years; the resolution would have greatly increased its impact on congressional politics too. With Congress voting up or down on the war every six months, debate could only have been intensified. Vietnam divided this country as no other issue has in recent memory; under the War Powers Act, that fissure would have widened into a chasm.

Speculation about the Future

Turning from the recent past to the near future, it may be instructive to speculate about the potential effects of the War Powers Act on the decision-making process in coming situations where the question of U.S. military intervention arises. Our crystal ball is by no means clear, however, and the following possibilities suggest themselves only as elements of a cloudy future.

One probable effect of the resolution will be to widen the circle of presidential assistants involved in a decision to use military force, and to color the bureaucratic politics from which the decision emerges. Not only national-security advisers but also legislative aides, political advisers, and speech-writers will have to be heard by a President contemplating military action, because they will have to prepare his report to Congress. Moreover, these aides will have grounds for opposing military action without appearing soft or disloyal: Whatever the merits, if Congress cannot be persuaded, the viability of the venture will be at risk. A second effect of the resolution will be to force Congress to act publicly whenever U.S. troops are engaged in hostilities that last as long as 60 days. This necessity that Congress vote for or against continuation of military action will frame a pervasive public debate about the decision—in Congress, in the press, and on television—a debate whose focus will be determined by the deadline requiring congressional action within 60 days. A third effect of the resolution will stem from its redistribution of influence within Congress—toward the Foreign Relations and International Relations committees, which have primary jurisdiction under the resolution. The character of discussion and hearings in those committees and the nature of the resolutions they will report out will be predictably more dovish than analogous discussions and resolutions of committees that authorize and appropriate funds for war. These three effects will create substantial incentives for a President to engage in extensive consultation with Congress before committing U.S. troops to combat; indeed, if there existed a congressional leadership capable of representing the institution and delivering most of the other legislators—a significant *if*—a President would have a powerful incentive to engage in *meaningful* consultation.

Several aspects of the President's response to these factors seem higher-confidence bets. One is that future military actions will be stage-managed to the fullest extent possible so as to induce a favorable public and congressional reaction. *Mayaguez* most likely provided a foretaste of things to come: The good news was trumpeted loudly, while the bad news was dribbled out in small doses; as a result, the administration's performance was acclaimed a great success, while in fact, in retrospect, it merits no such accolade. Another is that when the President is contemplating military action, two types of military operations will appear much more attractive than any other: those that promise quick victory, within the 60 to 90 days of grace, and those that can become national crusades. For the latter, he will be more likely to seek a formal declaration of war—to avoid the need to return to Congress every six months.

Perhaps the least certain element in assessing the likely impact of the War Powers Act concerns the role of Congress: the extent to which Congress will assert its authority. To date, the record is ambiguous. On the one hand, Congress's cutoff of funding for U.S. participation in the Angolan conflict reflected a widespread fear of "another Vietnam," however remote. Yet Congress raised no protest against President Ford's evacuations of U.S. and foreign citizens from Phnom Penh and Saigon, and it cheered his handling of the *Mayaguez* affair—despite the fact that these actions violated seven separate statutory provisions barring the use of funds "to finance military or paramilitary operations by the United States in or over Vietnam, Laos, or Cambodia."[30]

The Constitution is, in E. S. Corwin's famous phrase, an "invitation to struggle for the privilege of directing American foreign policy."[31] The War Powers Act does not alter that basic fact of the political landscape. It may serve as a potential weapon in that ongoing struggle, though for which side is not entirely clear. But the overall "correlation of forces" will be determined by the deeper undercurrents of American political life—among them, the "lessons of history" as etched on the popular mind. Before Pearl Harbor, what constrained Franklin D. Roosevelt was not only, or even mainly, words in statutes but, rather, the forbidding strength of isolationist convictions moving millions of his fellow citizens. What fueled their convictions? A deeply held impression that American involvement in World War I had been a needless waste, the result of a plot for profit. After World War II, the freedom, relatively speaking, felt and asserted by successive presidents reflected not only congressional but also widespread press and public sentiment. What fueled this permissiveness? Above all, "Munich" as remembered after victory in 1945. For the foreseeable future, the watchword of American foreign policy will be "to avoid another Vietnam." But whose version of the "lessons" of that conflict will become the prevailing reality? It is an entirely open question, but its answer will largely determine how the "balance" between the President and Congress in war-making will be struck.

Notes

1. See Glenn Tucker, *Dawn Like Thunder: The Barbary Wars and the Birth of the U.S. Navy* (New York: Bobbs-Merrill, 1963), *passim.*
2. Both quotations are taken from Arthur M. Schlesinger, Jr., *The Imperial Presidency* (Boston: Houghton Mifflin, 1973), pp. 41–42.
3. Public Law 87–733, 76 Stat. 697, October 3, 1962.
4. Schlesinger, op. cit., p. 176.
5. Public Law 88–408, 78 Stat. 384, August 10, 1964.
6. *New York Times*, August 19, 1967.
7. Richard M. Nixon, *A New Road for America: Major Policy Statements, March 1970–October 1971* (Washington, D.C.: Government Printing Office, 1972), pp. 675, 683.
8. *Myers* v. *United States*, 272 U.S. 52, 296 (1926).
9. For example, the American Enterprise Institute's analysis of the War Powers Bill lists 161 such incidents. See "The War Powers Bill," *Legislative Analysis No. 19*, April 17, 1972, pp. 47–55. Similarly, J. Terry Emerson, counsel to Senator Barry Goldwater, counts 199, up to and including

the Jordanian crisis of 1970; reprinted in *War Powers Legislation, 1973,* hearings before the Committee on Foreign Relations, United States Senate, 93d Cong. 1st sess., pp. 126–48.

10. See, for example, Barry M. Goldwater, "The President's Ability to Protect America's Freedoms: The Warmaking Power," *Law and the Social Order, Arizona State University Law Journal,* 1971, p. 423.

11. John Locke, *Second Treatise on Government,* ed. J. W. Gough (New York: Barnes & Noble, 1966), chap. 14.

12. Letter to W. C. Claiborne, February 3, 1807, in Thomas Jefferson, *Writings,* memorial ed. (Washington, D.C., 1905), vol. XI, p. 151.

13. Quoted in Schlesinger, op. cit, p. 58.

14. *Prize Cases,* 2 Black 635 (1863).

15. Quoted in Jacob Javits, *Who Makes War* (New York: William Morrow, 1973), p. 130.

16. Abraham Lincoln, *Collected Works,* ed. R. P. Basler (New Brunswick, N.J.: Rutgers University Press, 1953), VII, 281–82.

17. *Presidential Power,* 2d ed. (New York: Wiley, 1968), p. 212.

18. Schlesinger, op. cit., p. 161.

19. Public Law 88–408, 78 Stat. 384, August 10, 1964. Emphasis added.

20. Public Law 93–148, 87 Stat. 555, November 7, 1973.

21. *New York Times,* November 8, 1973.

22. Ibid.

23. Ibid.

24. Quoted in Schlesinger, op. cit., p. 304.

25. *Congressional Quarterly Weekly Reports,* October 13, 1973, p. 2743.

26. *New York Times,* November 8, 1973.

27. Michael J. Glennon, "Strengthening the War Powers Resolution: The Case for Purse-Strings Restrictions," 60 *Minnesota Law Review* No. 1 (November 1975).

28. See Federation of American Scientists, *Public Interest Report,* November 1975, p. 5.

29. Quoted in *Pentagon Papers,* Senator Gravel edition (Boston: Beacon Press, 1971), vol. IV, p. 204.

30. The language is taken from Section 30 of the Foreign Assistance Act of 1973. Cf. Glennon, *op. cit.,* p. 13.

31. E. S. Corwin, *The President: Office and Powers* (New York: New York University Press, 1940), p. 200.

13. A Symbolic Attack on the Imperial Presidency: An American "Question Time"

Philippa Strum

In 1961, Pakistan's President Mohammed Ayub Khan and his wife came to the United States for dinner. It was not one's everyday, garden-variety dinner, though it did take place on a lawn; it was part of the Khans' state visit to the United States, during which they were entertained by President and Mrs. John F. Kennedy. Bereft as our relatively young nation is of ancestral European castles, its President turned to Mount Vernon as the site of the evening's entertainment. That Buckingham-Palace-on-the-Potomac, however, was discovered to be overabundantly supplied with mosquitoes. For three days before the gala event, therefore, the Army Corps of Engineers sprayed four square miles around Mount Vernon with a pesticide designed to eliminate all mosquitoes, chiggers, ticks, and ants. But the insect problem was the least of the tactical difficulties encountered in planning the evening. Mount Vernon does not possess sufficient culinary equipment to cater to the needs of a large gathering of dignitaries. Chef René Verdon coped by preparing the evening's meal at the White House, and the completed dinners were rushed to Mount Vernon by a fleet of mobile army field kitchens. But while dead chickens, even when transformed into *poulet chasseur avec couronne de riz clamart*, presumably have no objection to being transported by army field kitchens, high government officials are something else again. The guests, therefore, assembled on the wharf of a naval-weapons plant in Washington, where they were piped aboard four immaculate navy ships, each containing its own complement of white-coated

Filipino waiters and strolling musicians. Having completed their music-lulled voyage, the dignitaries alighted upon the shore of Mount Vernon, up whose hill they were conveyed in black Cadillacs. The road was lined with marines in full dress. Mint juleps awaited the guests at the top of the hill, as did a pageant portraying the Revolutionary army's fighting techniques. Although Mount Vernon had been equipped with spotlights for the first time in its history, it was felt that electric lighting would not create the appropriate mood for *framboises à la crème Chantilly.* Thus the little dinner tables arranged under a tent were lit by candles. After the petits fours, the guests were treated to the National Symphony's rendering of Mozart and Gershwin, accompanied by champagne and Corona Coronas. The watery return to Washington was effected to the sounds of dance music, and the potential problem of the effect of cool river breezes on exposed arms was solved with the aid of the store of sweaters and jackets assembled by the First Lady's staff for the occasion.[1]

Were one to search through history for an occasion as sumptuous as the Khans' evening at Mount Vernon, he would have to turn from democracies to monarchies, and most probably to that at Versailles. While it is true that the Kennedys did not have brilliant fireworks displays, neither did any of the Louis have three days' worth of mosquito repellent.

The purpose of the anecdote is not to heap scorn upon the Kennedys, whose style bears comparison with their successors' preference for Grand Old Opry and Billy Graham, but to illustrate the monarchical character of presidential commands. The President decrees that mosquitoes shall cease to exist, and lo, the Army Corps of Engineers hastens to carry out what might be labeled its "scorched insect" policy. One could as easily cite the private helicopters, jet planes, and limousines enjoyed by any President, the kind of total service available to the families of White House incumbents, or the $3.3 million spent to refurbish the Nixon White House with such necessities as a $5,000 antique bed and $10,700 worth of curtains and bed coverings for the presidential bedroom.[2] The point to be made is: At both a ceremonial and a political level, we treat our President like a King; in so doing, we have destroyed something basic in the American democratic ideal; and one of the few remedies available to us is elimination of the imperial nature of the Presidency. It might be wise to consider adopting such European institutions as ombudsmen, permanent high-level civil-service officials, and the Scandinavian system of openness of public documents—all of which could help redemocratize the government. This essay, however, will focus on the specific remedy of the parliamentary-style question time, not as a procedure for information-gathering but as a symbolic attack on the monarchical trappings with which we have clothed our chief political official.

A number of assumptions underlie advocacy of the question time as a means of controlling presidential power:

1. *The existence of the imperial presidency is at least as much the responsibility of an unassertive Congress as it is of power-hungry presidents.* One need look only as far as the post-Watergate Congress, which, shrewd observers assured us, would reassert itself as an equal partner in the decision-making process. What we find, instead, is a Congress that cannot come up with a coherent energy policy, that withdraws in fright when one of its committees suggests contempt citations against Cabinet members who high-handedly refuse it information, that loudly trumpets its vitality in cutting off funds for use in Angola while obediently agreeing that the American people have no right to know where else such funds have been spent, that takes potshots at individual presidential appointments but seeks no answers to the policy problems that will fall by default to presidential appointees. None of this should come as a surprise. Members of Congress (of course, one must allow for the occasional and much welcomed exception) are egocentric individualists—for one does not normally run for office in the absence of a very healthy ego— responsive only to small numbers of constituents in a geographically large society and well aware that the bulk of their constituents consider it unnecessary for them to possess an overall view of American policy or any view whatsoever of American foreign policy. The existence of a Presidency to which Americans routinely turn for answers to whatever societal problems arise permits legislators the luxury of irresponsibility. Indeed, members of Congress are far more concerned with the members of the specific interest groups and bureaucracies with which their committees have mutually supportive relationships than with the electorate at large. They may snipe at the excessive power of the Presidency, but given the interests and habits of most members of Congress, one wonders whether, if the imperial Presidency did not exist, they might not wish to invent it.

We cannot rely on Congress for real limitations on the Presidency as long as the Presidency retains its popular mystique as the nation's problem-solver. Unless the mystique is destroyed and Congress is thereby forced to take action, Congress is likely to remain a major part of the problem rather than a part of the solution.

2. *The primary question is not how to limit executive power but the more difficult problem of how to guarantee the executive branch the flexibility it requires while making the executive consistently accountable.* One can attaik the idea of the imperial Presidency, that is, the unaccountable Presidency—without wishing to put limits on the open and democratic powers exercised by the President. President Gerald R. Ford's problems with Congress were the result in part of his

own inability to exercise his powers effectively and in part of his assumption that the federal government should not be very active in the domestic sphere. Nonetheless, we might well wonder whether a President with a coherent and positive domestic policy, determined to use his office as a vehicle for leadership, would possess sufficient power to carry out his program. Certainly the examples of the Kennedy and Johnson administrations indicate that Congress has far too great an ability to throw roadblocks in the path of even a popular President's domestic policies. James Sundquist has suggested that even Johnson's 1963–66 domestic-policy successes were due in large measure to the shock of the Kennedy assassination and the election of a heavily Democratic Congress as the voters' response to the specter of Barry Goldwater.[3] At the same time, Congress has shown itself unable to substitute its own program for that of the President. Given the size of Congress and the multitude of interlocking problems facing the American political system, it is logical for proponents of domestic change to turn to the Presidency. Indeed, if one looks at other political systems that have moved into the modern industrial era, one finds that both parliamentary and presidential systems invariably display a movement of power from the legislature to the executive. Extensive government involvement in the everyday life of the citizenry, whether under a capitalist or a socialist regime, coupled with technological complexities, world interdependence, and the concomitant importance of foreign affairs, makes the pre-eminence of the executive inevitable.

The failure of President Richard M. Nixon lay in his inability to use the possibilities for leadership inherent in the Presidency while at the same time he seized powers he did not legitimately possess. He was not a particularly strong leader; on the contrary, he attempted to circumvent the need to exercise leadership—in Richard E. Neustadt's formulation, to undertake the difficult task of convincing people that they wanted to do what he wanted them to do[4]—with secret tricks and dirty devices that have no place in a democratic system.

The objection to the imperial Presidency is not that it has too much power but that it has too much secret, unchecked, and unbalanced power. The problem is how to eliminate the mystique of the imperial Presidency, which almost enabled a President to survive his deliberate perversion of his office, while leaving intact the powers needed by future presidents for leadership. The object of the search is "conditional discretion," meaning that while limits would not be placed on the kind of discretionary powers needed by the President, he would be required to pay more attention to genuine before-the-fact consultation and less to after-the-fact explanations of unilateral actions. The result would be the elimination not of presidential power but of irresponsible power. Thus our focus must be accountability rather than limitation. It should be emphasized that we are not thereby discussing methods of achieving "good government" or specific desirable policies, though we may hope with the Founding Fathers that balanced power will be more likely to result in wise policies than will monopolistic control of power. Instead, our inquiry now centers on the procedures that should be followed in the exercise of power.

3. *What many perceive as the current most pressing problem of the American polity—that is, the electorate's lack of confidence in, and concern about, its government—is both a function of presidential unaccountability and a contributor to it.* Declining voter participation and scores of surveys attest to a deepening conviction on the part of the electorate that the government is inherently rotten and that there is virtually nothing the average citizen can do about it. This belief is popularly labeled "post-Watergate," but it actually appeared during the later years of the Johnson Administration. Apparently, most Americans believe that the government does not represent them. They may occasionally agree with government policies, but the similarities between policies and their own beliefs are viewed as a happy coincidence rather than as a matter of cause and effect. It is extraordinary that the most successful presidential challengers of the 1976 primaries were those who attacked not individual officeholders but "Washington," which in this context served as a symbol for egocentric and expensive bureaucrats too concerned with the expansion of their empires to consider the needs of the average citizen. One can only suggest, again drawing on the Founding Fathers, that a democracy in which the voters are alienated and policy decisions are in no way the reflection of voter opinion is no democracy at all.

Paradoxically enough, it is at times when the excesses of the imperial Presidency are given partial blame for voter alienation that the imperial Presidency is most likely to flourish. Let us remember that it was not the power possessed by Presidents Johnson and Nixon that alienated citizens, for it is highly doubtful that those presidents were perceived by the average citizen as possessing greater power than, for example, Franklin D. Roosevelt or Harry S. Truman, but, rather, the misuse of that power—specifically, Johnson's repeated lies to Congress and the public about the progress of the Vietnam War, and Nixon's utilization of his office to undermine the safeguards of our political system while cavalierly lining his own pockets. Individual misuse of power has contributed to electorate alienation; yet in 1976 the voters proved responsive both to a presidential candidate who told them little more than that he, as an individual, could be trusted and to a President whose primary strength was his possession of a reputation as a nice guy. The American voters today are looking not for particular policies but for a President who can restore their belief that "You have a friend in the White House." Long before Watergate, Murray Edelman wrote:

> Alienation, anomie, despair of being able to chart one's own course in a complex, cold, and bewildering world have become characteristics of a large part of the population of advanced countries. As the world can be neither understood nor influenced, attachment to reassuring abstract symbols rather than to one's own efforts becomes chronic. And what symbol can be more reassuring than the incumbent of a high position who knows what to do and is willing to act, especially when others are bewildered and alone? Because such a symbol is so intensely sought, it will predictably be found in the person of any incumbent whose actions *can* be interpreted as beneficent, whether it is because they are demonstrably beneficent or because their consequences are unknowable.[5]

Similarly, W. Lloyd Warner wrote of the human need for heroes as a source of "moral strength" to counteract the "disquiet of personal chaos."[6] The best indication that Americans are seeking the appearance of strength rather than the reality of any specific policy is, perhaps, the public reaction to presidential televison addresses, in the aftermath of which presidential popularity invariably rises no matter what the content of the address. It is precisely because Americans are alienated from the political process that it is necessary now to organize an attack on the imperial nature of the Presidency, lest we reach the point at which the imperial Presidency has become so synonymous with the Presidency that it is invulnerable. Hence, the third assumption of this paper: The alienation of the electorate, caused by Vietnam, Cambodia, Watergate, and the like, could too easily result in the unconscious search for an even more imperial and comfortingly omniscient President. A symbolic attack on the imperial Presidency is necessary to prevent this occurrence.

4. *An answer to the problem of monarchical presidents cannot be found by looking within the American political system as it currently exists.* Although the framers of the Constitution would be horrified at the development, American political institutions have come to be considered more as the embodiment of democracy than as mechanisms for the achievement of democracy. Democracy is viewed in the United States as an end product rather than a means. This is in large measure the result of an unexamined satisfaction with our economic system, which in spite of recessions and inflations has produced the world's highest living standard for the great majority of Americans. Economic satisfaction, in turn, is popularly attributed to the political system and accounts both for the more offensively smug manifestations of the belief that our political system is the biggest and the best and for the overwhelmingly nonideological nature of American politics. Systemic ideology is engendered by dissatisfaction, but as a

people, we bury our discontents under a satisfied cataloguing of our refrigerators, our cars, our color television sets, and our expectation that the next generation will have even more of them. Additionally, the truly heterogeneous nature of the American people and the possibility that the vague American liberal ethos does not contain answers to twentieth-century problems (whose existence Americans as a whole would rather not admit) lead us to avoid confrontation of our problems in favor of the eager assumption that we *have* democracy and to seek it would be superfluous. We destroy the balance of powers by making no demands on Congress. We destroy political parties by discouraging them from taking strong ideological stands and presenting meaningful alternative policies and programs. We manage to discern the existence of parties in the once-every-four-years gatherings that organize a competitive race for the Presidency, and vote down such suggestions as biannual national party conventions that would formulate policy.

Of course, there are peripheral reforms that can be made within the system. One, already in its infancy, is the establishment of congressional budgetary committees to view the budget as a unified whole and to allocate resources within established dollar limitations. Others, all in the area of the executive branch, might be placing an upper limit on the number of White House staff, specifying and making public the duties of each staffer, subjecting certain potential staffers (such as the chief of the Domestic Council and the Special Assistant for National Security Affairs) to Senate confirmation, and eliminating dual roles for White House assistants by forbidding them to hold office in any other part of the executive branch. These reforms are certainly desirable, but they are, nonetheless, peripheral, as they do not address the central problem of lack of presidential accountability. Reforms are necessarily peripheral if they do not attack the monolith created by the unification of the powers of chief of state and chief executive in one human being.

Let us turn for a moment to the combination of those two powers in the American Presidency. One of the factors that differentiates modern constitutional political systems from medieval monarchies is the functioning of the modern chief of state as little more than an integrative and ceremonial figure. The disparate members of the electorate are symbolically pulled together by the chief of state, who becomes the living embodiment of the ideals that underlie the political system. The abstract and difficult notions of popular sovereignty, republican representation, and extensive but limited individual liberties are made specific by their supposed embodiment in a human chief of state to whom one can relate with far more ease than one can to democratic principles. The chief of state as an integrative mechanism becomes all the more important when, as in the current United States, an extremely large and divided society faces a plethora of seemingly insoluble problems. The logical reaction to such threat and confusion is increased reliance upon the personification of the political principles that are believed to safeguard us. During the heyday of local political bosses, it was to them and their organizations that Americans were wont to turn; today, Americans turn to their President. If what they find is a lack of answers, or ineffectiveness, or corruption, their bewildered disappointment becomes skepticism and apathy about the political process.

Evidence of the extent to which the President, as chief of state, is indeed viewed as the personification of Americanism is to be found everywhere. One might begin with the magazines on sale at local newsstands, the covers of which indicate that the only threat to the primacy of movie stars comes from the family of the President. As their husbands and fathers occupied the White House, Jackie, John-John, Caroline, Lady Bird, Julie, Betty, Jack, Rosalynn, and Amy all occupied *their* places of honor on the covers of popular magazines. The wedding receptions of the Johnson daughters and of Tricia Nixon were televised media events. More recently, the nation was deeply embroiled in thrashing out the question of whether or not Susan Ford should be permitted to have an affair. Apparently the young lady herself was not consulted, presumably on the assumption that the lives of the royal family are too important to be left to their discretion. In a more somber vein, one might note the wounding spasm of national grief caused by the assassination of John F. Kennedy. It is difficult to remember, in the postdeification period, that Kennedy was neither an enormously successful nor an outstandingly popular President—in spite of the glamour of Camelot. Dwight D. Eisenhower was more consistently popular than Kennedy was—but the reaction to the latter's death was, in effect, a reaction to regicide: The king—the symbol of the nation—had been killed.

George Reedy, whose sojourn in the White House led him to dismiss the Presidency as an institution so tainted by the creeping growth of monarchy as to be unworkable, describes the imperial Presidency:

> By the twentieth century, the Presidency had taken on all the regalia of monarchy except the ermine robes, a scepter, and a crown. The President was not to be jostled by a crowd—unless he elected to subject himself to do so during those moments when he shed his role of chief of state and mounted the hustings as a candidate for re-election. The ritual of shaking hands with the President took on more and more the coloration of the medieval "king's touch" as a specific for scrofula. The President was not to be called to account by any other body (after the doctrine of executive privilege was established). In time, another kingly habit began to appear and presidents referred to themselves more and more as "we"—the ultimate hallmark of imperial majesty.[7]

James MacGregor Burns has noted the incongruity in hanging up icon-like pictures of the chief political officer of a democracy in every post office in the land.[8] Congressman Morris Udall has commented on the strange practice, unknown in the early days of the Republic, of having a band blare out "Hail to the Chief" whenever the President enters the room.[9] Citing a White House staffer who claimed President Nixon would go nowhere during the last days of his Presidency without having Stephen Bull announce his presence, Udall muses:

> He [Nixon] would go in at 9:30 in the morning to talk to Haldeman and Ehrlichman and maybe one other official, and first Stephen Bull had to go to the door and say, "Gentlemen, the President of the United States!"—as though his presence with his closest associates were some kind of historic event. I used to speculate that it probably got so bad that I could see Mr. Nixon at the bedroom door in his blue pajamas with the seal of the United States, with Stephen Bull rushing in to declare, "Mrs. Nixon, your husband, the President of the United States!"[10]

Studies of the political socialization of children invariably find, as did that by Robert Hess and David Easton, "a strong parental-like tie with respect to the President's role itself, developed before the child can become familiar with the conditions surrounding the incumbent of the office."[11] And lest the child-become-adult lose any awe for the chief of state, television is always present to reinforce the early image. As Fred Friendly says about presidential use of television, "No mighty king, no ambitious emperor, no pope, or prophet ever dreamt of such an awesome pulpit, so potent a magic wand."[12] The imperial Presidency would probably have been impossible without television. Now we are a nation of tube-watchers. Little wonder, then, that "My President, right or wrong," has become one of the more popular chants in what was envisioned as a society of independent, self-governing adults.

The treatment of a chief of state as a hero symbolic of the nation is not in itself dangerous, and to the extent that it is in fact an integrative technique, it may be extremely useful. What *is* pernicious is the granting of political power to the chief of state. One could argue that the move from absolute monarchy to constitutional monarchy consists in large measure of separating the king from any real political power. But in the President we find the combination of symbolism with power, and this, of course, is the problem.

Harold Wilson resigned in 1976 after having served for almost eight years as Britain's Prime Minister. The reaction of the British electorate was described by the *New York Times*: "There was scant talk of Mr. Wilson in the subway or pubs, and his imminent departure was viewed with curious dispassion. By mid-afternoon the political news about Mr. Wilson and his successor seemed to be overshadowed by headlines about a rumored separation between Princess Margaret and Lord Snowden."[13] The British, who have been far more successful than we in separating monarchy from politics, understood that Great Britain was not resigning; a new Prime Minister would assume power in due course, and life would continue. Contrast this with the departure from the White House of Richard Nixon. Even though he had been forced to resign under threat of impeachment, Nixon, instead of skulking out at midnight, coat collar up and hat brim down, commanded the television networks as he marched over a carpet to mount the presidential helicopter impressively stamped with the presidential seal. All around him the loyal wept as the monarch was escorted into exile. He had been expelled from the White House because of his misuse of power, but he left surrounded by the aura of a chief of state.

Although Nixon was, one hopes, an aberration among presidents, Watergate typifies the danger in the combination of chief of state and chief political officer. The most pernicious results are the President's lack of accountability and his control over the flow of information. The end result is the President's use of his role as chief of state for political purposes.

Reedy has described at length how the White House staff has been transformed into a palace guard that controls both personal access to the President and the information that reaches him, while constantly reassuring him of his wisdom.[14] Members of Congress, of interest groups, of the bureaucracy, and of the press can all be denied access to the President, which effectively prevents them both from bringing him information about the concerns of the people and from demanding information about his policies. Press conferences are held at the President's whim and scarcely live up to the name "conferences." Howard K. Smith, one of the news-hungry journalists whose communications are supposed to ensure the existence of an informed electorate, said, "The Chief of State is like the flag. You have to be deferential."[15] Gradually, press conferences have been replaced by televised presidential addresses to the nation. As manicured appearances in prime time increase, the number of press conferences decrease. President Nixon appeared on prime time during his first eighteen months in office as often as did Presidents Eisenhower, Kennedy, and Johnson in their first eighteen-month periods combined.[16] Kennedy receives high marks for having held 64 press conferences while making only 10 prime-time appearances.[17] This, however, should be contrasted with the 998 press conferences President Franklin Roosevelt held in a little over three terms.[18] Today, a President hires a full-time television adviser, contrives the most impressive and convincing setting possible, delivers a monologue to his subjects, receives the congratulations of his courtiers, and convinces himself that he and the populace have just engaged in communication. Even when the press is admitted, it becomes part of the charade. The White House flew more than 150 members of the press to Europe to cover President Ford's 1975 trip, and then ordered the United States Information Service to prepare for the President and Secretary of State every two hours summaries of the coverage given the trip by the United Press, the Associated Press, and Reuters.[19] Instead of gathering information, the media was being used to record an event designed as part of the 1976 campaign.

And what happens if members of Congress, whose power was meant to balance that of the President, are admitted to the Presence? When Gerald Ford delivered his first presidential address to Congress, the television cameras caught Carl Albert leaning over the podium to apologize to Ford, his junior colleague of two decades, for having inadvertently addressed him the preceding day by his first name. The Speaker of the House was paying public penance for having called the President "Jerry." Alexander Hamilton, monarchist that he was, must have been smiling.

Not all members of Congress are deferential, of course, but the experience of the last few years has taught them that they can be cut off from the White House if they are not. President Kennedy is remembered for having run an "open" White House, which is much to his credit—but laws and institutions are designed for precisely those situations in which the wielders of power are *not* open. More important than Kennedy's openness is the siege mentality, the tightly controlled White House, and the lack of both accessibility and accountability on the part of his successors. More important still is the realization that the very charm and style brought to the White House by Kennedy—one of the "good guys"—were major factors in the modern personalization of the Presidency. The Presidency as symbol now supersedes the individual President, which is another way of indicating that a President no longer has to do anything successful in order to be perceived as a leader, and he cannot help being viewed by the people as a hero even if he does not fall prey to the temptation to use his status as hero for political purposes. The individual President has become the captive of his imperial office.

What, then, is to be done? Somehow, the President must be removed from his throne. Somehow, the terrible deference accorded to the President must be exchanged for a demand that he be no less available and forthcoming than any other chief executive of a democratic state. Before this can be achieved, however, the mystique that surrounds the imperial Presidency must be destroyed.

Representative Henry Reuss of Wisconsin proposed a constitutional amendment that would create an office of Chief of State, separate from that of the President.[20] Passage of the amendment would solve the problem, but it is precisely because the electorate has been conditioned to view the President as chief of state that the amendment is likely to fail. There is another possible approach—one that is less dramatic, less overtly an attack on presidential power, and, therefore, one that can perhaps be implemented. It is the introduction of a question time.

At present, two kinds of question times exist in the Western world. The first, found in England, involves questions from members of the House of Commons,* submitted in advance and circulated in written form (called an "order paper") to both Parliament and the press. Each question is directed to a specific minister, with the Prime Minister expected to be on the floor of the House for the last fifteen minutes of the Tuesday and Thursday question hours. The answer is usually written as well as oral, and the questioning legislator is normally permitted one supplementary question. After that, recognition of additional questioners lies within the discretion of the Speaker, who technically refuses to permit "questions" that are speeches instead of quests for information but who actually attempts only to keep the occasionally wordy and convoluted speeches-*cum*-questions relatively short. The result of a question time may be real information or superficial avoidances, but it is in either event reported by the nation's newspapers and thereby made available to the entire electorate almost immediately. The press knows in advance what questions will be asked when, and, as recipients of the written answers, receives fast and convenient copy.†[21]

Although the simple question time described above is used by many Continental parliamentary systems, most of them also make provision, in one form or another, for "interpolations." These are questions submitted to ministers with the consent of the legislative body. They are answered during sessions that have no time limit, and during which free debate is permitted.[22] Interpolations thus differ from the British system of questions in creating a far greater possibility of information exchange. Even under the British system, however, it is not unknown for the minister being questioned to remain voluntarily after the question time to make a short statement and to permit further discussion. It is in this kind of session that Parliament often receives the bulk of its information during foreign crises.

While the introduction of such an interpolation into the American system would be of great informational use, especially if members of the Cabinet also appeared before Congress regularly, the simple question time would be equally successful in achieving the result

---

*A form of question time also exists in the House of Lords.

†Members may also submit questions for written rather than oral answers. Written answers are otherwise only given when the questioner is not in Commons during a question time to hear the answer or when the time allotted in a session does not permit oral answers to all the questions on the day's order paper.

aimed at here. If the Presidency becomes less imperial, presidents may become more responsive both to the question time and to other demands for information. The flow of information, however, is not the immediate point, especially as we have been taught by presidential press conferences that it is possible to reply to a question with a spate of impressive-sounding sentences that do not answer it. A question time as advocated here would be an attack on the symbolism of the Presidency. The President would appear before Congress regularly, at a time of its choosing, not his, and would be subjected to whatever questions his nominal peers decide to ask. Legislators would no longer be forced to await the imperial summons before being permitted to speak with the President. The electorate would no longer regard the emergence of the President from his palace as a major ceremonial event, and would become used to the now impossible idea that it is normal for the President to be accountable to Congress. Because the normal quickly takes on the coloration of the normative, it would, one hopes, not be too long before Congress and the electorate would feel that presidents should be accountable, and would respond with outrage rather than apathy to incidents of nonaccountability. Congress would presumably cease its schoolchildren's habit of jumping to its collective feet at the sight of the President, and it is barely possible that the President would begin to view himself as a putative leader in constant search of followers, rather than a ruler with automatic privilege—or, as ex-President Nixon would have it, a sovereign.

If part of our purpose is to end the sense of anomie and alienation so obviously current among the electorate, the extension of the question time to Cabinet members might be useful in ending their public anonymity and forcing them to assume responsibility for the actions of their departments. The consciousness of the British Cabinet of its liability to be questioned and of the publicity that its answers will receive is a major factor in the day-to-day workings of its bureaucracies.[23] In addition, questioning of the Cabinet by members of the out-party would permit the opposition a form of address to the electorate and the sort of opportunity to build issues for the next campaign now available only to the President.

Public questioning by Congress of top bureaucrats might produce more information, if not for the public, then for Congress itself. As elites are challenged most successfully by other elites, rather than by the public, the possession of information by the legislative elite might enable it to begin reasserting itself as a counterweight to the executive elite. This would constitute both a threat to the imperial nature of the Presidency and a return to the intentions of the Constitution. The division of the federal government into four institutions (the executive, the Senate, the House, and the Supreme Court) reflected the assumptions that even a concerned electorate with frequent recourse to the ballot box would not be sufficient to keep government honest and that the policies least harmful to the people would result from the struggle for power among competing institutions. The imperial Presidency has effectively taken Congress out of the competition.

How might a question time actually be implemented in the United States? One of the advantages of the question time, as opposed to some of the other suggestions that have been made for curbing the imperial Presidency, is that it would require no constitutional amendment. Article II, section 3, of the Constitution says of the President, "He shall from time to time give to the Congress information of the state of the Union." It was this passage, of course, that led to the tradition of the annual State of the Union Address, but it could as easily become the constitutional basis for the enactment of a statute mandating a question time. One half hour each week—let us say, arbitrarily and hypothetically, Tuesday afternoons from 3:00 to 3:30—could be allotted for presidential appearances before the House; another half hour—again hypothetically, Thursday afternoons from 3:00 to 3:30—for the Senate. Were the interpolation rather than the simple question technique to be adopted, questioning would begin at a stated hour but might well continue until adjournment for the day. (That in itself might be an argument against interpolation, given the already heavy schedule of the President.) Presumably much of the Washington press corps would be present, both to watch the proceedings and to receive the printed answers provided by the President. Another procedural possibility might be to limit participation to the party leaders of the two houses along with a small rotated group of members of both houses. This would permit situating the question time in a less barnlike location and might encourage more informal interaction between President and legislators. The question time could be held weekly for an hour, perhaps in one of the large committee rooms, with the chair held alternately by leaders of each house.

The Speaker of the House of Commons, who decides which and how many supplementary questioners to recognize, has gradually become an apolitical official. As this is not true of the officers presiding over Congress, allowing them the sole power of recognition might lead to charges of partisanship. To avoid this, the Speaker of the House and the Vice-President (who is, of course, the presiding officer of the Senate) might alternate in the chair with the key official of the other party, whether Majority or Minority Leader. Thus the Speaker would chair the Tuesday session one week and the Minority Leader would preside the following week. As is the case in Britain, legislators would take turns submitting questions. If the question time were extended to members of the Cabinet, their appearances before each house would also be rotated, and the members of the house could use their turns at questioning to address either the President or one of the Cabinet members.* Again as in Britain, an official of each house could tabulate the number of questions submitted to each Cabinet official, and if necessary, key officials such as the Secretary of State could be scheduled more frequently than those for whom there were fewer questions.

Should Congress choose to enact such legislation, it might consider the issue of televised proceedings. Congress has consistently kept television out of its deliberations, and the admission of cameras would certainly have some effect on the behavior of the participants. Nevertheless, the most recent examples of televised congressional hearings are instructive. Television made the names of Senator Sam Ervin and Representative Peter Rodino household words and gave boosts to the careers of such other members of their committees as Barbara Jordan. Expectations of the post-Nixon Congress ran unrealistically high in large part because the performances of the Ervin and Rodino committees were so impressive that the average viewer mistakenly thought that they reflected the norm for congressional activity. Although the solemnity of their tasks may explain the responsible demeanor of the two committees, it is also possible that the presence of the television cameras contributed its share. What developed was a mini–congressional mystique, and while one may doubt that Congress is capable of sustaining such a high level of knowledge and deportment, it is intriguing to wonder whether television could not aid in the creation of a congressional mystique that would help counter the presidential mystique already benefited so heavily by the existence of television. Congress does have its heroes and heroines; perhaps it would be good for the electorate to learn about them.

At some point, we must begin to wrestle with the larger problem embodied in the contradictory desirres for democracy and for centralization of power. Our assumption that the difficulties of the modern age necessitate quick answers flies in the face of our simultaneous insistence on the democratization of the policy-making process. This is a very basic and equally complex matter to which those concerned with our political system have paid insufficient attention. It is not argued here that anything as simple as the introduction of a question time will resolve this problem, nor will it by itself result in either

---

*Jimmy Carter's campaign autobiography, *Why Not the Best?* (New York: Bantam Books, 1976), includes this passage: "[I] believe that it would be helpful here to have members of the Cabinet appear before joint sessions of the Congress to answer written and verbal questions, preferably with live television coverage for the whole nation to view." (Pp. 144–45. The suggestion is repeated on p. 170.) The crush of legislators, press, camera crews, and so on, involved in televised joint sessions would probably foster dramatics rather than information flow. Carter did not mention similar presidential appearances. Cf. Walter F. Mondale, *The Accountability of Power* (McKay, 1975), pp. 148–51, 216.

accountability or wise policies. A wise government is something that can never be guaranteed, and a President well prepared by his staff and even minimally able to think on his feet can respond to questions without providing information. What we are dealing with here is symbolism—the need to alter the current symbols of the political system before we can attempt to alter the output of the system itself. To return to political scientist Murray Edelman:

> ... mass publics respond to currently conspicuous political symbols: not to "facts," and not to moral codes embedded in the character or soul, but to the gestures and speeches that make up the drama of the state.... It is therefore political actions that chiefly shape men's political wants and "knowledge," not the other way around.... Political acts and settings, leadership, and language all influence legitimations and assumptions about possibility.[24]

Therefore, we must alter the "conspicuous political symbols" by writing a new "drama of the state." The President must become symbolically accountable, through regular mandated appearances before Congress, before the expectation of real accountability can even arise. With its independent power base, and in a group setting where the presence of colleagues is likely to reinforce the will of the individual questioner, Congress is in a far better position than is the press to make the demands for information that will, at the same time, serve as symbolic attacks on the imperial Presidency. Congress is not particularly good at legislating, but it is quite adept at sniping. Its role as a sniper at presidents has traditionally been scorned by academics; perhaps it can now be put to use.

In June 1975, appearing before the National Press Club, Eugene McCarthy spoke of the personalized imperial Presidency and commented upon what could be expected of President Ford:

> President Ford has not shown any disposition to change the trend toward personalization of the Presidency. When asked last fall whether there would be a code of ethics for his administration, he replied that his example would be the guide. I might note that even Moses, when he came down from the mountain, had specific recommendations—carrying an endorsement other than his own.[25]

Even Moses had to leave his mountaintop and converse with the multitude. It is time for the President to follow his example.

Notes

1. Hugh Sidey, *John F. Kennedy, President* (New York: Atheneum, 1963), pp. 207–9.
2. *New York Times*, April 6, 1975, sec. I, p. 26, cols. 4–6.

3. James L. Sundquist, *Politics and Policy* (Washington, D.C.: Brookings Institution, 1968), pp. 68, 511.

4. Richard E. Neustadt, *Presidential Power* (New York: Wiley, 1960).

5. Murray Edelman, *The Symbolic Uses of Politics* (Urbana: University of Illinois Press, 1964), pp. 76–77.

6. W. Lloyd Warner, *The Living and the Dead: A Study of the Symbolic Life of Americans* (New Haven, Conn.: Yale University Press, 1959), p. 15.

7. George E. Reedy, *The Twilight of the Presidency* (New York: World, 1970), p. 9.

8. James MacGregor Burns, "Considerations on National Leadership," *Presidential Studies Quarterly* 5 (Fall 1975): 4, 9.

9. Morris K. Udall, "Some Thoughts from the Campaign Trail," *Presidential Studies Quarterly* 5 (Fall 1975): 36–37.

10. Ibid.

11. Robert D. Hess and David Easton, "The Child's Changing Image of the President," *Public Opinion Quarterly* 24 (Winter 1960): 632, 644.

12. Fred Friendly, "Foreword," in Newton N. Minow, John Bartlow Martin, and Lee M. Mitchell, *Presidential Television* (New York: Basic Books, 1973), p. vii.

13. *New York Times*, March 18, 1976, p. 3, col. 2.

14. Reedy, op. cit., chaps. 1, 7.

15. *Time*, January 18, 1971, p. 36.

16. Friendly, op. cit., p. ix.

17. Ibid.

18. Ibid.

19. Aaron Latham, *New York Magazine*, June 23, 1975, p. 64.

20. *Congressional Record* (House), July 21, 1975, p. 7162.

21. For a fuller description, see, for example, D. N. Chester and Nona Bowring, *Questions in Parliament* (Oxford: Clarendon Press, 1962); Patrick Gordon Walker, *The Cabinet: Political Authority in Britain* (New York: Basic Books, 1970); and John P. Mackintosh, *The British Cabinet*, 2d ed. (London: Stevens & Sons, 1968).

22. For a fuller description of interpolations in a variety of countries, see, for example, Inter-Parliamentary Union, *Parliaments* (New York: Praeger, 1963), pp. 262–72.

23. George W. Keeton, *Government in Action in the United Kingdom* (London: Ernest Benn, 1970), p. 59; Chester and Bowring, op. cit., p. 172.

24. Edelman, op. cit., pp. 172–73.

25. Quoted in *New Republic*, June 21, 1975, p. 17.

PART FIVE

Presidential Government Reconsidered

14. The President, Congress, and Legislation

H. G. Gallagher

The President's relations with Congress are a complicated business. Congress must pass the laws and fund and oversee the operations of the whole vast executive area of our federal government. Just how the executive and legislative branches interact cannot be reduced to formula and theory. Even so, certain general observations can be made that seem to hold true year in and year out—except during the Watergate years, which were different and must be considered on their own.

Watergate

The Bay of Pigs, the Cuban missile crisis, the Gulf of Tonkin, the bombing of Cambodia, the burning cities, the protest marches, the assassinations, the Vietnam War, and Watergate—the crisis of government, building to crescendo from the last half of the 1960s through the first half of the 1970s, distorted and might have destroyed the American federal system. During this dreadful period, it was not clear whether the checks and balances—which over the years, in their way, had prevented excesses of power—would suffice or even survive. It was a grim time for those who cared about the American system.

The President and Congress have always existed in controversy, competition, and jealousy. Comity and courtesy have been observed in their deliberations with each other. At times, Congress imposed its will upon the President; at other times, the President dominated Congress. The methods by which this was accomplished were not savory but were traditional: pork barrel, patronage, and propaganda. The years 1965–75 saw an escalation in this struggle and new weapons. The traditional means of American politics were replaced by some of the methods of a police state.

Presidents Kennedy, Johnson, and Nixon were obsessed by power. They were not obsessed by what could be achieved with power; they were interested in power itself. As policies crumbled and protests mounted, the obsession grew until, with Nixon, it became all-possessing and pathological. President Grant hated Senator Sumner and cursed him mightily. But Grant never tried to destroy Sumner by spying on him to expose his private life. This, however, was the policy of the Nixon Administration. The methods by which the President and his men imposed their will were not all new, but the intensity and the hostility with which they were applied were certainly new. It was a complete break with tradition. As the President did not know how to lead, he set out to destroy.

This is what the President did:

The President ignored Congress, or, at most, paid it lip service. Congress was excluded from the plans for, or the operation of, such major actions as the Bay of Pigs invasion, the Dominican Republic invasion, the Cuban missile crisis, the Gulf of Tonkin episode, the bombing of Cambodia. In fact, the whole Vietnam War was largely the result of the covert plans of the executive branch in which the legislative branch played no role. During the years 1965–75, Congress was not consulted on these foreign-policy matters. Congressional leaders did not advise on, or participate in, the plans and policy discussions. Congress was asked only to ratify steps already taken, to pay for commitments already made.

The President denied information to Congress. The important concept of national security was widely misused to keep embarrassing material from Congress, whose members were pressured not to speak their doubts or dismay on grounds that to do so would constitute acts of disloyalty or treason. "Did you hear the story," said boisterous Lyndon Johnson, "of the senator who thought he was smarter than his President?"

Worse yet, *the President and his administration lied to Congress.* The direct lies were numerous: They concerned the bombing of North Vietnam, the bombing and invasion of Cambodia, the invasion of the Dominican Republic, and the overthrow of the Allende government in Chile. Lies told about these events and the attitude toward the Congress that spawned these lies were just part of a general climate within the administration. Testimony to Congress, like the press release, was considered not as a source of information but as just another avenue for propaganda. During that dreadful decade, the communication lines between the two branches broke down—what with the lies, the propaganda, the rancor, and finally the hatred.

Last, *the President spied on Congress.* The police agencies of the federal government were turned on Congress. Phones were tapped, conversations were bugged, and agents were placed in jobs on the Hill to spy upon the members. The FBI developed dossiers on the members of Congress, including information on their drinking habits and their sex lives. The Internal Revenue Service investigated their tax records. The CIA opened their overseas mail and watched their movements abroad. President Nixon taped their every conversation with him, whether on the phone or in the privacy of the Oval Office. These taped conversations, not yet transcribed, lie ticking away like time bombs in the national archives. Information from secret administration files (or upon occasion information fabricated to suit the circumstances) was released to the press in efforts to embarrass an enemy politician into silence or to defeat an opposition senator.

All these things were done. They were not done as often or as regularly as in a police state. Nonetheless, they were police-state methods.

Furthermore, they were not done in the name of furthering a policy or serving legislative strategy. They were done for the subversion of one branch of the government by another. The modern presidents' search for power, begun by Franklin D. Roosevelt in 1933, by 1974 had at last lost all reason. Power once sought to press a legislative program through a recalcitrant Congress had become, over forty years, nothing more than naked power. Power had become its own excuse for being.

Almost until the end, Congress was passive. Only gradually did its members awaken to the assault being mounted against them. Accustomed as they were to the more traditional struggle between the branches of government, members of Congress were slow to perceive the seriousness and danger of the attack. Congress, after all, has its weapons. They are powerful and seldom used, but the authors of the Constitution provided them for just such occasions as the Watergate crisis. Congressional authority in a life-or-death struggle with the executive includes the power of the purse (the power to cut off funds to any executive agency, including the White House itself), the power to subpoena people or materials, the power to vote officials in contempt and to imprison them without recourse to the executive department, and, of course, the power to impeach and remove from office. Perhaps, as the unwinding of Watergate showed, the greatest power of them all is that of publicity. The Senate Select Committee and the House Judiciary Committee, by opening their proceedings to the television cameras, were able to present their case directly to the

American people. Presidents do this regularly (Wilson and the League, FDR and his fireside chats, Truman and the 1948 campaign), but it is not so easy for Congress. Congress is usually sharply divided and undisciplined. Only seldom can it produce the leadership, the unity of purpose, the consistency, and the clarity needed to make a substantial impact on public opinion. It did produce such an impact, and this is a measure of the staggering importance that Congress at last attached to the Watergate accusations.

During the investigation and the impeachment proceedings, there was no "politics as usual" on Capitol Hill. When Senator Barry Goldwater told President Nixon he had, at most, fifteen votes against impeachment in the Senate, the American federal system stood in its greatest danger since the South opened fire on Fort Sumter. Congress knew it and acted throughout in a highly responsible manner.

Post-Watergate and Before

Watergate is over, and once again Congress has brought the Presidency down to size—as it did after the Civil War, as it did after World War I. For some forty years, we were dazzled by the FDR vision of the President. Now, after Watergate, it is possible to place the Presidency in a more realistic perspective with Congress. If we stop looking at the President as some sort of colossus towering over Congress and the country and look at him, instead, as the man he is, we find him at the head of a coequal branch of our national government. He may propose legislation in the State of the Union message or otherwise. His proposals will be received by Congress, and, depending on a host of variables, Congress will give its attention to them. Sometimes he is more influential, sometimes less influential with Congress as it considers legislation. Sometimes his legislative proposals are innovative, sometimes not. Sometimes his authority is great in one policy area but not in others. Our system of government is not a seesaw, with the President up when Congress is down. It is a system that separates executive and legislative powers. In regard to his legislative powers, the President is a constitutional monarch with hardly more authority over Congress than Elizabeth II has over Parliament.

In the years since FDR, the executive branch has expanded immensely. The various departments have grown in size and responsibility; the Executive Office of the President has grown; and the White House staff itself is larger now than any Washington department was under Hoover. But this growth has not meant a growth in the power of the President. Far from it.

The President is not strong but weak: He has lost control of the departments, of domestic policy, and, as we see in Watergate, even of his own house. He has retreated into foreign policy, but even there he must share his authority with Congress.

So much attention has been given, in recent years, to the growth of executive power that an essential point has been overlooked. It is true the executive branch has taken upon itself extraordinary powers— war, peace, control of the economy. This does not mean, however, that the man elected by the people to the Presidency can actually wield these powers. If he is gifted in the art of leadership, he will be able to direct the agencies of government, but he will not control them. He reigns, but he does not rule.

It is axiomatic that, sooner or later, all presidents come to hate Congress. They have reason to do so. During the course of president- ial campaigns, the country is encouraged to hold the last President responsible for what happened in his administration and to expect the new President to produce on his promises under the new administra- tion. Clearly and repeatedly, Congress comes between the President and these promises. The President finds he cannot keep his promises to the people without the cooperation of Congress. This leads to presidential frustration of a high order.

In fact, there is very little left with which a President can influence a vote or reward a friend in Congress. Patronage and the Post Office are not the help they once were. An opportunity to share the presidential publicity spotlight for a few moments at a bill-signing ceremony is nice but brief. A presidential campaign swing through a member's district just before election is supposed to be of value, but anyone who has lived through such an exercise must have his doubts. The value of presidential endorsements, always debatable, has in re- cent years become largely discredited.

Yet, though the President has little to trade, he has a desperate need for congressional cooperation. Congress can undo him at every turn. It can make his program appear successful by approving it and funding it; it can turn it into disgrace by harassment, underfunding, and over- investigation.

For example, after the messianic first hundred days, even Roosevelt's relations with Congress settled down into the normal bad. After the great purge effort of 1938, they became worse and continued so until his death. After 1938, with the exception of declarations of war and other necessities, FDR received little congressional support for his innovative legislative and social proposals. It is true that Congress gave him the executive powers he sought in order to direct the war, but not fast enough to suit him. In a peculiar address to Congress, rather chilling in its overtones, Roosevelt said, in 1942, "in event that the Congress should fail to act adequately, I shall accept the responsi- bility and will act. . . . I have given the most thoughtful consideration to meeting this issue without further reference to Congress . . . when the war is won the powers under which I act automatically revert to the people to whom they belong."

Many a President has threatened to horsewhip congressmen, but this is, I believe, the only time a President has stood in the halls of Congress and threatened to abolish it.

Harry S. Truman, originally a Senate club member if ever there was one, ended up making his living by giving hell to the Eightieth, "Do Nothing," Congress—actually, a most responsible, productive Congress. Lyndon B. Johnson, after that year of wonders, 1964, during which he conducted Congress through its most productive session in history, came to despise congressional criticism. "Go ask Walter Lippmann for your appropriation," LBJ was overheard growling to a senator who had questioned his Vietnam policy.

No wonder Congress so often produces in a President rage at his own impotence. It is built into the system—it *is* the system—and we can perhaps take comfort in the thought that it is not new. When the Senate rejected not only his first but also his second nomination to the Supreme Court, President Nixon lashed out, accusing the Senate of action vicious, false, and hypocritical. It is, he said, the "constitutional responsibility" of the President to appoint members of the Court. The Senate's rejection of the nominations amounted to the substitution of the Senate's "own subjective judgment for that of the one person entrusted by the Constitution with the power of appointment . . . the fact remains, under the Constitution it is the duty of the President to appoint and of the Senate to advise and consent." Failure to consent, he said, placed the "traditional constitutional balance in jeopardy." The Senate was not impressed.

John Tyler, tenth President of the United States, would have had great sympathy with President Nixon's frustration, for certainly John Tyler was the all-time champion of bad relations with his Congress. A fine and decent Virginian, he became President by mistake, upon the death of William Henry Harrison, who died of a chill contracted while giving a lengthy inaugural address. Tyler had broken with the Jacksonian Democrats to accept second place on the Whig ticket with Harrison. The Whigs thought he would bring Virginia with him. He failed to do so. He was not a Whig; he was not a Democrat. He thus came to the White House with virtually no party support in Congress. There ensued three zany years in the history of the Republic.

When Harrison died, the congressional Whigs confidently expected Tyler to serve as acting President only. They soon found out how mistaken they were: "I am the President and am responsible for my administration."

The President vetoed the Bank bill. Congress promptly passed another Bank bill. The President vetoed it. The House of Representatives drew up a bill of indictment with intent to impeach the President. The President protested by message—a message the House refused to receive, let alone consider. The President's Cabinet resigned en masse, excepting only Daniel Webster, who had his own presidential ambitions. The charade reached its zenith—or perhaps nadir—over Senate confirmation of Tyler's appointments. In the last session of his administration, the Senate rejected four Cabinet nominations, four Supreme Court nominations, and nominations of ministers to France and Brazil, five marshals, one attorney, fourteen deputy postmasters, thirty-one customs officials, four receivers of public money, and four registrars of land offices. These figures must of necessity be approximate. The records are confused because several of the nominations were submitted and rejected a number of times.

President Tyler was a stubborn man.

On the last night of the session, as was the custom of the day, Tyler went to the President's Room adjacent to the Senate chamber, ready for battle. That night, the Senate received and rejected three times the nomination of Caleb Cushing to be the Secretary of the Treasury. That same night, Henry A. Wise was nominated three times to be minister to France, and rejected three times. Old Senator Benton reported that "nominations and rejections flew backwards and forwards as in a game of shuttlecock—the same nomination in several instances being rejected . . . within the same hour."

Never was a President more badly treated by a Congress.

And perhaps it can fairly be said that never was a Congress more badly treated by a President than through the actions of Abraham Lincoln. At the beginning of the Civil War, the President purposely delayed calling Congress into session to avoid the criticisms and delays that Congress invariably produces. To save the Union, President Lincoln used powers he did not have, knowingly and repeatedly overstepping the Constitution.

In a statement, breathtaking and sweeping, to Senator Chandler, Lincoln said, "I conceive that I may, in an emergency, do things on military grounds which cannot constitutionally be done by the Congress." Franklin D. Roosevelt threatened to assume powers held by Congress, but only Lincoln claimed powers held neither by Congress nor by the President. No wonder Senator Wade said the country was going to hell.

President Lincoln called up troops, drafted men, and spent unappropriated money that he had his own friends carry from the Treasury to pay arms and ammunition makers. He interned people of suspect loyalty and abolished habeas corpus.

As a politician, a candidate, and a President, he maintained his theory that it was best to watch and wait for the big event and to ignore the small, entangling ones. Using his concept of his war powers, against the advice of his Cabinet, without consulting Congress, he issued the Emancipation Proclamation. This action, its moral significance aside, abolished without compensation, at one fell swoop, considerably more than a billion dollars worth of personal property held by American citizens. He issued his Proclamation even as Congress was considering legislation of its own to provide for the freeing of the slaves.

As war President, Lincoln dictated the terms of the peace. He appointed military governors without congressional approval and declared what terms and procedures must be satisfied before returning Southern states could reassume their places in Congress and the Union. At the time of his assassination, he was preparing to implement his Reconstruction program, prepared without consulting Congress. Lincoln saved the Union but upset the comity between the President and Congress.

We have allowed strong presidents such as Lincoln to assume sweeping powers in times of great crisis. After the crisis, Congress has always moved to reassert itself, to bring the President down to size, to redress the balance. The danger of allowing a President like Lincoln to act without regard to constitutional restraints in a great crisis is that lesser men may take Lincoln as precedent in lesser causes.

In general, the President and his administration have always had to lobby Congress to obtain what they wished. Secretary of the Treasury Alexander Hamilton thought of himself as President Washington's Prime Minister and for five years lobbied Congress to obtain approval of the President's program. Congress has, from the beginning, been indignant at such interference in the legislative process. But to no avail; it still goes on.

The business of rallying support for the administration in a tight vote is an extraordinarily difficult thing to categorize. It involves all the things we read about in textbooks and newspapers—patronage, judgeships, projects, grants, bargains with labor, pressure from industry, swaps of support of dubious programs, appeals to one's higher instincts—and the President himself can play a central role. Grover Cleveland was once busy dispensing patronage in exchange for votes. When told he would not win until hell froze over, he replied, "Hell will freeze over in exactly twenty-four hours."

Woodrow Wilson is widely believed to have been the first modern President to use his officials to lobby Congress in any consistent, continuing manner. Albert Sydney Burleson, Wilson's Postmaster General, used the President's Room off the Senate chamber for his office as he lobbied the Wilson program through the Senate. Upon occasion, this room has seen presidents themselves pleading for their programs. Harding used it during his extraordinary efforts to defeat the soldier's bonus bill. President Grant lobbied in favor of his Santo Domingo Treaty from it.

Presidents have actually taken their lobbying to the floor of the Senate and occasionally to the floor of the House. There is nothing in the Senate rules that allows the President to speak. He has, however, never been denied the opportunity. Warren G. Harding spoke directly to the Senate as it was considering the bonus bill. In one extraordinary moment, Herbert Hoover pleaded with an unresponsive Congress for passage of his tax bill. In the depth of the Depression and the depth of his own despair, he appeared late one night, without previous notice, before the Senate to plead that "in your hands at this moment is the answer to the question whether Democracy has the capacity to act speedily enough to save itself in an emergency." In this case, the Democratic Congress cooperated. Otherwise, it was congressional politics as usual until Roosevelt took office.

The best-remembered case of an incumbent President's appearing before a congressional committee was unexpected, unannounced. The Joint Committee on the Conduct of the War was considering, in secret session, reports of treason within Lincoln's immediate family. Lincoln walked in, to the astonishment and dismay of the committee, told its members there were no traitors in the White House, turned, and left. This killed the investigation.

Presidential efforts at influencing committee investigations or congressional actions are seldom that effective. Perhaps the basic reason for this is that the President is a short-termer, while Congress, like the Civil Service, is a career. Of the thirty-six presidents preceding Nixon, only eleven, or fewer than one-third were elected to two consecutive terms. The popular conception that incumbent presidents tend to be re-elected is just not true. It was true through the first forty-eight years of the Republic, when five of the seven presidents were re-elected. Since then, there have been thirty presidents, and only six of these have been elected to two consecutive terms. Four were wartime leaders (Lincoln, McKinley, Wilson, and Roosevelt), and two were beloved war heroes (Grant and Eisenhower).

Congressional seniority is important to the balance of power between the executive and the legislature. Congressional leaders, with their years of seniority, full of "stubbornness and penicillin," as Senator Eugene McCarthy once put it, are cunning with experience. They have seen presidents come and go, but they remain. If a President does not get his legislative program—and, since Theodore Roosevelt, each President has had a program—approved by Congress in his first two years, he is likely to get very little of it approved. Woodrow Wilson pointed this out, and FDR used to quote Wilson on the subject, though, as his term wore on, he stretched Wilson's two years to four. In any case, by that time Congress has decided what it likes and will approve and what it will not. The President, without experience or very much influence, is seldom able to revive a program once it is bogged down in a recalcitrant Congress.

Legislative Procedure and Strategy

It is my impression that, on the whole, Congress has been more innovative and creative in proposing legislation than the President has. The root reason for this is a simple one. There is, after all, a basic difference between what the two branches do. To garble a Bernard Shaw quotation: The administration looks at things the way they are and tries to improve them; Congress looks at the way things should be and tries to achieve them.

There are intelligent, able men in both branches of government. Those in the executive branch are intent on keeping things from flying apart or from grinding at last to a full stop. The administration tries to administer rather than to innovate. Congress has the opportunity to act, not react—to create events. It can create new institutions; it can abolish old ones. It is not limited, as the administration is, to adjusting or perfecting the existing machinery of government.

Congress attracts intelligent individuals who in almost every case have competed strenuously to get there. It would hardly do so if it were but an empty honor. Intelligent men would not be content merely to ratify the President's ideas, appropriate him money, and go home. Not all of the 535 members of Congress may be intelligent, but all of them carry a degree of ambition. This combination of intelligence, ambition, and status encourages creativity. The disparate many in Congress are struggling for the respect of their peers, the approval of their constituents, and national recognition. This brings about a congressional search for new legislative possibilities that never ceases. Members of Congress and their staffs are ever looking for the issue that will catch on, the bandwagon that is going to go, the Big One. They are anxious to find an issue that will lead to an interview on "Meet the Press," an article in *Parade*, an item on the front page of the *New York Times*.

The story of each piece of legislation is different, but all arise out of a complicated power struggle involving public interest and private ambition. An innovative proposal will come from one or two or several voices in Congress. It may be an old proposal brought to life again, like revenue-sharing and the direct election of the President—ideas that date back at least to Andrew Jackson's first State of the Union message. It may be a new idea fresh from a sociology course or the mind of a congressman. The idea, once expressed, may cause discussion. If it is taken up by the press, debated by the intelligentsia, deplored by the establishment, there may come, in due course, serious congressional attention to the proposal. Hearings will be held. More discussion will be generated: Radicals will support it; the establishment will oppose it. In due course, it will pass from heresy to dogma. It will receive the presidential imprimatur, be mentioned in the State of the Union message, and become part of the official presidential legislative program.

The State of the Union message in which this program is set forth is largely an empty institution. It consists, normally, of harmless short sermons, one or two headline-grabbing innovative proposals, and a list of legislative items that, though not new, carry reasonable prospects of passage into law. These serve to maintain a fairly respectable presidential batting average. The message is usually universally ignored the week after it is given.

The writing and preparation of the actual bills and amendments have become a profession, and each branch of our government now has its experts in legislative preparation and interpretation. These experts often work together. The camaraderie that in many cases has grown up between the professional staff of a congressional committee and the career staff of the agency over which the committee has jurisdiction is a source of uneasiness both to the White House and to members of Congress—and properly so.

Each Senate or House committee is staffed with people having specialized knowledge in the area of the committee's competence. Each executive department or agency has its corresponding staff for legislative counsel and liaison. Over the years, they develop a working relationship that continues no matter what the election results. To check this intimacy, there is, within the Executive Office of the President, the Office of Management and Budget (OMB), a group of dedicated men with that "passion for anonymity" defined by Louis Brownlow. These men perform a service called "Legislative Reference." They are not political; they do not make policy. It is their duty to see that the legislative statements, testimony, and reports emanating from all of the many executive agencies reflect administration policy, are consistent, and are not contradictory. They serve as a clearing house, a court of appeal, a traffic cop. It is their duty not to question administration policy but simply to see that it is applied, to interpret and implement it throughout government. "Policy" itself is supposedly made across the street, in the White House, by the politicians, perhaps by the President himself. In fact, there are many times when there is *no* policy, and it is made consciously or unconsciously by the nonpolitical civil servants of Legislative Reference. These men see presidents come and go, and they have no great respect for the ability of the White House staff, whether it be Republican or Democratic. So, in the absence of policy, they often must make it—in order to keep the executive end of legislation functioning. They make it one way until someone tells them to make it another.

In this strange and shifting world of legislative policy, authority is there to be used by those who take it. Legislative Reference in OMB has the advantage and wiliness that come from years of experience.

Actually, it can be—and has been—overruled by a ribbon clerk in the White House who claims to be, and occasionally may be, close to the President. Most junior White House clerks, however, do not know they can do this, and by the time they learn, they are usually on their way back to private business or wherever else they came from.

Confrontation within an administration, of course, depends on the character of the administration. In recent administrations, not including Nixon's, the secretary of any department had the right to reject the pronouncement of the Office of Management and Budget on legislation or, indeed, on anything else. He could appeal directly to the President. This was done, often enough, in a state of high dudgeon. The strength, importance, and utility of the OMB depend on the ability of its director to get to the President *first*. A wise President supports his director, for the Office of Management and Budget offers his one last, sad hope of retaining control over that vast bureaucracy, the U.S. Government.

The presidents of the 1960s—Kennedy, Johnson, and Nixon— brought no training in administration with them. All three had been senators, two had been vice-presidents, but not one had ever run a government agency or met a payroll in the private sector. This showed. They did not know how to manage an organization. They had difficulty making the bureaucracy work for them; they were unwilling to trust career civil servants; they doubted the loyalty of all those people working for HEW and HUD, DOT and DOD. Instead of inspiring confidence and spirited teamwork, they sowed suspicion and mistrust. The presidents complained they had little control over the executive agencies, and they were right. As their terms wore on, Johnson and Kennedy developed methods and channels for coping more or less with this problem. Nixon never did; for him it just got worse. Nixon surrounded himself with zealous loyalists trained in advertising. He denied access to those he did not trust, and the number of those he did not trust grew and grew—until finally he was alone. The White House in those last Nixon years had at least as much difficulty with HEW professionals as it did with Viet Cong negotiators. The White House understood neither, and both were its enemies.

During the months of Watergate, the White House almost ceased to function on regular legislative matters. Congressional mail often remained unanswered. Legislative proposals from the agencies were not cleared. Requests from Congress for executive advice on pending bills were not answered. And what happened was interesting. Congress acted on bills without receiving executive advice. Agencies dealt directly with congressional committees on policy matters without executive clearance. The informal direct ties between Congress and the agencies were strengthened. The efforts of Presidents Polk,

Lincoln, Andrew Johnson, Wilson, Harding, and FDR to strengthen executive control over the agencies of government were weakened. Nixon, desperate to control the government, lost its direction. Unwilling to let Congress succeed where he had failed, he set out to destroy Congress and in the process was himself destroyed.

What Nixon erroneously perceived as a conspiracy against himself and his mistaken sense of the President's due was simply a fact of national political life. Any President in search of legislative achievement must buck Congress, the established civil service, the departments, and now the Executive Office itself. No wonder John Kennedy is reported to have said that he found "no pleasure" in the job.

Once a proposal is mentioned in the State of the Union message, it becomes part of the President's program. It gains in stature. Lobbyists and interest groups—including states, cities, and localities, federal agencies, and commissions—struggle over its terms. The professional syndicates take over—that is, the organizations, the clients, the lobbyists, the civil servants, the philanthropists, and the congressmen who are bound together by a common interest in education, mental health, the SST, or whatever. The bill may become a partisan issue. Democrats and Republicans vie to develop, according to their lights, a more acceptable version of the measure. Finally, it is passed, and its sponsors and cosponsors are invited to the White House to participate in the presidential signing ceremony. The President passes out pens to all concerned and makes a moving statement on the progress being achieved, a statement carried by all major networks on their evening news programs. And this is how the original idea of Congressman X becomes a major achievement in the record of the administration of the President.

The Legislative Box Score

In 1946, Lawrence Chamberlain of Columbia University published his book, *The President, Congress, and Legislation*. Professor Chamberlain analyzes the legislative history of ninety major pieces of legislation passed by Congress between the years 1880 and 1940. He has chosen measures in the fields of business, tariffs, labor, national defense, agriculture, federal credit, banking and currency, immigration, conservation, and railroads. Over the sixty years studied—including the New Deal years—Chamberlain finds, "Of the entire ninety laws no less than seventy-seven traced their ancestry directly to bills which originally had been introduced without administration sponsorship." He says, rather quietly, "These figures do not support the thesis that Congress is unimportant in the formulation of major legislation." Chamberlain contends that the creative role of Congress can not be denied, even in the major pieces of Roosevelt legislation: the National Industrial Recovery Act, the Securities and Exchange Act, the Agricultural Adjustment Act, the National Labor Relations Act, the Fair Labor Standards Act, the Social Security Act. "Most of the great mass of regulatory legislation of the past decade, popularly dubbed 'New Deal Legislation,' had a well-defined prenatal history extending back several years before it was espoused by the Roosevelt Administration. This is true not only of the more conventional fields such as banking, railroads and taxation but of the newer areas of social security, holding company regulation and security control." Political scientists Ronald C. Moe and Stephen C. Teel updated the Chamberlain study, and their valuable findings were published in the September 1970 *Political Science Quarterly*. Their appraisal of Congress through the 1960s confirms Chamberlain's observation—Congress remains the innovator.

In recent years Congress has provided initiative and incentive in several major policy areas: (1) oil price-control legislation; (2) land-use planning; (3) strip mining; (4) campaign financing; (5) day-care centers; and (6) consumer legislation—auto safety, consumer-product safety, consumer-protection agency, X-ray radiation standards, restrictions on pesticides and carcinogens. Major legislation over the last generation in civil rights, constitutional rights, education, environmental protection, Medicare, Medicaid, and federally financed medical research had its origins in Congress as well.

Since the debacles of Vietnam and Watergate, Congress has stepped up its investigative and oversight activities. These have led to tight congressional control over covert CIA activities; a halt to random CIA-FBI domestic surveillance activities; repeal of a multitude of emergency powers granted the President in war time; repeal of the Tonkin, Quemoy, Matsu, and Lebanon resolutions, which granted the President open-ended authority to act in these areas without consulting Congress; and the Congressional Budget and Impoundment Act of 1974, designed to provide Congress with economic and budgetary competence consonant with that of the executive.

Moe and Teel also take note of a most interesting and significant development. The President has found it increasingly difficult to exert leadership over the executive branch and its policies, let alone compete with or lead Congress as chief legislator. It appears that the President increasingly tends to retreat into foreign policy and world affairs—areas over which he has clear constitutional and historical dominion. Because of the realities of the United States as a great nuclear power and H-bomb missile technology, perhaps this is unavoidable, but every President since 1940 has devoted more time to foreign affairs than he has to domestic matters.

After the Vietnam disaster, the cries became general that Congress has relinquished its "traditional and constitutional" responsibility to share foreign policy-making with the President. This is said as though the President had deliberately and impudently seized powers in the field hitherto held by Congress. Such is just not the case.

Cecil Crabb, Jr., summarizes what has been happening since World War II: "A striking phenomenon associated with the control of foreign relations in recent American history is the expanded role of Congress in virtually all phases of external affairs." Moe and Teel quote Crabb and list the areas of dominance: economic-aid policy, military assistance, agricultural-surplus disposal, location of facilities, immigration and tariff policies. To this list may be added several other specific items: the Nuclear Test–Ban Treaty; the approval and withdrawal of the Gulf of Tonkin Resolution; the Lebanese and Quemoy and Matsu resolutions; the Fulbright Vietnam hearings, televised nationwide; the Pearl Harbor hearings after World War II; the hearings on the Dominican Republic invasion; and the congressional investigation related to the Pentagon Papers.

In spite of President Nixon's brilliant innovations in foreign policy, Congress continues to have a major say in national-security matters. The Senate insists on amending the SALT treaty; it blocks the Russian-trade détente. Congress forces the President to stop bombing Cambodia. Interference in Greek-Turkish relations, Angolan policy, and Chilean and Panamanian affairs illustrates, as did the activities of Woodrow Wilson's Senate, that the President *alone* cannot commit the United States to a foreign policy.

Even with regard to Vietnam, Congress condoned the President's policy by appropriation and resolution. When Congress finally withdrew its support, America's active involvement came to a virtual halt. This suggests that Congress plays a substantial role in American foreign policy-making—a role larger than that of confirming ambassadors and ratifying treaties. The President may have more power to act on his own initiative in this area, but even here, he is a limited constitutional monarch, with no more control over Congress than over his own departments.

The President of the United States has many titles, one of which is chief legislator. It is a paper title.

Congress legislates, and more often than not, the President has little to say about it. The origins of most of the innovative legislation in the last ten years, or the last century, can be found in Congress.

Presidents, like kings, provide a handy chronology. They are easy to remember. The personality of a king is more memorable than the multitudes of a parliament. To identify a measure as part of the Kennedy New Frontier program is to fix it in time as a silver spoon is fixed as Georgian. In most cases, upon examination, the Kennedy Administration had about as much to do with the initiation of the proposal as the Georges had to do with the design and craftsmanship of the spoon.

Congress is a small and diverse body. It is a career. It is run by old men at the top, with the young men at the bottom. The old have the experience of age; the young have the ideas of youth. These ideas are sifted by experience, and what results is usually timely and responsive.

Congress is close enough to the people to determine when change is necessary and, unlike the executive bureaucracy, small enough to provide it. Do not worry too much about Congress. It is doing its job.

If anyone is in trouble, it is the President, who is more in danger of losing control of his own executive branch than he is in a position to seize control of the legislative branch of our federal government. As the size and responsibilities of the federal government grow, the President's lack of control grows apace. This is, at heart, the story of Watergate—a weak man in a weak office trying to control events by using illicit dirty tricks to destroy those he takes to be his enemies.

The Presidency is a weak office. It always has been. Only very few men have transcended its weakness.

In 1838, James Fenimore Cooper wrote, "As a rule, there is far more danger that the President of the United States will render the office less efficient than was intended, than that he will exercise an authority dangerous to the liberties of the country."

This is still true.

15. The President and Constitutional Reform: Toward Presidential Leadership and Party Government

Charles M. Hardin

When the tide of evidence of Richard M. Nixon's presidential abuses reached its flood, a profound interest in reforming the presidency ripened.* Earlier, some scholars, politicians, and publicists had sought to strengthen the office by giving the President the item veto, by permitting him to raise and lower income taxes, by enlarging his power over personnel administration, by repealing the Twenty-second Amendment, and by equating presidential and congressional terms at four years while synchronizing elections.[1] After Watergate, commentators generally aimed at diminishing a President's power and increasing his accountability by requiring more information from him, by expanding the use of the concurrent resolution or congressional veto, by limiting his authority to appoint officials without senatorial approval, by shrinking his ability to impound appropriated funds, and by specific injunctions and restrictions attached to delegations of presidential power. Some proposed changes called for constitutional amendments—to lighten the burdens of the office while reducing its mystique by dividing ceremonial functions from those of the chief executive and vesting the former in a head of state;[2] to require the President regularly to submit to a question period, adapted from parliamentary regimes, in a political forum;[3] to substitute a vote of no confidence for impeachment as a means of evicting presidents;[4] and to limit the President to one term of six years, thereby

*Although the provocations had been much different, similar periods of reform proposals had occurred before. (Joseph E. Kallenbach, *The American Chief Executive* [New York: Harper & Row, 1966], pp. 566–67.)

expanding his time for carrying out programs while reducing his incentive to manipulate the next election.[5]

Then, with Nixon's resignation, many lost interest in reforming the Presidency. For them, "the system worked"; our framework of government and our political institutions had proved once more to be providential. But some still found their skepticism undiminished. My own misgivings are based on an interpretation of constitutional trends noticeable at least since the 1930s. In this perspective, Watergate becomes only one of the more ominous symptoms. The opportunity and the obligation to re-examine the system loom with rare urgency. I shall argue that we need to look at the Presidency, including its potential for good and evil, within the general structure of American Government. A strong and accountable Presidency is indispensable, and it requires a proper relationship to other institutions. After dwelling on relationships among the President, Congress, the bureaucracy, and the people, I shall suggest constitutional changes that would make the Presidency more accountable without sacrificing its effectiveness; that would do so by restructuring the separation of powers so that it becomes a separation between government and opposition rather than between the executive, the legislative, and the judicial; and that would be fulfilled through the emergence of more centralized and disciplined political parties.[6]

The Need for a Strong Presidency

The force of Alexander Hamilton's argument for a strong Presidency vested in one person is underlined in our era by the danger of wars of global annihilation, combined with the virtual disappearance of warning time between apprehension of the foreign threat and response. Just as we are compelled to concentrate military decisions to meet the ultimate danger, so also we must centralize the power to make lesser military and diplomatic responses to lesser dangers, because these must be examined to see whether they are integrally related to the ultimate danger. The need to fix great military and diplomatic powers in one man was happily condensed in Hamilton's epigram about the need to achieve "Decision, activity, secrecy, and despatch."[7]

Second only to national survival (and essential to it) is the nourishing of national prosperity, the result of a growing economy with high employment and fairly stable prices. Just as he is first in war and in diplomacy, so also the President is hailed as the "manager of prosperity." From the economic statutes of the New Deal to the Humphrey-Hawkins bill of 1976, Congress has sought to cope with economic problems by delegating sweeping powers to the President. True, the impressive presidential power in foreign and military policy has been diluted and compromised in domestic policy by the need to bargain with Congress and with vested interests;[8] nevertheless, the secular trend clearly favors presidential initiative, coordination, and synthesis—in reciprocal trade agreements, in the executive budget, and in planning and administering schemes for managing the economy and protecting the environment.*[9]

Recently the triumphant march of the planned economy and the welfare state has faltered. Taxpayers have begun to resist. A number of economists have urged that curing the economic ills of modern polities requires less emphasis on stimulating demand and more on increasing supply. Wholehearted commitment to extending and equalizing equities in the enjoyment of economic goods is not enough, they have said. Unless productivity is increased, the shares for all—including jobs, the most vital of all amenities—will shrink. Whatever turn economic policy takes—whether government's role will stress (1) manipulation of the economy in more and more detail to provide ever expanding equities in consumption or (2) the role of the private economy in the belief that production will increase and prosperity flourish in proportion to governmental wisdom not only in regulation but in forebearance—the need for centralized, organized, and disciplined government will remain. So will the need for a powerful executive. The issue between the two conceptions (it would be permissible to say "world views") was partly raised by the differences between the two candidates for the American Presidency in 1976 on whether controlling inflation or reducing unemployment should have priority. Similar issues have risen in several other countries, the more sharply in proportion to their degree of industrialization.†

Inadequate and Overzealous Presidents

The seemingly inexorable logic of fixing executive power in one person subjects the country to dangers arising from human frailty. A President may lose his grasp of events, his will, or his nerve. Or he may commit the country to reckless acts of war. As Winston Churchill

*Some (for example, Aaron Wildavsky and Donald E. Peppers) will demur from the assertion that the President's role is this significant. While conceding that the organization and culture of modern government introduce many obstacles between presidential directives and their implementation, I should argue that the inferences that the executive role is of little significance and that government action is essentially a complex of incremental departures and adjustments is misleading.

†The issue has been posed in Britain, France, and West Germany, as well as in a number of other countries. An analysis of the issue and the role of political-economic thought related thereto can be found in Theodore W. Schultz, "On Economics, Agriculture, and Political Economy," the Elmhirst Lecture, International Conference of Agricultural Economics, Nairobi, Kenya, 1976.

wrote, "The loyalties which center on number one are enormous. If he trips he must be sustained. If he makes mistakes they must be covered. If he sleeps he must not be wantonly disturbed. If he is no good he must be pole-axed."[10]

Only the United States among the large constitutional democracies is without an orderly, workable, and accepted means of replacing its chief executive. Nixon resigned to escape virtually certain impeachment and conviction. Eminent authorities agree that this resolution of the problem rested essentially on the tapes—especially the tape of June 23, 1972—hence on a kind of evidence never likely to be available again. As Raoul Berger put it, "It is of the nature of miracles that they are not recurrent."[11] It is by no means clear that impeachment will avail for anything other than common-law crimes. In the unwieldy procedures of the Twenty-fifth Amendment, the grounds for removing presidents are almost certainly confined to inability to serve—meaning physical or mental incapacity. Given the heavily legalistic approach that would be employed in any conceivable application of the amendment, it is unthinkable that the grounds would be expanded to include *political* incompetence or unreliability.[12]

Congressman Henry S. Reuss introduced an amendment to provide for a vote of confidence that would permit removing a President on political grounds and holding a new election—an imaginative proposal directed at the real problem. Some may demur because no British Government with a majority has lost a vote of confidence since 1885;[13] the rebuttal is that in crises a majority has not been needed to upset a government, as the examples of Asquith in 1916, Chamberlain in 1940, and Eden in 1956 show. What is crucial, and what the British have, is a constitutional understanding that provides a legitimate and orderly means of replacing leaders. The method should include the kinds of signals to leaders—even those with party majorities—that tell them when they should step aside. More typically, the Reuss proposal is attacked for violating the separation of powers and for advocating the vote of confidence, adapted from parliamentary systems where it requires strong, centralized, disciplined parties—notoriously absent in the United States—to make it work.[14] The counterargument, which will be expanded later, is to round out the Reuss amendment with other measures designed to promote the strength, centralization, and discipline of American parties; if successful, this course of action will preserve the principle of the separation of powers but change its nature—for the better.

Let me begin by noting that the threat of removing dangerously incompetent or overzealous presidents should be incorporated in the ordinary procedures of government by taking steps to stabilize and centralize the opposition. This course is advisable because the disease of presidential arrogance is chronic, fed by the unremitting inflation of the presidential ego.[15]

Countering Government by Presidential Whim

Presidents have acquired enormous powers over decisions, especially but not exclusively in foreign and military affairs. Often presidents tend to make decisions guided by their own whims, instincts, or mind sets. Our institutions protect the President from dissent and encourage him to follow his own predilections without the chastening influence of debate with someone who has a political base comparable to, and different from, his own. My introduction to the problem came in August 1943 from Chester C. Davis, then President of the Federal Reserve Bank of St. Louis, who had just resigned from his brief and unhappy service as President Franklin D. Roosevelt's War Food Administrator. Davis was full of the problems of the Presidency. He described a 1937 meeting in the Oval Office on the bill to enlarge the Supreme Court. President Roosevelt asked Davis, then head of the Agricultural Adjustment Administration, to encourage farm leaders to accept his proposal. Davis replied that farm leaders would oppose changes in the Supreme Court. "Roosevelt's eyes got glassy the way they always did when anyone disagreed with him."

That incident lodged in my memory to be joined by others until enough evidence accumulated to convince me that presidents are subject to the curse of expanding arrogance, continuously nourished by the climate of almost unrelieved agreement and, indeed, adulation, in which they operate.

Examples multiply of government by presidential whim, instinct, or mind set. To go no farther back, they can be discovered repeatedly in the actions of every incumbent from Franklin D. Roosevelt with his policies toward China, his Supreme Court plan, and his idiosyncratic economics to Gerald R. Ford with his precipitous pardon of Richard Nixon and his overreaction in the *Mayaguez* incident. Examples are most dramatic and disturbing in the fields of foreign and military policy, as the Pentagon Papers show, especially when supplemented by the Cambodian invasion of 1971 and the various military initiatives by President Nixon in 1972. But many significant examples arise in domestic policy, such as Harry S. Truman's support of inflationary monetary policy in 1950–51, Dwight D. Eisenhower's persistence in restrictive fiscal policy in 1959–60, and Lyndon B. Johnson's rejection of a surtax to finance Vietnam expenses in 1966–67.[16]

Many people experienced in presidential service will deny my assertion, insisting that people do argue with presidents, who thus are effectively exposed to varieties of viewpoints. Emboldened by my virtual innocence of working sessions with presidents, but also encouraged by reading and discussions,[17] I maintain that the typical life of a President is spent awash in agreement and that the more the chips are down—the higher the tension, the sharper the crisis, the greater the need for explicit confrontation and challenge—the stronger will be the tendency for staff members, friends, advisers, and the entourage generally either to cheer the President on to whatever he wants to do or to fall silent.

What is needed is a constitutional structure that will compel presidents to debate the issues couched in presidential terms, that is, the issues emerging from the presidential perspective—the synthesizing and combining comprehension of the problems of national survival *and* of prosperity *and* of the preservation of liberty—with all their mutual influences and interrelations. The President must have (or, at least, should have) programs to deal with these problems, and those programs need to be examined by all the force of logic human intelligence can muster. If the President is to debate, he must have a peer—someone with a political base comparable to, but different from, his own. The obvious peer would be the defeated presidential candidate, who should be given a seat in Congress, pre-emptive privilege on the floor and on all committees, an adequate staff, and an appropriate office with the obvious perquisites. Thus would be created a Leader of the Opposition whose office, supported by other changes to be mentioned later, would help enormously to group, coordinate, and discipline the opposition party—and hence to have the same effect on the party in power.[18] When the President speaks, the press would have someone to ask for an answer, someone who would be motivated and prepared to answer in the same presidential perspective but from the viewpoint of a different power base. The President would be forced to anticipate the reaction of the Leader of the Opposition; he would be subjected to the chastening influence of knowing that he would have to explain his proposals, not merely ritually to a pliant entourage but to a political opposition armed with live ammunition. Of great importance: Some members of his entourage, knowing that the President would be challenged, would be emboldened far more now to play devil's advocates.

Coping with an Overreaching Bureaucracy

Presidents do not monopolize the abuse of power. Especially since World War II, a relatively new political phenomenon has emerged, the concentration of semi-autonomous power in the American version of bureaucracy.[19] Examples multiply in water-resource agencies, in soil-conservation agencies, in environmental agencies or resource-management agencies, in agencies formed to provide public housing or public roads, and, above all, in the military. Once wars have begun, frequently by presidential initiative, the military bureaucracy has often acquired undue influence on the nature, extent, intensity, and duration of hostilities. Recent disclosures also show that the same phenomenon—the semi-autonomous agency dangerously free from responsible control—has appeared in intelligence and security agencies, notably, the FBI and the CIA.[20]

In this brief account, one illustration will have to suffice, to show the leverage of the military bureaucracy and the importance of the decisions that it may influence. I refer to the persistent aggravation of the arms race by the American military bureaucracy. A salient example occurred when the Kennedy Administration took office, after a campaign that had featured one of the greatest frauds ever foisted on the country by presidential politics, the "missile gap." Robert McNamara became Secretary of Defense. Because he was anxious above all to slow the nuclear arms race, McNamara's first intention was to cut back the manufacture of nuclear warheads. The presidential staff had suddenly discovered that 450 warheads, the number already deployed, were enough. By this time, however, McNamara had had a quick education in the power of bureaucracy. In White House conferences he conceded that 450 would be the greatest plenty, but he insisted that the administration must request 950. The Joint Chiefs of Staff were asking for 3,000, and they were working closely with their friends in Congress. Therefore, 950 was the "smallest number we can take up on the hill without getting murdered." Our move prompted the Russians to increase their manufacture of nuclear weapons, and the dismal race goes on and on.[21]

It is extremely important to recognize that the bureaucracy is not simply the administrative agencies. Rather, bureaucratic power is fashioned out of the interactions and understandings, tacit and otherwise, between agency leaders, those legislators who control agency funds or grants of power and (often) leaders of organized clientele groups. Our system of fragmented legislative power, coupled with vastly expanded government in recent decades, spawns numerous bureaucracies. Each must be studied to determine as exactly as possible the kinds of interrelationships existing among agencies, congressional leaders, and clientele groups. But the conception of an "iron triangle" is extremely useful.

Bureaucratic power is strengthened by competition between the President and Congress and within Congress itself. The President seeks to control the bureaucracy by centralizing power, by coordinating programs, and by forcing integration by means of budgetary and administrative limits and standards. In contrast, Congress seeks control by dividing policies and programs among agencies each beholden to specific committees or subcommittees. The agencies (and sometimes their congressional allies) become adept at playing Congress against President, House against Senate, and subject-matter against appropriation committee. Frustrated, the President and Congress square off against each other, and in the melee, the bureaucracy escapes control.

A leading analyst of the phenomenon of bureaucratic power urges that it be met by a union of presidential and congressional politicians.[22] His recommendation would best be realized through strengthening the ties of political parties to which both belong, and, more than that, through forging clear lines of mutual initiation and response between the central party and its field organizations; for the bureaucracies themselves are not confined to Washington but pervade American localities, where they often pre-empt the representative functions of elected politicians.

Presidents and the People

If politicians unite in political parties of sufficient strength, depth, purposes, and permanence to take and hold the field against the great bureaucracies, their power base will be the people. We come then to that mysterious entity, the people, the public, the populace, in whom ultimate sovereignty resides (if it resides anywhere)—"We, the People of the United States, in order to form a more perfect union. . . ."

Presidents are the only officials elected directly by the "people," a fact of awesome importance. Increasingly since 1948, with the resurgence of presidential primaries, presidents have also been nominated by the "people." More and more, freshly elected presidents fall heir to the prestige George Washington enjoyed even in 1787, when Gouverneur Morris was suddenly confronted and undone by Washington's embodiment of the "awful majesty of the American people" (all 3.7 million of them—a fifth being slaves). In 1898, Henry Jones Ford wrote, "The truth is that in the presidential office, as it has been constituted since Jackson's time, American democracy has revived the oldest political tradition of the race, the elective kingship."

The phenomenon has been central to the constitutional interpretations of eminent authorities. Edward S. Corwin views its effects on presidents with foreboding. Jackson's claim "to be the People's Choice has been reiterated . . . by successors many times, with decisive results for the presidential role."[23] Corwin is especially critical of Franklin D. Roosevelt for claiming that his "transcendent powers" derived from "some peculiar relationship between himself and the people."[24] By contrast, Richard E. Neustadt considers maintenance of strong rapport between presidents and public essential to the health of the Presidency and the well-being of the nation. Presidential prestige is necessary to ensure presidential leeway to choose among alternative policies in critical situations. The President's expertise consists of the ability to nourish his popular prestige (along with his reputation among "Washingtonians") in order to maintain a strong bargaining position that can be exploited to make choices in the public interest. "An expert in the White House does not guarantee effective policy, but lacking such an expert every hope is placed in doubt."[25]

Viewing the same phenomenon from the standpoint of the public, James David Barber writes that

> the Presidency is much more than an institution. It is a focus of feelings. In general, popular feelings about politics are low-key, shallow, casual. For example, the vast majority of Americans knows virtually nothing of what Congress is doing and cares less. The Presidency is different. The Presidency is the focus for the most intense and persistent emotions in the American polity. The President is a symbolic leader, the one figure who draws together the people's hopes and fears for the political future.

And he goes on to say that the President, "a special being with mysterious dimensions . . . helps people make sense of politics"; hence, his *"main* responsibilities reach far beyond administering the Executive Branch or commanding the armed forces. The White House is first and foremost a place of public leadership. That inevitably brings to bear on the President intense moral, sentimental, and quasi-religious pressures which can, if he lets them, distort his own thinking and feeling."[26]

In his speech accepting the Democratic presidential nomination in 1976, Governor Jimmy Carter made nineteen references to the people, identifying them as the base of power and the source of democratic values and qualities (decency, competence, strength, wisdom, courage, common sense, and exalted moral character), and five times he stressed the need for leadership, especially presidential leadership, which takes its strength from the people: "As I have said before, we can have an American President who does not govern with negativism and fear of the future, but with vigor and vision and aggressive leadership—a President who is not isolated from our people, but who feels your pain and shares your dreams and takes his strength and wisdom and courage from you."*[27]

Problems of the President-Populace Relationship

Carter's classic populism is diametrically opposed to the theory of human nature basic to the Constitution. According to James Madison, the latent causes of faction are sown in the nature of man. Human reason is fallible; reason and self-love are inextricably connected in all men, whose diverse faculties create numerous interests, many of

---

*A week later Carter was much more conciliatory at a New York luncheon with fifty corporate leaders, on whom he promised to depend "very heavily" once elected. (Albert P. Hunt, "Carter and Business," *Wall Street Journal,* August 12, 1976.) As Mr. Dooley observed of Theodore Roosevelt: "Th' thrusts," says he, "are heejous monsthers built up by th' inlightened intherprise ov th' men that have done so much to advance progress in our beloved country," he says. "On wan hand I wud stamp them undher fut; on th' other hand, not so fast."

them conflicting. Opinion, infused with passion, grows out of self-interest; numbers of citizens (minorities or majorities) form factions; that is, they are "united and actuated by some common impulse of passion, or of interest, adverse to the rights of other citizens, or to the permanent and aggregate interests of the community." "The regulation of these various and interfering interests forms the principal task of modern legislation, and involves the spirit of party and faction in the necessary and ordinary operations of government."[28]

Carter acknowledges evil in human nature but confines it to a "political and economic elite who have shaped decisions and never had to account for mistakes nor to suffer from injustice." When others have been unemployed, they have worked; when others have gone hungry, they have eaten. The mass of people, though suffering from injustice, are endowed with nobility. Instead of Reinhold Niebuhr's moral man and immoral society, we have moral people and immoral elites. Carter's assertion of the essential goodness of the common people recalls Abraham Lincoln's appeal in his first Inaugural Address to the "better angels of our nature"—which clearly implied, however, that our nature also harbors perverse angels. Lincoln was less pessimistic than Madison, who discerned a clear distinction between men and angels. The millennium may come with the solution of Carter's equation: justice = jobs + security + health care + respect for all. Until then, I shall accept Madison's view of human nature and his inferences, namely, that the government of men over men requires, first, the ability of the government to control the governed and, second, the obligation of the government to control itself.[29]

How does this analysis apply to President-populace relationships? Bearing in mind the need for a strong Presidency, one may hail the strength that presidents can draw from popular support. It is essential to the safety of the Republic. There are problems, however, that because of limitations of space, can be stated only dogmatically. First, American politicians are prone, at least in their public statements, to oversimplify and misrepresent the role of the public, which is repeatedly exhorted to act and is declared competent in knowledge, wisdom, and benevolence to find just solutions to all problems. Second, by contrast, a great deal of evidence confirms what experience tells us, that the public is ordinarily neither much interested in nor well informed about government and politics—until its attention is commanded by fear of serious reverses or deprivations. Third, painfully alerted, the public then attends the President, the one popularly elected leader, the one person with whom people generally can identify. Fourth, the President then has the opportunity, and is under compulsion, to respond, if possible with ameliorative actions, but also with explanations that will enlighten the public by showing to what degree its hardships are inevitable. The nation gains from the steadying of public resolve; the President gains by shoring up his prestige.[30]

This analysis of statesmanship in presidential education of the public has become classic. Less ideally, and yet in keeping with the psychological realities, presidents may try to manipulate to their advantage the gut issues that have suddenly brought them public attention. Recall presidential appeals to patriotism when the country was deeply divided by the Vietnam War, appeals often combined with fresh presidential initiation of aggressive action; recall the invocations of the fear of communism; and recall President Nixon's assiduous exploitation of the racial issue by attacks on "forced busing to achieve integration."

Fifth, despite everything the President may do to improve his standing with the public, he may lose support until his ability to lead is compromised — a dangerous thing for the country, whose need for a strong President is unabated. Of presidents between World Wars I and II, Woodrow Wilson and Herbert Hoover apparently suffered catastrophic and probably irreversible losses in public prestige. For obvious reasons, Warren G. Harding may be omitted. Only Calvin Coolidge, when it did not much matter, and Franklin D. Roosevelt, when it mattered a great deal, maintained their prestige. Since World War II, with the country's stakes in prestigious presidents rising, the record has been dismal. Harry S. Truman, Lyndon B. Johnson, and Richard M. Nixon suffered precipitous and permanent declines in prestige. Dwight D. Eisenhower was the great exception. John F. Kennedy's assassination eliminates him from consideration. Gerald R. Ford's position is equivocal because of the peculiarities of his ascension; his presidential leverage was manifested nearly entirely in his vetoes.[31]

Sixth, a danger emerges in precisely the opposite eventuality. A President may so solidify his prestige (or his sense of it) that the concentration of power in him (or his belief in its concentration) becomes disturbingly great. He may not remain long on the dizzy heights, but still long enough to do mischief. Recall the arrogance of Lyndon B. Johnson in 1965 or of Franklin D. Roosevelt in 1937. Indeed, with the exception of 1932, but with 1920, 1928, 1936, 1956, 1964, and 1972 in mind, one might say that landslide presidential elections bode more ill than good for the country. The ill may come not only in the sudden inflation of presidential prestige but also in its subsequent tendency to precipitous decline.

Proposed Constitutional Changes

Problems raised by president-populace relationships reinforce the reasons already set forth for changing the Constitution in ways that will encourage the emergence of two centralized and disciplined parties, one forming the government-of-the-day, the other the opposition. My preference would be to do the least possible by law (constitutional amendment) and let the new arrangements develop as much as they can by constitutional convention or custom.

I do not propose to develop reform proposals fully here;[32] my intention has been to focus discussion on some of the reasons for change, rather than on a set of specifics. Nevertheless, changes might include (1) "a marriage between presidential and congressional electorates, particularly at the stage of nomination"[33]—I suggest terms of five years, rather than four, for all, hoping that the custom will evolve of holding elections following dissolutions, usually in the fifth year; (2) provision for the nomination of presidential candidates by the nominees of the parties for Congress and for nomination of all national legislative candidates according to rules established by the national parties, which should retain a veto over candidates proposed by constituency parties; (3) establishment of the losing presidential candidate in the House of Representatives as Leader of the Opposition, with powers and perquisites already noted, with the added provision that the opposition party can remove him but must replace him with another leader; and (4) some adaptation of the Reuss vote-of-confidence amendment, changed to provide censure by an absolute legislative majority on a roll-call vote and also to provide that the President may call for a dissolution, including the dissolution of his own office, and a new election. (The government elected after a dissolution would have a five-year lease.)

Anticipated Criticisms

My proposals have been labeled an "exercise in political fantasy."[34] *Webster's* has six definitions of "fantasy," four of them pejorative. One, "daydreaming," may be justified because our world's nightmarish quality bedevils mainly our waking hours. With a daily diet of surrealistic disasters, fantasy becomes progressively harder to distinguish. It may be that clinging to the status quo is its worst manifestation. Many certainties that have blessed our lives are crumbling. Benevolent weather patterns show ominous portents. The continents and oceans are discerned to rest uneasily on shifting plates. Venerable social, economic, and political institutions tremble in resonance with disturbances of underlying structural faults. When hyperbole becomes nature's norm, calling my modest proposals fantasies involves a misplaced encomium. Ah, if they only were!

A second criticism is that the trip isn't necessary. With proper changes the present system can be made to work.[35] The War Powers Act of 1973, the Budget and Impoundment Act of 1974, and the organizational and procedural reforms in the majority party (the rise of the caucus, the diminishment of seniority) show that Congress is on its way to establishing a degree of centralization and hierarchy needed to obtain the overview of policies required by modern governments. Or so they say. This criticism challenges my entire analysis. I can only reiterate that the flaws in our present system are sufficiently serious to warrant a thorough, continuing examination of fundamental alternatives.

A third criticism is narrower, namely, that making the President accountable to the legislature will not work well when a powerful second chamber exists. Does he have to defend the life of his regime twice on every significant issue, in two bodies strikingly different in their electoral bases? The proposed changes should prompt the migration of presidential aspirants to the House of Representatives and in other ways lead to a diminution of the power of the Senate, but the problem would not be wholly solved.*

Fourth, the possibility would remain of a divided government, with a President of one party and Congress controlled by the other. The chance of dichotomy would be lessened by eliminating off-year congressional elections; the last twenty presidential elections have created divided governments only three times. Nevertheless, the possibility is disquieting.†

Fifth, a most telling charge is that, given the multitude of conflicting interests in the United States, our parties will remain "voter coalitions differently aligned for different offices in different places."[36] Hence no stable majority can be produced. "To overstate the point, every ally is sometimes an enemy and every enemy is sometimes an ally."[37] For many, this objection to the feasibility of party government is persuasive. To reduce a complex answer to an assertion: The effect of institutional changes on voting behavior, on the number of parties in the system, on party identification, and on the organization (and centralization and discipline) of parties can be powerful enough to make party government work even under American conditions.

*The trend in Britain, Canada, France, the Bonn Constitution of West Germany, the Netherlands, and Ireland has been to diminish the power of second chambers and to make the government responsible only to the first chamber (comparable to the House of Commons). New Zealand, Norway, Finland, and Sweden have unicameral legislatures. In Italy, either the Senate or the Chamber of Deputies can vote out a government, but none has since 1948; governments resign when coalitions fall apart. Australia, Belgium, Iceland, and Switzerland have accountability to both houses of bicameral legislatures. For the first time in history, the Australian Senate shared in ousting a government in 1975. (Fox Butterfield, in *New York Times*, December 12, 1975; cf. William D. Hartley, *Wall Street Journal*, December 11, 1975.)

†Elsewhere (*Presidential Power and Accountability*, chap. 10), I proposed the use of congressmen elected at large to ensure that the party winning the Presidency would also control the House of Representatives. The formula would have worked historically, but a Republican debacle in 1976 might have made it futile even if it were operative.

Potential Advantages of Reform

1. The proposed changes are guided by the ideals of constitutional democracy. They assume a view of human nature similar to the one that informed the *Federalist Papers*. They are consistent with James Madison's two principles that government must be able to control the governed and be obliged to control itself. The difference would lie in changing the functional separation of powers to a separation between the Government and the Opposition, each organized as a political party.[38] Power would still be checked by power. But now presidential government would be confronted and opposed by an opposition organized in a comparable fashion, oriented to the same set of problems, but with a different political base, a different perspective, and (quite possibly) a different ideology.*

2. An orderly means of quickly replacing inadequate or overzealous presidents would be provided. We could remove presidents without having to destroy them. Soon the method of change should become widely accepted, as has happened in England, West Germany, and Japan.

3. The vote of confidence together with the President's power of dissolution should facilitate a shift from elections on fixed dates to elections on dissolution, thus achieving three desirable results: (a) the escape from rigidly calendar-bound elections that increase America's vulnerability to attack and harassment from other countries; (b) drastically shortened campaigns replacing the endlessly protracted, occult, and demoralizing contests to which we are now subjected; and (c) elections in which the voters can clearly see that they are performing the one uniquely important function for which in a democracy they and they alone are qualified — the creation of a government and, equally significant, of an opposition.

4. Presidents would be both empowered and controlled. Except for those elected in divided governments, presidents would enjoy a much stabler popular support built on the stronger party loyalties the new system is expected to nourish. At the same time, presidents would be looked on as holding their position by virtue of their leadership of the

---

*Among the foremost political needs of the United States may be workable, believable ideologies that both stimulate and restrain each other by developing different (but not absolutely incompatible) perspectives on the great problems of equality versus liberty, of consumption versus production, and of human well-being versus the rights of property. (Aaron Wildavsky, in Aaron Wildavsky, ed., *Perspectives on the Presidency* [Boston: Little, Brown, 1975], p. 58.) Historically, one of the most impressive successes of the British political system has been its ability to produce such ideologies, and it has done so by means of party government. (Cf. Samuel H. Beer, *British Government in the Collectivist Age* [New York: Alfred A. Knopf, 1965], pp. 386–90 and *passim*. See also Samuel H. Beer, in Samuel H. Beer et al., *Patterns of Government*, 3d ed. [New York: Random House, 1973], pp. 277 ff. and *passim*.)

winning party, rather than as embodiments of the "people." Each President would face an opposition united behind a leader who commands organized, stable, popular support of a party only a little less numerous than the President's own. Finally, every President would have a peer, and a situation would soon develop conducive to presidential debate, not merely in presidential campaigns (where it has been exceedingly rare but would also be less valuable) but throughout the course of his administration when it is essential.

5. Among the most beneficial effects would be the restructuring of the role of the citizens, the voters, the public, the people. A sensible division of political labor should not only be created;* it should also be clearly perceived. By voting for governing parties, citizens can have not only some share in the election of a government but also in its operations, its successes and vicissitudes, or, of comparable importance to democracy, they can have a continuing, felt share in the function of opposition. At the same time, the change should give birth to a new concept of representation, one that includes a theory of what the whole is and how it is represented, along with a theory of the parts and how they are bespoken.[39] Implicit in this argument is the rationale for continuing and even strengthening those institutions that support two parties and handicap third parties. Voters would retain the right to try to throw out a hated government and to opt for the party that they think more nearly represents their interest. But they also would have the sense, largely vicarious though it would be, of sharing in the ongoing task of government, with all its ennobling, exhilarating, humiliating, and frustrating moments. Is this not the essence of participatory democracy? Would it not fulfill the lofty injunction of the Declaration of Independence that governments derive their just powers from the consent of the governed? Would it not be a reasonable road to the creation of the political community so unforgettably invoked at the 1976 Democratic National Convention by Barbara Jordan?

Conclusion

Continuing crisis propels the growth of the Presidency and subjects the central principle of the Constitution of 1787, the separation of powers between President and Congress, to great stress. It remains

---

*The division of political labor is among the most significant constitution-building concepts. (Cf. Ernest Barker, *Reflections on Government* [New York: Oxford University Press, 1942], pp. 37 and 43–44; Joseph A. Schumpeter, *Capitalism, Socialism and Democracy* [New York: Harper, 1942], chaps. 22 and 23; and Charles M. Hardin, *Presidential Power and Accountability* [Chicago: University of Chicago Press, 1974], p. 190).

eternally true that power must be checked by power. Logically, the best check to the executive would be provided by a comparable entity compelled to confront the Presidency on the same terms that the problems of modernity inexorably pose to modern governments. What is needed, therefore, is an opposition that, like the Presidency, is organized, centralized, equipped, and staffed to formulate an alternative program and to use it to subject the Presidency to continuing evaluation that will remind everyone that modern government, however necessary, is also contingent and experimental. Alas! Our present Constitution, with its contrived struggle for ascendancy between President and Congress, cannot generate this double-headed approach to things political. The Presidency can perform the governing task. Its nature is to synthesize, coordinate, centralize, and plan. By contrast, the nature of Congress is to handle problems by dividing them among committees; and many modern problems, if manageable at all, are intractable when fragmented. Congress cannot gestate an opposition that meets the President in the political arena fashioned by the pressures of modernity.

Solution of the problem of political power in the United States may come through devising institutions that will encourage party government. Parties could both provide the regime with reasonably reliable support and bolster an opposition capable of enforcing accountability. In this way, Congress could come alive politically in the sense demanded by modern conditions; it could develop its proper function of ventilating the central issues and forcing the regime—even the President himself—to debate them with the opposition and especially with its leader, whose eminence would be enhanced as he came to be identified through his party with the causes of the minority he represented.

In this way, too, the power of the President could be maintained and even increased while, at the same time, he could appear in a perspective that is much safer for the survival of democracy; he would be seen much more as the leader of a majority than as the personification of the sovereign people. Party government would happily divide that mysterious entity, the people, into two parts. The President would be subjected to the chastening requirements of debate that would force him to explain his acts under adversary conditions. Perhaps even more important than the rational values made possible by presidential debate would be the psychological gains achieved through forcing the President to recognize that he had a peer. Presidents are surrounded by all conceivable devices for ego expansion. Unless we elect only Hamlets to the office (and even Hamlet at last became a force of almost total destruction), we have to calculate as part of the price of a necessarily single chief executive a dangerous inflation of his ego. How proper then to oppose to the President not merely a debating skill that he must contemplate with some anxiety but also a man of flesh and blood, a physical rival who can inspire in him the thoroughly wholesome emotion of fear. Sweet are the uses of adversaries.

Notes

1. See, for example, Louis W. Koenig, *The Chief Executive* (New York: Harcourt, Brace & World, 1964).
2. See the constitutional amendment proposed by Congressman Henry S. Reuss, *Congressional Record* (House), II 7158, July 21, 1975, and literature there cited.
3. See Selection 13 above.
4. H. J. Res. 903 and H. J. Res. 1111, 93d Cong., 2d sess. (1974). See *George Washington Law Review*, symposium on the Reuss Resolution, vol. XLIII, No. 2 (January 1975), henceforth, cited as Reuss Symposium.
5. See "Altering the Term of Office: The Six-Year Term Proposal" in Thomas E. Cronin, *The State of the Presidency* (Boston: Little, Brown, 1975), pp. 298–306.
6. More elaboration is provided in Charles M. Hardin, *Presidential Power and Accountability* (Chicago: University of Chicago Press, 1974). An excellent presentation of the opposing view is in Samuel H. Beer, "Government and Politics: An Imbalance," *The Center Magazine*, March-April, 1974. See also Emmet John Hughes, *The Living Presidency* (New York: Coward, McCann & Geoghegan, 1973), chap. 8.
7. *The Federalist*, No. 70.
8. Aaron Wildavsky, "The Two Presidencies," *Trans-Action*, vol. IV, No. 2 (December 1966). Cf. Donald E. Peppers, "The Two Presidencies: Eight Years Later," in Aaron Wildavsky, ed., *Perspectives on the Presidency* (Boston: Little, Brown, 1975).
9. For two interpretations stressing the high significance of presidential roles in fiscal and monetary policy, see Walter W. Heller, *New Dimensions in Political Economy* (New York: W. W. Norton, 1966) and Herbert Stein, *The Fiscal Revolution in America* (Chicago: University of Chicago Press, 1969).
10. Winston Churchill, *The Second World War*, vol. II: *Their Finest Hour* (Boston: Houghton, Mifflin, 1949), p. 15.
11. *New York Times*, February 19, 1975. Leon Jaworski upholds similar views in *The Sacramento Bee*, August 8, 1975. Hans A. Linde, "Replacing a President: Prescription for a Twenty-first Century Watergate," and Arthur Selwyn Miller, "Cutting the Presidency Down to Size—but Not Too Much," in Reuss Symposium, p. 413, agree.
12. William F. Swindler, "Accountability: The Constitutional Goal," in Reuss Symposium.
13. Arthur M. Schlesinger, Jr., "The Search for a Better 'Ole," *Wall Street Journal*, April 4, 1974.
14. See the Reuss Symposium articles by Fletcher N. Baldwin, Jr., John H. Reese, and William F. Swindler respecting the violation of the separation

of powers, and articles by Baldwin, Jefferson B. Fordham, Louis W. Koenig, and Allan P. Sindler noting the lack of centralized, disciplined parties in the United States.

15. Hardin, op. cit., chaps. 2 and 3.

16. Note also reports of "political abuse of intelligence information," including abuse by some presidents and their close advisers, with examples going back to Franklin D. Roosevelt in 1940, in *Final Report*, Senate Select Committee to Study Governmental Operations with Respect to Intelligence Activities (the Church Committee), 94th Cong., 2d sess., No. 94-755 (1976), Book II, p. 225 and *passim* and Book III, pp. 392 ff.

17. *The Twilight of the Presidency* (New York: World, 1970). See also Selection 13 above and Donald Allen Robinson, "Presidents and Party Leadership . . ." a paper prepared for the 1974 annual meeting of the American Political Science Association, Chicago.

18. Norton E. Long, "Patriotism for Partisans: A Responsible Opposition," *Antioch Review*, December 1952, reprinted in Charles Press, ed., *The Polity* (Chicago: Rand McNally, 1962). On the need for presidential debate, see Alexander J. Groth, "Britain and America: Some Requisites of Executive Leadership Compared," *Political Science Quarterly*, vol. LXXXV, No. 2 (June 1970).

19. Of a number of models of the American bureaucracy, I have found that of Richard E. Neustadt most illuminating: "Politicians and Bureaucrats" in David B. Truman, ed., *The Congress and America's Future* (The American Assembly and Englewood Cliffs, N. J.: Prentice-Hall, 1965); cf. Hardin, op. cit., chap. 4–6.

20. See the Church Committee *Final Report* cited in note 16 above.

21. Hardin, ibid., pp. 113 and 220.

22. Neustadt, op. cit.

23. Edward S. Corwin, *The President: Office and Powers* (New York: New York University Press, 1957), p. 20.

24. Ibid., p. 252.

25. Richard E. Neustadt, *Presidential Power* (New York: John Wiley & Sons, 1960), chap. 5 and p. 193.

26. James David Barber, *Presidential Character* (Englewood Cliffs, N.J.: Prentice-Hall, 1972), pp. 4–5.

27. *New York Times*, July 26, 1976.

28. *The Federalist*, No. 10, and Benjamin F. Wright, "The Federalist on the Nature of Political Man," *Ethics*, January 1949, pt. 2.

29. *The Federalist*, No. 51. Cf. Robert Penn Warren, "Bearers of Bad Tidings: Writers and the American Dream," *New York Review of Books*, March 20, 1975.

30. Neustadt, *Presidential Power*, chap. 5; cf. Peter W. Sperlich, "Bargaining and Overload: An Essay on *Presidential Power*" in Wildavsky, *Perspectives on the Presidency*, especially pp. 409–10.

31. A number of recent analyses suggest a tendency, perhaps accelerating, for public support of presidents to decline over time: John E. Mueller, *War, Presidents and Public Opinion* (New York: John Wiley & Sons, 1973); Richard A. Brody and Benjamin I. Page, "The Impact of Events on Presidential Prosperity," Samuel Kernell, Peter W. Sperlich, and Aaron

Wildavsky, "Public Support for Presidents," in Wildavsky, *Perspectives on the Presidency;* also Wildavsky, "Introduction," and "Government and the People," same volume.

32. See Hardin, op. cit., chap. 10. Congressman Reuss's proposal for the creation of an office of a head of state and Professor Strum's for a question time would be compatible with my suggestions. See Reuss Symposium and Selection 13 above.

33. Neustadt, *Presidential Power*, p. 191.

34. Arthur M. Schlesinger, Jr., "Postscript" to *The Imperial Presidency* (Boston: Houghton Mifflin, 1974).

35. Cf. Beer, op. cit. and Hughes, op. cit.

36. Neustadt, *Presidential Power*, p. 188.

37. Robert A. Dahl, *Political Oppositions in Western Democracies* (New Haven, Conn.: Yale University Press, 1966), p. 54.

38. E. E. Schattschneider, *Party Government* (New York: Rinehart, 1942), chaps. 1 and 10.

39. Samuel H. Beer, "The Representation of Interests in British Government: Historical Background," *American Political Science Review*, September 1957; and A. H. Birch, *Representation* (New York: Praeger, 1971), p. 131.

16. On Bringing Presidents to Heel

Rexford G. Tugwell

Anyone who takes seriously the prevailing concern about the pre-eminence of the Presidency, and who accepts the necessity for change, must deal with the stubborn difficulties inherent in the alternatives proposed by critics. Certainly, executive operations have been enlarged, and this understandably has provoked strong reactions. It may be useful to summarize the complaints most often heard and, this done, look briefly at the suggested curtailments of the President's powers.

If it is concluded that the office has accumulated too many duties and has too much authority—perhaps the most frequent charge—such questions must be asked as: Where have the duties, and the authority to carry them out, come from? Why were they allocated to the President? To whom should they be entrusted, or with whom should they be shared if they are to be reduced?

If it is concluded that recent accumulations have caused a systematic neglect of traditional domestic duties—as is unquestionably true—then it has to be asked how the neglect can be remedied without, at the same time, risking the national security. This latter responsibility especially, it will be said, cannot be put aside for any other consideration.

Concerning the domestic duties of the office, the theory of the Constitution is that the President, through his departmental heads, will actually administer all the government's operations. But presidents are no longer able to follow agricultural, medical, or space research; they cannot judge the sufficiency of the government's elaborate welfare services, the effectiveness of its correctional efforts, or the adequacy of its efforts to curb exploitations of natural resources. Nor can they inform themselves, in any but the most superficial way, about progress in the sciences or the arts. Appointed officials act "for the President" in these and many other matters, but it is a fiction that they do so under his direction. In fact, as everyone knows, their relations with interested legislators are often closer than those they have with the President.

If, however, the usual assumptions concerning the distribution of power are no longer valid, it is mistaken to conclude that the President is no longer actually the chief executive. What must be understood is that he can no longer be the government's *administrator*. This is a distinction frequently either neglected or ignored.

The most pervasive criticisms of the President as chief executive, however, center not on those constitutionally assigned duties he seems to neglect but on the manner in which he conducts those affairs he does manage. Critics allege that he behaves as a dictator, consulting only his close personal aides. It is only fair to ask such critics how decisions can be made otherwise in the prevailing circumstances. Ought decisions to be concluded by a group, each having an equal vote, as is done by the Supreme Court, thus spreading both the management and the responsibility? Aside from questions of constitutionality, this method would involve an expectation of unanimity among several decision-makers. If agreement should not be reached, could the public be expected to have confidence in the policies agreed upon by a majority, with a minority of dissenters? Would it not be suspected that the minority may have been right, and that a wrong policy had been adopted? If this were so, might not the Presidency be paralyzed when it most needs to be capable of acting?

Particularly on the part of congressional committees probing the behavior of the administering branch, there is some attempt to break through closed decision-making by demanding access to the exchanges among presidential subordinates in the course of formulating policies. Such data have almost always been formally withheld. (They are often leaked or stolen, however, and then commentators end up as the judges of what is properly made public.) This withholding of information is a cause of repeated irritation and leads periodically to acidulous debates; all recent presidents, and most department heads, have been attacked for such refusals. They are decried as further evidence of a progression toward dictatorship. Actually, of course, they are not new. Many presidents have refused disclosure of data used for arriving at decisions. They have also refused to release the contingency plans required for possible future action.

The secrecy surrounding presidential decision-making becomes even more important because of the frequent assertion that the

President has intruded into the province of the legislature. He is not supposed to *make* laws, some complain, only to *execute* them, but, for many years, he has gone beyond the constitutional directive to "recommend . . . such measures as he shall judge necessary and expedient" and has used a variety of means to see that they are adopted. This includes a formidable lobbying staff and the use of his immense resources for bargaining.

Considering the accepted theory that Congress is to make laws and the President to execute them, it is amazing to what extent the rule is denied by the facts. Legislation is more apt to originate in the executive branch, and it is quite customary for legislators, under the rubric of oversight, to interest themselves in administration. Among the important pieces of legislation originating with the President there come to mind the TVA, AAA, and NRA of the New Deal, the supporting legislation for the cold war, and both the establishment and, later, the disestablishment of the Great Society in numerous separate acts. Congress has, in effect, been reduced to approving, disapproving, or negotiating for amendments. What would be the alternative, in view of the nature of the legislative process? Would it be to confine the President closely to the Constitution's "recommendation," prohibiting actual legislative proposals as well as maneuvers on his part to get them passed? If so, who would then originate projects, recalling that the President is still his party's head, with a fixed, four-year term, and recalling, also, the discouraging immobility of Congress as it is now organized?

At this late time, it is unlikely that the President will be excluded from the originating of legislation. This, however, is not the main concern of the critics. Their bitterest protest is that the President, proclaiming an emergency or asking a concerned—perhaps frightened—Congress to declare one, assumes that his powers as Commander in Chief allow him to use the armed forces at his discretion, thereby making, at an extreme, what amounts to war without consultation, or short of that, to dominate relations with other nations by brandishing America's military might.

It is frequently complained that there has been a growing tendency to ignore the "declaration of war" phrase in the Constitution. This was true of earlier, frequent interventions in Latin America, as well as of more consequential ones in Korea and Southeast Asia, not to mention incidents such as the temporary occupations of Lebanon and Santo Domingo. In all of them, the armed forces were deployed without the "declaration" mentioned in the Constitution and without much "consultation." Critics have demanded an end to executive war-making— and even to use of the military in making foreign policy. But they do not satisfactorily explain what might happen in a situation known to threaten the national security if instant action were not taken. Would they, for instance, really find a Communist government in Santo Domingo desirable? Or were they, when the question was being debated, opposed to support of the South Vietnamese, so widely considered a bulwark against Communist aggression? It was, it will be recalled, a time of excited concern about the "free world" and its vulnerability to subversion as well as actual attack. Self-determination was an accepted liberal cause.

There is another explanation concerning the delegation of powers to the President. The most skeptical critics are compelled to recognize that wars no longer begin by the slow deployment of troops, the gradual taking up of adversary positions, and, finally, when diplomacy fails, by the outbreak of fighting. In World War I, a whole year elapsed after the declaration of war before the armed forces could be prepared for deployment. Less time was required for engagement in World War II, but that was because Roosevelt had forced the pace of rearming— against an opposition of such strength that it was nearly successful. Recognizing that delayed reaction might result in fatal consequences, prolonged argument might, in certain circumstances, be fatal. The abdication of Congress in such circumstances is necessary to survival.

Critics who deny this usually do so in times of relative tranquillity, and, faced with a demand for alternatives, tend to avoid the real issue. They are, of course, able to argue that such emergencies are avoidable and would not occur if more wisdom were used in shaping peacetime policies. This, however, would require much more than restraints imposed by congressional committees; it would, indeed, require participation in the conduct of negotiations. The difficulties involved in this have been obvious since the Articles of Confederation were abandoned for the present Constitution. Possibly, these might be overcome, but only by more drastic changes than are usually contemplated.

In the past, irritation about this was less, because of a tradition that politics ended "at the water's edge," with members of all factions agreeing to close ranks behind the President in his dealings with other nations. Indeed, a generation ago, it was a custom never to mention foreign affairs in national campaigns. In 1932, for instance, Franklin D. Roosevelt assiduously avoided any reference to the pressure for settlement of the war debts, the impending World Economic Conference, and even the question of joining the League of Nations. The precedent had been established by his predecessors and was generally observed, except when war threatened, or when difficult and unpopular settlements had to be made.

The assumption that foreign affairs are exempt from politics was made untenable after Roosevelt, however, by the many differences concerning such issues as the containment of communism, the ambitions of American businesses to become international, and the support of self-determination for other nations—not to mention continual controversy as the many obligations of the United States as a great power appeared to expand indefinitely. Indeed, they were enlarged by every President after World War II until 1968. *Pax Americana* used to be confined to neighboring nations embraced by the Monroe Doctrine. It was extended, after 1945, to other continents and other seas. This was perhaps a consequence of American campaigns during the war on the continents of both Asia and Europe and of a two-ocean fleet to control the waters reaching those shores. At any rate, the policy afterward took the armed forces, in new engagements, into Southeast Asia, the Mediterranean, the Indian Ocean, and Africa—a responsibility that eventually strained even the immense resources of the American economy and became a furiously debated issue no candidate could ignore. The Nixon Doctrine of withdrawal was an admission that the massive postwar obligations had become insupportable. The extension of these responsibilities had been largely a presidential initiative; retreat from them was likewise an exclusively presidential decision.

The extension of partisan politics to foreign relations reinforces another concern of some critics: that the President, having been a party candidate, remains a party man. They suggest that some other way of choosing presidents must at least be considered, one that ensures the support essential to leadership and provides the lead time necessary for national policy-making but avoids the divisiveness inherent in party politics.

There is certainly a dilemma here: A candidate, after a partisan campaign, suddenly becomes President of all the people, not just the leader of his party. This, if regarded as an absolute, would separate him from the permanent organization needed for party control, if not for his own re-election. The maintenance of party solidarity in the legislature and elsewhere admittedly makes for easier passage into law of whatever program seems to have been approved by the President's election.

That these abandonments of political ties are often more talked about than acted on, however, is shown by the party's influence in choosing the White House entourage. If it is assumed that, once in office, a chief executive is President of all the people, how is it that members of other parties and independent opponents are so generally excluded from employment?

And a final question: Does this partisan selection process result in the best possible President? It is charged that most presidents have not been the best available selections to take on the awesome duties they must assume, and there is much evidence that this is so. Historians generally agree that those who cannot be rated as successful outnumber those considered to have been adequate. If this is a reliable assessment, it brings into question the whole selection process and opens a vast area of democratic dogma to exploration. It goes not only to the determination of qualifications for suffrage but to the electoral processes. But does anyone demand that the electorate be purged or that nominations come under federal law?

A Pattern

It is not intended here to imply that, in all controversies about policy, presidents have been wise, but a pattern does seem to exist: Repeated assumptions of power are followed each time by a chorus of criticism. No President escapes furious castigation. The critics, however, are conspicuously negative. The means they offer for reducing the powers of the President and easing the differences between his power and that of the other branches are hopelessly inadequate for the purpose. More drastic changes are needed than are offered as alternatives.

There are, to summarize, specific complaints of dictatorial behavior, invasion of legislative prerogatives, inadmissible uses of the armed forces, monopolization of new government concerns (the economy, welfare, consumer protection, environmental dangers, scientific and cultural activities), and even control of discussion about public policy. There are other complaints as well, some variations of these and some combinations of several. Each has a tendency to gather others about itself, and usually, as complaints mount, all are justified by the assiduously conducted campaigns of political antagonists.

Presidents are so exposed, and so apt to make decisions with consequences found intolerable by vociferous critics, that the heroic stature of their first months almost inevitably becomes diminished so seriously as to make them antiheroes before they have been long in the White House.

Some years ago, it might have seemed exaggerated to speak of a crisis in constitutional divisions of power, but suddenly, during Lyndon B. Johnson's Administration, such a concern did not seem exaggerated at all. For Johnson, or so it seemed during his first three years, was able to turn Congress into a rubber stamp that gladly approved nearly all his directives. Something, it was agreed, must be done about the Presidency, but the suggestions most often heard were neither useful appraisals nor workable correctives. Mostly, the offerings were palliatives. Even after a quarter century of growing distrust, nothing really remedial emerged.

This meant that Richard M. Nixon, after the deplorable history of the Johnson years, would not even be permitted to try new approaches if his detractors could prevent it, and very often they could.

He was more inventive than his predecessors. He delegated many of his duties and concentrated on his own judgment about policies, with such information as his helpers provided. When he emerged from his characteristic solitary sessions with such startling decisions as the reversal of the quarter-century policy of containment and of traditional economic laissez-faire, his critics were infuriated but speechless, since he had clearly co-opted the issues they had hoped would embarrass him.

The dangers in his procedural changes were, of course, illustrated by the discovery that he had chosen unprincipled subordinates and allowed them too much authority, but it had at least been an effort to solve the central problem of decision-making.

Would Nixon's method have been improved by the confrontation so ardently advocated as a corrective to his habit of acting in isolation? Who would confront him? Only members of Congress were in a position to do so, and it must be said that debates did take place. He lost most of those on domestic matters and won most of those on foreign policy, but most presidents have had this experience. It would certainly have been more agreeable to the press if it had been known in advance that he intended to propose new initiatives, but there did have to be a feeling-out process, and if he had been repulsed in the midst of public furor, it could hardly have furthered the cause of peace.

On certain issues, there had obviously been compromise with congressional leaders in advance. Because of this, some parts of the President's program were canceled by other parts. The likelihood that his economic measures would cure inflation was as doubtful as their effect on unemployment, but relief from either or both would have been even more remote if he had waited for debate with peers— whoever they might be. If arrangement for confrontation had existed, his chance of making any effort at all would have been prevented. In any case, it would have been too late; the confronters would have disagreed in about the same proportion as the dissenters did when he announced the effort, and their power of delay would have been fatally effective.

When, in his attempt to control inflation, he used a permissive law passed earlier to absolve Congress of responsibility for economic distresses, there was a stunning effect. When he announced an immediate freeze on both wages and prices, it was recognized that debate would have made these measures far less effective. This, indeed, was an example of the need for presidential freedom in an emergency. With the emergency already recognized, he was able to move into a deteriorating situation and establish a block. Discussion could follow; if it had preceded action, chaos might well have ensued.

It soon became clear that the economic troubles were the result of mistaken policies of long standing. These were not amenable to emergency reversal, but something did have to be done, and the President had to do it. Corrective measures would run deep and be bitterly opposed. His critics, however, paid little attention to past mistakes. They were acidulous about the handling of the crisis and chary of helpful suggestions about alternatives.

It has to be recognized that every minute of every presidential day is occupied by the duties of office. Those who would insist on open debates about controversial presidential actions at the critics' convenience, and presumably at length, before decisions on policy innovations are taken would force the neglect of still more duties. It is already well known that, even in quiet times, the President knows what goes on in the departments only as he is told in rare conferences with their heads, and his directions to them are channeled through his subordinates, who, it is suspected, are really their originators. Only the more serious problems are even known about by him, and then only when trouble impends. His knowledge is so superficial that mistakes of judgment are not just likely but, indeed, probable.

At the most extreme, critics suggest confrontation concerning all important policies, domestic as well as foreign, thus putting the President in the position of defending many determinations about which he cannot possibly be informed. Actually, what happens at present is that subterranean relations are established between congressional committees and bureau or agency chiefs, the President and his office being bypassed. Confrontation would be ineffective in reducing this undercover bargaining. If it did take place, it would be superficial and unreal on both sides.

It is not, of course, about domestic issues that the demand for presidential response to critics mostly arises; it is about foreign policy, the commitments made for the nation by its chief of state. The most controversial of these, in recent years, concerned the use of the armed forces. It is argued that before these forces are deployed abroad, the President should consult with others. Those others, unless there should be constitutional change, would be legislators. The legislators could not well be *all* 535 senators and representatives. They would, presumably, be the members of the committees (most importantly their chairmen) assigned to deal with foreign policy.

The fact is, however, that committee chairmen already argue with the President and his lobbyists, especially when majorities are not of the President's party. This is well known but it is evidently not enough for advocates of confrontation. They would prevent the President from acting without explicit consent, even after an effort at justification. By the time hearings are held and debates occur, they say, commitment has already been made. Certainly, it could not be contended that hearings, as traditionally conducted, have the effect sought. Committeemen frequently are patently partisan. They are more often interested in promoting themselves or their parties than in clarifying issues, and, of course, what they get from the President's defenders is not offered in good faith, either.

The frequently repeated suggestion that the defeated candidate in the last election be given a legislative seat and adequate means for informing himself, with the purpose of opposing the incumbent, assumes that the duty of legislators is not to pass laws but to contest those proposed by the President. To accept this scheme would also be to abandon the theory that, once elected, a President represents all the people, not only those who voted for him. Because this is an essential attribute of a chief of state, the proposal would seem to be a denial of an important tenet of our Constitution.

Here, it must be noted that there are enormous differences between crises requiring instant response and gradually developing ones requiring permanent changes in policy. The slowly developing ones may, if neglected, turn into emergencies, but they ought to be preceded by discussion of alternative suggestions for remedy, and they usually are.

Concerning long-range commitments, the lack of adequate consultation is, without any doubt, something requiring remedy. When a new general position is adopted, not previously debated and not generally understood, it ought not to be effectuated until there is substantial consent. Lacking this, there will sooner or later be acrimonious dissent. How is this to be arranged? Or, to put it another way, how is the President to know whether he has approval? It is not enough to depend on campaign debates; many important issues are never touched in the quadrennial appeals, one reason being that the candidate who is assured by the polls that he is in the lead will avoid advocacy of any policy likely to arouse the opposition of any large group of voters—ethnic, economic, social, or other—and so will come to office without instructions from the electorate. Similarly, the candidate who is running behind is likely to concentrate on criticisms ("Throw the rascals out") and will be even more likely to avoid proposals for any substantial change.

Because he has made no commitments or, at the most, only very general ones, and because he will have four years in office anyway, a President feels free to adopt policies not previously debated. He may even make dispositions certain to alter relations with other nations, and these may, at the most extreme, amount to alliances or provocations leading to rupture. Presidents will do this believing they are acting in the best interest of the nation, and because they believe themselves chosen to make just such decisions.

Those who complain of such presidential exclusiveness and who advocate confrontation are in a weak position if they are unwilling to designate those with whom the President should be required to argue and the conditions requiring such discussions. Some have done this, but they characteristically refuse to go outside present institutional limits, and this confines them to demanding that he consult legislators, or some of them—usually the committeemen who deal with foreign relations. It is to most people an appalling thought that the senators who are heard from most often, as things are, should have a decisive voice in really vital matters. Their chosen role is critical; their habit, probing; their purpose, exposure; their attitude, self-righteous. They represent districts or states, not the whole nation, as does the President. When things go wrong, they become invisible. Something quite different from this is needed—but it *is* needed.

As for confrontation with peers, there is a curious refusal to say who these peers might be. If they do not exist in any part of Congress as it is now constituted, their creation would obviously require constitutional amendment. If that should happen, would the newly created peers be associate presidents, would they be a court of appraisal—or what? How would such a group operate? Would its members actually share the President's decision-making, perhaps voting on policies to be adopted? Nothing less would seem to suffice.

Perhaps what is being edged toward is a plural, or collegial, Presidency. This is an arrangement that is not new to political literature. It even exists in smaller countries—Switzerland, for instance, where it is so successful that there is no desire for change. Plurality would provide one species of confrontation. Policies would be discussed among a group of whatever size was decided on. It would not, however, satisfy minorities who could never be sure that their point of view had been adequately represented. It would also suffer from the same lack of unity that reduces the authority of the Supreme Court. When four members dissent from the majority opinion of five, the fallibility of judgment, and even the possibility of future reversal, is all too obvious.

Yet, it has become impossible for the President to meet his constitutional responsibilities. The burden and complexity have outrun his human capacities. Perhaps a plural or collegial Presidency will have to be turned to as the only real alternative. As things are, the President has no one to share his responsibility. Only he represents all the people. The creation of peers would require that they have the same representative legitimacy. No constitutional amendment to effectuate such a change is suggested by the critics, but what it must be like is quite obvious. Others at his level of authority must be chosen. Why do the advocates of confrontation avoid this conclusion?

Credibility

Is the President justified in deception when, in his judgment, it is necessary in the public interest? This is by now a familiar question. It is evident that what honorable people would not do in their private capacities they frequently do in their public ones. All find themselves, sooner or later, compelled to choose, and they all choose, at least, to dissimulate if not so often to deceive.

"Credibility" became a familiar word during the Johnson Administration, and "credibility gap" was used to describe the claim that what was being told to the public by the President and his associates was untrue. Because there was nothing novel about this, the charge had its force from the flagrancy of the particular offense. It had to do with an extremely unpopular foreign involvement, and exposure of deception was too well authenticated for effective denial.

Operations in Southeast Asia were being portrayed in ways calculated to support policies and actions decided on and carried through by both military and civilian officials, and approval was unlikely if the facts about the situation were understood by the public. Reporters in the battle areas and around headquarters insisted that damaging facts were being concealed. The invasion, they consistently maintained, was going badly. Both the strategy and the tactics were mistaken. Decisions were made in secrecy and then denied (such as the support of small armies in Laos and Cambodia), and both people and land in the areas of engagement were being ruthlessly sacrificed.

Complaints about the cover-ups concerning Southeast Asia were of the same nature. In spite of massive evidence, Johnson refused to admit that there had been grievous errors in decision-making and execution. The list of his sins became long and tended, moreover, to be exaggerated. There was a concerted search for the bad news he was trying to conceal. Naturally, it was found, and his discredit eventually became politically insupportable, making it impossible for him to continue in office.

Had these defensive presidential representations become characteristic of the office? Sadly, these deceptions had only become more professional. Their use to defend a costly and unpopular foreign involvement was peculiarly offensive to legislative critics, who were not entirely innocent themselves. It was suddenly discovered that legions of public-relations men attached to the military were engaged in interpretation of repeated failures as a succession of victories. So few, in fact, were deceived that persistence in keeping on with attempts to deceive seemed an insult to public intelligence. What had been a well-understood and fairly tolerable style of defending executive behavior became, in Johnson's case, so exaggerated as to be wholly unacceptable.

Besides, it began to be noted, this kind of manipulation was not peculiar to the military. The same sorts of specialists were attached to other agencies of government. They were, in effect, being paid by the taxpayers to befuddle rather than to inform them. This was more reprehensible than the similar operations of large corporations. They, of course, could deduct such expenses from their tax bills and so charge them to consumers who were being deceived, but their operations were not quite so direct, nor did they have so obvious a bearing on public policy.

It would not be at all difficult to list manifestly self-serving statements issued in numerous administrations since Washington's— in practically all of them, in fact. Approaches to both world wars, for instance, were marked by hardly forgivable declarations by Wilson and Roosevelt that they were firm opponents of involvement. They would not send American boys to fight in foreign wars, they said, and it appeared soon afterward that they had intended all along to do just that. Abuse of the FBI also goes well back before the Johnson and Nixon episodes.

Retrospect turns up this kind of thing too late, in most instances, to be really embarrassing, or, if what was done appears to have been wise and farsighted, the deceptions are forgotten or forgiven. Neither Wilson nor Roosevelt suffered politically: Wilson was justified by victory and the Kaiser's abdication; Roosevelt's repeated declarations that he only meant to defend the nation were forgotten after Pearl Harbor and were excused as part of his foresighted approach to joining the Allies and achieving victory.

Considering what a long list there is of such representations by presidents of actions whose failure they have preferred not to disclose, how often they have tortured the facts into justifications, and how often they have actually been untruthful, it must be concluded that, as a rule, presidents do not hesitate to deceive when it seems necessary to get their way or to defend themselves. This is not attributable to faults of character or to doubtful personal morals. With one or two exceptions, they have been upright men who found themselves in positions that offered them no alternative. It must be expected that future presidents, given similar circumstances, will behave in the same way.

The alternative most frequently suggested is the obvious one: Make deceptions impossible by arranging for full disclosure of the facts. Recent "sunshine" and open-meetings laws move us in this direction. Still there is an old aphorism that truth is elusive and appears different to different people. There is also the well-known propensity for self-deception, heightened by the weight of great responsibility. Presidents usually seem to believe what they say, even when it is patently false, and this weakness is apparently worsened when national interests are involved. It is probable that they do not regard themselves as taking moral risks, even in outright lying, if essential purposes are to be served. In such situations, preferred beliefs or settled convictions appear to be extremely resistant to controverting evidence, and because, in complex matters, it is possible to claim exclusive knowledge, and often the support of dependent experts, a chosen policy is easy enough to defend—until it collides with reality and collapses!

An illustration on the grandest scale is available in the quarter century of hostility to communism after Roosevelt's death. It was supported by massive compilations of evidence that a nation given over to communism could not succeed. During that period, however, the Soviet Union grew in strength, until it finally became an undisputed superpower and challenged the position of the United States in the world. But, given the widespread—almost unanimous—assumption of the system's weakness embedded in American opinion, no political leader saw fit to associate Soviet growth with virtue. The system was manifestly capable of progress because it had progressed, but in American opinion—reinforced by presidential rhetoric—it continued to be at once feeble and dangerously strong.

There arises a question: Where, in all that time, were newspapers, magazines, and television broadcasters, who so often profess devotion to informing the public? If the public had the right to know, its right was not respected. When successive presidents reiterated their interpretation of events, they were joined almost unanimously by communicators. This long deception was certainly assisted by a failure of reporting.

It is even more revealing to ask where were the legislators who had at least some knowledge of growing Soviet power? They were even more assiduous than presidents in disseminating a deception that must eventually be revealed for what it was.

There are so many illustrations of official deception, and of the concurrence of those who might have objected, that we need to ask whether Johnson's departures from veracity concerning Southeast Asia appear in perspective as different in kind. Were they really much worse, in effect, than familiar ones in the past? Harry S. Truman justifying the use of the atom bomb by concealing efforts of the Japanese to surrender, Dwight D. Eisenhower plainly lying about overflights of the Soviet Union by spy planes, John F. Kennedy sending troops to Vietnam disguised (for the benefit of the public) as observers (or, perhaps, advisers)—these are only a few recent incidents of this kind. None of those was unknown to legislators or reporters. Apparently, it is only when hostility to a policy becomes general that the media begin to find and disseminate evidence that the public is being deceived.

As long as the shapers of public opinion have strong preferences about policy and use the instruments they control to support those preferences, they will not serve as a source of public enlightenment. When they prefer one candidate to others, or find an official agreeable to their interests, they do not complain about "credibility gaps" and violations of the "public's right to know." It is all too evident that newspapers and television will not, in all circumstances, expose the elaborate fictions of presidents defending doubtful policies. They have biases and interests of their own, and they have their own means of protecting them. Morality becomes an issue much more easily when presidential behavior is displeasing to them.

Incompetence

Americans find it almost impossible to admit, despite incontrovertible evidence, that the present selection system sometimes results in the election of presidents who, however upright, are simply incompetent for what is expected of them, and often of presidents whose abilities are much inferior to those of some of their contemporaries who were available. Some were incompetent even for the far simpler presidential duties before the great wars and the Depression. Van Buren, Harrison, Taylor, Fillmore, Pierce, and Buchanan—the line preceding the Civil War—all failed to reach even a minimal standard of effectiveness. After Lincoln, there were Andrew Johnson, Grant, Hayes, Garfield, and Arthur. Then, after Theodore Roosevelt, there were (omitting Wilson) Taft, Harding, and Coolidge, and after Franklin D. Roosevelt, there was Truman. All of these are usually judged to have been less than adequate for the office.

No one, at this distance, would defend any one of these as the best available choice. To take Harding and Coolidge, for illustrative purposes, recall what the consequences were. Harding demeaned the office and left a record of scandal; Coolidge passively allowed the development of the economic catastrophe that swamped his successor, Hoover. Instead of Harding, Governor Lowden of Illinois was an available alternative, an able and trusted state executive, but not likely to have been amenable to control by the old guard of his party. The instance of Coolidge is somewhat less illustrative, because, as Vice-President, he succeeded at Harding's death, but in the next election (1924), he was preferred to John W. Davis, the Democratic nominee, and, before that, he had been preferred to several Republicans for the nomination, any one of whom—Hoover or Hughes, for instance—was highly visible and, moreover, known to be more competent.

These presidents were selected in a process with no other constitutional legitimization than that in the Twelfth Amendment (ratified in 1804 to supplement sections 2 and 3 of Article II in the original), providing that electors chosen in the states would meet and make choices later to be counted in Washington.

The framers of the Constitution did not anticipate any such gradual degradation of representation as has taken place. Because, in their time, only a small percentage of the adult male citizens could vote (at most 15 percent), the select few were to choose a still more select group in each state as electors, and these were to make the final choice. When suffrage was extended, first to nonproperty owners, then to former slaves, to women, and, finally, to eighteen-year-olds, the entirely new situations made changes in procedures obviously necessary, but none was provided for by amendment.

When, from a few voters—leading citizens in each community—the choice in elections passed to the millions newly enfranchised, new kinds of appeals had to be made. The wealthy and wellborn have different standards from what those who are poor and undistinguished have. The electors, when they were actually functioning, had chosen Adams. It is doubtful whether any of the early presidents, except Washington and perhaps Jefferson too, would have been nominated at any time after 1838, and certainly the original Electoral College would not have chosen half or more of the succession that began then—perhaps none of them, as the successes in that line had, besides. unexpected abilities, the necessary touch of demagoguery and a willingness to compromise with the demands of the bosses.

The original Electoral College soon fell into desuetude because of the rise of parties, but it continued to exist, functioning in a pro forma way. The electors no longer exercised any choice. The substitute process consisted of conventions to nominate candidates and nationwide voting in a contest among them for votes, so that electors have been reduced to merely registering the results in their respective states.

What explains the curious disarray of election procedure is this growth, without legitimization, of an entirely new selection process to take the place of the one originally provided for in the Constitution. Direct election has been proposed over and over again, but no proposal has been adopted by Congress for submission to the states as a constitutional amendment. Even if one had been adopted, however, and ratified, the quality of the candidates chosen by the conventions would not have been improved.

There were some years, early in the nineteenth century, when congressional caucuses provided candidates. These were superseded by conventions called by various organizations, and gradually took on forms provided for by their own resolutions. They thus made laws for themselves. They were nearly always controlled by small groups of professional politicians—usually state or city bosses—and the candidates they provided were mostly mediocre.

Most delegates to these conventions now come from states with presidential primaries, but some of these primaries do no more than indicate preferences, and the selection of candidates has remained, at least in part, a privilege of those who, by assiduous management of local party machinery, are able to have themselves designated as delegates. Conventions, at least until recently, have been bargaining sessions among these self-chosen power brokers, who settle finally on a candidate they believe will take advice concerning policy and will distribute favors according to the agreements reached at the convention. They prefer one who has at least a chance to win, but this is often less important to them than the fortunes of their local organizations.

A process controlled in such ways is bound to produce a fair percentage of incompetent presidents. It is not always convenient to select from among the possibilities a person who will promise not to disturb the existing arrangement of privileges, but one is often found. It has lately become essential, as well, for him to have access to the huge funds necessary to conduct modern campaigns. It is understood that there will be some sort of compensation for campaign contributions or, at least, that the interests of those making them will not be jeopardized. The professionals realize this, and, even given recent laws limiting contributions, the subtle corruption of candidates made possible by contributions to party funds begins at the outset of the selection process. No one will be put forward who is unacceptable to those financing his campaign.

Such a set of requirements promises nothing in the way of managership for the vast service departments of government, for the making of foreign policy, or for the complex business of achieving stability in a privately managed economy. The infrequent exceptions to the rule of mediocrity—Wilson, Hoover, and the Roosevelts, for instance—are accounted for by unusual circumstances: Theodore Roosevelt by the death of McKinley, Wilson by a split in the Republican Party, Hoover by his great wartime reputation as an administrator, and Franklin D. Roosevelt by the discrediting effect on Hoover of the Great Depression. The exceptions do not vitiate the rule.

It is often pointed out that ten of the largest contributors to Nixon's campaign funds became ambassadors, but so did the most generous of Roosevelt's financial backers. Besides, the cabinets of both presidents were chosen largely to please the conservative elders of their respective parties. Their administrations were indifferently equipped for their tasks.

Turning from senatorial activities to administration requires a most unlikely transformation. The management of a bureaucracy comprising perhaps thousands of careerists will be, at best, nominal; the agency heads will inevitably outmaneuver a politician-secretary. Presidential orders transmitted through such channels are mysteriously changed to suit the bureaucracy's preferences. Policies persist from one administration to another remarkably unchanged. Resistance to change is also reinforced by alliances between bureaucrats and the appropriate congressmen. Altogether, it requires a most sophisticated and determined President to effect any changes at all.

At the very time when most can be accomplished, new presidents, even those who have had long experience, are apt to be incapable of getting anything done. This was conspicuously true of Truman and Kennedy, for instance, but Eisenhower also did not discover for a long time how different being President was from being a general. Johnson was an exception, of course, but his notable honeymoon record is accounted for by the overwhelming majority of liberal legislators who came into office when he did. His ability to carry Congress with him stopped abruptly in 1966, when the midterm elections returned the old guard and their army of lobbyists to power. Nixon's early difficulties were of a different sort. He was much more experienced and realistic but had a hostile Congress to contend with and an unusually rapacious coterie of campaign contributors who expected returns in government favors. This is only to speak of legislative accomplishments. As an administrator, neither Johnson nor Nixon appears to have had much interest in faithful execution. Johnson's spate of welfare laws proved to be badly coordinated, and many became objects of ridicule; they seemed to Nixon, in his time, ready for transformation by the simplistic formula of "revenue-sharing." His success in this was no greater than Johnson's in his War on Poverty.

Since the probability that the present selection process will produce mediocre presidents is high, why has it been allowed to develop and continue? The answer is, of course, that it is natural to an enormously expanded electorate more or less at the mercy of those with special interests to be served and with control of the mass media. Party membership is open; loyalists become fewer and fewer; and those who are unreliable have no standing in the organized nucleus. The masses of voters cannot be counted on for support, and they have no influence at nominating conventions, except as the polls give some indication of their preferences.

Better Presidents

To provide the United States with a Presidency competent for the responsibilities it must carry, fairly obvious changes will have to be made. They will be drastic—that is to say, constitutional—and will not only affect the processes of selection and the activities of the office but also alter the position of the Presidency within the government.

First, no individual and no interest can be allowed to hold the office in its debt. The 1974 Campaign Finance Act goes a long way, but not far enough, in this direction. Equally important, the workings of the whole party system will have to be democratized, so that anyone with political talents will be able to begin at the local level and rise to positions of more and more responsibility.

Once it is made less likely that Hardings and Coolidges will become presidents, the more capable incumbents will have to be relieved of all duties not essential for the President himself to carry—specifically, administration of the proliferating service functions characteristic of the welfare state. This will allow him time and energy for the unavoidable duties, those having to do with the security and good prospects of the nation.

For these major tasks, he must have the support of his wide constituency and the assistance of peers. He will have been elected by all the people. He must keep their trust by sounding their wishes and by explaining his formulations of policy. He must also have the critical appraisal and the cooperation of the legislative branch. These can be had only by ensuring, in the selection process, that some part, at least, of the legislature will be chosen for the same reasons as he himself and with the same ends in view.

A President, as things are, succeeds or fails largely because he can or cannot persuade Congress to accept his leadership and assist in developing common policies. The legislature, however, is so positioned that it has aims other than those of the President. He represents all the people; members of Congress represent smaller, localized constituencies. Congressmen, in the belief that their time and effort are best spent in pleasing their constituents, inevitably form an opposition, and one intensified by the likelihood that a majority of them will belong to another party. If some representatives were elected at large, and on the same ticket with the President, cooperation rather than obstruction would be more likely.

The President, being responsible for dealings with other nations and for future domestic policies, should be given the assistance of a planning agency devoted not only to the calculations necessary for the formulation of national needs and the resources available for meeting them but also to bringing into its deliberations the expertise of the scientific and technological community. Thus reinforced, a President could exert leadership with greater confidence that large mistakes would be avoided and future prosperity made more likely.

Decisions arising out of recurring environmental and technological changes must now be made by the President alone, and largely on the basis of instinct tempered only by the advice of department heads and intelligence services. Because of this situation, there have been costly errors, such as the depopulation of the American countryside and the proliferation of urban slums, or the undertaking of the long and exhausting cold war, which led into the involvement in Southeast Asia.

Such decisions could benefit from reliance on a peer group for advice, but the President now has no peers. It is suggested that the Senate, having been originally the result of compromise and being unnecessary for legislation, should be transformed into a House of National Concern. If its members were appointed from panels of citizens with proved ability and were forbidden any other employment, they would be as nearly peers of the President as could be devised without actually making them voting associates. A select body of these senators might be chosen to join in certain of his crucial decisions, such as the deployment of the armed forces abroad or in far waters, thus avoiding the near approach to dictatorship clearly developing in recent years.

These changes are indeed drastic, and they require changes in a basic law that has been essentially unchanged for nearly two centuries, except for the extrapolations of the Supreme Court. That law might regain its credibility and usefulness by such a reconstitution.

17. Reforming the Presidency: Problems and Prospects

Norman C. Thomas

When historians examine twentieth-century American politics, they doubtless will take special notice of the decade 1965–75, a period that witnessed the end, at least temporarily, of American liberalism's fascination with the heroic Presidency and of its view that presidential power was the only effective means of achieving the goals of liberal democracy. The shock waves that emanated first from America's protracted involvement in Vietnam and then from the Watergate affair contributed to sharp reductions in both the public's trust in government and its confidence in the major government institutions. The disenchantment of liberal politicians and scholars gave rise to a revisionist approach that urged abandonment (or at least reappraisal) of the "textbook Presidency," an idealized model that had been extensively nurtured in the media and in high school and college classrooms.[1]

The reformers, though not always in full agreement with each other, directed the bulk of their proposals at the abuse of presidential power. They compared the Presidency to a medieval court, noted its swollen size, and complained about a constitutional imbalance as illustrated in an undeclared, presidentially initiated war, questionable impoundment of congressionally appropriated funds, and claims of an absolute executive privilege. Most reformers viewed the so-called imperial Presidency as the culmination of a process of presidential aggrandizement and institutionalization begun under Franklin D. Roosevelt and given impetus by a series of difficult and often intractable economic and social problems, an ever expanding international role, and a breathtaking surge of technological advances. As former LBJ aide Joseph A. Califano has so aptly stated, the United States has become more a "Presidential nation" than a "republic of deliberately fragmented power."

After an initial round of proposals for systemic change (such as introduction of parliamentary government), reform suggestions focused more on improving presidential accountability than on diminishing presidential power. Even Arthur Schlesinger, Jr., whose scholarly polemic against the Johnson and Nixon presidencies, *The Imperial Presidency*, set the revisionist tone for popular consumption, cautioned that a "pogrom against the Presidency was not the answer" and warned against "stripping the President of all independent authority." Indeed, only a few reforms have been accomplished since Richard M. Nixon's fall, and the actual effects of the major reform statutes remain in question.

Specifically, the War Powers Act of 1973 did not prevent a response with force in the *Mayaguez* incident, and its ability to restrict the President's war-making powers in similar crisis situations is doubtful.[2] The Budget and Impoundment Control Act of 1974 got off to a promising beginning in 1975 when the Congressional Budget Office and House and Senate Budget committees were established and a dry run was conducted on the fiscal 1976 budget. Whether this legislation will have the desired effect of making Congress an equal and independent participant with the Presidency in controlling federal spending remains to be seen; it appears to have succeeded in curtailing the use of impoundment for purposes of controlling policy, but at the cost of considerable paperwork and some ambiguity. Plainly, recent reforms of campaign finance are far-reaching changes, but the effects of the Federal Elections Campaign Act Amendments of 1974 on presidential politics will not be clearly known for a few more years.[3]

Is there, then, much prospect of substantial reform of the Presidency and readjustment of balance within the political system? Perhaps not, but the fact that many of the conditions that gave rise to the Vietnam War and Watergate remain substantially unchanged and that the phenomenon of a powerful institutionalized Presidency is still very much with us—together with the question of how well equipped the nation is, under the Constitution, to cope with the challenges of a society and a world in flux—demands that we give serious attention to these matters.

Problems

It is taken for granted among students of American politics that the modern Presidency began under Franklin D. Roosevelt, as the nation met, fairly successfully, the challenges of depression and war, expanded and grew under Harry S. Truman and Dwight D. Eisenhower as we looked increasingly to the President to maintain economic stability and prosperity at home, and reached imperial proportions as we expected later presidents to make America the dominant nation in world affairs. The problem of the contemporary Presidency has several dimensions, depending on who is diagnosing it. According to Arthur Schlesinger, the "underlying issue" is the "expansion and abuse of presidential power." Thomas E. Cronin sees two challenges: making the "Presidency more manageable and presidential leadership more effective" and "making the Presidency safe for democracy." Many others regard inadequate personalities as a major aspect of the problem but are equally concerned with the impact of the institutionalized Presidency, particularly as it leads to secrecy, the isolation of the President from constructive criticism, and the inability of the President to maintain control over the evolution of policy because of his dependence on staff and the expertise of others.

The prevailing view is that, because presidential power is extensive (some say excessive), its exercise should be more tightly restrained and made more accountable to Congress and the people. The Presidency's critics also tend to agree that the need for effective presidential leadership remains unabated. A few conservatives have, on the other hand, explained liberal disenchantment in terms of the rise of a "new class" of upper-middle-class professionals and intellectuals who regard the Presidency as unresponsive to their needs and values. Thus, political scientist Paul H. Weaver argues that presidential power has diminished because of the rise in the influence and independence of the media, the growing inability of presidents to control the bureaucracy, the decline of political parties as vehicles for mobilizing presidential support, and the resurgence of Congress as a policy innovator.[4] He sees Congress replacing the Presidency as the vehicle for pursuit of new-class policy objectives. However, Weaver reaches his conclusion by misinterpreting the relationships between Congress and the causal factors he identifies. As an indication that he recognizes the wishful nature of his analysis, he hedges his bet by observing at the end that the Ninety-fourth Congress has not been doing a very good job and that, perhaps, a strong Presidency is the only really effective means of achieving new-class goals.

The problem presented by the Presidency has three dimensions: expanded presidential power and the potential for its abuse, the consequences of a swollen institutionalized presidency, and the need to find a means of coping with the first two problems while preserving free government. The problem arises from four sets of interrelated factors, which can be termed societal, political, programmatic, and governmental.

The *societal* factors include conditions that have resulted in demands for increased government activity and more presidential leadership. Presidents and would-be presidents have had to address such matters as the claims of minorities to equal treatment in American social and economic life and access to, and full participation in, political decision-making processes hitherto closed to, or at least severely restricted for, them. The social turbulence resulting from the unmet demands of emerging interest groups has altered the nature of presidential politics. Economic factors have also had major consequences. Increased economic interdependence both domestically and internationally places limits on the options open to government. The interrelated problems of increasing environmental pollution and decreasing supplies of energy impose a "politics of resource constraint" that makes wise and courageous presidential leadership more needed than ever.

American presidents have been more than willing to claim that they have the answers to such problems and to promise that, if elected, they will restore life to simpler, more manageable proportions. An inflation of *political* promises and expectations has taken place, especially accelerated by presidential use of television to communicate with the public. Since John F. Kennedy, chief executives have seldom hesitated to pre-empt prime time in order to promote their policies and upstage their rivals. Television gives the President an unparalleled instrument for enhancing his power. It also increases the temptation to present things in the most favorable light possible and to shade, hide, or distort the truth. Television has reduced presidential dependence on political parties. Moreover, the public's disenchantment with the two major parties, as suggested by the rise in the number of independent voters and the decline of party loyalties, has further contributed to their disarray.[5] The long-standing indifference of Americans toward politics has, then, been reinforced by the advent of television, which operates in a dual manner, through exposure and manipulation. The beneficiary of these developments, at least until now, has been the Presidency. Its power to shape opinion and influence policy has been positively enhanced through increased communication capability, and the negative restraint of the political parties has been substantially weakened.

The cost of this increased power has been an apparent decline of public support for presidents. Presidents are increasingly unable to meet the inflated expectations held for them and thus suffer sharp losses in support as the public learns to distinguish between promise and performance.

The *societal* and *political* factors that contribute to the problem are accompanied by *the consequences of expanded government programs*. The massive increase in demands for government action that began during the Great Depression and continued through the 1960s produced a wide array of federal grant-in-aid *programs* designed to meet diverse needs. The expansion of federal programs, activities, and services resulted in increased *governmental* complexity—the growth of bureaucracies that, in turn, fostered specialized clientele groups, which functioned as supportive constituencies for major programs and nurtured development of a proprietary interest in the programs and the agencies that administer them on the part of congressional subcommittees having jurisdiction over them. These symbiotic triangular relationships, often referred to as subgovernments, constitute autonomous centers of power that presidents largely have been unable to control or even penetrate.

This phenomenon of "interest-group liberalism" provoked presidents to develop means of control through expansion of Executive Office staff units, the assignment of program-management responsibilities to presidential assistants, and the designation of Cabinet officers as presidential counselors. These efforts culminated in Nixon's highly centralized "administrative Presidency," which was aborted by the unraveling of the Watergate affair.[6] The principal devices that President Nixon and his top-level aides employed to bring the "permanent government" under control included extensive budget impoundments, sweeping personnel shifts at the Cabinet and sub-Cabinet levels that made loyalty to the President the principal criterion for appointment, use of the reorganization power to increase the authority of the President's lieutenants, and the revision of agency regulations under White House direction.

Presidents responded to these complex societal, political, programmatic, and governmental problems in ways that tended to increase their power relative to other political institutions and forces, that expanded their staff support and furthered institutionalization of the Presidency, and that increasingly tended to isolate them from all but their closest advisers. The more they attempted to do independently, the greater the risks they assumed for their personal popularity and the more they jeopardized public support for the Presidency. Charges of presidential arrogance, manipulation, and, ultimately, "high crimes and misdemeanors" led to calls for reform. To determine whether a cure is in the offing, we must examine the objectives of reform and the reform agenda.

Reform

The modern reform movement in American politics and political science can be traced to political scientist Woodrow Wilson. He countered his disenchantment with the congressional supremacy of the late nineteenth century with the hope that a strong Presidency, which he saw emerging under Grover Cleveland, would result in more responsible government. Wilson left as his main legacy to future reformers an admiration of the British form of parliamentary government. He recognized, however, that it could not be transplanted intact to the United States, and he sought ways to graft various of its features onto the American constitutional system. Many of Wilson's twentieth-century successors in the reform enterprise have shared his fascination with parliamentary government and urged that its essentials be incorporated through devices such as a system of government by programmatic, issue-oriented parties[7] and various suggested methods of fusing legislative and executive leadership.[8] More sweeping proposals for an American parliamentary system have neither been well received nor given vigorous consideration.[9] Reform suggestions that take the British model as their point of departure place a high value on securing a direct, responsive linkage between public opinion and public policy. They seek to strengthen popular control and democratic accountability. Either explicitly or by implication, they regard the constitutional system of separated and balanced powers as wholly or partially dysfunctional for the achievement of their goal.

There has also been a sustained effort to improve the efficiency of government operations through administrative reforms that date from the establishment of federal civil service in 1883. These administrative reforms have focused on structure, procedure, and personnel. Usually they have been preceded by study commissions that have recommended changes, some of which have been adopted. Most significant for the development of the modern Presidency was the 1937 report of the President's Committee on Administrative Management (the Brownlow Committee), the basic theme of which was embodied in its statement that the "President needs help." The principal consequences of the Brownlow Committee's efforts were establishment of the Executive Office of the President, transfer of the Bureau of the Budget from the Treasury Department to the Executive Office, and empowering of the President to reorganize administrative agencies subject to congressional veto. Since then (1939), there have been occasional minor changes in government organization and a wide range of reorganization proposals that have followed the periodic reports of prestigious study commissions. Indeed, as Harold Seidman observes, "reorganization has almost become a religion in Washington [and it] is deemed synonymous with reform and reform with progress."[10]

Administrative reform movements that seek to enhance economy and efficiency through structural changes have been supplemented in recent years by procedural revolutions such as systems analysis, the Program, Planning, and Budgeting System (PPBS), Management by Objectives (MBO), and most recently, various "sunshine" bills designed to open government processes to public view. Some see administrative reform as the constant pursuit of a single objective, efficiency, while others regard it as a continuous swinging back and forth between such values as efficiency, representativeness, and decisive leadership.

Historically, political reform proposals have tended to emphasize responsiveness and accountability. The most recent wave of reform proposals, those immediately inspired by Vietnam and Watergate and growing out of the development of presidential government, have a set of objectives that combine some of the goals of earlier political and administrative reform movements and that address the special problems of the current malaise. Contemporary political reform proposals retain the long-standing concern over democratic accountability and have adopted the administrative reform goal of efficiency. In addition, they seek to restore the constitutional balance between the executive and the other branches of government and to regain a sense of public trust in government that has been lost in recent years. To summarize, the goals of current political reform proposals are (1) to increase responsiveness and accountability, particularly of the Presidency, (2) to increase government efficiency and effectiveness, (3) to restore constitutional balance, and (4) to restore trust in government.

The Reform Agenda

In spite of various calls for drastic constitutional changes, it is apparent, if the past is a valid guide, that only a modest portion of the extensive reform agenda proposed for the Presidency will be adopted. But aside from whether they would pass or not, what are the proposals' merits, and what would be their probable consequences? Answers to these questions must, of course, be speculative. A change in one dimension of our institutions or patterns of political behavior may produce unanticipated changes in the others that lead to results that are quite different from those originally intended. Reforms never are neutral, they necessarily affect who gets what, when, and how. In short, reform is complex and unpredictable, and it is unlikely that there will be any simple proposals that will neatly accomplish its objectives and its objectives only.

Reform proposals can be brought into sharper perspective and evaluation of them is assisted through the use of the simple visual presentation that follows. The proposals seem to lend themselves to classification according to two distinctive variables, level and focus. Either they deal with two or more elements of the entire political system or, at a lower level, with the institution of the Presidency. Their focus is either on government structure or on procedures, that is, on the organizational framework within which political behavior takes place or on the behavior itself. Proposed government-wide reforms tend to focus primarily on structure rather than procedure,

Classification of Presidential Reforms by Level and Focus

LEVEL \ FOCUS	Structural[a]	Procedural[b]
Systemic[c]	1. Parliamentary system 2. Parliamentary variants 3. Initiative and recall 4. Council of state 5. Cabinet upgrading 6. National planning agency 7. Altered presidential selection 8. Six-year presidential terms 9. Congressional reform 10. Party-system overhaul	1. War Powers Resolution (1973) 2. Budget and Impoundment Control Act (1974) 3. Campaign Finance Act (1974) 4. National planning bill (proposed 1975, 1976) 5. Restriction of executive-privilege claims
Institutional[d]	1. Collegial executive 2. Limited size and function of presidential staff 3. Strengthened presidential planning and evaluation staffs	1. Explicit delegations of presidential functions to staff 2. Requirement of presidential-powers impact statements, specific reports with State of Union message, and annual national-posture statement 3. Multiple advocacy

[a] Structural: the way in which the parts and elements of the governmental organization are arranged.

[b] Procedural: forms and methods of conducting the business of government.

[c] Systemic: having to do with the overall political system in the United States.

[d] Institutional: having to do with the established organization of the Presidency.

especially when directed at conditions that cut across political institutions. Proposals directed solely toward the Presidency are understandably less sweeping and contain a more even balance between structural and procedural changes. The various structural reforms would, if adopted, have greater impact than most procedural changes because they would alter the rules of the game, institutional resources, and the organizational terrain on which the political struggle is waged. Procedural reforms are necessarily more sharply focused and tend to be less sweeping in potential impact.

Structural Systemic Reforms

The most far-reaching reform proposed for the Presidency is that hearty perennial, parliamentary government, an often mentioned alternative that implicitly, if not explicitly, denies the virtues claimed for separated powers and a balanced constitution.[11] Its advocates claim that an American parliamentary system would achieve democratic responsiveness and accountability, and also that it would increase governmental legitimacy by improving the linkage between public opinion and public policy. Presumably a smoothly functioning parliamentary system would also make government more effective and bring the federal bureaucracy under tighter political control. The case against parliamentary government for America seems more persuasive. Such a system would reduce the direct accountability of the President and the executive branch to the national electorate and substantially eliminate constitutional checks and balances. The fusion of executive and legislative leadership is no guarantee of governmental effectiveness. In all probability, it is argued, an American parliamentary system would be characterized by a multiplicity of political parties, given our social pluralism, and hence it might encourage chronic instability like that of the French Fourth Republic or the current Italian Republic.

Short of a total collapse of our constitutional system, parliamentary government as a systemic reform is unlikely; however, its discussion is useful not only for the stark contrast it provides but also because it is the source of a variety of less sweeping, more plausible proposals. Two reforms suggested in the mid-1970s derive from parliamentary government: (1) a no-confidence vote as a means of presidential removal on policy and performance grounds, without the elaborate procedural requirements of impeachment, coupled with a provision for dissolution of Congress and the conduct of special presidential elections,[12] and (2) a requirement that the President and the principal department and agency heads appear before congressional bodies and respond to questions.

The proposal for a congressional no-confidence vote attempts to increase presidential responsiveness and accountability. It would also tilt the constitutional balance away from the President toward Congress. The principal advocates of this reform have been James L. Sundquist of the Brookings Institution[13] and Democratic Representative Henry L. Reuss of Wisconsin, who in 1974 introduced a proposed constitutional amendment that would establish it.[14] The no-confidence proposal is directly linked to suggestions for dissolution of Congress and the conduct of new elections. A variety of possibilities exist: The President could be required to resign, to face a new election, or to run against his record. In the Reuss resolution, Congress would be required to dissolve itself and face new elections along with the President. Also open to variation is the type of majority that would be required; a simple majority of those present and voting or a more demanding vote, say, 60 percent of those present and voting as in the Reuss resolution. The mechanics of a no confidence–dissolution reform are not as important as its potential consequences. Sundquist argues that it would force the President to "maintain the confidence of the country and the Congress." It would certainly require more presidential-congressional consultation and provide a method of ending deadlocked or leaderless government such as occurred in 1919–20, 1931–32, and 1973–74.

The primary argument against the no confidence–dissolution reform is that impeachment and other available checks and balances can and do work. Moreover, it is argued that the device would severely cripple the Presidency without increasing the capacity of Congress to govern. Finally, the potential for both congressional and presidential manipulation of the procedure for short-run political advantage makes it unduly risky.

The efficacy of impeachment as demonstrated in the events leading to the Nixon resignation seems to be a thin reed on which to rest the goal of greater presidential accountability. What future President is likely to provide taped evidence of his indictable conduct and simultaneously mount frontal assaults on Congress, the bureaucracy, the courts, the media, the electoral process, and his own political party? A no confidence–dissolution procedure offers the possibility of realizing in varying degrees the four goals of the current reform thrust without abandoning the basic constitutional structure. The change, however, would be substantial, but the immediate impetus for it (Nixon's conduct in office) is a fading and unpleasant memory. As in the case of the periodic drives for Electoral College reform, once the immediate danger has passed, prospects for change wane rapidly. Only when the system misfires badly, as in the election of 1800, is structural change likely (witness the Twelfth Amendment). Otherwise, inertia prevails.

The proposal for mandatory congressional questioning of the President and the principal department and agency heads has not attracted much support. In part, it may have been defused by President Gerald R. Ford's voluntary appearance in late 1974 before the House Judiciary Committee to explain his pardon of former President Nixon. Still, as Philippa Strum argues, the suggestion requires serious consideration because of the exaggerated claims of executive privilege and the excessive preoccupation with secrecy during the Johnson and Nixon administrations, as well as the reluctance of high-ranking officials such as Secretary Henry Kissinger to appear before congressional committees, together with their insistence on stipulating the subjects they will discuss if and when they do so. In addition to being a symbolic attack on the "imperial Presidency," this proposal would serve at least two reform goals, restoration of constitutional balance and increased accountability. But it can be argued that the cost in terms of policy effectiveness would be too great and that the reform would result in renewed executive efforts at secrecy or, alternatively, in so much exposure that legitimacy might be further eroded. Most objectives of a mandatory question procedure could probably be achieved by legislation defining the scope of executive privilege and the conditions under which it can be invoked. (This would be a systemic change with a procedural focus.) Professor Strum suggests that Article II, section 3 of the Constitution can be interpreted as providing a basis for a statute mandating a "question time." Such a statute would, however, be difficult to enact because of the inherent congressional-presidential conflict it would entail.

An American-style alternative to the no confidence–dissolution reform as a means of increasing accountability and responsiveness is the proposal for national initiative and recall procedures as suggested by the People's Lobby, a California populist organization.[15] The technology exists to enable the national electorate to vote on legislation initiated by petition and to decide on whether to remove or retain the President. Ample precedents for mass referenda can be found in several state constitutions. Certainly the use of national referenda for initiative and recall would increase popular control of government. The experiences with direct democracy at the state and local levels suggest, however, that such a reform would create more problems than it would solve. The proposal raises questions that cannot be answered: Who would decide what issues to submit and under what circumstances? How would the referenda weigh the intensity of voter opinions? What would happen if voters adopted contradictory or even regressive laws that increased social, economic, and political polarization? So far, no major political forces have emerged to support any form of national referenda.

Two structural reform proposals with system-wide consequences are concerned with advising the President and readjusting his relationship to the executive branch. The Constitutional Convention of 1787 considered the creation of a Council of State to comprise the Chief Justice, the President of the Senate, the Speaker of the House, and the heads of the executive departments. The framers rejected the idea on the ground that the President ought to be free to choose his advisers. Political scientist Edward S. Corwin suggests that the President "construct his Cabinet from a joint Legislative Council to be created by the two houses of Congress."[16] He sees such a Cabinet as being capable of controlling as well as supporting the President. Its advantages would be that its members would not be wholly dependent on the President and that its decisions would represent a wider consensus than the President could supply himself. Several modern-day students of the Presidency have re-examined the Council of State and other proposals for a plural executive and concluded that they would only increase the difficulty of affixing presidential accountability.

Thomas E. Cronin has recently called attention to a proposal for Cabinet consolidation designed to strengthen the position of department secretary "institutionally."[17] This would be accomplished by reorganization of the executive branch along the lines of President Nixon's 1972 proposal for new departments of Community Development, Natural Resources, Human Resources, and Economic Affairs, and retention of the existing departments of State, the Treasury, Defense, Justice, and Agriculture. Cronin suggests that the "central conflict in White House–departmental relations does not lie between the President and his Cabinet heads so much as between general and special interests." Consolidation would facilitate resolution of such conflicts within departments, thus strengthening department heads and enabling them to function as advisers to the President as well as advocates for their departments. This, in turn, would reduce pressures for the presidential staff to direct administrative operations from the White House.

Cronin's proposal has a certain logic, but its chance of success is cast in doubt, as he himself acknowledges, by the difficulties encountered in managing the two existing superdepartments, Defense and Health, Education, and Welfare. If Cabinet consolidation could realize the aspirations Cronin holds for it, opportunities for increased governmental efficiency and effectiveness and executive accountability would be substantially enhanced.

Another proposal with potential to increase the effectiveness of national policy leadership calls for the establishment of an Economic Planning Board and the creation of a national planning process that would coordinate congressional, presidential, and executive-branch responsibilities. The Humphrey-Javits balanced growth and economic planning bill introduced in 1975 and the Humphrey-Hawkins full employment and balanced growth bill of 1976 initiated a lively dialogue on the subject of planning.[18] Liberals argue that national economic planning would lead to increased responsiveness and accountability and improved congressional-presidential cooperation. Conservatives see it as socialism in action and fear it would lead to the destruction of economic freedom. Some form of comprehensive planning may eventually be adopted, but only after extended debate and substantial compromise.

No discussion of systemic reform proposals would be complete without reference to presidential selection. Leaving aside the matter of campaign finance, which Congress addressed in the 1974 legislation on the subject, the range of proposals includes such well-worn suggestions as direct election of the President and various overhauls of the Electoral College, as well as newer ones for national and regional primaries. In addition, both major parties have altered their national conventions' delegate-selection rules and procedures so as to provide greater opportunity for participation by women and minorities. The recent spread of presidential primaries and the opening of convention delegations to individuals and groups outside local and state party leadership cadres seek to increase responsiveness and legitimacy. Whether these goals have been achieved and the extent of their impact on party politics and political leadership have yet to be determined. One study of the 1972 California Democratic National Convention delegation concludes that the new rules may have helped George McGovern to secure the nomination, but they hindered his efforts in the election.[19] My tentative impression is that these reforms have weakened the parties without effectively broadening popular control. They have shifted the balance of power within the parties away from established organizational leaders toward newer, primarily issue-oriented leaders.

Proposals for reforming or abandoning the Electoral College deserve serious consideration if only because the potential for breakdown—either a minority-supported President or a deadlocked election in the House of Representatives—remains very real. It is difficult to imagine the extent of possible damage to confidence in our government should 1824, 1876, or 1888 occur in this era of instant mass communication. Unfortunately, though substantial agreement appears to exist that changes are necessary, consensus on a desired alternative has thus far been unobtainable.[20]

The idea of a single national primary or a series of regional primaries to replace the lengthy sequence of individual state primaries extending from late February to early June may gain support as the public wearies of prolonged preconvention campaigning. However, it seems unlikely that the parochial desires of the states to be distinctive (New Hampshire is the primary example) will be easily overcome. Rationalization of presidential primaries would almost certainly improve responsiveness and contribute to greater governmental legitimacy, but the forces and values of localism will probably prevail for some time to come.

Unfortunately, none of the reforms relating to the selection of the President appears directed toward broadening the net cast for potential nominees or improving the quality of the people ultimately chosen to serve as President and Vice-President. The question at issue may be unanswerable: How can we minimize the possibility of choosing another compulsive or rigidity-prone President (or, in James David Barber's terms, an "active negative"—as described in his book *The Presidential Character*), guard against the near disaster of having convicted bribe-taker (Spiro Agnew) succeed to the Presidency, and avoid another Thomas Eagleton fiasco? More careful background investigations of all presidential candidates would reduce the possibilities of error—if we could agree upon an agency to conduct the inquiries in an impartial manner. Little or no support exists, however, for requiring psychiatric testing of candidates. There are some risks that a free society simply must run in choosing its leaders.

Closely related to reform of the selection process is the proposed single six-year term for the President. This idea, which had been advocated by Lyndon B. Johnson and Senator Mike Mansfield (among others), has attracted surprisingly substantial support in recent years.[21] The rationale for the change is that a President freed of the concerns of re-election and partisan politics would be able to provide more effectively rational, objective national policy leadership. The six-year-term reform is a deliberate attempt to take party politics out of the Presidency. It assumes that "politics" is incompatible with the proper discharge of the President's constitutional duties. The argument is also made that four years are not a long enough time for a President to plan, secure the adoption, and supervise the implementation of his major policy objectives.

The six-year term would have the effects of reducing the amount of political expediency that enters the President's policy decisions and of removing the advantage of incumbency from presidential election campaigns. Its disadvantages, however, would be extensive. The President would be a lame duck from the moment of his election, and his political leverage would be reduced accordingly. He would still have to engage in political bargaining in order to fashion winning congressional coalitions, but his resources would be less than if he could stand for re-election. Also, the single six-year term would make presidential accountability and executive-branch responsiveness more difficult to achieve than at present. What if an incompetent were elected? Then the nation would be stuck for six years rather than four. If four years are not enough time for the accomplishment of a President's plans, what assurance is there that six would suffice?

Two of the most important suggestions for systemic reform involve institutions other than the Presidency: Congress and the political parties. Most advocates of presidential reform eventually come around to the position that unless Congress, the party system, or both can be strengthened substantially, no amount of tinkering with the structure and powers of the Presidency will provide an effective means of restraint and achieve the major reform goals.

However, the prognosis for politically significant congressional and party reform is not very bright. Although Congress has adopted several changes since 1970, many, if not most, of the structural and procedural reforms have had contrary results.[22] Some reforms have increased congressional capacity to act expeditiously and on the basis of better information—for example, for the curbing of committee chairmen, the strengthening of party machinery, and improved staffing for information retrieval and analysis—while others have further diffused and fragmented institutional power in the name of openness and democratization—for example, increased public scrutiny and reduction in the number of leadership positions an individual member may hold. The most encouraging developments, such as the creation of the Congressional Budget Office and the excellent performance of the House Judiciary Committee in the 1974 impeachment hearings, are counterbalanced by the increased importance of incumbency for winning re-election and by the low apparent correlation between changes in congressional membership and changes in public opinion. Most observers believe that Congress has far to travel if it is to acquire the courage and the capacity to counterbalance the executive branch effectively for an appreciable length of time. On most matters, the problem with Congress is not its lack of power but, rather, the need to find ways in which it can use its power effectively.

If reforming Congress appears difficult, revitalization of the parties is even a much tougher undertaking. The long-range trend throughout this century has been toward increasing debility of the major national parties. In spite of the increase in issue-based voting, party loyalty among the electorate is declining and the number of people who register as independents is rising. Optimistic speculations that a more issue-oriented electorate would provide the opportunity for party reform have not begun to be realized. Party organization remains fragmented and decentralized. Since 1952, presidential nominees of the two major parties have divorced management of their campaigns from the operations of the national committees of their parties. Once elected, presidents have found that they needed the support of their parties much less than the parties needed them and that often partisan demands were an embarrassment. Parties still serve Congress mainly as voting cues for members, not as active and publicly visible formulators of party policy.

The weakness of the parties and their ineffectual performance of the active policy-leadership role assigned them by democratic theory reflect the deep hostility of the American people to politics. Dorothy B. James accurately assesses the problem: "Those who desire rapid strengthening of American parties face a version of *Catch 22*: It takes strengthened parties to inform and activate opinion but such a change is blocked by public opinion."[23]

Many of the recent political reforms—such as some aspects of the Campaign Finance Act of 1974, the revised rules for nominating conventions, and the opening of numerous primaries to voters other than party members—threaten to weaken the parties further. In our zeal to restrain such abuses traditionally associated with partisanship as bossism, patronage, and graft, we have almost rendered the parties incapable of effective performance as the main vehicles for collective political action. Reforms that would strengthen party discipline and organization and enable the parties to serve as a basis for translating issue concerns into government programs have not been seriously considered. The reforms that have been adopted recently have given attention to expanded political expression, but they have neglected the need to provide a means for translating that expression, through the parties, into electoral success and public policy.

Procedural Systemic Reforms

Most reforms adopted in recent years have dealt with government procedures rather than structural arrangements. Their thrust has been to limit the powers of the President and increase congressional power by prescribing specific procedures. The War Powers Act of 1973 is an attempt to curtail, within broad boundaries, the capacity of the President to involve the nation in war without the full participation of Congress in the decision. The difficulty with the legislation is that in taking into account the inherent limitations of Congress, it necessarily leaves a broad scope for the exercise of presidential discretion. As events in May 1975 revealed, this new provision is not adequate for preventing American involvement in international incidents (such as that involving the *Mayaguez*) that could quite conceivably lead to military action on an extensive scale. On the other hand, the congressional power of the purse, which Congress has always possessed, was quite sufficient to prevent American involvement in the 1976 Angolan civil conflict. The War Powers Act is, then, a symbolic congressional affirmation of the ultimate constitutional power to declare war. Its success as an attempt to restore the congressional-presidential balance and increase legitimacy is largely problematic.

The Budget and Impoundment Control Act of 1974 holds greater promise as a means to the achievement of the same reform goals. It gives Congress the capacity to participate on an equal basis with the President in the formulation and execution of fiscal policy, and it has scaled down impoundment from a major policy weapon to its original function of returning unexpended funds to the Treasury. If Congress has the will and self-discipline to abide by its new budget process, this reform could prove to be the most significant consequence of the Nixon Presidency.

The consequences of the Campaign Finance Act of 1974 have yet to be fully felt. Presidential candidates have made disclosures of their personal finances that previously would have been unthinkable. It is not yet apparent whether the legislation will reduce substantially the influence of large "fat cat" donors in presidential politics. Given the limited success of past efforts in this area, it is perhaps wise not to be too hopeful.

National economic planning, if adopted along the lines proposed in the Humphrey-Javits and Humphrey-Hawkins bills, would have profound effects on the role of the federal government in managing the economy. In terms of our reform model, the goals to be served by a planning process would be restored congressional-presidential balance through participation in economic policy-making and increased governmental effectiveness. As indicated above, heated debates about national economic planning have just begun.

A final procedural reform with systemic consequences involves limitations on governmental and presidential secrecy. The extensive claims of executive privilege after 1964 attracted the attention of the Senate Subcommittee on Separation of Powers chaired by Senator Sam Ervin of North Carolina, well before the revelations of Watergate.[24] Senators Ervin and J. William Fulbright of Arkansas, who appeared as witnesses, argued that executive evasion and denial of congressional requests for information, as well as unilateral executive determination of which officials would testify before congressional committees, were clear violations of the powers of Congress. The issue of executive privilege came to a climax in 1974 during the controversy over the House Judiciary Committee's request for the tapes of President Nixon's Oval Office conversations. The Supreme Court ruled that a President does not have an absolute privilege of immunity and ordered Nixon to surrender the tapes.[25] However, the Court did not definitively dispose of the issue of executive privilege.[26] Rather, it found a constitutional basis for the doctrine, suggested that it could be applied broadly, but declined to specify the conditions under which it may be asserted. If those conditions are to be stipulated, the task will have to be performed by Congress.

Reforms designed to provide greater openness in the conduct of national policy-making are not easily devised and are even more difficult to enact. This is clearly an issue when "where you stand depends on where you sit." Somehow Congress and the President must establish conditions and procedures for the assertion of executive privilege and the release of information. It must also be recognized that when disagreement arises, the courts will necessarily act as arbitrators. The development of more precise statutory provisions in this area would be an important step toward the reform objectives of improved presidential accountability and increased governmental legitimacy.

Structural Institutional Reforms

Reform proposals that concentrate primarily or entirely on the Presidency emphasize the goals of increased presidential accountability and improved governmental effectiveness. Some proposals in this category would, however, work at cross-purposes with others if all were to be adopted. A long-standing structural reform suggestion is the establishment of a plural executive. The rationale is that the burdens of office are so great that they should be shared and responsibility placed on more than one person. The concept of a plural executive received consideration at the Constitutional Convention of 1787, and Alexander Hamilton's classic statement against it remains persuasive today:

> ... the plurality of the Executive tends to deprive the people of the two greatest securities they can have for the faithful exercise of any delegated power, first, the restraints of public opinion, which lose their efficacy as well as on account of the division of the censure attendant on bad measures among a number, as on account of the uncertainty on whom it ought to fall; and, secondly, the opportunity of discovering with facility and clearness the misconduct of the persons they trust, in order either to their removal from office, or to their actual punishment in cases which admit of it.[27]

There are numerous variations on the plural-executive concept—some derived from the parliamentary model, others that seek direct electoral selection of several national executives as is done in most of the states, and some more modest suggestions for one or two additional vice-presidents with specific functional responsibilities.[28] The plural, or collegial, executive has attracted little support and almost no sustained interest. Its potential defects are competition and conflict within the executive, further growth of upper-level executive staffs, and a diffusion of responsibilities and accountabilities. Pluralization of the executive short of Cabinet government would only compound the problems of the Presidency. Further, present structural arrangements result in a form of collective leadership, and a President can achieve many of its alleged advantages through use of his high-level assistants.

The presidential staff is, however, an object of major concern to reformers. Here we find somewhat contradictory proposals calling, on the one hand, for limiting the size and functions of the Executive Office and on the other for strengthening presidential planning and evaluation staffs. The two suggestions are not wholly in opposition, however. In essence, both argue that the principal functions of the White House staff and Executive Office units should be to assist and advise the President and not to attempt to run the government in his place. If Congress were to enact legislation that more precisely defined the functions of the institutionalized Presidency, leaving its internal structure and procedures to presidential discretion, the goals of increased responsiveness and accountability and improved governmental effectiveness would come more within reach. This is not an unachievable reform, but it will require presidential willingness to curtail the size of the Presidency and to limit its functional responsibilities within the executive branch.

Proposed structural reforms of the Presidency, then, offer limited assistance for the achievement of reform goals. The most promising, and also the most modest and the most likely to be adopted, would strengthen presidential planning and evaluation staff services while limiting the institutionalized Presidency to advisory functions.

Procedural Institutional Reforms

Of equal, perhaps greater, potential as means for achieving reform objectives are proposals that focus on the processes and powers of the Presidency. Disturbed by the claims of former Nixon aides John Ehrlichman and H. R. Haldeman that they acted on the basis of "delegated presidential authority," some writers have recommended legislation that would restrict, and require publication of, delegations of authority within the White House. Specifically, they call for publication in the *Federal Register* of (1) the functions assigned to White House units, (2) the names and duties of White House personnel, (3) delegations of authority within the Executive Office, and (4) the titles of officials to whom the delegations have been made.[29] This reform would not impair presidential leadership performance to any significant degree, though it might have cramped the freewheeling styles of some recent presidents, and it should directly increase presidential accountability.

Of greater potential value for the achievement of several reform goals is a set of suggestions offered by Joseph A. Califano, Jr., President Johnson's principal domestic-policy aide. Califano calls for (1) a Presidential-Powers Impact Statement Act, which would require an analysis by the executive branch and Congress of the "impact of each significant new legislative program on the powers of the Presidency"; (2) legislation requiring that "certain specific reports" covering matters such as social programs and national-security policy accompany the annual State of the Union message; and (3) a presidentially prepared annual National Posture Statement that compares executive-branch program performance with statutory goals and presidential claims for the programs.[30] The proposed impact statements might result in more careful delegations of legislative authority to the President and curtail thoughtless aggrandizement of presidential power. Requiring the President, in effect, to document and substantiate the State of the Union message and annually to measure program performance against congressional and presidential objectives and promises could substantially reduce the dangers to governmental legitimacy caused by unmet expectations of the masses resulting from exaggerated promises by their leaders. The contributions of these reforms to the restoration of governmental legitimacy and constitutional balance and to increased presidential accountability could be substantial. They could be accomplished through legislation and would probably strengthen rather than impair the effectiveness of presidential leadership.

A third set of suggested procedural changes involves presidential decision-making. Aware of the dangers that inhere in presidential isolation, on the one hand, and the pressures for conformity within the Presidency, on the other, political scientist Alexander George and social psychologist Irving Janis, in separate treatises, call for decisional processes that guarantee that the President will receive adverse information and critical analysis of the principal policy alternatives before taking critical decisions.

George calls for the development of a formal "multiple advocacy" process that would assign individuals specific responsibilities, to bring a wide range of advisers and bargaining resources into the ambit of presidential decision-making.[31] The key role in George's multiple-advocacy process is that of a staff aide who would be a neutral, objective guardian responsible for ensuring the maintenance of a balance of advice and information. The difficulty with multiple advocacy is that it cannot realistically be imposed on a President; he must find it compatible with his style and want to operate with it. It is doubtful that many presidents would find it attractive or be comfortable with it, given the time constraints under which they must operate and the challenges it would continually pose to their self-images.

Janis addresses the problem of "groupthink" in decision-making bodies, which results from pressures toward conformity and tendencies to suppress unpleasant and unpopular views and information. He calls for the independent analysis of policy questions by several planning and evaluation subgroups and for the specific assignment of devil's-advocate roles when decisions are made.[32]

Both George and Janis emphasize confrontation in a collegial presidential decision-making process. There are serious limitations to these kinds of reforms. How willingly would any President assent to a process that exposed him to charges of not being able to control his own shop? Secondly, even if the principle of competition and confrontation among advisers and high-level subordinates were to be followed, a President would still be ultimately responsible and on a higher plane of authority. Who would confront him? Is it realistic to assume that he can be confronted when he has no peers? Over time, could his advisers and subordinates be prevented from courting his favor, and could he be expected to resist indefinitely the blandishments of those who stroke his ego and play to his prejudices?

The success of multiple advocacy and other schemes for improved collective decision-making would depend on the highly unpredictable factor of presidential personality. In theory they make sense, but it does not seem advisable to place a high degree of hope in them. Some presidents with great self-confidence and emotional stability have successfully employed competition among their advisers and even allowed subordinates occasionally to confront them directly, but it is not likely that even they would have found full implementation of a multiple-advocacy process very congenial. Much depends, then, on the personalities and leadership styles of future presidents.

Prospects

Given the problems of curbing the growth and preventing the abuse of presidential power, what are the prospects for achieving the objectives of the various reform proposals examined here? On balance, I conclude that though some changes have been made in the past few years and a few more may be forthcoming, we should not expect too much. The proposals that would contribute most to the realization of the reform goals involve far-reaching structural changes in the Presidency and the political system. None has yet been adopted in the aftermath of Watergate and Vietnam. As we recede from the anguish of the turbulent 1965–75 decade, the impetus for radical change wanes.

The obstacles to major change seem almost insurmountable. The diversity of American society and politics impedes the formation of majority coalitions for the passage of much substantive legislation and vastly increases the difficulty of building the sizable coalition required to amend the Constitution. In spite of growing distrust of government, a strong popular demand for radical reform of the Presidency and the political system as a whole is yet to emerge.

What, then, is the future of the Presidency? The public will expect presidents to do more, not less, than at present. Presidential power will increase in the absolute sense, though not necessarily in relation to other political institutions and forces. Presidents will encounter increasing frustration as they attempt to solve problems, manage events, and change conditions that are beyond their control. As Aaron Wildavsky forecasts, "Presidents will be more important but less popular than they are today."[33] It may even be more difficult than at present to secure responsible exercise of presidential power. A few years from now, we may witness a return to the imperial Presidency, perhaps with a vengeance.

This unhappy scenario need not take effect, however, if the nation—the public and its leaders—will heed the lessons of the immediate past. The most important lesson is "not that the Presidency should be diminished but [that] other institutions should grow in stature."[34] We urgently need to strengthen the forces that restrain the President, and thus re-establish the balanced Constitution of the framers. The basic changes that might alter the conditions that trouble us most must concentrate on the party system. Unless we can find ways to revitalize the parties, achieve much higher measures of party responsiveness to the electorate and party control over public policy, and bring the President and his party closer together in seeking office and running the government, we appear destined to continue the march toward an American version of the Gaullist republic.

Cronin summarizes the task well when he observes that we need to "put the Presidency back into politics."[35] We also need to develop effective party leadership in Congress.

The history of the Republic and the structure of its Constitution indicate that there is no foolproof method of guaranteeing that presidents will possess the appropriate combination of functional skills and moral responsibility that the office requires. We are left to rely on our own capacity to judge character and on an ultimate belief that the American voter is discerning. The electorate has chosen both wisely and mistakenly in the past, and it will undoubtedly continue in this pattern. Perhaps the best guide to the future is to be found in a remark of James Madison's: "A dependence on the people is, no doubt, the primary control on the government; but experience has taught mankind the necessity of auxiliary precautions."[36] If we are to benefit from our recent experiences, we must move to enhance and maintain the effectiveness of the "auxiliary precautions"—Congress, the party system, and the press—and thus re-establish the balanced Constitution of Madison and the framers.

Notes

1. Illustrative revisionist statements include James David Barber, *Presidential Character* (Englewood Cliffs, N.J.: Prentice-Hall, 1972); Thomas E. Cronin, *The State of the Presidency* (Boston: Little, Brown, 1975); and Henry Fairlie, *The Kennedy Promise: The Politics of Expectation* (Garden City: Doubleday, 1973).
2. See Michael J. Glennon, "Strengthening the War Powers Resolution: The Case for Purse-Strings Restrictions," *Minnesota Law Review*, November 1975, reprinted in the *Congressional Record*, daily edition, February 25, 1976, pp. S2307–S2318; and Graham T. Allison, "Making War: The President and Congress," Selection 12 above.
3. *Buckley* v. *Valeo* 46 L. Ed. 2d 659 (1976). See, in general, *Political Finance: Reform and Reality*, (The Annals of the American Academy of Political and Social Science, May 1976).
4. Paul H. Weaver, "Liberals and the Presidency," *Commentary*, October 1975, pp. 48–53.
5. See Walter Dean Burnham, *Critical Elections and the Mainsprings of American Politics* (New York: W. W. Norton, 1970); David S. Broder, *The Party's Over* (New York: Harper & Row, 1972); and Norman Nie, Sidney Verba, and John Petrocik, *The Changing American Voter* (Cambridge, Mass.: Harvard University Press, 1975).

6. Richard P. Nathan, *The Plot That Failed: Nixon and the Administrative Presidency* (New York: John Wiley & Sons, 1975).
7. See, for example, E. E. Schattschneider, *Party Government* (New York: Henry Holt, 1942); "Toward a More Responsible Two-Party System: A Report of the Committee on Political Parties, American Political Science Association," *The American Political Science Review* supplement, September 1950; James M. Burns, *The Deadlock of Democracy* (Englewood Cliffs, N.J.: Prentice-Hall, 1963); and Charles M. Hardin, *Presidential Power and Accountability* (Chicago: University of Chicago Press, 1974).
8. See Edward S. Corwin, *The President: Office and Powers*, 4th ed. (New York: New York University Press, 1957), pp. 297–99.
9. For example, little has happened to the suggestions of Henry Hazlitt in *A New Constitution Now* (New York, 1942), Thomas K. Finletter in *Can Representative Government Do the Job?* (New York, 1945), or Rexford G. Tugwell in *The Emerging Constitution* (New York: Harper's Magazine Press, 1974).
10. Harold Seidman, *Politics, Position and Power*, 2d ed. (New York: Oxford University Press, 1975), p. 3.
11. One of the most thoughtful recent proposals of this type is that of Professor Charles M. Hardin. See Selection 15 in this volume and his *Presidential Power and Accountability*. Hardin would retain the President but make radical changes in the structure of the national government, the most important being the implementation of "party government" and the subordination of the Senate to the House of Representatives.
12. See "Symposium on the Reuss Resolution: A Vote of No Confidence in the President," *George Washington Law Review*, vol. XLIII, January 1975, pp. 327–503. The authors who contributed to the symposium varied widely in their support for, or opposition to, the proposal.
13. James L. Sundquist, "Needed: A Workable Check on the Presidency," *Brookings Bulletin 10*, no. 4 (Washington, D.C.: Brookings Institution).
14. House Joint Resolution IV, August 15, 1974.
15. See Thomas E. Cronin's discussion in *The State of the Presidency*, pp. 295–98.
16. Corwin, op. cit., p. 297.
17. Cronin, op. cit., p. 272.
18. For a positive assessment, see Robert L. Heilbroner, "The American Plan," *New York Times Magazine*, January 25, 1976, reprinted in the *Congressional Record*, daily edition, January 26, 1976, pp. E164–E166. A thoughtful negative appraisal is Herbert Stein, *Economic Planning and the Improvement of Economic Policy* (Washington, D. C.: American Enterprise Institute for Public Policy Research, 1975). See also Otis Graham, *Toward a Planned Society* (New York: Oxford University Press, 1976).
19. William Cavala, "Changing the Rules Changes the Game: Party Reform and the 1972 California Delegation to the Democratic National Convention," *American Political Science Review*, March 1974, pp. 27–42. But also see William Keech and Donald Matthews, *The Party's Choice* (Washington, D.C.: Brookings Institution, 1976).
20. One of the more comprehensive analyses of the Electoral College and efforts at reform concludes with a strong appeal for the direct popular vote

alternative. See Neal R. Peirce, *The People's President* (New York: Clarion Books, 1968). For a defense of the Electoral College, see Wallace Sayre and Judith Parris, *Voting for President* (Washington, D.C.: Brookings Institution, 1970).

21. See the discussion in Cronin, op. cit., pp. 298–306.

22. See Leroy Rieselbach, "Congressional Reform: Some Policy Implications," *Policy Studies Journal*, Winter 1975, pp. 180–87.

23. Dorothy B. James, *The Contemporary Presidency* 2d ed. (New York: Pegasus, 1974), p. 294.

24. U.S. Senate, Subcommittee on Separation of Powers of the Committee on the Judiciary, "Executive Privilege: The Withholding of Information by the Executive," *Hearings* on July 27, 28, and 29, and August 4 and 5, 1971 (Washington, D.C.: Government Printing Office, 1971).

25. *United States* v. *Nixon* 418 U.S. 683 (1974).

26. For a thorough analysis of the case, see "Symposium on *United States* v. *Nixon*," *UCLA Law Review*, vol. XXII, October 1974, pp. 4–140. The distinguished law professors who contributed to the symposium tended to agree that the decision was more political than legal. They also tended to view the Court's opinion as "soft" law in that it gave explicit constitutional sanction to the doctrine of executive privilege where none had previously existed. The consensus of the scholars seemed to be that though Nixon lost, the Presidency won.

27. Alexander Hamilton, *The Federalist*, No. 70 (New York: Modern Library, 1937), pp. 460–61.

28. See Thomas E. Cronin's discussion of proposals for a collegial presidency, op. cit., pp. 263–68.

29. Frederick C. Mosher et al., *Watergate: Implications for Responsible Government* (New York: Basic Books, 1974), pp. 33–34.

30. Joseph A. Califano, Jr., *A Presidential Nation* (New York: W. W. Norton, 1975), pp. 283–87.

31. Alexander L. George, "The Case for Multiple Advocacy in Making Foreign Policy," *American Political Science Review*, September 1972, pp. 751–85.

32. Irving L. Janis, *Victims of Groupthink* (Boston: Houghton Mifflin, 1972).

33. Aaron Wildavsky, "The Past and Future Presidency," *The Public Interest*, No. 41 (Fall 1975), p. 57.

34. Ibid., p. 74.

35. Thomas E. Cronin, "Putting the Presidency Back into Politics," *Washington Monthly*, September 1973, pp. 7–12.

36. James Madison, *The Federalist*, No. 51 (New York: Modern Library, 1937), p. 337.

Bibliography

This listing of the important monographs and studies of the Presidency as an institution makes no attempt to be exhaustive. Rather it is offered for readers who want to know the standard works in the field as well as those that develop at greater length some of the themes that have been raised in this volume.

ALLISON, GRAHAM T., *Essence of Decision: Explaining the Cuban Missile Crisis* (Boston: Little, Brown, 1971).

ALLISON, GRAHAM T., and PETER SZANTON, *Remaking Foreign Policy: The Organizational Connection* (New York: Basic Books, 1976).

ANDERSON, PATRICK, *The President's Men* (New York: Doubleday, 1968).

ASHER, HERBERT, *Presidential Elections and American Politics*, (Homewood, Ill.: Dorsey, 1976).

BAILEY, THOMAS A., *Presidential Greatness* (New York: Appleton-Century-Crofts, 1966).

BARBER, JAMES DAVID, *The Presidential Character*, rev. ed. (Englewood Cliffs, N.J.: Prentice-Hall, 1977).

———, ed., *Choosing a President* (Englewood Cliffs, N.J.: Prentice-Hall, 1974).

BERGER, RAOUL, *Executive Privilege: A Constitutional Myth* (Cambridge, Mass.: Harvard University Press, 1974).

———, *Impeachment: The Constitutional Problems* (Cambridge, Mass.: Harvard University Press, 1973).

BERNSTEIN, CARL, and BOB WOODWARD, *All the President's Men* (New York: Simon and Schuster, 1974).

BINKLEY, WILFRED E., *President and Congress*, 3d rev. ed. (New York: Vintage, 1962).

BRANT, IRVING, *Impeachment: Trials and Errors* (New York: Knopf, 1972).

BRODER, DAVID S., *The Party's Over* (New York: Harper & Row, 1971).

BROWNLOW, LOUIS, *The President and the Presidency* (Chicago: University of Chicago Press, 1949).

BUNDY, MCGEORGE, *The Strength of Government* (Cambridge, Mass.: Harvard University Press, 1968).

BURNS, JAMES M., *Presidential Government* (Boston: Houghton Mifflin, 1973).

CALIFANO, JOSEPH, *The Presidential Nation* (New York: Norton, 1975).

CHAMBERLAIN, LAWRENCE H., *The President, Congress and Legislation* (New York: Columbia University Press, 1946).

CLARK, KEITH, and LAURENCE LEGERE, eds., *The President and the Management of National Security* (New York: Praeger, 1969).

COCHRAN, BERT, *Harry Truman and the Crisis Presidency* (New York: Funk & Wagnalls, 1973).

CORNWELL, ELMER E., *Presidential Leadership of Public Opinion* (Bloomington: University of Indiana Press, 1962).

CORWIN, EDWARD S., *The President: Office and Powers*, 4th ed. (New York: New York University Press, 1957).

COTTER, C. P., and J. M. SMITH, *Powers of the President during National Crises* (Washington, D.C.: Public Affairs Press, 1961).

CRONIN, THOMAS E., *The State of the Presidency* (Boston: Little, Brown, 1975).

CRONIN, THOMAS E., and SANFORD D. GREENBERG, eds., *The Presidential Advisory System* (New York: Harper & Row, 1969).

CUNLIFFE, MARCUS, *The American Heritage History of the Presidency* (New York: American Heritage, 1968).

DEAN, JOHN, III, *Blind Ambition* (New York: Simon & Schuster, 1976).

DESTLER, I. M., *Presidents, Bureaucrats and Foreign Policy* (Princeton, N.J.: Princeton University Press, 1972).

DONOVAN, JOHN C., *The Policy-Makers* (New York: Pegasus, 1970).

DUNN, CHARLES W., ed., *The Future of the American Presidency* (Morristown, N.J.: General Learning Press, 1975).

DUNN, DELMER D., *Financing Presidential Campaigns* (Washington, D.C.: Brookings Institution, 1972).

FAIRLIE, HENRY, *The Kennedy Promise: The Politics of Expectation* (New York: Doubleday, 1973).

FENNO, RICHARD F., *The President's Cabinet* (New York: Vintage, 1959).

FINER, HERMAN, *The Presidency, Crises and Regeneration* (Chicago: University of Chicago Press, 1960).

FISHER, LOUIS, *President and Congress* (New York: Free Press, 1972).

———, *Presidential Spending Power* (Princeton, N.J.: Princeton University Press, 1975).

GOLDMAN, ERIC F., *The Tragedy of Lyndon Johnson* (New York: Knopf, 1969).

GOLDSMITH, WILLIAM, *The Growth of Presidential Power* (3 vols.; New York: Chelsea House/Bowker, 1974).

GRABNER, DORIS, *Public Opinion, the President and Foreign Policy* (New York: Holt, Rinehart & Winston, 1968).

HALBERSTAM, DAVID, *The Best and the Brightest* (New York: Random House, 1972).

HALPERN, PAUL J., ed., *Why Watergate?* (Pacific Palisades: Goodyear, 1975).

HARGROVE, ERWIN C., *The Power of the Modern Presidency* (New York: Knopf, 1974).

HELLER, FRANCIS, *The Presidency* (New York: Random House, 1960).

HENRY, LAURIN L., *Presidential Transitions* (Washington, D.C.: Brookings Institution, 1960).

HERBERS, JOHN, *No Thank You, Mr. President* (New York: Norton, 1976).

HERRING, PENDLETON, *Presidential Leadership* (New York: Farrar & Rinehart, 1940).

HESS, STEPHEN, *Organizing the Presidency* (Washington, D.C.: Brookings Institution, 1976).

HOFSTADTER, RICHARD, *The American Political Tradition* (New York: Vintage, 1948).

HOLTZMAN, ABRAHAM, *Legislative Liaison: Executive Leadership in Congress* (Chicago: Rand McNally, 1970).

HOOPES, TOWNSEND, *The Limits of Intervention* (New York: McKay, 1969).

HUGHES, EMMET JOHN, *The Living Presidency* (New York: Coward, McCann and Geoghegan, 1973).

———, *The Ordeal of Power* (New York: Dell, 1962).

HYMAN, SIDNEY, *The American President* (New York: Harper, 1954).

JAMES, DOROTHY B., *The Contemporary Presidency*, 2d ed. (New York: Pegasus, 1974).

JANIS, IRVING L., *Victims of Groupthink* (Boston: Houghton Mifflin, 1972).

JOHNSON, DONALD B., and JACK L. WALKER, eds., *The Dynamics of the American Presidency* (New York: Wiley, 1964).

JOHNSON, LYNDON B., *The Vantage Point* (New York: Holt, Rinehart & Winston, 1971).

KALLENBACK, JOSEPH E., *The American Chief Executive* (New York: Harper & Row, 1966).

KEARNS, DORIS, *Lyndon B. Johnson and the American Dream* (New York: Harper & Row, 1976).

KEECH, WILLIAM, and DONALD MATTHEWS, *The Party's Choice* (Washington, D.C.: Brookings Institution, 1976).

KENNEDY, ROBERT F., *Thirteen Days: A Memoir of the Cuban Missile Crisis* (Norton, 1969).

KESSEL, JOHN, *The Domestic Presidency* (North Scituate, Mass.: Duxbury, 1975).

KOENIG, LOUIS, *The Chief Executive*, 3d ed. (New York: Harcourt, Brace & World, 1975).

LAMMERS, WILLIAM W., *Presidential Politics: Patterns and Prospects* (New York: Harper & Row, 1976).

LASKI, HAROLD J., *The American Presidency* (New York: Grosset & Dunlap, 1940).

LUKAS, J. ANTHONY, *Nightmare—The Underside of the Nixon Years* (New York: Viking, 1976).

MCCONNELL, GRANT, *Steel and the Presidency* (New York: Norton, 1963).

——, *The Modern Presidency*, 2d ed. (New York: St. Martin's Press, 1976).

MCGINNISS, JOE, *The Selling of the President 1968* (New York: Trident Press, 1969).

MATTHEWS, DONALD R., ed., *Perspectives on Presidential Selection* (Washington, D.C.: Brookings Institution, 1973).

MILTON, GEORGE F., *The Use of Presidential Power* (Boston: Little, Brown, 1944).

MIROFF, BRUCE, *Pragmatic Illusions: The Presidential Politics of John F. Kennedy* (New York: McKay, 1976).

MOE, RONALD C., ed., *Congress and the President* (Pacific Palisades, Calif.: Goodyear, 1971).

MONDALE, WALTER F., *The Accountability of Power: Toward a Responsible Presidency* (New York: McKay, 1975).

MORGAN, RUTH P., *The President and Civil Rights* (New York: St. Martin's Press, 1970).

MOYNIHAN, DANIEL P., *The Politics of a Guaranteed Income* (New York: Random House, 1973).

MUELLER, JOHN E., *War, Presidents and Public Opinion* (New York: Wiley, 1973).

MULLEN, WILLIAM F., *Presidential Power and Politics* (New York: St. Martin's Press, 1976).

NATHAN, RICHARD P., *The Plot That Failed: Nixon and the Administrative Presidency* (New York: Wiley, 1975).

NEUSTADT, RICHARD E., *Alliance Politics* (New York: Columbia University Press, 1970).

———, *Presidential Power*, rev. ed. (New York: Wiley, 1976).

NOVAK, MICHAEL, *Choosing Our King* (Macmillan, 1974).

PATTERSON, BRADLEY H., Jr., *The President's Cabinet: Issues and Questions* (Washington, D.C.: American Society for Public Administration, 1976).

PATTERSON, C. P., *Presidential Government in the United States* (Chapel Hill: University of North Carolina Press, 1947).

PEIRCE, NEAL R., *The People's President* (New York: Clarion, 1968).

POLLARD, JAMES F., *The Presidents and the Press* (Washington, D.C.: Public Affairs Press, 1964).

POLSBY, NELSON W., *Congress and the Presidency*, 3d ed. (Englewood Cliffs, N.J.: Prentice-Hall, 1975).

POLSBY, NELSON W., and AARON WILDAVSKY, *Presidential Elections*, 3d ed. (New York: Scribners, 1976).

POPPER, FRANK, *The President's Commissions* (New York: Twentieth Century Fund, 1970).

RATHER, DAN, and GARY PAUL GATES, *The Palace Guard* (Harper & Row, 1974).

REEDY, GEORGE E., *The Presidency in Flux* (New York: Columbia University Press, 1973).

———, *The Twilight of the Presidency* (New York: World, 1970).

ROBERTS, CHARLES, ed., *Has the President Too Much Power?* (New York: Harper's Magazine Press, 1974).

ROSE, RICHARD, *Managing Presidential Objectives* (New York: Free Press, 1976).

ROSSITER, CLINTON, *Constitutional Dictatorship* (New York: Harcourt, Brace, 1948).

———, *The American Presidency* (New York: Harcourt, Brace & World, 1960).

ROURKE, FRANCIS E., *Bureaucracy, Politics and Public Policy* (Boston: Little, Brown, 1969).

SAFIRE, WILLIAM, *Before the Fall* (Garden City, N.Y.: Doubleday, 1975).

SCHLESINGER, ARTHUR M., JR., *A Thousand Days: John F. Kennedy in the White House* (Boston: Houghton Mifflin, 1965).

———, *The Imperial Presidency* (Boston: Houghton Mifflin, 1973).

SCHLESINGER, ARTHUR M., JR., and ALFRED DE GRAZIA, *Congress and the Presidency: Their Role in Modern Times* (Washington, D.C.: American Enterprise Institute, 1967).

SCHUBERT, GLENDON, *The Presidency in the Courts* (Minneapolis: University of Minnesota Press, 1957).

SCIGLIANO, ROBERT, *The Supreme Court and the Presidency* (New York: Free Press, 1971).

SINDLER, ALLAN P., *Unchosen Presidents: The Vice President and*

Other Frustrations of Presidential Succession (Berkeley: University of California Press, 1976).

SORENSEN, THEODORE C., *Decision-Making in the White House* (New York: Columbia University Press, 1963).

———, *Kennedy* (Harper & Row, 1965).

———, *Watchmen in the Night: Presidential Accountability after Watergate* (Cambridge, Mass.: M.I.T. Press, 1975).

STRUM, PHILIPPA, *Presidential Power and American Democracy* (Pacific Palisades, Calif.: Goodyear, 1972).

SULZNER, GEORGE, and STANLEY BACH, eds.n *Perspectives on the Presidency* (Boston: Heath, 1974).

SUNDQUIST, JAMES L., *Politics and Policy: The Eisenhower, Kennedy and Johnson Years* (Washington, D.C.: Brookings Institution, 1968).

THACH, CHARLES C., JR., *The Creation of the Presidency, 1775–1789* (New York: Da Capo Press, 1969).

THOMAS, NORMAN C., and HANS W. BAADE, eds., *The Institutionalized Presidency* (Dobbs Ferry, N.Y.: Oceana, 1972).

THOMAS, NORMAN C., ed., *The Presidency in Contemporary Context* (New York: Dodd, Mead, 1975).

THOMPSON, HUNTER S., *Fear and Loathing: On the Campaign Trail '72* (San Francisco, Calif.: Straight Arrow Books, 1973).

TUGWELL, REXFORD G., *How They Became President* (New York: Simon & Schuster, 1965).

———, *The Democratic Roosevelt* (New York: Doubleday, 1957).

———, *The Enlargement of the Presidency* (New York: Doubleday, 1960).

VINYARD, DALE, *The Presidency* (New York: Scribners, 1971).

WANN, A. J., *The President as Chief Administrator* (Washington, D.C.: Public Affairs Press, 1968).

WHITE, THEODORE H., *The Making of the President, 1960* (New York: Atheneum, 1961).

———, *The Making of the President, 1964* (New York: Atheneum, 1965).

———, *The Making of the President, 1968* (New York: Atheneum, 1969).

———, *The Making of the President, 1972* (New York: Atheneum, 1973).

———, *Breach of Faith: The Fall of Richard Nixon* (New York: Atheneum, 1975).

WILDAVSKY, AARON, ed., *The Presidency* (Boston: Little, Brown, 1969).

———, *Perspectives on the Presidency* (Boston: Little, Brown, 1975).

WILLS, GARY, *Nixon Agonistes* (Boston: Houghton Mifflin, 1970).

WISE, SIDNEY, and RICHARD F. SCHIER, eds., *The Presidential Office* (New York: Crowell, 1968).

WOLANIN, THOMAS R., *Presidential Advisory Commissions: Truman to Nixon* (Madison: University of Wisconsin Press, 1975).

YOUNG, JAMES S., *The Washington Community, 1800–1820* (New York: Columbia University Press, 1966).

Note: Readers who want to keep informed about the Presidency will also want to consult the following journals: *Congressional Quarterly, National Journal, Presidential Studies Quarterly, The Washington Monthly,* and *Weekly Compilation of Presidential Documents.*

The Contributors

THOMAS E. CRONIN, a former White House Fellow and White House
staff assistant in the mid-1960s, has taught political science at the
University of North Carolina, Brandeis University, and the University of Delaware. He has served on the staffs of The Brookings
Institution and the Center for the Study of Democratic Institutions
and is author of *The State of the Presidency* (1975) and co-author of
several other works including *Government by the People* (1975)
and *America in the Seventies* (1977).
REXFORD G. TUGWELL, former Professor of Political Economy and
Planning at Columbia University and the University of Chicago,
was a member of President Franklin D. Roosevelt's "Brains Trust."
He also served as Under-Secretary of Agriculture and as the wartime Governor of Puerto Rico. A long-time senior fellow at the
Center for the Study of Democratic Institutions, he is the author of
more than a score of books, among them *The Democratic Roosevelt*;
The Enlargement of the Presidency; *The Emerging Constitution*;
and his latest, *The Compromised Constitution* (1976).
C. HERMAN PRITCHETT, long-time professor and Chairman of the
Department of Political Science at the University of Chicago, has
taught in recent years at the University of California at Santa Barbara. A past president of the American Political Science Association, he is the author of numerous books including *The Roosevelt
Court*; *The American Constitution*; *The American Constitutional
System*; and the co-author of *Courts, Judges, and Politics*, 2d ed.
(1974).

353

PHILIP SHABECOFF is a veteran reporter for the *New York Times*, most recently serving as a White House correspondent. He has also served as a foreign correspondent in Europe and Asia and has covered labor and economic policy for the *Times*. He has contributed articles and essays to numerous magazines and journals including *The Nation*, *The New York Times Magazine*, and *Pacific Community*.

WILLIAM R. KEECH teaches political science at the University of North Carolina at Chapel Hill and is the author of numerous essays and research studies. The author of *The Impact of Negro Voting* and co-author of *The Party's Choice* (1976), he is a frequent contributor to major political science journals and has served on the staff of The Brookings Institution.

DORIS KEARNS teaches American politics and government at Harvard University. A former White House Fellow, she worked with President Johnson during his last months in the White House and assisted in the preparation of his memoir *The Vantage Point*. Author of the best-selling *Lyndon Johnson and the American Dream* (1976) she has also written several articles and commentaries on contemporary American politics.

FRANCIS G. HUTCHINS, former Lecturer on Government at Harvard University, is the author of *India's Revolution: Gandhi and the Quit-India Movement* and *The Illusion of Permanence: British Imperialism in India*. He has also written a number of articles dealing with American and South Asian politics. Currently, he is a Research Fellow at the Institute for Advanced Study, Princeton, New Jersey.

DOM BONAFEDE is senior editor and White House correspondent for *The National Journal*. A veteran reporter, he has served with *The New York Herald-Tribune*, *Newsweek*, and is a frequent contributor to numerous journals and newspapers such as *The Washington Post*, *The Progressive*, *The Nation*, and *Washingtonian*.

DANIEL P. MOYNIHAN, currently a United States Senator from New York, is a former ambassador to India, a former Harvard University professor, member of the sub-Cabinets of Presidents Kennedy and Johnson and the Cabinet of President Nixon. He is the author of *Maximum Feasible Misunderstanding*; *Beyond the Melting Pot* (with Nathan Glazer); *Coping*; and several other books. He has also been a frequent contributor to *Commentary* and *The Public Interest*.

GEORGE E. REEDY, former White House Press Secretary and former Staff Director of the Senate Democratic Policy Committee, is now Dean and Nieman Professor of the College of Journalism, Marquette University. He is the author of *The Twilight of the Presidency* (1970) and *The Presidency in Flux* (1973).

ARTHUR SCHLESINGER, JR., a Presidential Assistant from 1961 to 1964, is now Albert Schweitzer Professor of Humanities at City

University of New York. Among his many books are the three volumes of *The Age of Roosevelt*; *The Age of Jackson*; and *A Thousand Days: John F. Kennedy in the White House*, of which the last two received Pulitzer prizes. His provocative book *The Imperial Presidency* (1973) has won significant praise.

GRAHAM ALLISON is Associate Dean of the John F. Kennedy School of Government at Harvard University. The author of *The Essence of Decision: Explaining the Cuban Missile Crisis* (1971) and co-author of *Remaking Foreign Policy: The Organizational Connection* (1976), he is a frequent contributor to *Foreign Policy* and other foreign-policy and international politics journals.

PHILIPPA STRUM has taught at Rutgers University and currently teaches at Brooklyn College of the City University of New York. Author of *Presidential Power and American Democracy* (1972) and *The Supreme Court and Political Questions*, she is a frequent contributor to several academic journals.

H. G. GALLAGHER is the author of several books, including *Advise and Obstruct: The Role of the United States Senate in Foreign Policy Decisions* and *President Hoover: A Biography* (1977). He has served as a legislative assistant to several members of Congress and is currently a Washington-based writer and consultant.

CHARLES M. HARDIN is Professor Emeritus at the University of California at Davis. A long-time professor at the University of Chicago, he is the author of several books, including *The Politics of Agriculture* and *Presidential Power and Accountability* (1974).

NORMAN C. THOMAS is Professor of Political Science at the University of Cincinnati. He has previously taught at the University of Michigan and Duke University and been a Guest Scholar at The Brookings Institution. He is the author or editor of a number of books, among them *Education in National Politics* (1975); *The Presidency in Contemporary Context* (1975); and *The Institutionalized Presidency* (1972).

Index

Case, Clifford, 213
Case Act (1972), 13
Central Intelligence Agency (CIA), 269
  appropriations for, 20, 21
  Congressional oversight of, 215, 280
  covert activities of, 21, 29, 215
  Eisenhower and, 214
Chamberlain, Lawrence, 279–80
character of the President, *see*
    personal characteristics of the
    President
checks and balances, 128
  isolation of the President and,
    192–94
  war-making powers and, 232
Chief administrator, the President as,
  18–19
chief of state, the President as, *see*
    head of state, the President as
China
  intervention in (1900), 208
  normalization of relations with,
    102–3
Church, Frank, 209
Churchill, Winston, 285–86
CIA, *see* Central Intelligence Agency
civil rights
  Carter on, 65
  as issue in elections, 101–2
  Lyndon Johnson and, 102, 122
Civil Rights Act (1964), 102
civil service, *see* bureaucracy, federal
Civil War, 205–6
Clark, J. Reuben, 208
Clark, Joseph, 116
classified information, *see* executive
    privilege; press, the, leaks to;
    secrecy
Cleveland, Grover, 96, 274
Clifford, Clark M., 155
coalition, electoral vs. governing, 82
coercion, Johnson's use of, 113–14,
  125, 127, 130
Cohen, Benjamin V., 226
Coffin, Frank, 217
cold war, 214, 215
collegial executive, 311
  rejected by Founders, 4–5, 8
  see also plural Presidency, proposals
    for
Colonial period, executive powers as
    seen in, 3–4
Colson, Charles, 164
comity, rule of, 157

Commager, Henry Steele, 212, 220,
  233*n*
Commander in Chief, the President
    as, 7, 10–13, 20, 135, 215, 220
  "faithful execution of the laws"
    clause and, 10, 13
  war-making powers and, 10–11
Commission on Freedom of the Press,
  186–87
communications media, *see* news
    media
confidence, vote of, 286, 294, 296
confrontation, reform proposals to
    increase, 308–11; *see also* Leader
    of the Opposition
Congress
  appointing power of the President
    and, 9
  Carter on role of, 42
  election of the President by,
    rejected by Founders, 5–6, 8
  legislative initiative and innovation
    by, 279–82
  personal qualities that make for
    success in, 127
  proposed reforms of, 334–35
  question-time proposal and, 259–63
  removal of officials by the President
    and, 10, 13
  representativeness of the President
    and, 134
  seniority system of, 113, 115,
    146–47, 275
  strengthening of, 146
  Vietnam War and, 125, 216–19, 281;
    see also Tonkin Gulf Resolution;
    War Powers Act
  war-declaring power of, *see*
    war-declaring power of Congress
  war-making power of the President
    and, 10–12
  White House staff expansion and,
    156–57
  Wilson's view of, 134
  see also House of Representatives;
    legislation; Legislature; *and*
    specific topics
Congressional Budget and
    Impoundment Control Act (1974),
    18, 30
congressional relations with the
    President, 267–82, 319
  in budget process, 30–31
  bureaucratic power and, 289–90

THE PRESIDENCY
REAPPRAISED

Presidential Power

The President's Constitutional Position, *C. Herman Pritchett/* Appraising Presidential Power: The Ford Presidency, *Philip Shabecoff/*The Carter Presidency: Plans and Priorities, *pre-presidency interviews with Jimmy Carter by Neil R. Peirce*

The Presidency and American Politics

The Presidency and Its Paradoxes, *Thomas E. Cronin/*Selecting and Electing Presidents, *William R. Keech/*Lyndon Johnson's Political Personality, *Doris Kearns/*Presidential Authority in America, *F. G. Hutchins*

The Institutionalized Presidency Reappraised

White House Staffing: The Nixon-Ford Era, *Dom Bonafede/* The President and the Press, *Daniel P. Moynihan/*On the Isolation of Presidents, *George E. Reedy*

The Imperial Presidency Reappraised

Congress and the Making of American Foreign Policy, *Arthur Schlesinger, Jr./*Marking War: The President and Congress *Graham T. Allison/*A Symbolic Attack on the Imperial Presidency: An American "Question Time," *Philippa Strum*

Presidential Government Reconsidered

The President, Congress, and Legislation, *H. G. Gallagher* The President and Constitutional Reform, *Charles M. Hardin* On Bringing Presidents to Heel, *Rexford G. Tugwell/*Reforming the Presidency: Problems and Prospects, *Norman C. Thomas*